Changing Governance and Public Policy in East Asia

The search for good governance has become an increasingly important element of public policy and public management and is high on the political agenda of East Asian countries. The need for robust governance structures and institutions was brought into sharp focus by the Asian Financial Crisis which adversely affected most East Asian societies. Since then they have begun to look for ways to restructure their public administration and political systems in order to develop new mechanisms and structures to promote good governance. This book focuses on how selected Asian states have responded to the growing impact of 'liberalizing and marketizing trends' in public policy formulation and public management. To what extent is the 'state-guided' regime in Asia still relevant to governing public policy / public management? What are the policy implications for a growing number of Asian states which are pursuing more pro-competition policy instruments? The book is a timely and important collection that offers critical analysis of the search for new governance in Asia and compares and contrasts experiences in selected Asian societies such as China, Japan, Hong Kong, Taiwan, South Korea, Singapore, and other parts of South East Asia. Chapters are written by leading scholars in the fields of comparative development, policy and governance studies from Hong Kong, Macau, Taiwan, China, Singapore, Japan and the United Kingdom.

Ka Ho Mok is Associate Dean and Professor, Faculty of Social Sciences, The University of Hong Kong. He has researched and published in the fields of comparative education, public policy and governance and social development in East Asia. Most recently, he has been appointed as Visiting Professor of the University of Bristol, Distinguished Professor of National Chiao-Tung University, Taiwan and International Advisor of the National Taiwan University.

Ray Forrest is Professor of Urban Studies and Associate Director of CEAS, University of Bristol. He is also co-director (with Professor Ade Kearns, University of Glasgow) of the ESRC Centre for Neighbourhood Research. Ray is currently a Visiting Professor at the Department of Urban Studies at Glasgow University and Adjunct Professor at the City University of Hong Kong. He has published extensively on urban and housing issues and his current research interests focus on the role and meaning of neighbourhood in the contemporary city; housing markets, the macro economy and globalization; and housing policy and social inequalities.

Comparative Development and Policy in Asia Series
Series Editors
Ka Ho Mok (Faculty of Social Sciences, The University of Hong Kong, China)
Rachel Murphy (Oxford University, UK)
The Centre for East Asian Studies, University of Bristol, UK

Cultural Exclusion in China
State Education, Social Mobility and Cultural Difference
Lin Yi

Labour Migration and Social Development in Contemporary China
Edited by Rachel Murphy

Changing Governance and Public Policy in East Asia
Edited by Ka Ho Mok and Ray Forrest

Changing Governance and Public Policy in East Asia

Edited by Ka Ho Mok and Ray Forrest

Routledge
Taylor & Francis Group

LONDON AND NEW YORK

First published 2009
by Routledge
2 Park Square, Milton Park, Abingdon, Oxon OX14 4RN

Simultaneously published in the USA and Canada
by Routledge
270 Madison Ave, New York, NY 10016

*Routledge is an imprint of the Taylor & Francis Group,
an informa business*

Typeset in Times New Roman by
RefineCatch Limited, Bungay, Suffolk
Printed and bound in Great Britain by
MPG Biddles Ltd, King's Lynn

British Library Cataloguing in Publication Data
A catalogue record for this book is available
from the British Library

Library of Congress Cataloging-in-Publication Data
Changing governance and public policy in East Asia / edited by Ka Ho
    Mok and Ray Forrest.
        p. cm. – (Comparative development and policy in Asia series)
    Includes bibliographical references and index.
    1. East Asia–Social policy.   2. Public administration–East Asia.
I. Mok, Ka-Ho, 1964–   II. Forrest, Ray.

HN720.5.A8C43 2008
320.6095–dc22   2008019825

ISBN10: 0–415–41596–9 (hbk)
ISBN10: 0–203–88821–9 (ebk)

ISBN13: 978–0–415–41596–5 (hbk)
ISBN13: 978–0–203–88821–6 (ebk)

Contents

List of figures and tables   viii
List of contributors   xi
Foreword   xvii
Preface   xix

Introduction: the search for good governance in Asia   1
KA HO MOK AND RAY FORREST

PART I
Changing policy paradigms   23

1 **Interpreting East Asian social policy development:**
   paradigm shifts or policy 'steadiness'?   25
   ANTHONY B. L. CHEUNG

2 **Redefining development in China: towards a new**
   policy paradigm for the new century?   49
   KINGLUN NGOK

3 **Empowering the public and the policy science of**
   democracy from a post-modernist perspective   67
   WEIQING GUO

4 **Japan's changing domestic governance and its**
   impact on foreign policy   81
   ITO GO

PART II

Changing policy instruments and regulatory regimes   97

5 Competition and control in public hospital reforms
   in Hong Kong and Singapore   99
   M. RAMESH

6 Pro-competition policy tools and state capacity: the
   corporatization of public universities in Hong Kong and
   Singapore and the implications for Asia   117
   KA HO MOK

7 Comparative welfare policy instruments in East
   Asia: embedding trust in policy   140
   YEUN WEN KU

8 Regulatory reform and private sector development
   in China: a case study of downsizing administrative licences   159
   BILL CHOU

PART III

The changing role of the private sector in public policy   183

9 Accommodating business interests in China and
   Hong Kong: two systems – one way out   185
   RAY YEP

10 From developmental regimes to post-developmental
   regimes: business and pension reforms in Japan,
   South Korea and Taiwan   206
   YOUNG JUN CHOI

11 Private education policy at a crossroads: comparing
   Hong Kong and Singapore   228
   MICHAEL H. LEE

12 Struggling among economic efficiency, social
   equality and social stability: housing monetarization reform
   in China   253
   YAPENG ZHU

PART IV

The challenge for urban governance 285

13 **Managing the chaotic city–social cohesion: new forms of urban governance and the challenge for East Asia** 287
RAY FORREST

14 **The governance of urban renaissance in Tokyo: post-urbanization and enhanced competitiveness** 303
YOSUKE HIRAYAMA

15 **Urbanization, low-income housing and urban governance in South Korea** 326
SEONG KYU HA

Index 347

List of figures and tables

Figures

  8.1 Distribution of licensing items among central bureaucracies (%)   171
12.1 Composition of sources for housing subsidy in enterprise in
     the East   266
12.2 Composition of sources for housing subsidy in enterprise in
     the Middle   267
12.3 Composition of sources for housing subsidy in enterprise in
     the West   267
12.4 Composition of housing funds for housing subsidy in the East   268
12.5 Composition of housing funds for housing subsidy in the
     Middle   269
12.6 Composition of housing funds for housing subsidy in the West   269
14.1 Redevelopment priority zones in Tokyo, designated by the
     Urban Renaissance Special Measure Law   309
14.2 Redevelopment priority zones in Tokyo, designated by the
     Urban Renaissance Special Measure Law completions and
     projected completions of tower condominiums, Tokyo   311
14.3 Number of high-rise buildings by height   312
14.4 Number of high-rise buildings by ratio of floor space to plot
     size   313
14.5 Number of urban redevelopment projects by the height of the
     tallest buildings in the project   314
14.6 Number of urban redevelopment projects by ratio of total
     floor space to land plot size   315

Tables

  1.1 Total government expenditure and major social policy
     expenditures, as percentages of GDP, in the late 1990s   28
  1.2 Public expenditure as percentage of GDP, 1996–2005   40
  2.1 Paradigmatic phase I: catching up development (1949–1978)   53

2.2 Paradigmatic phase II: economic growth (GDPism)
(1978–2003) 55
2.3 Paradigmatic phase III: people-centred development
(2003–) (in progress) 62
4.1 US methods of maintaining leverage 94
5.1 Health status 101
5.2 National healthcare expenditures 102
5.3 Public health expenditures, percentage of GDP, annual
average 102
5.4 Physicians and hospital beds, per 1000 persons 103
6.1 Comparing the corporatization projects of Hong Kong and
Singapore 128
6.2 Different modes of governance 131
7.1 Welfare instruments and their characteristics 145
7.2 Welfare instruments by country and contingency 146
7.3 Welfare instrument mixes in East Asia 147
8.1 A comparison of selected indicators of business regulations
in eight developing countries in 2003 161
8.2 A comparison of the minimum capital requirement in eight
developing countries in 2003 161
8.3 The number of licensing items in selected governments 167
8.4 Surveys of managers on business environments 169
8.5 Distribution of licensing items among central bureaucracies 172
9.1 Shares of state sector in China's economy in 1985 and 2000 194
9.2 Growth of private enterprises in selected years 196
9.3 Growth of rural enterprises in selected years 196
11.1 Primary schools in Hong Kong, 1992–2004 232
11.2 Secondary schools in Hong Kong, 1992–2004 233
11.3 Primary schools in Singapore, 1960–2005 234
11.4 Secondary schools in Singapore, 1960–2004 235
11.5 Private school education in Hong Kong and Singapore 242
12.1 Comparison of two housing reform approaches 260
12.2 Implementation situation in prefecture-level cities 264
12.3 Implementation situations in counties (county-level cities) 264
12.4 Situation of provision of housing subsidy in the 35 major
cities 265
12.5 Sources of funds for provision of housing subsidy in SOEs
and institutions funded by themselves 266
12.6 Sources of funds for provision of housing subsidy in
government departments and institutions in the 35 major cities 268
12.7 Space of public housing in the 35 major cities sold and
chengben price in major cities (March 2000) 272
12.8 Rent for the public housing sector in provinces and major
cities in 2000 273
15.1 Population growth in SMR 328

15.2 Concentration in SMR (2000)   328
15.3 Population, households and housing indicators, 1980–2000   330
15.4 NGOs by year of foundation (%)   334
15.5 The relative performances of urban governance goals in Korea   340

Contributors

Anthony B. L. Cheung is President of the Hong Kong Institute of Education. Prior to January 2008 he was Professor of the Department of Public and Social Administration and Associate Director of the Governance in Asia Research Centre at the City University of Hong Kong. He has written extensively on privatization, civil service and public sector reforms, government and politics in Hong Kong and China, and Asian administrative reforms. His recent books are *Governance and Public Sector Reform in Asia: Paradigm Shift or Business As Usual?* (co-edited, London: RoutledgeCurzon, 2003) and *Public Service Reform in East Asia* (edited, Hong Kong: Chinese University Press, 2005). An ex-civil servant and a former legislator, Professor Cheung is now a Member of Hong Kong's Executive Council, and Chairman of the Consumer Council. He was the founding chairman of the policy think-tank SynergyNet and sits on the board of directors of the Hong Kong Policy Research Institute.

Young Jun Choi is a Lecturer in International Social Policy at the University of Bath, UK. He is also a founding member of East Asian Social Policy research network (EASP) and is serving as the Secretary of EASP. His research interests are in East Asian welfare regimes, ageing and pensions, welfare politics, and comparative research methods. His recent work has been published in *Ageing and Society*, *Policy and Politics*, *Journal of Social Policy* and *Labor Studies*.

Bill Chou is an Assistant Professor in the Department of Government and Public Administration, University of Macau. He obtained a bachelor's and a master's degree from the City University of Hong Kong and a doctoral degree from the University of Hong Kong. He has held visiting positions at the Asian Development Bank Institute, the National University of Singapore and the City University of Hong Kong. His research interests include governance and public sector reform in China, Hong Kong and Macau. His publications have appeared in *Communist and Post-Communist Studies*, *International Journal of Public Administration*, *Journal of Contemporary China*, *China Information* and *Public Administration and Policy*.

Ray Forrest is Professor of Urban Studies in the School for Policy Studies, University of Bristol, UK. From 2001–2005 he was co-Director of the ESRC Centre for Neighbourhood Research and is currently Acting Director of the Centre for East Asian Studies at Bristol. He has held visiting appointments at the Universities of Glasgow, Hong Kong and the City University of Hong Kong. He is a founding member of the Asia-Pacific Network of Housing Researchers and is co-editor of *Housing Studies* and *Asian Public Policy*. Current research interests include an ESRC project (with Dr Misa Izuhara) on Housing Assets and Inter-generational Dynamics in East Asian Societies.

Ito Go is a Professor of International Relations at Meiji University in Tokyo, Japan. He is currently one of Japan's leading experts on national and international security studies, more specifically on US-China-Japan relations, US policy toward East Asia, Asian regionalism, and Japanese foreign and security policy. He has received several domestic and international honours for his work, including Eisenhower Fellowships and the Yasuhiro Nakasone Award. As a prolific writer, he has published *Alliance in Anxiety: Détente and the Sino-American-Japanese Triangle* (New York: Routledge, 2003), 'Japan's Participation in UN Peacekeeping Operations' in *Japan in International Politics* (Boulder: Lynne Rienner, 2007), and numerous other articles in *Journal of East Asian Studies* (Lynne Rienner), *Policy and Society* (University of Sydney Press), *Liaison* (Center of Excellence in Disaster Management and Humanitarian Assistance, Honolulu), and others.

Weiqing Guo is Professor of Political Science and Public Policy at the School of Government at Sun Yat-Sen University (China) and a Member of the Chinese Association of Political Science. He is a chief editor of the annual journal *Chinese Public Policies Review* (Guangzhou) and one of the main contributors to the annual journal *Analysis of Public Policies of China* (Beijing). His current main research interests are in the role of policy networks in policy making and the changing structures of governance, the dimension of globalization in analysing various issues in public policy, and the new developments in social policy in China. His most recent publication is *Studying Public Policy* (co-authored, Southern Daily Express, 2007). He is also actively involved in promoting public education. Since 2004 he has been writing columns for *Nanfang Metropolis News, Guangzhou Daily* and *Yangcheng Evening*. His latest public lecture was *China's New Employment Laws and the Changing Relationships between Employers and Labourers* presented at the Southern China Public Forum.

Seong Kyu Ha is Professor of Urban Planning and Housing Policy in the Department of Urban and Regional Planning at Chung-Ang University, Korea. He received a master's degree in City Planning from Seoul National University in 1979, a master's degree from the London School of

Economics in 1981, and a doctorate in Urban and Regional Planning from University College London in 1984. In addition to his academic position, he was Dean of the Graduate School of Social Development, Chung-Ang University, and Director of the Korea Center for City and Environment Research in Seoul, Korea. Professor Ha also serves as President of the Korea Association for Housing Policy Studies. He has published two books in Korean, *Housing Policy* (Bakyoungsa, 1995) and *Urban Management* (Hyungseol, 1992). He also edited the English-language volume *Housing Policy and Practice in Asia* (Croom Helm, 1987). He has written many articles in Korean and in English on housing and urban redevelopment problems in Korea and elsewhere in Asia.

Yosuke Hirayama is Professor of Housing and Urban Studies at the Graduate School of Human Development and Environment, Kobe University, working extensively in the areas of housing and urban regeneration, home ownership and social change, as well as comparative housing policy. His work has appeared in international journals such as *Housing Studies* and *Urban Studies* and he is a co-editor of *Housing and Social Transition in Japan* (with Richard Ronald, Routledge, 2007). He has received academic prizes from the City Planning Institute of Japan, the Architectural Institute of Japan and Tokyo Institute of Municipal Research. He is also a founding member of the Asia-Pacific Network for Housing Research and chaired its 2005 international conference on Housing and Globalization.

Yeun Wen Ku is a Professor in the Department of Social Work, National Taiwan University. He was awarded his PhD at the University of Manchester, and then taught social policy in the Department of Social Policy and Social Work, National Chi Nan University, Taiwan for many years. After stepping down as Department Head, Professor Ku moved to the National Taiwan University and became involved in the establishment of the Social Policy Research Centre. He has written widely on welfare development and policy debates in Taiwan, including comparative studies on East Asian welfare. His publications include *Welfare Capitalism in Taiwan* (Macmillan, 1997), many collected volumes (for example, *Welfare Capitalism in East Asia*, Palgrave, 2003) and journal papers in both English and Chinese. He is also currently the Secretary-General of the Taiwanese Association of Social Policy (TASW) and the editor for *Social Policy and Social Work*, which is the most respected social policy journal published by TASP in Taiwan.

Michael H. Lee is an instructor in the Department of History, the Chinese University of Hong Kong. His research interests include education policy and reform, comparative education, higher education studies, history of modern Singapore, and history of education in Hong Kong, Singapore and Malaysia. He has published in international journals such as *Asia Pacific Education Review*, *Asia Pacific Journal of Education*, *Australian*

Journal of Education, Education and Society, Higher Education Policy and *Higher Education Research and Development*.

Ka Ho Mok is Associate Dean in the Faculty of Social Sciences, University of Hong Kong, China. Before he joined the University of Hong Kong, he was Chair Professor in East Asian Studies and Founding Director of the Centre for East Asian Studies at the University of Bristol, UK. He has researched and published extensively in the fields of comparative education policy and governance and contemporary China studies. His most recent books include *Education Reform and Education Policy in East Asia* (Routledge, 2006) and *Globalization and Higher Education in East Asia* (Marshall Cavendish Academic, 2005). He has also published in internationally refereed journals such as *Comparative Education, Comparative Education Review, International Review of Education, Journal of Education Policy, Higher Education, Governance* and *Policy & Politics*. His forthcoming book is *Challenges for the Regulatory State in Asia: Governance Change in Telecommunications, Higher Education and Health Management* (co-authored with Martin Painter and M. Ramesh, Routledge and Centre for East Asian Studies, forthcoming).

Kinglun Ngok is currently Research Fellow at the Center for Public Administration Research and Associate Professor in the School of Government, Sun Yat-Sen University, Guangzhou, China. His research interests focus on public policy and administration in China. His academic articles appear in international journals such as *International Review of Administrative Sciences, Problems of Post-Communism, Chinese Law & Government, Issues & Studies* and *Asia and Pacific Education Review*. His recent publications include *Chinese Public Policy Review* (2007), *Labour Policy in China: Marketization and Globalization Perspectives* (2007) and *Social Policy in China: Development and Wellbeing* (2008).

M. Ramesh is a leading expert on social policies in East and Southeast Asia. He is the author or co-author of *Social Policies in East and Southeast Asia* (2004), *Welfare Capitalism in Southeast Asia* (2000), *Studying Public Policy* (2003) and *The Political Economy of Canada* (1999). He has also been the editor of the *Policy and Society* journal. His research focuses on comparative political economy and public policy in Eastern Asia. His teaching interests are concentrated on public policy process, social policy, and government and business. Ramesh has held teaching or visiting appointments in Australia, Canada, Hong Kong, New Zealand, Norway and the USA.

Ray Yep is an Associate Professor in the Department of Public and Social Administration, City University of Hong Kong. He publishes extensively on market reforms and rural development in China in leading journals such as *China Quarterly, Journal of Contemporary China* and *Public Administration Review*. He also wrote *Management Empowerment in China: Political Implications of Rural Industrialization in the Reform Era*

(RoutledgeCurzon, 2003). His current research project focuses on the colonial governance of Hong Kong.

Yapeng Zhu is Associate Professor at the School of Government/Centre for Public Administration, Sun Yat-Sen University, Guangzhou, China. His research focuses on public policy and housing studies in China. His main publications include *Housing Reform in China: Policy Innovation and Housing Inequality* (Sun Yat-Sen University Press, 2007) and 'Urban governance, neoliberalism and housing reform in China' (with James Lee), *Pacific Review* (2006).

Foreword

Interest in Asian experiences of development has never been higher. The appetite of scholars and practitioners for knowledge and understanding of China has increased alongside its re-emergence as a global player and its unparalleled growth rates – its economy will overtake that of the USA by 2038. The Indian economy is also showing renewed dynamism. Japan has genuinely recovered from economic downturn in the last two years. Meanwhile the Asian tiger economies have experienced rapid economic recovery and dramatic political shifts in the wake of the 1997 financial crisis. Asian co-operation to solve regional and global development problems is on the increase. Policy learning among Asian countries, for example Vietnamese learning from China's reforms and China's learning from Singapore's governance and India's IT sector, is dynamic. Targeted Asian and Western policy learning to promote development is also an important driver of change. Given that all predictions point to Asia as the future engine of economic growth, we should know more about regional patterns of co-operation and competition; opportunities for constructive engagement; the factors underpinning the immense economic achievements of different countries; the social, political, cultural and environmental implications of the economic restructuring; and the fate and political impact of people who have been excluded from the growth.

It is against this wider political economy context that the HKU-Oxford-Bristol Book Series on *Comparative Development and Policy in Asia* has been initilated and developed since 2006. Since the launch of this series, we have been able to attract a number of manuscripts which attempt to address critical development issues, public policy and governance strategies in Asia. The present volume *Changing Governance and Public Policy in East Asia* was started about two years ago. The chapters in this volume were selected from the papers presented at three international conferences, including the 'Second Congress of Asian Political and International Studies Association' held at the City University of Hong Kong and the 'International Conference on Changing Governance and Public Policy Paradigms: Asian Perspectives' in Guangzhou, China in November 2005, as well as the international conference on 'GDPism and Risk: Social Development Challenges and Changing Governance in Asia' held in July 2006 at the University of Bristol.

The contributors to this volume identify major issues and discuss challenges that their countries are now confronting in terms of public policy formulation and the choice of policy options and policy instruments. Major attention will be focused on how selected Asian states have responded to the growing impact of 'liberalizing and marketizing trends' in public policy formulation and public management. To what extent is the 'state-guided' regime in Asia still relevant to governing public policy / public management? What are the policy implications for a growing number of Asian states which are pursuing more pro-competition policy instruments? The volume is thus a timely and important collection that offers critical analysis of the search for new governance in Asia and will compare and contrast experiences in selected Asian societies such as China, Japan, Hong Kong, Taiwan, South Korea, Singapore, and other parts of South East Asia. The present volume puts together leading scholars from Hong Kong, Taiwan, China, Japan, Singapore, South Korea and the United Kingdom to engage in critical analysis of how globalization has challenged Asian societies and in what way nation states in the region have responded by searching for better governance strategies in handling the increasingly complex social, economic and political issues in Asia.

Preface

In the post-Cold War era since the late 1980s, the Washington consensus has given way to the supranational organizations in shaping and determining global social, economic and political agendas. Nonetheless, this powerful agenda has encountered its critics. A number of scholars suggest that the implementation of the consensus in many countries, especially in developing or less-developed countries, around the world has led to a situation where there is 'global governance without global government'. Similarly, the proposal to reduce state activity by the Washington consensus has been relentlessly attacked by other scholars as an irresponsible act, particularly when many countries of the developing world conceive the reduction of state activity as an effort to cut back state capacity across the board (Fukuyama 2005: 20). The growing popularity of the ideas and practices of neo-liberalism and neo-liberal institutionalism, coupled with the negative consequences emerging from the process of reducing state activity in the developing world, have aroused concerns about state capacity in managing an increasingly complex and globalizing world. Unlike the neo-liberalist ideas that play up the role of the market at the expense of the state, the state capacity literature argues for 'stateness' as the basis for effective governance.

In view of the growing influence of the neo-liberalist project in advocating the reduction of the state in public management and governance, Fukuyama has recently argued that 'the state-building agenda, which was at least as important as the state-reducing one, was not given nearly as much thought or emphasis' (2005: 7). Well aware of the problems when the state lacks the capacity to govern complex economic, social and political issues in the globalizing economy context, Fukuyama calls for a better understanding of the difference between the *scope* of state activities, which means the different functions and goals taken on by governments, and the *strength* of state power, which refers to the ability of the state to plan and implement its policies and political agendas. He also highlights the confusions in the understanding of stateness, especially when 'the word *strength* is often used indifferently to refer both to what is here labeled *scope* as well as to *strength* or *capacity*'. The distinction between the scope of state activity and the strength of state power would enable us to develop a better understanding of the notion of stateness in the contemporary world.

The current book project was initiated and developed when I served as the Founding Director and Chair Professor of the Centre for East Asian Studies, University of Bristol. Throughout the editorial process of this volume, I have received very positive support from all the contributors. I am particularly grateful that Mr Peter Sowden from Routledge approached me regarding launching a new series on *Comparative Development and Policy in Asia*. Since the launch of the new series, we have been able to attract some high quality manuscripts for inclusion in the series. I am delighted to present the current volume as part of the series. Throughout the last few years, I have been strongly supported by a team of colleagues working closely at the Centre for East Asian Studies, University of Bristol, Faculty of Social Sciences, the University of Hong Kong and the Department of Public and Social Administration, City University of Hong Kong. We would like to thank Emma Holland, Will Lo, Kinglun Ngok, Ray Yep and Ian Holliday for their assistance in turning the papers into a coherent volume. We would like to thank the Japan Foundation, London and National Chi Nan University, Taiwan for supporting one of the conferences held at Bristol in 2006.

My sincere thanks must be extended to all the authors in this volume. Without their contributions, we would not be able to develop all these papers into a coherent book. The present book was completed when I took up a new position at the Faculty of Social Sciences, the University of Hong Kong in late 2007. The completion of this volume marks a new stage in my academic journey and I would like to dedicate it to all colleagues, academic friends and researchers who are interested in governance issues in Asia.

Last, but not least, I express my gratitude to Jasmine, my beloved wife, and Esther and Lucinda, my lovely daughters, for their unfailing love during my years in Bristol and their full support when I decided to join the University of Hong Kong.

Ka Ho Mok
Hong Kong, 2008

Reference

Fukuyama, F. (2005) The imperative of state-building, *Journal of Democracy*, 15(2): 17–31.

Introduction

The search for good governance in Asia

Ka Ho Mok and Ray Forrest

Global challenges and common agenda: the search for good governance

The search for good governance has become an increasingly important element of public policy and public management and is high on the political agenda of East Asian countries. The need for robust governance structures and institutions was brought into sharp focus by the Asian financial crisis (AFC), which affected adversely most East Asian societies. Since then they have begun to look for ways to restructure their public administration and political systems in order to develop new mechanisms and structures to promote good governance. When reflecting upon the notions of good governance, most Asian countries refer to the quality of the relationship between government and the citizens whom it exists to serve and protect (Asian Development Bank 2007). As Howell (2005: 1) rightly argues, 'taking the spotlight away from ideology and global political divisions, the good governance agenda focused its attentions on the internal failure of states in the South'. If we follow the definitions proposed by major international organizations such as the World Bank or the International Monetary Fund, good governance refers to institutionalizing processes for achieving effective, efficient, transparent and accountable government. Turner and Hulme (1997: 229–231) develop a close relationship between good governance with the established processes and mechanisms for holding public servants responsible for their actions, a legal framework for development, decentralization, micro-level accountability to consumers, and making information available for policy analysis and debate. Like their western counterparts, Asian governments have tried hard in recent years to benchmark using the four pillars of good governance, which are related to accountability, transparency, predictability and participation.

We have also witnessed the growing influence of neo-liberalism on public policy decision making and social service provision. In recent decades, privatization and marketization have become common strategies in shaping patterns of government–business relations not only in the West but also in East Asia (Gouri et al. 1991; World Bank 1995). And pressure for broad governance changes has been strong, coming to a head with the financial crisis of 1997. A feature of these pressures is the increasing presence of influential inter-national agencies such as the International Monetary Fund (IMF) and the World Bank. Their preferred models of governance reflect these neo-liberal influences: *a less interventionist and arbitrary state; a strengthening of 'juridical' forms of regulation (often associated with fundamental legal reform); more disaggregated and decentralized forms of government, including partnerships and a stronger 'co-production' role for civil society groups; and a preference for market-like mechanisms over bureaucratic methods of service delivery.*

Instead of relying solely upon government bureaucracy for the delivery of goods or services, there has been a massive proliferation of tools and policy instruments, with a dizzying array of loans, loan guarantees, grants, contracts, insurance, vouchers etc. to address public policy problems. Such diversified policy tools and instruments may render the conventional governance model inappropriate. It is particularly true when many of these tools are highly indirect. They rely heavily on a wide assortment of 'third parties' such as commercial banks, private hospitals, industrial corporations, universities, social service agencies and other social organizations (Salomon 2002). There-fore, networks and partnerships supplant hierarchical command and con-trol (Bache 2003; Rhodes 1997, 2000). This book is set in the wider policy context outlined above to examine how the selected Asian governments have responded to the globalization challenges and what strategies they have adopted in reforming their public administration and social policy in promoting good governance

The origin, major focuses and structure of the book

The chapters in this volume were selected from the papers presented at three international conferences, including the 'Second Congress of Asian Political and International Studies Association' held at the City University of Hong Kong, the 'International Conference on Changing Governance and Public Policy Paradigms: Asian Perspectives' in Guangzhou, China in November 2005 and the international conference on 'GDPism and Risk: Social Devel-opment Challenges and Changing Governance in Asia' held in July 2006 at the University of Bristol. The contributors to this volume identify major issues and discuss challenges that their countries are now confronting in terms of public policy formulation and the choice of policy options and policy instruments.

Major attention will be focused on how selected Asian states have responded to the growing impact of 'liberalizing and marketizing trends' in public policy formulation and public management. To what extent is the 'state-guided' regime in Asia still relevant to governing public policy/public management? What are the policy implications for a growing number of Asian states that are pursuing more pro-competition policy instruments? The volume is thus a timely and important collection that offers critical analysis of the search for new governance in Asia and will compare and contrast experiences in selected Asian societies such as China, Japan, Hong Kong, Taiwan, South Korea, Singapore, and other parts of South East Asia. The present volume is organized into four parts, covering sub-themes including 'globalization challenges, state capacity and changing policy paradigms', 'changing policy instruments and regulatory regimes', 'the changing role of the private sector in public policy' and 'the challenge for urban governance'.

Globalization challenges, state capacity and changing policy paradigms

The four chapters in Part I address this sub-theme. Authors in the first part focus on how different Asian states have responded to the growing impacts of globalization on governance by changing social policy paradigms or searching for new strategies in improving public sector management. Cheung's chapter reviews critically East Asian social policy development, pointing out that despite the arguments for the eroding role of state-led developmentalism in Asia, East Asian states still maintain a strong bureaucrat-dominated form of public policy making. He also points to the interconnections between East Asian welfarism and the growth of East Asian capitalism. Just as Marxists and neo-Marxists have explained the relationship between western capitalism and its welfare state, the East Asian social policy discourse cannot be decoupled from the larger developmentalist paradigm. Cheung echoes the recent debates regarding the demise of the East Asian developmental state in accounting for future success and development in Asia. In response to the competitive pressures of globalization a growing number of Asian states have followed global trends in public governance by transforming themselves into new forms of regulatory states by adopting far more pro-competition policy instruments in enhancing the performance and efficiency of public sector management or social policy delivery (Gill 1995; Jordana and Levi-Faur 2005; Moran 2002). However, this does not necessarily mean that the state capacity of these Asian economies has been reduced. Indeed, recent research has indicated that governments across different parts of the globe, facing similar competitive pressures, have undertaken regulatory reforms such as privatization or corporatization of state-owned industries or public-owned organizations like post offices and universities, opening up new markets to multiple providers and the introduction of new regulatory regimes under the control of independent regulators (Drahos and Joseph 1995; Levi-Faur 1998; Scott 2004). Similarly, a growing number of East Asian governments have also subscribed to these 'international norms' and successfully reinvented themselves after the financial crisis of 1997 with strengthened governing capacity (Asia Development Bank 2007; Cheung and Scott 2003; Shimomura 2003).

Unlike the regulatory state in America, which evolved against a liberal market economy context, the regulatory state in Asia has emerged in the context of a combined strong state and a free market economy, by which the state ideologically commits to an 'authoritarian liberalism'. As Jayasuriya has rightly pointed out, 'this authoritarian liberalism presupposes the existence of a strong (or better described as politically illiberal) state with a capacity to regulate the economy' (2000: 329). In order to enhance their global competitiveness, many of these Asian states have attempted to transform themselves into 'market accelerationist states' (Mok 2006a). The market accelerationist state has the features of a 'dualistic state', which Fraenkel (1941) described as a strong state combined with a liberal market economy. With this kind of state architecture in place, the success of the markets rests heavily upon the presence of strong regulatory institutions. The strong regulatory role of the state is to prevent the market from unnecessary domestic political interference. Thus it is not simply a market-embracing model of the state. Instead, the market accelerationist state operates according to the logic of the market but intervenes in markets in order to remove inefficiencies (Mok 2005; Painter and Wong 2005; Weiss 1998).

It is against this wider socio-economic and socio-political context that East Asian governments have introduced reforms or restructuring exercises to enhance their economic and political institutions to compete in the global marketplace. Transforming social policy delivery and reforming public sector management with a neo-liberal orientation may not necessarily weaken the state capacity because the long-standing bureaucrat-dominated nature of public policy making remains in place (Cheung 2005). Therefore, we should not simply interpret such changes as paradigm shifts. Instead, Cheung argues that Asian governments have tactically maintained the status quo during these transformative processes, which has contributed to policy steadiness.

Like its neighbouring East Asian countries, China seems to have adopted similar development strategies. The economic success enjoyed by China in the last few decades suggests that a combination of fundamental and selective interventions can be highly effective (Angresano 2005; Brahm 2002). By concentrating its full attention on modernization and economic transformation projects since the late 1970s, China has significantly transformed the country not only in terms of the economic sphere but also in cultural, political and social domains (So 2003; Tang and Holzner 2007; Tubilewicz 2006). Technological advancement in post-Mao China, especially the rapid development of high-tech industries, and the expansion of higher education have generated substantial changes in the employment structure. New professions and new status groups are on the rise, such as accountants, engineers, lawyers, managers, stock-brokers, speculators, and so on (Li 2003). These developments are indicative of new forms of social differentiation and heterogeneity in post-Mao China (So 2003). Moreover, decentralization, enterprise reforms and the success of township enterprises have greatly expanded the size of the new middle class (corporate professionals such as mid-level managers and accountants). The expansion of higher education institutions and the service sector has also greatly expanded the size of another segment of the new middle class (service professionals such as teachers and journalists). Other social groups such as private entrepreneurs have benefited from the same social and economic change processes and have become rich in the process (Lippit 2005; So 2005).

Nonetheless, these same change processes have also intensified social inequalities and widened regional disparities in China (Hu et al. 2001; Keng 2006; Zhang 2006; Zhu 2005). Although the Chinese government has made attempts to alleviate absolute poverty since 1949, the problems related to relative poverty and social exclusion have become so acute that they threaten rising social instability and political crisis in China (Mackerras 2006; Schweickart 2006; Walder 2007). As Robert Weil has recently suggested,

> the capitalist system [in China] is devouring its own and rapidly generating ever-wider groups of the alienated. . . . The worsening conditions of the working classes are pushing them rapidly in a more radical and militant direction. Within the ranks not only of the workers and peasants, but among many intellectuals and at least some of the broader new middle class as well, there is a deep and growing understanding that global capitalism has no answer to their situations, and that the revolutionary socialism that they built under Mao offers at least the outline of another way forward today.
>
> (2006: 6)

In response to the diversified social interests and the growing social contradictions in China, the Chinese government has recently proposed a scientific approach to development by promoting the importance of 'social harmony'. In specific policy terms, the government has made attempts to rectify the problems resulting from the marketization and privatization of social policy by adopting a more welfare-based orientation (Li 2007).

It is against this policy background that Kinglun Ngok examines the changing social policy paradigm shifts in China by making use of Peter Hall's concept of policy paradigm to analyse different phases of development policy in China. Ngok argues that with the growing tensions among different social groups, coupled with the rising discontent in relation to widening income gaps and social injustice, the new generation of Chinese leaders led by President Hu Jintao and Premier Wan Jiabo has attempted to rectify the problems and crises generated from the quest for GDPism over the last two decades. In order to sustain further development, both Hu and Wan have adopted a more 'people-centred' development orientation. This is welfare-based instead of the social policy approach solely determined by the drive for marketization and commodification (CCCCP 2003; Ngok, this volume). Although the central government has attempted to move from the market-oriented social policy paradigm to a more welfare-based and people-centred paradigm, Ngok believes the institutionalization of the new paradigm will take a long time to make such a shift because of the complex central–local relations in the Chinese political system and the increasingly powerful and strong localities.

After reviewing the work of Fischer and Forester (1993) regarding the 'Argumentative Turn', coupled with the analysis of Wildavsky's thought on the roles and norms (1992), Weiqing Guo provides a framework for analysing the processes in making public policy. Believing in the significance of transparency and citizen participation in the policy-making process, the empowerment of the public in the public policy discourse has received more attention in recent years. Although the present Chinese political regime remains socialist, the new generation of Chinese leaders is well aware of the importance of identifying good practices elsewhere to promote good governance. Although there are serious problems of malpractice, rent-seeking, inefficiency and corruption in China's public administration (Howell 2005; Lieberthal and Oksenberg 1998; Yeo and Pearson 2007), the policy-making processes in general and public sector management in particular have gradually improved, especially when the central government has attached more weight to accountability and anti-corruption. In the context of the transitional economy, China has made attempts to strengthen its legal systems, reform its institutional framework for market forces and promote efficiency in its public service units (Howell 2005; OECD 2005).

Analysing public policy paradigm shifts from another perspective, Weiqing Guo argues that Chinese residents on mainland China have been empowered in influencing the processes of public policy making in China. Unlike the notions and forms of democracy in western societies, Guo argues that through a close scrutiny of gradual changes in public policy making in the post-Mao era from a policy science perspective, we can easily observe the ways in which public policy management differs significantly from previous periods, especially with more professional input generated from academics and think tanks. Other scholars even argue that China is transforming towards a consultative rule of law regime and the political regime is evolving toward soft authoritarianism (Pan 2003; Pei 2000). Comparing China's citizen empowerment experiences with the western democracies, there is clearly substantial room for improvement. Nonetheless, the pace and extent of changes which have taken place over the last two decades in China is striking, especially when the Hu and Wan leadership has given greater credence to the advice given by academics. The policy-making process has embraced more policy research, and the approach has shifted toward a more humanitarian orientation, with the senior leaders recognizing the growing social inequalities and intensified regional disparities that have emerged through the drive for GDPism.

If we follow the discussions in the chapters mentioned above, it is evident that the orientations of public policy and the choices of policy option have been increasingly shaped by popular global trends. For example, no matter how hard Japan has tried to preserve its very rich traditions and practices, Ito Go argues in his chapter that Japanese society is at a crossroads. Despite the fact that the Koizumi government attempted to 'contain' the effects resulting from the introduction of 'structural reform' on the politics and society of Japan, the country has been constrained in its policy options because the economic engine in Japan is no longer as powerful as it once was a few decades ago. Although Japan has experienced gradual economic recovery in recent years, Go argues that the Japanese government has to make a very difficult decision as to whether to go along the US route and maintain its close association with the developed economies in Europe or to identify Japan with neighbouring countries and better integrate with the Asian community. In addition, he argues that a better understanding of public policy making in Japan could be obtained by analysing the domestic–international nexus. Despite the fact that the government does not intend to interrupt the fundamental structure of 'embedded liberalism', such a system has been challenged in the last decade, particularly given the uncertainties as to whether Japan can maintain its economic growth (Flath 2005; Kikkawa 2005). Calculating the political risk, the government led by Koizumi had started to adopt far more pro-competition policy instruments to transform the public sector and the employment systems have changed significantly in the last decade (Rebick 2005; Stockwin 2006).

More importantly, whether the anticipated economic growth could sustain a society with growing but competing social demands remains in question. After experiencing economic downturn, coupled with rapid social and demographic changes, contemporary Japanese society is confronted with intensified income disparities, a growing ageing population, late marriage, unemployment and other social problems (Izuhara 2003; Rebick and Takenaka 2006; Retherford et al. 2001). In this connection, Go argues in his chapter that the choice of public policy is determined not only by domestic developments but also by Japan's foreign relationships with the US, China and its neighbours in the Asian region. What really constrains Japan's choice is that whenever it has attempted to take a more proactive approach in engaging with the Asian community, some of the countries in the region are still wary of Japan's intentions because of the negative legacy of Japan's colonization (McCargo 2004). At the same time, there is a growing nationalist movement in Japan, which has inhibited the government from making drastic changes in foreign policy to engage with China, especially when some local political forces have attempted to play up the 'China threat' issues (Cheng 2007). With the rise of China and the business opportunities offered, the Japanese government is now caught between remaining in the European club and joining the Asian one. In short, Ito Go's chapter demonstrates that the extent and nature of public policy paradigm shifts depend not only on domestic conditions but also on international relations.

Changing policy instruments and regulatory regimes

In addition to the changing policy paradigms, modern states have attempted to reinvent themselves by moving beyond the welfare state to become the competition state in response to the growing pressures generated by the forces of globalization (Gill 1995; Jordana and Levi-Faur 2005; Moran 2002). To enhance the efficiency of public policy and public management, modern states may deregulate in some areas while enforcing competition in others, hence becoming a facilitator or even a generator of markets. Thus, it is common for reregulation or recentralization in the processes of market restructuring to be accompanied by the emergence of strong regulatory and entrepreneurial states (Chan and Tan 2006; Ng and Chan 2006).

The four chapters in Part II examine how selected East Asian governments have transformed their regulatory regimes by adopting far more pro-competition policy instruments in promoting good governance. Ramesh's chapter focuses on public hospital reforms in Hong Kong and Singapore. The comparative study of the hospital reforms between these two city-states has shown that centralized coordination and planning afforded by public ownership allows the government to correct many failures in the healthcare market. According to Ramesh, efforts to promote competition among hospitals in Singapore have had added benefits for those unable to pay. In addition, the case of Hong Kong indicates that competition is not as central to efficient management of hospitals as suggested by the New Public Management (NPM) protagonists and mainstream health economists. In his chapter, Ramesh sets out the comparative study very neatly by referring to the global trends in healthcare reforms. He makes it clear that there are three major reform strategies in healthcare, namely: autonomization, corporatization and privatization. Autonomization involves increasing management autonomy for managers, while privatization involves complete divesture (Preker and Harding 2003). Realizing the social and political costs to pay, most governments would opt for corporatization of healthcare, somewhere in-between the autonomization and privatization options. Corporatization entails transforming public hospitals into autonomous state enterprises with considerable operational autonomy and significant exposure to market competition but avoids the political and technical difficulties associated with privatization.

Ramesh's chapter shows clearly that the adoption of market-oriented approaches in transforming the healthcare sectors in Hong Kong and Singapore may not necessarily reduce the control of the state. He even argues that centralized planning would enhance Hong Kong's ability to deliver a highly effective but relatively comprehensive healthcare system. This comparative study offers a significant alternative approach to those of mainstream health economists and NPM protagonists by arguing that good planning and professional management can substitute for the market. After comparing Hong Kong with the Singapore case, Ramesh believes that the Hong Kong healthcare management approach offers more useful lessons for developing countries than Singapore. The constant monitoring and improvements necessary to correct undesirable developments show that greater reliance on the market in the healthcare sector can only be achieved if accompanied by a high level of bureaucratic capability and willingness on the part of the government to use it. Relying solely upon the market for healthcare would not fulfil the social objectives. Without a strong state that can intervene to protect public interests, profit motives are likely to overwhelm social objectives. Such situations can be easily found in the case of China, where healthcare is highly marketized resulting in growing complaints from citizens about excessive medical charges and health financing burdens (Mok 2006a; Zhu 2005).

Similar to the healthcare reforms, higher education systems in East Asia have also experienced drastic restructuring, particularly when governments are keen to promote the global competence of their university graduates and to improve the global ranking of their universities. Being part of the larger public sector, higher education has never been immune from the same reinventing government project. In order to improve university governance, universities in East Asia have been experiencing the incorporation and corporatization processes. Significantly influenced by the popular tide of neo-liberalism and particularly by the university models offered by the US, higher education systems in Asia have started restructuring and reforming exercises to 'displace political sovereignty with the sovereignty of "the market"' (Comaroff, cited in Giroux 2002: 5). Instead of being closely directed by the Ministry of Education or equivalent government administrative bodies, state universities in Asia are now required to become more proactive and dynamic in seeking their own financial resources. Being dissatisfied with the conventional model along the lines of 'state-oriented' and 'highly centralized' approaches in higher education, Asian governments have recently tried to 'incorporate' or introduce 'corporatization' and 'privatization' measures to run their state/national universities, believing that these transformations could make national universities more flexible and responsive to rapid socio-economic changes (Mok 2006b; Oba 2006).

Ka Ho Mok's chapter critically examines how universities in Hong Kong and Singapore have been transformed in line with the ideas and practices of neo-liberalism. He clearly demonstrates how university governance is increasingly directed by corporate values and cultures, especially when public universities face state budget cuts. Without sufficient resources, public universities have to diversify resources by engaging in other income generation projects or developing closer partnerships with business and industry. University presidents or vice-chancellors are heavily occupied with fund-raising activities, while university curriculum design and even faculty appointments are increasingly influenced by corporate interests, with more reliance on research contracts, social donations and endowment chairs (Mok 2007). Whether the introduction of competition to the university sector and the corporatization of public universities have really enabled university administrators to have more autonomy and flexibility in university governance is subject to debate. Recent comparative studies have suggested that academics generally feel academic freedom under threat and collegial relationship deteriorating as a result of growing corporate influences on university governance

(Giroux 2002; Lynch 2006; Petersen and Currie 2007). Mok argues that the adoption of far more pro-competition policy instruments along the lines of corporatization, commodification and privatization in East Asian higher education is set against a strong state interventionist context. Contrary to the regulatory regime in the US, the corporatization drives in East Asian higher education systems have resulted in increased control; academics complain about lack of autonomy because of corporate governance, while the implementation of decentralization in university governance has led to the 'centralized decentralization' phenomenon (Lee 2004; Lee and Gopinathan 2007; Mok 2006a).

Like Ramesh and Mok's chapters, Yeun Wen Ku compares different welfare policy instruments in East Asia and discovers that policy instruments have been diversified and mixed. The varied welfare instrument mixes in East Asia have clearly shown the different choices that have been made by governments during the process of instrument selection. Placed against a highly politicized environment, the choice of welfare policy instruments should be acceptable to citizens. More specifically, the transformation from authoritarianism to democracy has inevitably made the public/social policy-making processes more political. Political leaders, therefore, must be sensitive to the sentiments and moods of society. Ku's chapter highlights the importance of the changing relationship between the state and the people, which involves citizens' feelings, public opinions and expectations in policy options. Walker and Wong also believe that, 'neither capitalism nor democracy are necessary conditions for constituting a welfare state or explaining its development' but non-capitalist and authoritarian states like the former Soviet Union and pre-reform Maoist China could implement many essential social policies in promoting social welfare similar to the welfare state in the West (2005: 4–5). Similarly, Ku argues that democratization does not imply that welfare development is mandatory. Instead, it opens opportunities for policy-makers, stakeholders and the people to rethink the welfare instruments they would prefer. Therefore, communication between the government and the people is extremely important, while trust becomes a crucial element in determining such a relationship. But the most crucial issue is how to cultivate a relationship based on 'trust' between the rulers and the ruled, which would eventually shape the choice in welfare instruments (Ku, this volume). One of the major contributions of Ku's chapter is to highlight the importance of the politics of welfare instrument selection in Asia, reminding us to be sensitive about how complicated are the processes in making welfare policy options.

Neo-liberalist globalization proponents and pluralist economic actors have never been satisfied with the way the Chinese government handles the market because of 'unnecessary' state regulations. Moreover, foreign investors and industrial firms have seldom valued Chinese state regulations, particularly when preferential treatment for Chinese companies is discovered. Struggling for 15 years to gain accession to the World Trade Organization (WTO), China began to act in accordance with its agreed market liberalization rules in 2001. It is against this wider policy context that the Chinese government has adopted far more pro-market measures to transform the state economy, public administration and public management in the last few decades (Burn 2005; Pistor and Xu 2005; Shafaeddin 2004; Zhang 2003). Bill Chou's chapter addresses an important development issue in China by examining a case study of downsizing administrative licenses to promote changes in the regulatory regime in the private sector. Based upon an institutional perspective, Chou argues that the institutional features of China's bureaucracy have shaped the incentive to keep burdensome licensing systems for pursuing local economic growth. There are major barriers involved in policy coordination and monitoring and hence local public officials are able to hide their activities from their principals' scrutiny and ignore the central directives that are in conflict with local agendas.

Potentially, administrative license downsizing could improve the business environment and contribute to a change in public officials' attitudes towards private businesses. In addition, the downsizing can reduce the use of an overly complicated licensing system for rent seeking by removing the licensing authority of local public officials, which they use to create market barriers. Nonetheless, the mixed success of downsizing administrative licenses has clearly shown that the masterminds behind the policy have not adequately considered local institutional features when designing the policy. Since the policy entails numerous ill-coordinated implementers with diverse interests, a top-down approach of downsizing neither solicits voluntary compliance from implementers nor provides adequate information for policy-makers to supervise policy implementation and exercise sanctions. More importantly, the incentive systems at local levels go against the downsizing policy (Zhong 2003). The performance appraisal systems of local leaders encourage them to focus on the short-term economic growth of small localities but ignore the collective benefits of improving the wider investment environment. Hence, licensing authority conducive to achieving the immediate result of economic growth by fending off competition against local enterprises and their products is much sought after. With the potential of the licensing authority to form an important source of revenue, local governments are given strong incentives to thwart administrative license downsizing. Chou's chapter once again shows the politics of public policy making in China. Even when there are good policy objectives, policy goals will be misplaced if the processes of implementation have not been well handled. This is particularly critical for China when the country is struggling to shift from a planned to a market economy (Yang 2004).

The changing role of the private sector in public policy

Part III examines the changing role of the private sector in public policy, with particular reference to examining how the prominence of neo-liberalism and the growing popularity of corporate ideas and practices have affected public policy formulation and social policy delivery in Asia. In order to offload the cost of public services such as housing, education, transport, care services and other social protection services, privatization, marketization, commodification and corporatization strategies have become increasingly popular policy tools adopted to transform public sector management and social service delivery. Citizens now have to buy these services at market value rather than have them provided by the state. The growing prominence of neo-liberalism and the popular practices of marketization, commodification and privatization in the public sector have significantly changed cultures and beliefs, hence creating a potential threat to critical voices and undermining the social and public functions performed by the public institutions (Harkavy 2006; Lee 2007; Lynch 2006; Marginson 2006).

In view of the global corporate influences penetrating public sector management and social policy developments, critical analysts have repeatedly argued that neo-liberalism is the most dangerous ideology of the current historical moment. Giroux, for example, believes that 'civic discourse has given way to the language of commercialization, privatization, and deregulation and that, within the language and impacts of corporate culture, citizenship is portrayed as an utterly privatized affair that produces self-interested individuals' (2002: 1). Even those market fundamentalists such as Milton Friedman, Robert Nozick and Francis Fukuyama argue that, 'neo-liberalism attempts to eliminate an engaged critique about its most basic principles and social consequences by embracing "the market as the arbiter of social destiny"' (Rule 1998: 31). Despite the invaluable role of non-commodified public spheres in history (Herman and McChesney 1997), corporate culture extends even deeper into basic institutions of civil and political society. Corporate culture and neo-liberalism involve a simultaneous diminishing of non-commodified public spheres, in which organizations such as public schools, churches, non-commercial public broadcasting, libraries, trade unions, and various voluntary institutions are reduced in importance, becoming less engaged in addressing the relationship of the self to public life and social responsibility to the broader demands of citizenship (Giroux 2002: 4).

Ray Yep's chapter compares China and Hong Kong in terms of how the governments of these two Chinese societies have responded to the growing corporate influences. Although mainland China is still practising a socialist market economy while Hong Kong has long been market capitalist, Yep demonstrates that the business sectors are finding ways to influence the making of public policy in both these societies. Both systems, however, are confronted with the challenge of how to accommodate the interests of capitalists. According to Yep, such business-bias leads to distrust of public authority on the political front and suspicion regarding the existence of a level-playing field in the economic realm. In addition, the continual exclusion of non-state capitalists in the policy process in mainland China not only obstructs further progress in market reforms but also affects long-term political stability. In order to address the growing corporate influences in public policy decision-making processes, Yep believes there is only one way out, which is to implement political reforms in both societies by institutionalizing democratic political systems.

Choi's chapter focuses on business structure and power politics developments resulting from pension privatization in Japan, South Korea and Taiwan. Choi's discussion not only offers comparative insights enabling readers to develop a more comprehensive and critical understanding of the role of the private sector in pension provisions in the selected Asian societies; it also highlights the increasing privatization in social provision in Asia. Will these Asian economies continue to transfer the welfare mix to other social/public policy areas? What relationship will exist between the state and other non-state sectors, particularly when the private sector has begun to play an increasingly important role in social policy governance. This comparative study on the changing role of business in pension provision raises important political questions.

Analysing education policy change in Hong Kong and Singapore, Michael Lee argues that the introduction and implementation of a private education policy in these Asian city-states have resulted in policy dilemmas confronting both governments. In his chapter, Lee critically reviews the development of and major changes in private education policy in these two Asian tigers. The comparative study finds that Hong Kong enjoys more autonomy, flexibility and diversity after private education has been introduced. The introduction of private education to the schooling in Hong Kong has fulfilled the policy objectives of promoting more diversity in the education system and creating more choices for students and parents. For Singapore, the introduction of private education is unquestionably a breakthrough since the city-state has long been practising a state-dominated model in education (Mok and Tan 2004). Through the institutionalization of independent and autonomous schools, some traditional prestigious schools can reinforce their own social status and outstanding academic and non-academic performance and thus keep their comparative advantage in the local education market. But what is equally true is that the same policy has widened the gap between these independent or autonomous schools and the others, especially when there is a widespread prejudice among students and parents against non-independent and non-autonomous schools. In this connection, Lee questions whether the introduction of market forces to drive competition among schools in Singapore would create a conducive environment for promoting a higher quality of education.

Most important of all, Lee's comparative study of Hong Kong and Singapore again raises the concerns of the negative influences of neo-liberalism on educational development. Although the growing prominence of privatization in education could promote diversity and choice in education, we must critically examine the issues of 'choice for whom' and 'for whose interests'. Undoubtedly, more private schools can provide parents or families who are rich enough with more choices, but the same education change processes have also socially marginalized those who cannot afford to pay for private education. In addition, established public schools could choose to opt out from the government/public sector and establish themselves as private/independent/autonomous schools. Thus, the privatization of education has inevitably resulted in the stratification of schools. Lee's chapter delivers a cautious note to public administrators: when making decisions and policy choices, they have to strike a balance between efficiency, equality and equity issues.

Considering the comparative study of Hong Kong and Singapore in relation to other Asian countries such as China and other Southeast Asian countries, we should be aware of the policy implications for the privatization of education or any other public/social policies. The evidence is overwhelming that in an economically unequal society like transitional China, only those with sufficient resources can make choices and those who are poor have no choices at all (Mok and Lo 2007; Reay and Lucey 2003). In this regard, whether people can exercise choice becomes a secondary consideration when the primary concerns of quality, affordability and access in education have not been properly addressed (Lynch and O'Riordan 1998). Part III concludes with an intellectually stimulating chapter by Yapeng Zhu, who has attempted to critically examine housing monetarization reform in China, with particular reference to how the government has struggled to balance economic efficiency, social equality and social stability. Housing policy, as with education, has been affected by the market forces and privatization strategies that have been adopted to transform the sector in mainland China.

Zhu's chapter focuses on housing monetarization reform in China. As a result of the emphasis placed on economic efficiency when the policy was initially implemented, it produced negative policy consequences, including worsening housing inequalities, and Chinese society is confronted with political instability. In order to rectify the problems of housing privatization, Zhu believes the alternative model is to revamp the social welfare-based approach in meeting people's housing needs. Zhu's chapter echoes Kinglun Ngok's argument in this volume, that the Chinese leaders are attempting to move beyond the market-oriented social policy paradigm to a more people-oriented and welfare-based approach (see also, Mok 2006a). In light of problems resulting from the marketization and commodification of social policy in the last two decades (Wong and Flynn 2001), the Chinese regime is caught between promoting economic efficiency and social equality. Zhu's chapter once again points out the importance of the adoption of a development strategy that would sustain long-term social and economic developments. Therefore, we should be careful when adhering to the principles and practices of neo-liberalism in transforming public sector management and social policy delivery.

The challenge for urban governance

Part IV focuses on the governance of cities. Consistent with the institutional and policy developments described above, the management of cities has experienced substantial transformation over the last two decades driven primarily by a neo-liberal agenda in which social investment became increasingly subservient to the imperatives of competition and growth. Indeed, cities have been at the forefront of the modernization agenda in terms of the privatization, deregulation and fragmentation of municipal services, as the test beds for policy and institutional innovation, and as the powerhouses of national economies (Kearns and Paddison 2000). In a globally integrated economy, the major cities have vied for competitive position and have become increasingly disconnected from their national hinterlands. The dominant policy discourse has revolved around ideas of the entrepreneurial city in which business and commercial interests have taken precedence (Hall and Hubbard 1998; Harvey 2002; Wu 2003). At the same time and partly as a consequence, old ideas of top-down municipal government have given way to notions of urban governance, partnerships and networks in which a diversity of urban stakeholders are involved in shaping the policy agenda. 'Good' urban governance has become synonymous with the implementation of this kind of policy mix (Jessop 2002).

Cities have also been at the forefront of demographic and social changes that have produced a whole new set of policy challenges. These include an ageing population, smaller households, shifts in employment patterns and changes in broader social norms. These developments combined with the exigencies of economic globalization have impacted on different cities in different ways, with evident contrasts between more mature urban settlements and those experiencing rapid economic development and population immigration. East Asian societies encompass a wide variety of cities but most have experienced substantial population growth in recent decades, amidst dramatic economic progress as well as periods of severe economic disruption, most notably and pervasively during the AFC. The AFC, in particular, had a major impact on the infrastructures and patterns of opportunity in cities in countries such as South Korea, Thailand and Hong Kong, and posed new questions about the need for a greater balance between economic objectives and social investment in urban policy. There is now a greater policy emphasis on issues of social inclusion, social cohesion and democratic participation – albeit against a tide of rampant development, which is too often acting to widen inequalities and reduce access for some groups to decent health, housing and education.

The three chapters in Part IV approach the question of urban governance from different perspectives. Forrest's paper sets the discussion of urban governance in the context of the broader urban experience. If 'good governance' is about creating the 'good city', what qualities should we be trying to create? In posing the question in terms of how to manage the 'chaotic' city, he argues that an element of chaos is a positive urban quality rather than necessarily a problem to be addressed. Some level of disorder is quintessentially urban in the sense that overplanned and overcontrolled urban environments may in the end lose their competitive edge. Moreover, a uni-dimensional city geared too self-consciously to the needs of inward investment and the business sectors runs the risk of losing the qualities that provide the energy and creative edge to great cities. And if social cohesion is one of the primary aims of urban policy, how should that be achieved and what would it look like? Here, again, there are potential contradictory processes at work on different spatial scales.

Forrest then proceeds to explore the issue of urban social cohesion in relation to some of the distinctive drivers of urban change in East Asian societies and contrasts the experiences of western cities when they faced similar pressures of urban–rural migration and rapid economic development. The cities of East Asia, as in many other parts of the world, are expanding in a very different global context from those of nineteenth-century Europe and face the combined challenges of social and environmental sustainability. He argues, however, that the urban social fabric can show a high degree of resilience even in the midst of dramatic social and economic transformations. For example, drawing on a study of Guangzhou, he demonstrates that contrary to some previous work there is evidence to suggest a robustness of social ties, traditional forms of reciprocity and mutual trust despite considerable spatial and social disruption. Forrest argues that it is these subtle qualities of urban life which good urban governance has to maintain and nurture – working with, rather than against, the grain of communities. The pace of development combined with growing economic resources in East Asia provides the opportunity for enlightened urban governance to create cities that are socially vibrant, environmentally sustainable and globally competitive.

Yosuke Hirayama's chapter focuses on the redevelopment of Tokyo and the way in which the city has been positioned at the forefront of attempts to reinvigorate the Japanese economy. In doing so, he engages with the broader question of metropolitan dominance and spatial inequalities. Prior to the 1980s, Tokyo's redevelopment was very much a top-down affair in which business interests were protected within a state driven and dominated framework. Since then, and with reduced urban pressures, more weight has been given to local decision making, wider participation and bottom-up approaches. However, Hirayama demonstrates that a new aggressive individualism and competitiveness lies at the heart of the urban renaissance of twenty-first century Japan and this reflects a broader prescription for the reshaping of Japanese society in the global age. The creation of a more competitive, outward-oriented Tokyo with a more individualistic social ethos is central to the broader project of lifting Japan out of the economic doldrums of the 1990s. As a consequence, the social and economic distance between the Tokyo region and the rest of the country is widening. And the encouragement of commercial and prestige developments in central Tokyo is creating contrasting fortunes within the city. Hirayama contrasts these 'hot spots' of strategic urban investment designed to demonstrate Tokyo's global city credentials with the 'cold spots' of disinvestment and decay on the periphery. He also points to the urban impact of Japan's ageing society, in which a large section of Tokyo's workforce will move into retirement. With that inevitable occurrence, the infrastructure currently being created for the younger, 'global' citizen may prove to be inappropriate and financially unsustainable. For Hirayama, a fundamental question is whether this new Tokyo offers an attractive vision for citizens of a new Japan or whether there will be a growing backlash to the widening and evident economic divisions of this version of urban renaissance.

Seong Kyu Ha's chapter addresses one of the enduring problems for urban policy, which is the provision of housing for lower income groups. Ha explores the changing relationships between urban governance and low-income housing in Korea through a period of developments in relation to five normative goals: participatory democracy, decentralization, efficiency, equity and security. In doing so, he is concerned to address two key questions. First, do the poor benefit from economic growth in general and urban regeneration in particular? Second, what scope is there for lower income groups to influence the urban policy agenda? The discussion is set against a background in which, echoing earlier comments in other contexts, housing policy in Korea has until relatively recently been shaped by the imperative of efficient economic development. Moreover, in the aftermath of the AFC, the scope for direct intervention to address the needs of the poorest sections of Korean society was heavily constrained by neo-liberal structural adjustment measures.

As Ha emphasizes, Korea has faced the challenge of an enormous housing shortage and has made considerable progress in tackling these problems. However, the poor have consistently lagged behind and the market-oriented reforms following the AFC have exacerbated their position and have in some instances been associated with fairly brutal methods of relocation to make for new developments. Ha's overall conclusion is that judged against his five normative goals for good urban governance, equity and security for the low-income poor remain extremely problematic. He is, however, more positive in his assessment in relation to decentralization and participative democracy and in the growing role for NGOs and community organizations in the policy process. As regards his central question as to whether the poor derive real benefits from economic growth, much depends on the evolving governance arrangements and the extent to which communities are meaningfully heard and their needs acted upon. Absolute housing conditions have improved substantially with economic progress in Korea but relative differences remain unacceptably wide. For Ha, good urban governance must fully embrace a broader civil society and develop a truly citizen-centric, community-oriented policy agenda. Korea has made significant shifts towards such an agenda in recent years, particularly in relation to the provision of affordable housing, and is in many ways bucking international trends.

Conclusion

The overall message from the contributions throughout this volume is that the governance agenda is now moving into a new phase. It may be premature to label it as post neo-liberal but it is evident that the consequences of policies of privatization, re-regulation and deregulation are now presenting a new set of challenges to East Asian societies in which issues of fairness and social cohesion at least sit more prominently alongside concerns with competitiveness and economic efficiency.

References

Angresano, J. (2005) China's development strategy: a game of chess that countered orthodox development advice, *Journal of Socio-Economics*, 34: 471–498.

Asian Development Bank (2007) What is governance?, *Governance in Asia: From Crisis to Opportunity*, at: www.adb.org/Documents/ Reports/Governance/gov.

Bache, I. (2003) Governing through governance: education policy control under new labour, *Political Studies*, 51: 300–314.

Brahm, L.J. (2002) *Zhu Rongji and the Transformation of Modern China*, Singapore: Wiley and Pte Ltd.

Burn, J. (2005) Civil service governance reform, in J. Howell (ed.), *Governance in China*, Lanham: Rowman & Littlefield.

Central Committee of the Chinese Communist Party (CCCCP) (2003) *The Communique of the Third Plenary Session of the Sixteenth Central Committee of the Chinese Communist Party*, 14 October.

Chan, D. and Tan, J. (2006) Privatization and the rise of direct subsidy scheme schools and independent schools in Hong Kong and Singapore, paper presented at the Asia Pacific Educational Research Association International Conference, 28–30 November, Hong Kong.

Cheng, J. (2007) China's Asian policy: multipolarity, regionalism and peaceful rise, paper presented at the Centre for East Asian Studies Seminar Series, University of Bristol, 26 February, University of Bristol.

Cheung, A. (2005) Bureaucrats: enterprise negotiation in China's enterprise reform at the local level: case study in Guangzhou, *Journal of Contemporary China*, 14(45): 695–720.

Cheung, A. and Scott, I. (eds) (2003) *Governance and Public Sector Reform in Asia*, London: Routledge.

Drahos, P. and Joseph, R. (1995) Telecommunications and investment in the great supranational regulatory game, *Telecommunications Policy*, 188: 619–635.

Fisher, F. and Forester, J. (eds) (1993) *The Argumentative Turn in Policy Analysis and Planning*, Durham and London: Duke University Press.

Flath, D. (2005) *The Japanese Economy*, second edition, Oxford: Oxford University Press.

Fraenkel, E. (1941) *The Dual State*, translation from the German by E.A. Shils, in collaboration with E. Lowenstein and K. Knorr, Oxford: Oxford University Press.

Gill, S. (1995) Globalization, market civilization and disciplinary neoliberalism, *Millennium*, 24(3): 399–423.

Giroux, H. (2002) Neoliberalism, corporate culture and the promise of higher education: the university as a democratic public sphere, *Harvard Educational Review*, 72(4): 1–52.

Gouri, G. et al. (1991) Imperatives and perspectives, in G. Gouri (ed.), *Privatisation and Public Enterprise*, New Delhi: Oxford and IBH Publishing.

Hall, T. and Hubbard, P. (1998) *The Entrepreneurial City: Geographies of Politics*, Chichester: Wiley.

Harkavy, I. (2006) The role of universities in advancing citizenship and social justice in the 21st century, *Education, Citizenship and Social Justice*, 1(1): 5–37.

Harvey, D. (2002) From managerialism to entrepreneurialism: the transformation in urban governance in late capitalism, in G. Bridge and S. Watson (eds), *The Blackwell City*, Oxford: Reader Blackwell.

Herman, E. and McChesney, R. (1997) *The Global Media: The New Missionaries of Global Capitalism*, Washington, DC: Cassell.

Howell, J. (ed.) (2005) *Governance in China*, Lanham: Rowman & Littlefield.

Hu A.G., Zou, P. and Li, C.P. (2001) The regional disparity in economic and social development in China between 1978 to 2000, in X. Ru, X. Lu and T. Shan (eds), *Zhongguo Shehui Xingshi Fenxi Yu Yuce* [*Analysis and Forecast of Social Conditions in China, 2002*], Beijing: Social Science Documentation Publishing House.

Izuhara, M. (ed.) (2003) *Comparing Social Policies: Exploring New Perspectives in Britain and Japan*, Bristol: Policy Press.

Jayasuriya, K. (2000) Authoritarian liberalism, governance and the emergence of the regulatory state in post-Crisis east Asia, in R. Robertson et al. (eds), *Politics and Markets in the Wake of the Asian Crisis*, London: Routledge.

Jessop, B. (2002) Liberalism, neoliberalism, and urban governance: a state-theoretical perspective, *Antipode*, 34(3): 452–472.

Jordana, J. and Levi-Faur, D. (2005) Preface: the making of a new regulatory order, *Annals of the American Academy of Political and Social Science*, 598: 1–6.

Kearns, A. and Paddison, R. (2002) New challenges for urban governance, *Urban Studies*, 37(5–6): 845–850.

Keng, C.W. (2006) China's unbalanced economic growth, *Journal of Contemporary China*, 15(46): 183–214.

Kikkawa, T. (2005) Toward the rebirth of the Japanese economy and its corporate system, *Japan Forum*, 17(1): 87–106.

Lee, H.H. and Gopinathan, S. (2007) University restructuring in Singapore: amazing or a maze, *Journal of Comparative Asian Development*, 6(1): 107–142.

Lee, M.N.N. (2004) *Restructuring Higher Education in Malaysia*, Penang: School of Educational Studies, Universiti Sains Malaysia.

Lee, W.O. (2007) Lifelong learning in Asia: eclectic concepts, rhetorical ideals, and missing values: implications for values education, paper presented at the Biannual Conference of Comparative Education Society of Asia, 8–10 January, University of Hong Kong.

Levi-Faur, D. (1998) The competition state as a neo-mercantalist state: understanding the restructuring of national and global telecommunications, *Journal of Socio-Economics*, 27(6): 655–686.

Li, P.L. (2003) A few issues related to China's social stratification, in H. S. Zheng (ed.), *Studies for Changing Trends of Social Structure in China Today*, Beijing: People's University Press.

Li, R. (2007) Casualties of the rush to profit from schooling, *South China Morning Post*, 27 January.

Lieberthal, K. and Oksenberg, M. (1998) *Policy Making in China: Leaders, Structures and Processes*, Princeton: Princeton University Press.

Lippit, V. (2005) The political economy of China's economic reform: observations on China and socialism, *Critical Asian Studies*, 37(3): 441–462.

Lynch, K. (2006) Neo-liberalism and marketisation: the implications for higher education, *European Educational Research Journal*, 5(1): 1–17.

Lynch, K. and O'Riordan, C. (1998) Inequality in higher education: a study of class barriers, *British Journal of Sociology of Education*, 19: 445–478.

Mackerras, C. (2006) Critical social issues, in C. Tubilewicz (ed.), *Critical Issues in Contemporary China*, London: Routledge and Hong Kong: Open University of Hong Kong Press.

Marginson, S. (2006) Putting public back into the public university, *Thesis Eleven*, 84: 44–59.

McCargo, D. (2004) *Contemporary Japan*, second edition, Basingstoke: Palgrave Macmillan.

Mok, K.H. (2005) Riding over socialism and global capitalism: changing education governance and social policy paradigms in post-Mao China, *Comparative Education*, 41(2): 217–242.

Mok, K.H. (2006a) Embracing the market: changing social policy paradigms in post-Mao China, paper presented to the GDPism and Risk: Challenges for Social Development and Changing Governance in East Asia conference, July, University of Bristol.

Mok, K.H. (2006b) Varieties of regulatory regimes in Asia: the liberalization of the higher education market in Hong Kong, Singapore and Malaysia, paper presented at the Asia Pacific Educational Research Association International Conference, 28–30 November, Hong Kong Institute of Education, Hong Kong.

Mok, K.H. (2007) When neo-liberalism colonizes higher education in Asia: bringing the public back into the contemporary university, in D. Rhoten (ed.), *Critical Issues and Challenges for Higher Education in the Contemporary Period*, New York: Social Science Research Council.

Mok, K.H. and Lo, Y.W. (2007) Embracing the market: the impacts of neo-liberalism on China's higher education, *Journal for Critical Education Policy Studies*, 5(1), at: http://www.jceps.com/index.php?pageID=article&articleID=93.

Mok, K.H. and Tan, J. (2004) *Globalization and Marketization in Education: A Comparative Analysis of Hong Kong and Singapore*, Cheltenham: Edward Elgar.

Moran, M. (2002) Review article: understanding the regulatory state, *British Journal of Political Science*, 32: 391–413.

Ng, P.T. and Chan, D. (2006) A comparative study of Singapore's school excellence model with Hong Kong's school-based management, paper presented at the Asia Pacific Educational Research Association International Conference, 28–30 November, Hong Kong Institute of Education, Hong Kong.

Oba, J. (2006) Incorporation of national universities in Japan and its impact upon institutional governance, paper presented at the International Workshop on University Restructuring in Asia, 16 January, Hiroshima, Japan.

Organization for Economic Co-operation and Development (OECD) (2005) *Governance in China*, Paris: OECD.

Painter, M. and Wong, S.F. (2005) Varieties of regulatory state? Government–business relations and telecommunications reforms in Malaysia and Thailand, *Policy and Society*, 24(3): 27–52.

Pan, W. (2003) Towards a consultative rule of law regime in China, *Journal of Contemporary China*, 12(34): 3–30.

Pei, M.X. (2000) China's evolution towards soft authoritarianism, in E. Friedman and B. MaCormick (eds), *What if China doesn't Democratize? Implications for War and Peace*, New York: M.E. Sharpe.

Petersen, C. and Currie, J. (2007) Higher education restructuring and academic freedom in Hong Kong, *Journal of Comparative Asian Development*, 6(1): 143–164.

Pistor, K. and Xu, C.G. (2005) Governing stock markets in transition economies: lessons from China, *American Law and Economics Review*, 7(1): 184–210.

Preker, A.S. and Harding, A. (eds) (2003) *Innovations in Health Service Delivery: The Corporatization of Public Hospitals*, Washington, DC: World Bank.

Reay, D. and Lucey, H. (2003) The limits of choice: children and inner city schooling, *Sociology*, 37(1): 121–142, at: http://dx.doi.org/10/1177/0038038503037001389.

Rebick, M. (2005) *The Japanese Employment System: Adapting to a New Economic Environment*, Oxford: Oxford University Press.

Rebick, M. and Takenaka, A. (eds) (2006) *The Changing Japanese Family*, London: Routledge.

Retherford, R.D., Ogawa, N. and Matsukura, R. (2001) Late marriage and less marriage in Japan, *Population and Development Review*, 27: 65–102.

Rhodes, R.A.W. (1997) *Understanding Governance*, Buckingham: Open University Press.

Rhodes, R.A.W. (2000) Governance and public administration, in J. Pierre (ed.), *Debating Governance*, Oxford: Oxford University Press.

Rule, J. (1998) Markets, in their place, *Dissent*, Winter: 31.

Salomon, L.M. (ed.) (2002) *The Tools of Government: A Guide to the New Governance*, Oxford: Oxford University Press.

Schweickart, D. (2006) China: market socialism or capitalism?, at: http://www.solidarityeconomy.net/2006/11/01/china-market-socilism-or-capitalism.

Scott, C. (2004) Regulation in the age of governance: The rise of the post-regulatory state, in J. Jordana and D. Levi-Faur (eds), The Politics of Regulation: Institutions and Regulatory Reforms for the Age of Governance, Cheltenham: Edward Elgar, 145–174.

Shafaeddin, S.M. (2004) Is China's accession to the WTO threatening exports of developing countries?, *China Economic Review*, 15: 109–144.

Shimomura, Y. (2003) *The Role of Governance in Asia*, Singapore: Institute of Southeast Asian Studies.

So, A.Y.C. (2003) The changing pattern of classes and class conflict in China, *Journal of Contemporary Asia*, 33(3): 363–376.

So, A.Y.C. (2005) Beyond the logic of capital and the polarization model: the state, market reforms, and the plurality of class conflict in China, *Critical Asian Studies*, 37(3): 481–494.

Stockwin, J.A.A. (2006) To oppose or to appease? Parties out of power and the need for real politics in Japan, *Japan Forum*, 18(1): 115–132.

Tang, W.F. and Holzner, B. (eds) (2007) *Social Change in Contemporary China*, Pittsburg: Pittsburgh Press.

Tubilewicz, C. (ed.) (2006) *Critical Issues in Contemporary China*, London: Routledge and Hong Kong: Open University of Hong Kong Press.

Turner, M. and Hulme, D. (1997) *Governance, Administration and Development: Making the State Work*, Basingstoke: Macmillan.

Walder, A. (2007) Social stability and popular protest in China: how serious is the threat?, key-note speech at the International Conference on Contemporary China Studies, 5–6 January, University of Hong Kong.

Walker, A. and Wong, C.K. (2005) Introduction: East Asian welfare regimes, in A. Walker and C. K. Wong (eds), *East Asian Welfare Regimes: From Confucianism to Globalization*, Bristol: Policy Press.

Weil, R. (2006) Conditions of the working classes in China, *Monthly Review*, 58(2), at: http://canadiandimension.com/articles/2006/07/29/596.

Weiss, L. (1998) *The Myth of the Powerless State*, New York: Cornell University Press.

Wildavsky, A. (1992) Speaking truth to different subjectivities, in W. Dunn and R. Kelly (eds), *Advances in Policy Studies since 1950*, New Brunswick: Transaction Publishers.

Wong, L. and Flynn, N. (2001) *The Market in Chinese Social Policy*, Basingstoke: Palgrave Macmillan.

World Bank (1995) *Higher Education: The Lessons of Experience*, Washington, DC: World Bank.

Wu, F. (2003) The (post-) socialist entrepreneurial city as a state project: Shanghai's reglobalisation in question, *Urban Studies*, 40(9): 1673–1698.

Yang, D.L. (2004) *Remaking the Chinese Leviathan: Market Transition and the Politics of Governance in China*, Stanford: Stanford University Press.

Yeo, Y.Y. and Pearson, M. (2007) Regulating decentralized state industries: China's auto industry, paper presented at the Workshop on Decentralization and Varieties of Regulatory Capitalism in China, 29–30 January, City University of Hong Kong.

Zhang, X.B. (2006) Fiscal decentralization and political centralization in China: implications for growth and inequality, *Journal of Comparative Economics*, 34: 713–726.

Zhang, Y.J. (2003) Reconsidering the economic internationalization of China: implications of WTO membership, *Journal of Contemporary China*, 12(37): 699–714.

Zhong, Y. (2003) *Local Government and Politics in China: Challenges from Below*, Armonk: M.E. Sharpe.

Zhu, Q.F. (2005) Social and economic indicators: analysis and assessment, in X. Yu et al. (eds), *Analysis and Forecast on China's Social Development 2006*, Beijing: Social Sciences Academic Press.

Part I
Changing policy paradigms

1 Interpreting East Asian social policy development

Paradigm shifts or policy 'steadiness'?[1]

Anthony B. L. Cheung

Introduction

There are two ways of interpreting the rapid expansion of social policy in East Asian developed societies. A 'universalist' interpretation would consider it in line with a path of modernization comparable to that in the West, where post-war economic and social changes constituted interlinked aspects of a singular process of transformation leading to policy convergence in the form of the 'welfare state'. The productivist explanation sees development in East Asian social policy as somewhat of an adjunct, as well as an instrument, of economic growth (Holliday 2000). If so, a logical question in the aftermath of the 1997 Asian financial crisis is whether policy reversal or paradigm shift has been triggered by an erosion of the previous East Asian developmental model by the economic slowdown and the rise of neo-liberalism as a prescription for economic problems. Holliday (2005) re-examined his productivist thesis recently but suggested it was too early to write it off, even though he found it impossible to reach a definitive conclusion.

This chapter argues that the East Asian social policy experience has displayed policy continuity and 'steadiness', which can be explained by the long-standing bureaucrat-dominated nature of public policy making in addition to the state-led economic development approach to policy interventions. Some public services had historically been developed and expanded not for the sake of any entrenched social policy values, but as instrumentalist complements to the developmental agenda and related political objectives. Welfare provisions had mostly been introduced not out of welfare ideology considerations, as some suggested to be the case in the formation of the welfare state in the West (Marshall and Bottomore 1992; Pinker 1979), but as a result of a fiscally and economically driven social development programme, in which case economic slowdown and recession could arguably cause a temporary readjustment, but still within the same logic. Developmentalism is still the foundation of the East Asian public policy discourse. New social policy development in some East Asian states like South Korea after democratization can be seen as indicative of the rise of 'welfare developmentalism'.

East Asian welfare states: nature and evolution

The developmental state

Before the 1997 Asian financial crisis (AFC) cast doubt on the prospect of the post-war developmental-state mode (Wong 2004: 345–56), the conventional wisdom in understanding the system of governance in East Asia lay in the 'East Asian economic miracle' thesis (World Bank 1993), under which the success of the East Asian growth economies (Japan, Taiwan, Singapore and South Korea) until the 1990s was attributed largely to the presence of a strong, and often authoritarian and corporatist, 'developmental state'. Johnson (1982) portrayed Japan as a pioneer model of the developmental or 'plan-rational' state. The very idea of the developmental state, as reflective of conceptions and intellectual traditions concerning the purpose of public policy and the con-comitant role of government, fundamentally differed from that prevalent in the Anglo-American nations and could be traced to the Meiji Restoration in the 1860s, when the modern Japanese nation-state was created as a response to the challenge (and threat) posed by western capitalist expansion (Beeson 2003: 26). Wade's (1990) seminal study of Japan, South Korea and Taiwan summarized East Asian developmentalism as the 'governed market'.

Among the newly developed East Asian economies, Hong Kong under British colonial rule (until 1997) was arguably an exception as it had all along been held as the last bastion of the free market (Friedman 1981: 54), practising a philosophy of 'positive non-interventionism' (Haddon-Cave 1984). Whether or not Hong Kong was the reverse proof of a successful non-intervention free market economy depends on how intervention (or non-intervention) was interpreted. Hong Kong's colonial government in reality had displayed some unusual instruments for influencing industrial activities, so that the economy worked very differently from the textbook picture of a free market economy or from those economies of the Anglo-American kind (Wade 1990: 331–33). Though not of a western welfare state type, the gov-ernment was active in regulative controls and had extensive involvement in social and community services, relying on land revenue instead of heavy taxation as the principal means of supporting these services. To that extent, Hong Kong was recognized by some as having developed a unique model of growth where the state still played a role (Schiffer 1983).

Though the East Asian developmental states used public policy instruments to allocate productive resources rather than relying solely on the market, sometimes playing a 'big' leadership role in prospecting potentially lucrative industrial sectors, they were still social welfare laggards in the sense that their economic policy, including industrial policy, was primarily geared toward maximizing national productivity, i.e. rapid economic growth, with distribu-tive consequences being considered secondary (Wong 2004: 349–52). The state was historically anchored as a 'hard' or 'soft' authoritarian one, attesting to Evans' (1989, 1995) notion of an 'embedded autonomy', giving the state the capacity to combine two apparently contradictory aspects, namely, 'Weberian bureaucratic insulation' and 'intense immersion in the surrounding social structure' (Evans 1989: 561). Thus it possessed what Weiss called the 'transformative' capacity, insulated from undue special interests but firmly embedded in society, and maintaining effective linkages with industry and other societal/economic actors to ensure the happening of things through 'governed interdependence' (1998: Chapter 2).

Expansion of the residualist welfare regime

Japan and, subsequently, other East Asian developed economies had historically exhibited a residual form of social welfare based more on family and corporate welfare than on state protection (Pierson 2004: 11). Ironically their 'welfare state'[2] was set up and expanded over the last few decades 'by conservative governments with clear antiwelfare ideologies' (Aspalter 2002a: 2). Hence, even in the heyday of the East Asian miracle towards the end of the 1990s, public social expenditures in East Asia were considered very low on a world scale (according to Gough (2004), though he included some Southeast Asian countries within the 'East Asia' sector (p. 171)). The figures were slightly higher in the developed East Asian states, but still low by western European and North American standards – see Table 1.1. However, rapid economic growth in the booming decades had resulted in a faster expansion in real resources devoted to the social sector than in most countries (Gough 2004). Rather than an ideological offshoot, the welfare state in Japan, South Korea, Hong Kong, Taiwan and Singapore was explained as largely a result of social protests, political pressures, competition in democratic elections, and particular demographic changes (ibid.).

Japan subordinated social policy to the logic of nation (re-)building through economic development, with a high economic growth strategy built around full (male) employment (Pierson 2004: 11). Relying on a network of communal and family social support, Japanese governments were able to keep to a minimum the state's responsibility for personal social services. Such a welfare regime was sustained by the anti-welfare stance of the dominant parties (in particular the Liberal Democratic Party, LDP), though demographic and social changes in recent years had seen the gradual rise of some new pro-welfare women-friendly social policies (Peng 2002). Until democratization in the late 1990s, **South Korea** and **Taiwan** shared the features of a system where an authoritarian state, acting closely with business interests and in a weak-unions context, fashioned a strategy for national economic development. Though social welfare was not a priority, it was improved through enlarging the economic pie, and maximizing employment. In **South Korea**, the development of the welfare state had an underlying logic of politics (Kwon 2002). The 1997 economic crisis forced the government to reform social security schemes and employment programmes as a way to enhance its political legitimacy and broaden electoral appeal. In **Taiwan**, demographic

Table 1.1 Total government expenditure and major social policy expenditures, as percentages of GDP, in the late 1990s

East Asian developed economies	Total government expenditure	Education	Health	Social security
	1997–98	*1995–97*	*1997–98*	*1990–97*
Japan	29.4	3.7	5.3	6.7
Singapore	16.8	1.8	1.2	0.8 (2.2[1])
Hong Kong	14.5	2.6	1.7	1.2
Taiwan	22.7	5	3.5	2.2
South Korea	17.4	3.7	2.2	3

Selected Western countries	Government expenditure	Education	Health	Social security transfers
	1999	*1998*	*1998*	*1998*
Australia	31.9[2]	4.34	5.9	8.4
Sweden	55.1	6.59	7.0	19.3
United States	32.7[3]	4.82	6.1	12.6[3]
UK	37.8	4.65	5.6	13.6
Germany	44.8	4.35	7.9	19.0

Notes:
1 Including social-related withdrawals from the Central Provident Fund.
2 1998 figure.
3 1997 figure.

Sources: Figures on the five East Asian developed economies are from Gough (2004, Table 5.2); figures on the five selected OECD developed economies are from: for general government expenditure: OECD (2001a: 36–37, unnumbered table), for public expenditure on education institutions: OECD (2001b: 80, Table B2.1a), for public expenditure on healthcare: OECD (2001a: 8–9, unnumbered table), and for 'social security transfers': OECD (2002: 67, Table 6.3).

changes reduced the role and capacity of the family as the most important provider of welfare, and the rise of public pressure, social movements and ultimately party competition within a growingly democratic political environment following the demise of Kuomintang (KMT, Nationalist Party) authoritarianism had driven the state into the establishment of social insurance and health insurance schemes (Ku 2002). Under positive non-interventionism, colonial **Hong Kong** traditionally had a typical system of residual welfare, though education and healthcare had evolved to become almost universal. Political factors – such as pressure groups and social movements, politicians' agitations, and the government's need for legitimacy – had pushed for expanding welfare provision (Chan, R. 2002). **Singapore**, despite its 'soft' paternalistic state, largely depended on the contributory Central Provident Fund (CPF) to provide for various accounts and schemes of retirement protection, healthcare and even home purchase (Aspalter 2002c).

Convergence towards western welfare state or productivist
welfare capitalism

As East Asian welfare states came to maturity in the 1990s upon reaching a developed economy stage, an obvious question is whether they would have eventually converged into the typical welfare state model of the West if not for the disruption by the 1997 Asian financial crisis. The answer depends on whether there exists some kind of established welfare state modernization path spurred by economic growth, given that the emergence of a globalizing economy has prompted policy convergence towards international policy benchmarking and the use of similar policy tools in the face of perceived common challenges from globalization (Harrop 1992: 263).

The OECD experience, however, does not attest to such inevitability. Castles' (1998) comparative study of OECD post-war transformation discovered that even European public policy development had not evolved along uniform patterns. Cross-national patterns of social and economic policy outcomes were in a constant state of flux as they were shaped by a wide range of economic, social, cultural, political and policy factors, which all altered over time. He tested the thesis of policy convergence amongst Western European nations and concluded that 'the story revealed . . . was of *a modernity fractured by major political, demographic and cultural fault lines,* cross-cutting each other in different ways in different nations and, potentially, making for considerable policy diversity' (p. 301, emphasis added). Modernity could be characterized by quite different age and occupational structures across nations, so much so that the story became that 'of a modernity with many mansions' (p. 305). Castles suggested there were thresholds of modernity in the sense that all these nations had moved into certain government programmes (such as universal health coverage and social security, which were typical of the welfare state), but once such thresholds were reached, nations might differ in their policy options and outcomes even if they were of comparable economic development. Economic and social development thus acted more as a *constraining* rather than determining factor in public policy choices.

Mirroring Esping-Andersen's (1990) typology of three 'worlds' of welfare capitalism (namely, Liberal, Conservative and Social Democratic), Castles identified four 'families of nations' among OECD countries, whose policy development differences could be defined in terms of common cultural, historical and geographical features, namely: English-speaking; Scandinavian; continental Western European; and Southern European (1998: 8–9). Japan was deemed to be outside such categorization and to belong to a new family of newly industrialized nations with East Asian cultural (or Confucianist) features. East Asian social policy scholars have also sought to delineate an 'East Asian experience . . . distinctive, differing decisively from the Euro-American models current in social policy discourse' (Kwon 1998: 27; also see Kwon 1997). Citing its unique politics of welfare, Miyamoto (2003) further disputed treating Japan in the same way as other East Asian states, arguing that neither the welfare state regime theory *a la* Esping-Anderson nor an East Asian model could fully capture the features of the Japanese welfare state. Cultural explanation aside, the argument for a unique East Asian social policy route rests its case on an economic thesis of productivism.

Holliday, when proposing a fourth world with *productivist* features, recognized three distinct subsets. While all three place social policy subordinate to economic policy, they differ in the state–market–family relationship – market-prioritized in the 'facilitative' type (Hong Kong), state underpinning market and families with some universal programmes in the 'development-universalist' type (Japan, South Korea and Taiwan), and state directing social welfare activities of families in the 'developmental-particularist' type (2000, Table 2). He argued that productivist welfare capitalism could not be fully explained by a unique East Asian social base of political superstructure, such as the typical 'Confucian welfare state' argument (Jones 1993) or developmental state argument (Kwon 1997; Ramesh 1995), but had to be seen as a result of bureaucratic politics that drove social policy development. Those technocrats and elite policy-makers staffing key East Asian economic agencies were central to the pursuance of particular social and economic policy (Holliday 2000: 717).

Impact of economic crisis and globalization

Irrespective of whether and how the different East Asian developed economies' experiences can be captured by a uniform conceptual framework surrounding a strong or interventionist state, a key question since the 1997 Asian financial crisis has been whether any previous paradigm of East Asian social policy development is being eroded by the impact of globalization, economic crisis and political changes (such as democratization in South Korea and Taiwan in the 1990s).

Two trajectories

If it is accepted that welfare provisions in East Asian countries had been embarked upon not out of welfare ideology considerations, but as a result of a fiscally-driven social programme funded by economic growth, then it is conceivable that economic slowdown and recession can easily trigger a reversal shift. In Hong Kong, there was observation that financial austerity prompted the state to adopt social policy reforms through re-commodification and cost containment, resulting in the retrenchment of the residualist welfare state (Lee, E.W.Y. 2005). The fact that Hong Kong society had never before engaged in real ideological debates on social policy or the role and functions of the state also means that mainstream public sentiments could easily be won over to a fiscally driven readjustment of public service. However, it is still too early to drive home such a re-commodification argument, partly because bureaucratic conservatism and caution would see that any reversal in service provision is less dramatic than if induced by mainly ideological or political objectives, and partly because there is still a developmentalist function to be served by the welfare system, even during economic recession.

Critics considered globalization not simply a market-driven economic phenomenon, but also very much a political and ideological phenomenon, underpinned by the 'transnational ideology of neoliberalism which seeks to establish its ascendancy world-wide' (Mishra 1999: 7). Robison and Hewison (2005) reviewed the impact of neo-liberalism on East Asian and Southeast Asian states following the 1997 Asian economic crisis. While it seemed true that the economic crisis had accelerated the restructuring of state and economic power, and offered an opportunity for neo-liberal policies to be strengthened – such as more market reforms promoted by international financial institutions as an alternative to the 'Asian capitalism' – such crisis had not succeeded in achieving a grand convergence. In reality, neo-liberalist motivated processes had been *'highly contested*, leading to contradictory, ambiguous and sometimes surprising outcomes' (ibid.: 191; emphasis added). Political regimes were also found to have subverted or hijacked neo-liberal agendas in some circumstances for their own policy and institutional goals.

An alternative view, in contrast, sees the Asian crisis as actually helping to spur welfare expansion rather than retrenchment. The argument is this: the East Asian welfare regimes 'had relied on optimistic assumptions of decade-long high economic growth rates, and a high and lifelong male labour market participation' (Croissant 2004: 520). The crisis was compounded by: increasing urbanization that resulted in demographic changes and weakened the 'familialistic' foundations of the welfare regimes, democratization which brought about rising welfare demands, and globalization that eroded 'enterprise-based welfare'. The previous welfare regimes proved to be unsustainable in the post-crisis environment. 'Since no actors other than the state will be able to fill the gaps in the welfare system, an increasing role for the state is likely' (op. cit.), to the extent that the debate about reform of the welfare system 'is already increasingly shaped by European models' (op. cit.). Examining the politics of welfare in Japan, Miyamoto (2003: 21) similarly argued that post-industrialization and globalization did not automatically result in welfare retrenchment. While it was true that there were strong tendencies towards financial austerity, the concern about increasing social instability amidst economic uncertainties gave rise to pressure for welfare expansion. The ageing society had also built up the need for lessening the family burden and increasing welfare protection for the elderly, who now constituted a growing portion of the electorate.

Gough (2004), too, saw the possibility of 'the transformation of East Asian productivist welfare regimes into productivist welfare *state* regimes' with an increasing statist orientation (p. 201). The East Asian welfare regime was an outcome of rapid social development coupled with a residual welfare system highly vulnerable to external shocks (Gough 2001: 177–181), hence the aftershock of the Asian economic crisis would leave East Asian welfare states with two possible trajectories (Gough 2004: 199–200). One is towards privatization coupled with persistent informalization, but this would face the resistance to 'de-statize' from an essentially developmentalist regime. The other trajectory is towards a more universalist social investment state with more government provision and redistribution. Three reasons can be given for the potential of such a direction (ibid.: 200–201):

- Globalization and increased competition demand moving into higher-technology and higher-productivity production, requiring more public investment in social policy, infrastructure and planning.
- The very weakness of existing social stratification effects among welfare recipients and of path-dependency effects in the regime as a whole may permit a statist turn.
- The impact of rising democracy in East Asia, notably in Taiwan and South Korea.

Taking the line of a post-crisis transformation of East Asian welfare systems, Peng (2004) suggested that even if they were previously productivist, such productivism might have by now outlived its time. She questioned if the logic of 'economy first, redistribution later', which underlined the productivist thesis, could still be sustained in light of the increasing challenge from three contending factors in recent years, namely: political and regime changes; the expansion, rather than retrenchment, of social welfare programmes in response to recent economic crises, which were not necessarily productivist in nature; and new welfare emphasis grounded in family and demographic considerations rather than economic ones.

Decline of productivism?

Based on the experience of Japan and South Korea, Peng argued that the East Asian welfare state configuration was no longer as economically determined, but was also mediated by social, structural and domestic political factors. In both countries, 'the politics of the welfare state changed as political regimes and political conditions changed' (Peng 2004: 408). During the 1990s, the end of LDP's one-party dominant rule in Japan caused political realignments, creating openings for policy innovations and allowing new civil society groups to enter the policy-making arena. Meanwhile, the 1997 economic crisis and the onset of democracy facilitated the process of political realignment in South Korea, which saw the Kim Dae Jung government embarking on both economic liberalization and welfare expansion (ibid.: 415–416). The new social policy was thus no longer exclusively confined to protecting and privileging the traditional productive sectors, and financial reform necessitated by economic crisis had actually led to the demise of company welfare, thereby triggering growing political demands for state welfare interventions.

What Peng and Gough have alluded to are important developments in the East Asian social policy discourse. However, it remains debatable if East Asian welfare states like Japan and South Korea have already moved beyond the stage of productivism and developmentalism or, as Peng herself has also allowed for, such changes are no more than a reorientation of the productivist logic under different social and structural conditions (ibid.: 416). Irrespective of the future shifts, if developmentalism continues to be the foundation of policy governance, which we would argue to be the case, then its welfarist component will remain an offshoot of economic development and thus fiscal accumulation, rather than the outcome of a political ideology of collectivist welfare. After all, the role of family and individual efforts are still the key elements of the East Asian social philosophy that underpins state–society interaction and the state's response to social demands. The post-crisis emphasis on education and economic and industrial policy reforms is geared towards revitalizing state-led developmentalism in the new environment of the knowledge economy and opened-up markets. Policy making in East Asia has always been dominated by a developmentalist bureaucracy keen on state-building. The social policy and social development agenda is determined neither by economics nor politics alone, but also by bureaucracy-mediated goals of the political economy that embrace both economic (productivist) and political (social stability, distributive and redistributive) imperatives.

Recent social policy reforms: policy shifts rather than policy reversals

Education reforms

All five East Asian states (Japan, South Korea, Taiwan, Singapore and Hong Kong) seem to have been most active in steering the education sector forward, through wide-scale school education reform (spanning the areas of curriculum reform, school management, and improvement in teacher quality), the expansion and liberalization of the tertiary sector, and the promotion of lifelong education, in order to create a larger and better educated workforce to cope with the challenges of the new knowledge-based economy under globalization and the information technology (IT) revolution.

Japan launched the Educational Reform Plan for the Twenty-first Century in 2001, and Compulsory Education Reform in 2004. **Hong Kong** encouraged the setting up of private schools and 'direct subsidy schools', and adopted a school-based management regime for all government-subsidized schools. In higher education, corporatizing state universities and encouraging private investment seemed a common direction. **South Korea** merged ten national universities into five as part of higher education reform, and launched a seven-year 'Brain Korea (BK) 21' project in 2005 to develop world-class research-centred universities. **Taiwan** promoted the corporatization of public universities and amended its University Law in 2005 to enable public universities to select their own presidents. **Singapore** too upgraded its universities aimed at creating a higher education hub within Asia by building a fifth polytechnic and three new junior colleges. More autonomy was given to public universities as they were corporatized. Though private involvement is enlarged in the provision of education, this has not diluted the proactive role of the state, which is closely aligned with its objectives to achieve economic restructuring and adjustment, and to build a more adaptive and knowledge-based workforce. However, as Gough (2004: 171) observed, while 'East Asian governments have consistently emphasised the central role of education in economic development, ... this is not matched by a higher-than-average expenditure for middle-income countries.'

Healthcare reforms

In healthcare, all five states have striven to maintain the universal coverage of their medical system, mostly through an extended insurance scheme, but also seeking to raise enough premiums and means-tested user fees to meet rising medical costs and patient demands, and to encourage private sector involvement. **Singapore** has continued with its policy path dating from the 1980s to expect citizens to save more to cater for housing and medical needs through the CPF vehicle, and made compulsory health insurance and savings a growing feature of its healthcare system through the Medishield and Medisave schemes, respectively. Medishield was reformed in 2004 to raise claims for deductibles and prevent the medical insurance industry from being too selective. Means testing was extended to general hospitals. **Hong Kong** still operates a predominantly government-funded public healthcare system, but is actively reviewing health finance arrangements with the aim of introducing some form of health insurance and/or savings schemes, and increasing user charges. Following the completion of the Harvard Study to review healthcare finance in 1999, which proposed setting up compulsory insurance-cum-savings accounts, but found resistance in public opinion, the government renewed its efforts in healthcare reform by publishing a consultation paper in 2005 to advocate more public–private interface and the introduction of a 'family doctor' scheme. The Hospital Authority adopted a standard drug formulatory to help reduce expenditure on prescriptions.

Even in **Taiwan**, where a comprehensive national health insurance system was implemented in 1995, there have been steady increases in insurance premiums in order to cope with rising medical costs. Planning for a second-generation national health insurance system was started in 2002 (Shin and Shaw 2003), but progress has been hampered by increasing political uncertainties facing the prospect of the new Democratic Progressive Party (DPP) government. Similarly, **South Korea** and **Japan** also face the problems of better funding insurance schemes in order to cope with rising demands and pooling community risk. **South Korea** extended its National Health Insurance to universal coverage in 1989. In 2000, it consolidated various health insurance agencies into one single organization to facilitate more equitable risk pooling. **Japan's** healthcare system was historically highly regulated by government and combines a mainly private provision of services with mandatory health insurance, with medical fees approved by government (Imai 2002). Employees of large companies were covered by company-based insurance societies, while those of small and medium enterprises (SMEs) were covered by one big subsidized central government insurance scheme and most others by schemes run by municipalities (some 3,250 of them). Under the 1997 Revision of Health Insurance Law, only 80 per cent of the medical costs were to be reimbursed to the insured. Patients' cost-sharing was increased in 2000, and Medical System Reform in 2002 sought to increase the contribution rate of citizens insured by society-managed health insurance from 20 per cent to 30 per cent, to be on a par with that under government-managed health insurance, but patient charges on prescription drugs were repealed (Fukawa 2005). A separate old-age nursing care insurance was introduced in 2000 (Imai 2002). Recently public–private partnership in the form of private finance was introduced in the management of public hospitals.

Housing reforms

In housing, while no significant policy reversal is observed in the five states' pre-existing housing policy regimes, the recent trend has been to stabilize the housing market and to encourage more private sector provision. **Singapore** is the only country still pursuing active and extensive state-subsidized housing provision in line with its national development agenda since independence. State housing was stepped up in recent years through the provision of new categories such as luxurious apartments for higher-income citizens and upgrading existing public housing estates. In 2003, the government replaced the Small Families Improvement Scheme by a new HOPE ('Home Ownership Plus Education') programme to help these families build up their self-reliance and break out of the poverty trap. A new CPF Housing Grant Scheme for lower-income families who buy Housing Development Board flats was implemented. In **Hong Kong**, the Housing Authority continued to reduce the waiting time for public rental housing, improve management and maintenance, and enhance the rent relief scheme. The post-1997 housing reform agenda – with an ambitious annual new build target of 85,000 units – to bring down an overheated property market was, however, brought to a drastic halt because of the Asian financial crisis which caused property prices to plummet. In 2002, the government made an important retreat by terminating its Home Ownership Scheme (introduced in the late 1970s) and sale of public rental housing to sitting tenants (Tenant Purchase Scheme, introduced in 1997), in order to rescue the private property market, even though its commitment to public rental housing remains intact. In 2006, a review of domestic rent policy for public housing was conducted.

In **Taiwan, South Korea** and **Japan**, private sector housing has always dominated housing provision. The situation has not changed following the Asian crisis – for example, even now public renting housing represents only 3 per cent of all housing units in South Korea (Lee, K.B. 2005). To cope with the post-crisis economic situation, though, their governments have provided various support measures to lower-income households, mainly in the form of housing loans and some limited public rental housing. In **Taiwan**, since the early 1990s, the government had encouraged the private sector to build housing units for some 20 categories of labourer, with conditions on repayment period, interest rate and upper ceiling of loans similar to those for public housing (Chen 2002). The Six-Year Housing Plan (1996–2001) allowed the majority of public housing units to be purchased from the market and the provision of government subsidized loans (ibid.). In 2004, a Home Finance Loan scheme was introduced to benefit 120,000 households. In **South Korea**, a price ceiling was introduced in 1997 for new residential housing units, and the Korea Housing Finance Cooperative was established in 1999 to allow government participation in housing consumer protection measures (Lee 2002). More budget allocations were given to the National Housing Fund. The long-term loan systems for small-sized rental houses for needy citizens and for the middle class were revitalized. The government also introduced measures on real estate stabilization, with a new Real Estate Reform Policy to curb speculation. In **Japan**, the Seventh Housing Construction Five-year Plan (commencing in 1996) promoted the building of good quality housing, targeting 7.3 million units by 2000, with 3.5 million units funded through public finances (Hayakawa 2002). A fixed-term rental rights system was introduced in 1999. On the other hand, the Government Housing Loan Corporation ceased to issue new loans in 2001 and was abolished in 2004 in order not to be seen as competing with the private sector in the housing finance market.

Welfare and labour protection reforms

In the area of welfare and labour protection, welfare reviews and reforms with a view to containing expenditure growth, as well as attempts to provide relief and minimum living support allowance schemes, are taking place concurrently across East Asia, underlining the impact of fiscal and economic pressures and the states' objective of maintaining a sufficiently harmonious society for the purpose of economic growth. **Hong Kong** has been trying to contain the growth of social security expenditure – through the review of CSSA (Comprehensive Social Security Assistance) eligibility and allowance rates – but welfare expenditure (including unemployment benefits and old-age allowance) has still escalated because of economic downturn. Voluntary and third-sector participation was encouraged through a Community Investment and Inclusion Fund set up in 2002. In 2005, the government was forced by political and public pressures to set up a Poverty Commission. Despite its non-interventionist policy orientation, the administration of newly installed chief executive, Donald Tsang, is prepared to support a community-wide debate on a mandatory minimum wage and standard working hours, which trade unions have been demanding for a long time but which business and employer interests have always resisted. In **Singapore**, no new social security programme involving significant additional public expenditure has been established since the 1960s (Ramesh 2003: 83) and government has focused on wage reform and CPF reform. As relief measures in the aftermath of the Asian crisis, various shorter-term initiatives were introduced – such as the Eldercare Fund; Children Development Co-Savings Scheme (known as Baby Bonus) and CPF top-ups for all citizens in 2000; the Economic Downturn Relief Scheme and 'New Singapore Shares' in 2001; and the 'Economic Restructuring Shares' from 2003 onwards (to offset the increase in the goods and services tax rate from 3 to 5 per cent). The objective is to achieve a new social compact to cope with the challenge of a new economy. The Workforce Development Agency was set up to enhance employability, and new measures were introduced in 2006 to support low-wage workers. Both city-states are giving greater emphasis to voluntary and third-sector involvement in welfare and community service provision.

Regime change and democratization of the political system in **South Korea** and **Taiwan** in the late 1990s coincided with the advent of the Asian financial crisis and the rising challenge of globalization. As a result, both have engaged more actively in providing unemployment benefits and some form of minimum living allowance/social assistance schemes, as well as labour protection measures, for political and social policy reasons. Since the ascendancy of the first democratically elected president, Kim Dae Jung, in 1997, **South Korea** has implemented a series of initiatives and reforms to protect the elderly, the underprivileged, and low-income families:

- Establishment of a tripartite Employees–Employers–Government Commission (1998).
- Introduction of 'minimum living standard guarantee' scheme (2000).
- 'Protection-first system' (2005) for elderly and other disenfranchised citizens.
- Review of National Pension Programme with new fiscal measures.
- 'Social Safety Plan 2005' to expand financial support for low-income families.
- Presidential Commission on Low Birthrate and Aged Society (2005).
- Pilot project on long-term care system.
- Measures to reduce income gap between irregular and regular workers.
- Plan to rationalize wage determination system to transit from seniority-based to productivity and job-based wage system (2005).

In **Taiwan**, the Social Assistance Law was passed in 1997, and an Employment Insurance Programme introduced in 1999. After regime change from

KMT to DPP, the labour pension system was reformed in 2001, with ongoing attempts to amend the 'three labour laws' (Trade Union Law, Collective Bargaining Law, and Industrial Disputes Settlement Law) (still pending in the legislature because of partisan disagreement). Temporary Provisions for Elderly Welfare Subsidy were promulgated in 2002, and reform introduced to the retirement pensions system, with the provision of unemployment benefits in 2002. The unemployment benefits scheme and existing training scheme were integrated into the Employment Insurance Programme in 2003, and the Employment Protection Law enacted in 2004. Elderly welfare allowance and living support allowance for the children of medium- to low-income families were also introduced. The Labour Standard Law was expanded and a Labour–Management–Government Committee established (Shin and Shaw 2003). In **Japan**, welfare laws have been revised and the social security system revamped because of increased unemployment and the ageing population. The Long-term Care Insurance Law was enacted in 1997, taking effect in 2000. Pension reform has been ongoing – raising the starting age for payment of employee pensions in 1994; amending the Public Pensions Law in 1998 to set maximum pension premiums, increase pensionable age, stop wage indexation, and introduce old-age pensions for active workers in their late sixties; and further raising the contribution rate and reducing pension benefits in 2004. The Social Insurance Agency Reform in 2004 responded to corruption scandals and demands to eliminate mismanagement of pension insurance premiums.

Economic and fiscal policy reforms

The 1997 regional economic crisis has also resulted in stepped-up measures in economic and fiscal policy reforms. Fiscal reform, deregulation and economic revitalization are among the key items of the government policy agenda in the five East Asian states. All have engaged actively in: financial services sector regulatory reform, coupled with the establishment of proper supervisory/regulatory institutions (such as a Financial Supervisory Commission/Agency) to promote better corporate governance; tax review or reform to secure a steadier and broader taxation base;[3] and new initiatives to nurture entrepreneurship and innovation, especially IT development. Special importance is attached to IT in order to respond to the challenges of the new knowledge economy and to open up a new frontier for the next round of economic expansion, as it is no longer realistic to rely on the traditional export-oriented manufacturing and service industries for growth and prosperity. Such developmentalist strategy ties in closely with the direction of educational reforms.

In **Japan**, an Industrial Revitalization Corporation was set up in 2003 to provide assistance to small and medium enterprises (SMEs). **South Korea** similarly placed the thrust of economic policy on nurturing SMEs and their IT capabilities as the next-generation growth engines. **Taiwan** extended credit support to traditional industries and SMEs and established research and development (R&D) centres and free trade zones. A strategy for a technology-based new economy was adopted. **Singapore** set up a Research, Innovation and Enterprise Council, and a National Research Foundation to fund long-term research in strategic areas in 2005. Strong support was provided to the internationalization of its government-linked companies (GLCs). **Hong Kong** established a Commission on Innovation and Technology and an Innovation and Technology Fund in 1998, followed by an SME Financial Assistance Scheme in 2001. There was greater emphasis on promoting cultural and creative industries. All five states have also strengthened their fair trade and pro-competition regimes (in terms of legislation and enforcement structure). Both **Japan** and **South Korea** amended their anti-monopoly legislation. **Singapore** enacted a Competition Law in 2004, while **Hong Kong** is debating on the need for legislation.

Policy shifts rather than policy reversals

In short, economic challenges such as globalization and the Asian financial crisis, and political challenges like regime change with democratization (South Korea and Taiwan) or without democratization (Hong Kong), and the gradual rise of new politics (Japan included), together with increasing fiscal/budgetary pressure (notably in Japan, Taiwan and Hong Kong), have together helped to induce public policy rethinking on the part of East Asian governments. All have to rise to the demand for policy shifts (and even policy reversals in some cases). New initiatives and modifications have been launched (such as towards contributory support of public healthcare, withdrawal from state-subsidized home ownership in Hong Kong, and a wider acceptance of minimum living standards and incomes).

Policy shifts there certainly are, but evidence thus far as enumerated above does not point to clear trends of policy reversals per se, such as in drastically 'privatizing' state responsibilities. At best, governments have only resorted more to regulating corporate and private resources on welfare, and imposing legislative frameworks for welfare schemes. The mode of policy delivery governance has, however, seen some notable changes, such as moving increasingly from state provision to shared responsibility (compulsory insurance/ savings schemes, public–private partnerships and more voluntary/third-sector involvement) and contracted-out provision and private sector production. Such shifts in public management systems, however, have not fundamentally eroded the 'old' regime of East Asian governance, nor diluted (not to say negated) state domination, except with reference to Hong Kong, which has all along been a muddled type of deviant among the East Asian states. Path dependency is still very much at play, sustained by institutional continuity. Policy changes have not moved significantly beyond the original policy path, which is still essentially productivist and conforms to the East Asian model of state developmentalism. State policy-makers and managers continue to espouse strong developmentalist thinking (despite the advent of new democratic regimes in Taiwan and South Korea). Even Hong Kong's post-colonial regime has become more proactive in economic and industrial policy because of business pressure and political motives (Cheung 2000).[4]

The picture is not complete without tracking the fiscal performance of the East Asian states. Over the past decade, public expenditure as a percentage of GDP had not recorded any pattern of substantial contraction – see Table 1.2, though fiscal stress created by economic fluctuations after the Asian financial crisis had accounted for some adjustments. Even Japan had managed to maintain a relatively stable level of public expenditure since the mid-1990s despite the bursting of the economic bubble in the beginning of the decade. It is interesting to note that in the case of South Korea, Taiwan and Hong Kong, public expenditure had actually taken up a higher proportion of GDP since the Asian crisis, which hit them more severely than Singapore. In a way, the fiscal picture corroborates the path of public policy developments.

Explanations of East Asian policy 'steadiness'

Path of East Asian public policy governance

The developmentalist nature of East Asian states has to be understood not just as an economic management strategy, but as historically path-dependent,

Table 1.2 Public expenditure as percentage of GDP, 1996–2005

Public expenditure as percentage of GDP	Japan	South Korea	Taiwan	Singapore	Hong Kong
1996	36.5*[1]	14.0	14.8	n.a.	17.7
1997	35.3	14.1	15.6	18.4	17.5
1998	42.7*	16.4	12.7	18.0	17.5
1999	n.a.	16.6	13.8	18.1	20.8
2000	36.4*	15.1	15.9[4]	17.5	21.6
2001	38.0*	15.9	17.1	18.1	21.1
2002	38.1*	15.9	15.3	17.1	20.9
2003	n.a.	16.3	16.0	16.8	22.2
2004	36.9*	15.2	15.2	15.6	20.7[2]
2005	n.a.	16.6	16.0	14.8[3]	n.a.

Notes:
n.a. = figures not available.
1 All figures are for financial years except for most years in Japan, marked *.
2 Estimates.
3 Preliminary figure.
4 From July 1999 to December 2000.

Sources: Japan – Ministry of Finance (various issues); Ministry of Finance (various years); South Korea – Ministry of Planning and Budget (2006); Taiwan – Directorate-General of Budget (various years); Singapore – Ministry of Trade and Industry (various years) [figures calculated by author based on official GDP (current market prices), government operating expenditure, and government development expenditure figures]; Hong Kong – Information Services Department (various years).

which contributes towards policy 'steadiness'. Public policy governance is grounded in a strong tradition of centralized, politics–administration fusion. Both Singapore and Hong Kong are typical 'administrative states', where either the bureaucracy runs the state (as clearly in colonial Hong Kong) (Harris 1988: 72–76) or the ruling party and the bureaucracy are one (Singapore) (Chan 1975). Taiwan until the late 1990s was under KMT one-party rule, where bureaucrats were at the same time KMT functionaries (Cheng 1993; Gold 2000). Things should have changed after the DPP came to power in 2000, but there seemed a tendency for the DPP to follow in the footsteps of KMT in 'politicizing' the bureaucracy and public corporations to create yet another interlocking model of governance similar to the past. In Japan, the bureaucracy has been a strong staying force in government deci-sion making, which, despite a long history of administrative reforms, makes the reform experience mostly a slow and somewhat hesitant process because of the previously successful inter-locking array of institutions resistant to rapid change (Beeson 2003). Reforms were more often than not a compromise with the agency bureaucrats, known as 'pre-emptive bureaucrats' (Ito 1995: 251). The same scepticism applies to South Korea, where bureaucrats generally saw reform activities as a source of instability and uncertainty (Hahm and Kim 1999: 491).

The East Asian bureaucracy is a modernizing and developmental force, in line with the nature of the state. Public management reforms have been pursued mostly to secure new or reinvented structures and systems of oper-ations that can improve the capacity of the state (and of the bureaucracy), so as to better lead nation-building and economic development efforts. Thus administrative reforms have tended to adopt a pro-bureaucracy or at least bureaucracy-friendly orientation, and are usually bureaucrats-driven. In the aftermath of the Asian financial crisis, as global competition intensifies resulting in greater economic pressures, national reform agendas might have embraced more overt managerial, fiscal and economic objectives seeking to make the bureaucracy less bloated and more efficient, to cope with fiscal stress, but this is far from trying to erode public bureaucratic power. Despite the apparent similarity of the East Asian governance and public sector reforms to the OECD-pioneered 'New Public Management' reforms, their political and institutional settings remain quite distinct (Cheung 2005b).

Bureaucrat-dominated policy making

A key reason for policy 'steadiness' in East Asian public policy governance – including social policy making – is thus the bureaucrat-dominated nature of public policy making, *in addition to* the state-led economic development approach to policy interventions, which sees things in an economic/develop-mental perspective rather than as strict welfare versus market dichotomies. Bureaucrats who have always been the driving force in public policy formula-tions are not accustomed to drastic changes that upset the *status quo* too much. Their preferred mode of operation is policy modifications and readjust-ments along the original policy path, or as Hogwood and Peters (1983) describe it, 'policy succession'. Bureaucrats, and politicians thinking like them or in alignment with them, tend to see the world as more static and policies as vehicles to help achieve stable development. Once settled in state-led developmentalism, or in Hong Kong's case a kind of growth-oriented positive non-interventionism, they are unlikely to change course substantially even amidst economic crisis because of the complexities and, at times, the inertia imposed by inter-locking interests between state, society and industry.

Besides, the recalcitrance of bureaucrats who are inherent stakeholders of existing policies and the *modus operandi*, as well as the opposition or some-times open 'revolt' by other stakeholders who feel affected by drastic policy changes, such as teachers, healthcare workers, social workers, and civil servants at large, would serve to prevent too much deviation from pre-existing policy governance. The fierce resistance of civil servants to pay reductions and contracting out in Hong Kong (Cheung 2005a), and that of Taiwanese teachers to education reform,[5] are cases in point. In Japan, as well as South Korea and Taiwan, both of which were previously colonized by Japan and have inherited a public administration system whereby legislative approval of detailed policy programmes and administration organizational plans is man-datory, executive-legislative gridlock grounded in factional politics is yet another cause of slow policy making. This has resulted in a high degree of policy continuity and slow incremental policy change. Despite the 2004 elect-oral system reform in Japan, which some presume to have weakened trad-itional factions within the ruling LDP, factional politics have not diminished. As Krauss and Pekkanen (2004: 1) pointed out, '[u]nexpected, *kōenkai* [i.e. factions] have grown stronger because they perform new functions.' LDP's Policy Research Council remains a major avenue of career advancement and specialization for Diet members and an important, if now challenged, struc-ture for policy making. Its structure and norms are still a means for special-ized *zoku giin* ('Policy Tribes' Diet members) to function as 'gatekeepers' over the policy and legislative agenda of individual members and the bureaucracy in LDP's and government's legislative process (p. 23).

Accumulation and legitimation in East Asian capitalism

Various functionalist theories and conflict theories of both Marxist and non-Marxist orientation have explained the emergence of the welfare state as part of western capitalism (Aspalter 2002b). Market and capitalism, like any institutions, are politically and culturally embedded in society. As Gray (1999) argued, it is a mistake to assume that capitalism everywhere 'will come to resemble the highly individualist culture of England, Scotland and parts of Germany and the Netherlands. It has not done so in France or Italy' (pp. 191–192). Polanyi (1944) similarly pointed out, much earlier, that market institutions did not emerge spontaneously, but rather often depended heavily on state actions. Indeed the creation of national markets in the West had historically coincided with the constitution and expansion of state institutions (UNDP 1999). In the same vein, the welfare state is a construct of state actions within a historically and nationally specific cultural, political and social context.

There are thus different forms of welfare state, embodying different forms of social policy development, inasmuch as there are different forms of capitalism. As 'market capitalism . . . is not an abstracted final stage of economic evolution' (Robison 2003: 168), so the western welfare state model is not the ultimate destiny of a welfare state development trajectory that all welfare states – European, American and Asian, etc. – had to converge to. Even globalization does not necessarily end up in convergence, either towards a universalist welfare regime or a neo-liberal economic regime sceptical of welfare. As an old Chinese philosophical saying put it: 'A white horse is not a horse', so the impact of globalization may bring about divergence as much as convergence. Indigenous values and projects count more than simply emulating some external models even as the process of policy learning and diffusion takes place. Whether globalization can predetermine the specific context and agenda of policy making at the national level is therefore problematic. Even if policy ideas may get transferred globally, policy making and politics are always *local*.

Social policy regimes are the outcome of institutional pathways, which in themselves are constructs of social processes and of historical evolution. In the western experience, if one were to employ the Marxist functionalist interpretation, capitalism came to a point where it suffered from the crisis of accumulation (i.e. continued growth and capital accumulation) and the crisis of legitimacy (of the capitalist mode of production). The role of the state in serving the ultimate interest of the logic of capitalism is to promote both economic growth ('accumulation') and the stability of the social and political order ('legitimation'), through extensive social policy provisions and the construction of a welfare state that helps to reduce class confrontations and political challenges to the capitalist system (Gough 1979; O'Connor 1973; Offe 1984). Among East Asian states, *developmentalism* (subsuming both economic and political *productivism*) can similarly be understood as an array of state actions and interventions in promoting and bolstering a unique form of market capitalism (which some describe as 'state-led' for economies like South Korea and Singapore, and others depict as 'predatory' or 'clientelist' for countries like Indonesia and Thailand).

In the aftershock of the Asian financial crisis, facing increasing pressure from globalization as well as the domestic politics of democratization, the developmental welfare states of both South Korea and Taiwan have clearly become more inclusive. According to Kwon (2005), the socially inclusive welfare regime helped these two states to come out of the economic crisis without suffering too many adverse social effects, such as a sharp rise in poverty or serious worsening of income inequality (p. 495). Granted, social policy helps to mitigate the impact of economic setback and uncertainty, and enables the society to regain cohesion and the collective capacity to pursue economic development, with still strong productivist connotations. In any case, the need for sustained growth (or 'accumulation' in the Marxist sense) and political legitimacy ('legitimation') would make it imperative for an increased state role for East Asian states in social policy development despite a cultural and social context that had traditionally assigned welfare functions to the family, the clan and the corporate sector (as in Japan). The core idea of the East Asian welfare state to facilitate the growth of East Asian capitalism would, resembling how Marxists and neo-Marxists had explained the relationship between western capitalism and its welfare state, support a social policy discourse that cannot be decoupled from the larger developmentalist paradigm.

Notes

1 The assistance of Lo Oi Yu, senior research assistant of the Governance in Asia Research Centre, City University of Hong Kong, in researching country data for the production of this chapter is most gratefully acknowledged.
2 The term 'welfare state' is used here as a general term not necessarily denoting any particular form of welfare state such as that in some European countries. As the later discussion explains, there are different forms of welfare state.
3 Both Japan and Singapore increased their consumption tax/goods and services tax (GST) from 3 to 5 per cent, while Hong Kong's government is consulting the public on the introduction of GST.
4 On 11 September 2006, Hong Kong's Chief Executive Donald Tsang announced that 'positive non-interventionism' was no longer the government's policy; instead government would adhere to the principle of 'big government, small government' (*South China Morning Post*, 2006).
5 They accused the reformers of only resorting 'to using political means and mobilizing the government's administrative power, assuming these to be sufficient to solve education problems' – see 'Rebuilding Education Declaration', Taiwan: www.highqualityeducation.com.

References

Aspalter, C. (2002a) Introduction, in C. Aspalter (ed.), *Discovering the Welfare State in East Asia*, Westport, CT: Praeger.
Aspalter, C. (2002b) Exploring old and new shores in welfare state theory, in C. Aspalter (ed.), *Discovering the Welfare State in East Asia*, Westport, CT: Praeger.
Aspalter, C. (2002c) Singapore: a welfare state in a class by itself, in C. Aspalter (ed.), *Discovering the Welfare State in East Asia*, Westport, CT: Praeger.
Beeson, M. (2003) Japan's reluctant reformers and the legacy of the developmental state, in A. B. L. Cheung and I. Scott (eds), *Governance and Public Sector Reform in Asia: Paradigm Shifts or Business As Usual?*, London: RoutledgeCurzon.
Castles, F.G. (1998) *Comparative Public Policy: Patterns of Post-war Transformation*, Cheltenham: Edward Elgar.
Chan, H.C. (1975) Politics in an administrative state: where has the politics gone?, in C. M. Seah (ed.), *Trends in Singapore*, Singapore: Institute of Southeast Asian Studies.

Chan, R. (2002) The struggle of welfare development in Hong Kong, in C. Aspalter (ed.), *Discovering the Welfare State in East Asia*, Westport, CT: Praeger.

Chen, H.N. (2002) Taiwan, in R. Agus, J. F. Doling and D. Lee (eds), *Housing Policy Systems in South and East Asia*, Basingstoke: Palgrave Macmillan.

Cheng, T.J. (1993) Taiwan in democratic transition, in J. W. Morley (ed.), *Driven by Growth: Political Change in the Asia-Pacific Region*, Armonk, NY: M. E. Sharpe.

Cheung, A.B.L. (2000) New interventionism in the making: interpreting state interventions in Hong Kong after the change of sovereignty, *Journal of Contemporary China*, 9(24): 291–308.

Cheung, A.B.L. (2005a) Civil service pay reform in Hong Kong: principles, politics and paradoxes, in A. B. L. Cheung (ed.), *Public Service Reform in East Asia: Reform Issues and Challenges in Japan, Korea, Singapore and Hong Kong*, Hong Kong: Chinese University Press.

Cheung, A.B.L. (2005b) The politics of administrative reforms in Asia: paradigms and legacies, paths and diversities, *Governance*, 18(2): 257–282.

Croissant, A. (2004) Changing welfare regimes in East and Southeast Asia: crisis, change and challenge, *Social Policy and Administration*, 38(5): 504–524.

Directorate-General of Budget, Accounting and Statistics, Executive Yuan of Taiwan (various years), Central government expenditure as percentages of gross domestic product in major countries (Zhuyao Guojia Zhongyang Zhengfu Zhichu Zhan Guonei Shengchan Maoe), at: http://win.dgbas.gov.tw/dgbas03/bs8/world/expgdp.htm.

Esping-Andersen, G. (1990) *The Three Worlds of Welfare Capitalism*, Cambridge: Polity Press.

Evans, P.B. (1989) Predatory, developmental and other apparatuses: a comparative political economy perspective on the third world state, *Sociological Forum*, 4: 233–246.

Evans, P.B. (1995) *Embedded Autonomy: States and Industrial Transformation*, Princeton, NJ: Princeton University Press.

Friedman, M. (1981) *Free To Choose*, Harmondsworth: Penguin.

Fukawa, T. (2005) Some structural issues in the Japanese social security system, *Japanese Journal of Social Security Policy*, 4(2): 67–75.

Gold, T. (2000) The waning of the Kuomintang state in Taiwan, in K. E. Brodsgaard and S. Young (eds), *State Capacity in East Asia: Japan, Taiwan, China, and Vietnam*, New York: Oxford University Press, 84–113.

Gough, I. (1979) *The Political Economy of the Welfare State*, London: Macmillan.

Gough, I. (2001) Globalisation and regional welfare regimes: the East Asian case, *Global Social Policy*, 1: 163–189.

Gough, I. (2004) East Asia: the limits of productivist regimes, in I. Gough, G. Wood et al. (eds), *Insecurity and Welfare Regimes in Asia, Africa and Latin America: Social Policy in Development Context*, Cambridge: Cambridge University Press.

Gray, J. (1999) *False Dawn: The Delusions of Global Capitalism*, London: Granta Books.

Haddon-Cave, P. (1984) The making of some aspects of public policy in Hong Kong (Introduction to the first edition), in D. G. Lethbridge (ed.), *The Business Environment in Hong Kong*, Hong Kong: Oxford University Press.

Hahm, S.D. and Kim, K.W. (1999) Institutional reforms and democratization in Korea: the case of the Kim Young Sam administration, 1993–1998, *Governance*, 12(4): 479–494.

Harris, P. (1988) *Hong Kong: A Study in Bureaucracy and Politics*, Hong Kong: Macmillan.

Harrop, M. (1992) *Power and Policy in Liberal Democracies*, Cambridge: Cambridge University Press.

Hayakawa, K. (2002) Japan, in R. Agus, J. F. Doling and D. Lee (eds), *Housing Policy Systems in South and East Asia*, Basingstoke: Palgrave Macmillan.

Hogwood, B.W. and Peters, B.G. (1983) *Policy Dynamics*, Brighton: Wheatsheaf.

Holliday, I. (2000) Productivist welfare capitalism: social policy in East Asia, *Political Studies*, 48: 706–723.

Holliday, I. (2005) East Asian social policy in the wake of the financial crisis: farewell to productivism?, *Policy and Politics*, 33(1): 145–162.

Imai, Y. (2002) *Health Care Reform in Japan, Economic Department Working Papers, No. 321*, Paris: Organization for Economic Cooperation and Development.

Information Services Department, Government Hong Kong Special Administrative Region (various years), *Hong Kong Year Book*, at: http://www.info.gov.hk/yearbook.

Ito, M. (1995) Administrative reform, in H. K. Kim, M. Muramatsu, T. J. Pempel and K. Yamamura (eds), *The Japanese Civil Service and Economic Development: Catalysts of Change*, Oxford: Clarendon Press.

Johnson, C. (1982) *MITI and the Japanese Miracle*, Stanford, CT: Stanford University Press.

Jones, C. (1993) The pacific challenge: Confucian welfare states, in C. Jones (ed.), *New Perspectives on the Welfare State in Europe*, London: Routledge.

Krauss, E. and Pekkanen, R. (2004) Explaining party adaptation to electoral reform: the discreet charm of the LDP?, *Journal of Japanese Studies*, 30(1): 1–34.

Ku, Y.W. (2002) Towards a Taiwanese welfare state: demographic change, politics, and social policy, in C. Aspalter (ed.), *Discovering the Welfare State in East Asia*, Westport, CT: Praeger.

Kwon, H.J. (1997) Beyond European welfare regimes: comparative perspectives on East Asian welfare systems, *Journal of Social Policy*, 26: 467–484.

Kwon, H.J. (1998) Democracy and the politics of social welfare: a comparative analysis of welfare systems in East Asia, in R. Goodman, G. White, and H. J. Kwon (eds), *The East Asian Welfare Model: Welfare Orientalism and the State*, London: Routledge.

Kwon, H.J. (2002) The Korean welfare state: development and reform agenda, in C. Aspalter (ed.), *Discovering the Welfare State in East Asia*, Westport, CT: Praeger.

Kwon, H.J. (2005) Transforming the development welfare state in East Asia, *Development and Change*, 36(3): 477–497.

Lee, D. (2002) Korea, in R. Agus, J. F. Doling and D. Lee (eds), *Housing Policy Systems in South and East Asia*, Basingstoke: Palgrave Macmillan.

Lee, E.W.Y. (2005) The renegotiation of the social pact in Hong Kong: economic globalization, socio-economic change, and local politics, *Journal of Social Policy*, 34(2): 293–310.

Lee, K.B. (2005) The effects of the August 31 real estate measures, *Korea Policy Review*, October, 50–53.

Marshall, T.H. and Bottomore, T. (1992) *Citizenship and Social Class*, London: Pluto Press.

Ministry of Finance, Government of Japan (various years), *Public Finance Related Information*, at: http://www.mof.go.jp/jouhou/syukei/siryou/sy_new.htm.

Ministry of Finance, Government of Japan (various years) *Understanding the Japanese Budget*, at: http://www.mof.go.jp/english/budget/budget.htm.

Ministry of Planning and Budget, Government of Republic of Korea (various years) *Annual Budget Expenditures, FY1996–FY2006*, at: http://www.mpb.go.kr/english.html.

Ministry of Trade and Industry, Government of Singapore (various years), *Economic Survey of Singapore*, at: http://app.mti.gov.sg/default.asp?id=123&cat=2.

Mishra, R. (1999) *Globalization and the Welfare State*, Cheltenham: Edward Elgar.

Miyamoto, T. (2003) Dynamics of the Japanese welfare state in comparative perspective: between three worlds and the developmental state, *Japanese Journal of Social Security Policy*, 2(2): 12–24.

O'Connor, J. (1973) *The Fiscal Crisis of the State*, New York: St. Martin's Press.

Offe, C. (1984) *Contradictions of the Welfare State*, in J. Keane (ed.), Cambridge, MA: MIT Press.

Organization for Economic Cooperation and Development (OECD) (2001a) *OECD in Figures 2001*, at: http://www.sourceoecd.org.

OECD (2001b) *Education at a Glance: OECD Indicators*, at: http://www.sourceoecd.org.

OECD (2002) *OECD Historical Statistics 1997–2000*, at: http://www.sourceoecd.org.

Peng, I. (2002) Gender and welfare state restructuring in Japan, in C. Aspalter (ed.), *Discovering the Welfare State in East Asia*, Westport, CT: Praeger.

Peng, I. (2004) Postindustrial pressures, political regime shifts, and social policy reform in Japan and South Korea, *Journal of East Asian Studies*, 4: 389–425.

Pierson, C. (2004) *Late Industrializers and the Development of the Welfare State*, Social Policy and Development Programme Paper No. 16, September, Geneva: UN Research Institute for Social Development.

Pinker, R.A. (1979) *The Idea of Welfare*, London: Heinemann Educational.

Polanyi, K. (1944) *The Great Transformation: The Political and Economic Origins of Our Time*, Boston, MA: Beacon Press.

Ramesh, M. (1995) Social security in South Korea and Singapore: explaining the differences, *Social Policy and Administration*, 29: 228–240.

Ramesh, M. (2003) Globalization and social security expansion in East Asia, in L. Weiss (ed.), *States in the Global Economy: Bringing Domestic Institutions Back In*, Cambridge: Cambridge University Press, 83–100.

Robison, R. (2003) Looking back on the Asian crisis: the question of convergence, *Asian Journal of Social Science*, 31(2): 162–171.

Robison, R. and Hewison, K. (2005) Introduction: East Asia and the trials of Neo-liberalism, *Journal of Development Studies*, 41(2): 183–196.

Schiffer, J.R. (1983) *Anatomy of a Laissez–faire Government: The Hong Kong Growth Model Reconsidered*, Hong Kong: Centre of Urban Studies and Urban Planning, University of Hong Kong.

Shin, C. and Shaw, I. (2003) Social policy in South Korea: cultural and structural factors in the emergence of welfare, *Social Policy and Administration*, 37(4): 328–341.

South China Morning Post (2006) Tsang tosses out hands-off economic policy, 12 September.

United Nations Development Programme (UNDP) (1999) *China Human Development Report 1999: Transition and the State*, New York: United Nations.

Wade, R. (1990) *Governing the Market: Economic Theory and the Role of Government in East Asian Industrialization*, Princeton, NJ: Princeton University Press.

48 *Anthony B. L. Cheung*

Weiss, L. (1998) *The Myth of the Powerless State*, Ithaca, NY: Cornell University Press.

Wong, J. (2004) The adaptive developmental state in East Asia, *Journal of East Asian Studies*, 4: 345–362.

World Bank (1993) *The East Asian Economic Miracle: Economic Growth and Public Policy*, New York: Oxford University Press.

2 Redefining development in China

Towards a new policy paradigm for the new century?

Kinglun Ngok

Introduction

Although market-oriented economic reforms in the past 20-odd years have brought unprecedented economic growth, and improved the living standards of over one billion people in China, the unilateral focus on economic growth (GDPism) by the governments at all levels has adverse developmental implications. It has led to a serious imbalance among economic growth, environmental protection and social equality. That imbalance is apparent in a widening gap between the rich and the poor, an increasing urban–rural divide, and destabilizing regional disparities. Population expansion, escalation of conflicts between economic development and the ecological environment and natural resources, a backward mode of economic growth, poor performance, and low competitiveness of the overall economy have further compounded such an imbalance. These developments and the grievances of those who have lost ground as a result of the economic reform process have led to widespread civil unrest in China (Cheng and Ngok 2004). Reflecting on these contradictions and problems in the course of China's rapid economic development over the past two decades, especially on the bitter experiences of the SARS crisis, the new generation of Chinese leadership led by Hu Jintao sought to redefine the concept of development in China. As a result, the 'scientific approach to development' (*kexue fazhanguan*) was formulated in late 2003. This new approach to development calls for 'people-centred development, which is comprehensive, coordinated and sustainable, for the promotion of overall harmonic development of economy, society and human beings' (CCCCP 2003). Since then, the so-called 'scientific approach to development' has become a buzzword nationwide. In the official discourse, this new approach has been hailed as the latest development of Marxism in pace with the times, and its effective implementation is conceived as being crucial for solving all the social problems accumulated in China. On 17 December 2005, when he conducted inspection in Qinghai, one of the poorest regions in northwest China, Hu Jintao further clarified his 'people-centred' development conception. Borrowing the usage of Abraham Lincoln's 'government of the people, by the people, for the people', Hu advocated a 'development for the people, by the people, and of the people'. This is the concise expression of the 'people-centred development' conception.

With the emergence of policy sciences in China in the late 1990s, studying public policy has become a hot field of academic activities. Theories and concepts of public policy developed by western scholars have been applied widely in the studies of public policies in China. Making use of Peter Hall's concept of the policy paradigm, this chapter argues that the new notion of 'scientific approach to development' indicates the emergence of a new policy paradigm in the reforming China. The formulation of the 'scientific approach to development' reflects not only the efforts made by the new Chinese leadership to revise and redefine the development policy launched by the late paramount leader Deng Xiaoping and continued in the era of Jiang Zemin, but also a new direction of public policy, especially policies in the development field. With the implementation of the new approach to development since 2003, Chinese policy-makers have started to revisit the policy problems facing the country, reset the policy goals, make use of new policy instruments, and even practise a new policy-making style.

To contextualize the emergence of the new policy paradigm revealed by the 'scientific concept of development', this chapter tries to outline the paradigmatic changes in the field of development policy in China since 1949. It argues that three paradigmatic phases of development policy may be distinguished in China: the paradigm of catching-up development policy (until the late 1970s); the paradigm of unilateral economic growth (GDPism) policy (1978–2003); and the current phase (from 2003 onwards) in which a new policy paradigm is taking shape. As development policy has a wide coverage, paradigms identified in this field can be, to a large extent, extended to China's public policy in general.

Policy paradigm and paradigm shift

Thomas Kuhn (1970) identified the notion of scientific paradigms. A paradigm refers to a set of integrated ideas that stand together to define a territory of understanding. Basically, a paradigm is regarded as the philosophical and theoretical framework of a scientific school or discipline within which theories, laws and generalizations, and the experiments performed in support of them, are formulated. Broadly, a philosophical or theoretical framework of any kind can be called a paradigm. Though paradigms have their own integrity, values and assumptions, they are not free of challenges. A once-stable paradigm might begin to weaken if it ceased adequately to provide solutions for problems; a shift of paradigm will then occur. Kuhn defined a paradigm shift as a new conceptual tradition, a radical change in interpretation, whereby science takes a wholly new and changed perspective towards an area of knowledge and activity.

Making use of the advantage of Kuhn's concept of scientific paradigm, Peter Hall first introduced the concept of 'policy paradigm' in studying the learning process in public policy making (Hall 1993). For Hall, the learning process may take different forms, depending on the kinds of change in policy that are involved. Hall sees policy making as a process that usually involves three central variables: the overarching goals that guide policy in a particular field; the techniques or policy instruments used to attain those goals; and the precise settings of these instruments. Based on these distinctions, Hall identifies three distinct kinds of change in policy: changes to the setting of existing policy instruments; changes in the basic instruments used to attain policy goals; and changes in all three components of policy. He further labels these three kinds of change 'first order change', 'second order change' and 'third order change', respectively. First order change refers to changes in the levels (or settings) of the basic policy instruments. Second order change refers to changes in the basic techniques used to attain policy goals, that is, adoption of new policy instruments. Third order change refers to changes in all three components of policy, that is, policy goal alteration. For Hall, the process of 'social learning' in policy making involves these three levels or order.

For Hall, the process of first order change is likely to display the features of incrementalism, satisficing and routinized decision making that people normally associate with the policy process. Second order change and the development of new policy instruments may move one step further in the direction of strategic action. Third order change is the most fundamental since it represents a marked shift in the intellectual framework within which policy is made. This framework, Hall argued, is 'policy paradigm', that is, 'a framework of ideas and standards that specifies not only the goals of policy and kind of instruments that can be used to attain them, but also the very nature of the problems they are meant to be addressing' (ibid.: 279).

Policy paradigm has become an important concept in policy sciences. It captures the idea that the established beliefs, values and attitudes behind understandings of public problems and notions of the feasibility of the proposed solutions are significant determinants of policy content (Howlett and Ramesh 2003). A policy paradigm represents a 'set of cognitive background assumptions that constrain action by limiting the range of alternatives that policy-making elites are likely to perceive as useful and worth considering' (Campbell 1998, quoted in Howlett and Ramesh 2003: 232). It shapes the broad goals policy-makers pursue, the way they perceive public problems and the kinds of solutions they consider for adoption. An easy way to understand a policy paradigm is to relate it to traditional philosophical notions of 'ideologies', or more recent sociological notions of 'discourses' or 'frames' (ibid.: 233).

In Hall's analysis, while first and second order changes are equivalent to Kuhn's 'normal science', third order change reflects a very different process, marked by the radical changes in the overarching terms of policy discourse associated with a 'paradigm shift' (Hall 1993: 278–279). First and second order change took place within a relatively closed policy network and did not cumulate into third order change. The latter displayed particular features. Paradigm shift is a process initiated by a specific kind of event, namely, by events that proved anomalous within the terms of the prevailing paradigm. As anomalies accumulated under the prevailing paradigm, policy-makers altered instrument settings and experimented with new policy instruments as they tried to correct the problem. If these efforts failed, policy failures would occur, which would discredit the old paradigm and lead to a wide-ranging search for alternatives and to a process of experimentation with modifications to policy (Oliver and Pembeton 2003).

> Central to this process was a shift in the locus of authority over policy. Shifts in the locus of authority seem to be a critical component of the process whereby paradigms shift. Finally, the process leading to changes of this magnitude could not be confined inside the state itself; it was ultimately effected by means of electoral competition and a broader societal debate.
>
> (Hall 1993: 291)

Paradigmatic phases of development policy in post-Mao China

Policy paradigms can be identified in a country over time in general or in a particular policy arena. According to Hall, a policy paradigm is an intellectual framework embedded in the minds of policy-makers, which governs not only the goals of policy and the choice of instruments and settings to achieve these goals, but also policy-makers' perception of the very problems they are meant to be addressing (Oliver and Pembeton 2003). A policy paradigm represents a framework for policy action and it can be identified in terms of how policy-makers set policy goals, choose policy instruments and define policy problems.

Utilizing Hall's concept, this chapter tries to distinguish policy paradigms in the field of development policy in China. Basically, three paradigmatic phases of development policy may be distinguished in China, as described earlier in this chapter. In identifying the policy paradigms in China, on top of policy goal, policy instrument, and policy problem definition, we also take into account some other factors, such as policy orientation, policy-making style and policy language.

The first paradigmatic phase of development policy in China is labeled 'catching-up'. Table 2.1 illustrates the basic features of this policy paradigm. As a result of the humiliating history suffered by the Chinese people since the mid-nineteenth century, characterized by poverty, economic backwardness and brutal foreign aggressions, the newly created Communist government under the leadership of Mao Zedong determined to build a prosperous and strong new China. In doing so, a state-led catching-up development model (Lin et al. 1994) was undertaken in China with the ambition of transcending the United Kingdom and catching up with the United States (*chaoying*

Table 2.1 Paradigmatic phase I: catching up development (1949–1978)

Policy paradigm	Catching-up development
Problem definition	A poor and weak China was bullied by the great powers
Policy goal	Nation-centred: • Enhancing nation-building • Generating employment • Reducing inequality • Promoting nation capacity and building up a strong country
Policy orientation	State-led policies: • Nationalization of foreign and private ownership • Preferred investment in heavy industries • Enhancing self-reliance • Public provision of welfare
Policy instrument	State-centric instruments: • Establishment of public enterprises • Expansion of state agencies • Elimination of market forces • Political mobilization and class struggle
Policy-making style	Elite-dominated policy-making: • The state dominating in planning development, formulating development policies, and carrying out development programmes and projects • Policy-making by the key leaders
Policy language	Red language: • Surpassing UK and catching up with US • Revolution • Class struggle • Rebellion • Great leap forward

ganmei). Based on development initiatives, the Chinese government managed to achieve the objectives of overcoming foreign ownership and domination, enhancing economic self-reliance, accelerating industrial growth, especially heavy industries, generating employment, redistributing income, developing infrastructure, and so on. In accordance with the ideology of socialism, China adopted various interventionist, state-led policies, including the establishment of state-owned enterprises, expansion of state sectors, nationalization of private economy, elimination of market forces, control over export and import, and prohibition of foreign investment. These policies were introduced to achieve major developmental goals set by national development plans. However, the Chinese leadership failed to separate economic principles from political passions, and tried in vain to utilize political means, for instance class struggle and mass mobilization, to achieve economic growth.

Chinese people had made huge sacrifices for the catching-up development policy. For instance, more than 40 million people died from famine in the late 1950s and early 1960s due to the catastrophe that resulted from the irrational Great Leap Forward strategy. The Cultural Revolution further destroyed Chinese economic and social development. Mao Zedong's radical political ideology and his launching of relentless political campaigns ultimately disrupted the catching-up policy paradigm for development. When Mao died in 1976, China was still a poor and weak country in which the people languished in poverty and starvation due to the shortage of necessities. Public dissatisfaction with the poor economic conditions and the repressive political environment peaked after Mao was dead. People's grievances, Mao's death and the ensuing leadership succession opened a window for a policy paradigm shift in the late 1970s. Deng Xiaoping's political revival in the late 1970s and the nationwide debate on the issue of the criterion of truth testing in 1978 marked the formation of a new locus of political authority.

Given the economic backwardness and poor economic performance of the state sector, the post-Mao leadership, led by Deng Xiaoping, shifted their focus on economic growth from the class struggle in late 1978 when the reform and open-door policy was adopted. Emphasis on economic growth signals a paradigm shift from the catching-up strategy in the development policy domain in China (see Table 2.2). While an open-door policy was adopted to attract foreign investment and advanced technology, the market-oriented reform strategy was launched to revive the poor national economy. To destroy the egalitarian legacy of the Maoist era, unbalanced growth theory and pragmatic principles were justified. New policy slogans became popular, such as 'getting rich is glorious', 'let a few people get rich first', and 'No matter it is white or black, those who can catch mice are good cats'. Economic growth became the paramount policy goal of the party-state and the source of its legitimacy. As Deng Xiaoping put it, '(G)rowth is the hard truth' (*fazhan shi yingdaoli*).

In the Deng Xiaoping era, the importance of economic building was emphasized in relation to the narrow economic dimension. As a result, the measurement of GDP (gross domestic product) became the dominant concern when adopting national development plans. GDP per capita has since been treated as the primary measure of development objectives, economic success, government's performance and citizens' national welfare. In line with the decentralization policy, the growth of GDP and the measurement of GDP per capita have been used to determine the economic status and rank of local governments in the overall hierarchy of national development. They are even used as the most important indicators to measure the performance of local leaders. In other words, GDP has been used to determine the career development of local officials. As a result, the pursuit of GDP has become the central task of officials at all levels. Officials have been participating in a national campaign of GDP production. No matter how parochial, superficial and misleading the GDP measurement may be, economists, politicians and

Table 2.2 Paradigmatic phase II: economic growth (GDPism) (1978–2003)

Policy paradigm	Unilateral economic growth (GDPism)
Problem definition	Economy of shortage eroded the party-state legitimacy
Policy goal	Goods-centred: • Overcoming economic backwardness • Improving economic performance in terms of greater efficiency, growth and competitiveness • Speeding up economic growth • Increasing GDP figures
Policy orientation	Market-oriented policies: • Downsizing public sector • Developing private economy • Deregulation of market controls • Liberalization of trade and foreign investment • Separation of government and enterprise
Policy instrument	Market-driven instruments: • Decentralization • Privatization • Deregulation • Liberalization • Marketization • Macro-economic control
Policy-making style	State-structural: • The state still the main actor in socio-economic development • Increasing role of economic elites in policy-making • Heavy involvement of experts, especially the economic experts in policy-making
Policy language	Yellow language: • A few people get rich first • Getting rich is glorious • GDP and GDP per capita • Economic growth

ordinary people in certifying the rank of a county, city or province in national economic order have effectively used it. It has been widely and explicitly observed that GDP is accepted as the principal indicator of economic progress, sign of wellbeing, yardstick of success, performance of local leaders and basis of policy debate in post-Mao China, especially in the 1990s. As a result, inappropriate development policies and strategies were launched to boost GDP nationwide.

Apparently, China's market transition since the late 1970s is parallel with the worldwide dominance of market-driven neo-liberal thinking. Since the early 1980s, in the global atmosphere dominated by the neo-liberal market ideology and neo-classical approach, there has been a fundamental pro-market shift in the policy orientation of developing nations. China is no exception, though it has a totally different starting point. For the purpose of improving the dire economic performance and providing Chinese people with enough food, the post-Mao Chinese leadership, with Deng Xiaoping at the core, decided to abandon the traditional socialist planned economy through the adoption of reform and opening-up policy in the late 1970s. In doing so, China began to embrace a new set of market-led policies, such as the creation of the private market, privatization of state enterprises, downsizing of the state sector, deregulation of market controls, liberalization of trade and foreign investment and withdrawal of welfare subsidies. These changes in policy have been pursued in order to enhance market competition, increase economic efficiency and accelerate economic growth. Although the state still plays the principal role in policy making, newly emerged interest groups, especially the political and economic elites, have a role to play. Since market institutions are underdeveloped, political power is still monopolized by a few political and economic elites, and interests are not fully organized. These elites could use development programmes to make economic gains and legitimize their repressive rule. As a result, the development initiatives can become an instrument of state domination.

In the absence of market transparency and competitive local buyers, valuable public assets have often been sold at nominal prices to the vested interests associated with the policy-making elites, without much concern for public accountability. The policy of streamlining the state sector and reducing welfare subsidies has adverse impacts on low-income citizens. The retreat of the government from fields such as education, health, housing and so on, represent a major challenge to the realization of basic needs for poorest households. Low-income citizens, mainly unemployed urban people, urban–rural migrant workers and peasants, cannot afford education, healthcare and housing. Patients without money are rejected by the hospitals and poor students are not allowed into schools and universities. Property prices are so high that only a few rich people can buy. The neglect of the basic needs of ordinary people has invited much social unrest. Since the late 1990s onwards, the unilateral economic growth paradigm has been facing serious challenge and public opposition in China. All these factors indicate that a new shift in policy paradigm is unavoidable.

Economic growth (GDP), social inequality and the accumulation of anomalies

Traditionally, politicians use GDP as an indicator of public wellbeing or the lack of it. In general, the GDP of a country or region represents the total money value of annual goods and services produced in that country or region. The obvious limitation of GDP measurement is that it is incapable of measuring the non-economic (social) dimension of human welfare, which constitutes an essential part of overall development. In addition, GDP overlooks the issue of income distribution: any economic gains made by a few high-income households may be understood as benefits to all; it does not make a distinction between the winners and losers of higher economic growth.

Within the unilateral economic growth (GDPism) paradigm, China has achieved huge growth in GDP. Between 1978 and 2004, China's GDP increased from US$147.3 billion to US$1.6494 trillion, with an average annual growth rate of 9.4 per cent. Its foreign trade rose from US$20.6 billion to US$1.1548 trillion, averaging an annual growth rate of over 16 per cent. China's foreign exchange reserve increased from US$167 million to US$609.9 billion. The number of rural poor has dwindled from some 250 million to 26 million (Hu 2005). Nevertheless, the unilateral economic growth policy has worsened income inequality, social erosion, environmental degradation and ecological crisis. Not only has social tension among different social groups been intensifying, there have been worsening forms of environmental degradation, such as air and water pollution, land degradation, deforestation and biodiversity loss. As Liou (2000) points out, China's economic reforms have also resulted in problems of social control, official corruption, social inequality, urban–rural conflict, social unrest and crime. These problems are especially noticable in such service areas as public education, public health and customer protection.

Social inequality in China is first demonstrated by income inequality. Before the economic reforms, income inequality in China was relatively low, but the Gini co-efficient, a common indicator of income inequality with zero representing absolute equality and one representing absolute inequality, has been rising rapidly since the economic reforms, with widening income gaps between rural and urban areas, and between the prosperous coastal region and the interior. Based on estimates made by some scholars about national income inequality during the early years of reform, the Gini coefficient was 0.30 (Yang and Xin 2002). According to data from the first household survey conducted by the income distribution research team of the Institute of Economics, CASS, the national Gini co-efficient was estimated at 0.382 in the late 1980s. The same research team conducted another national household survey in 2002, showing that the national Gini co-efficient for that year was close to 0.46. By comparison, we find that the Gini co-efficient in China has increased from 0.3 in the early 1980s to 0.46 in the early twenty-first century. That means China's national income inequality has widened by more than 50 per cent in the last two decades (UNDP 2005).

The impressive reforms have produced a huge gap between the rich and poor. Currently, China ranks ninetieth among 131 countries in terms of the Gini co-efficient for income distribution. Based on the national samples, the income share of the highest-income group in 1988 was 7.3 times that of the lowest-income group. When comparing the income shares of different income groups in 2002, the 1 per cent with the highest income controlled 6.1 per cent of the total. The top 5 per cent controlled nearly 20 per cent of total income, while the top 10 per cent controlled nearly 32 per cent. The average income of the highest-income decile group is 11 times that of the lowest-income decile group. The widening was more evident in rural income inequality in the late 1980s, in urban income inequality in the early 1990s, and in the urban–rural income gap since the late 1990s (ibid.).

Along with increasing income inequality, a substantial underclass of about 40 million rural poor people and 10 million urban poor has been produced. Among them, laid-off workers, the unemployed, retirees, workers in poorly run enterprises, poor peasants, migrant workers and land-expropriated farmers are worst affected. Although official poverty lines have been set locally since the mid-1990s, many living under the lines have not been offered official relief. An official survey conducted in 1999 revealed that the per capita monthly income was less than 100 yuan for 6–10 per cent of all urban families. Those in the top 20 per cent secured 42.4 per cent of the total income of the country, while the bottom 20 per cent earned just 2.2 per cent of the total income (Yang and Xin 2002).

Despite economic growth, the urban–rural divide has been an enduring problem in China, and it now has the biggest urban–rural gap in the world; per capita income among urban residents is approximately four times that of rural residents, compared with the global average ratio of approximately 1.5. Rural income has been in decline since 1997 (ibid.) and the urban–rural income gap has led to a large-scale migration from the villages to the cities. In the largest internal migration in the world in peacetime, 100 million peasants now move from city to city looking for work in the so-called mangliu (blind flow).

Wide disparities also exist between the coastal and inland regions, especially regions with substantial ethnic minorities. Some scholars described China as 'a country with four worlds'. The first world refers to the most prosperous urban areas; the second, the relatively prosperous coastal provinces; the third, the poor interior provinces; and the fourth, the poverty-stricken border regions and rural areas dominated by ethnic minorities. In 1999, average income in Shanghai (US$15,516) was 12 times that in Guizhou province (US$1,247), an interior province in the 'fourth world' (Hu et al. 2001).

This imbalanced development has resulted in rising tension in Chinese society, and increasing worries concerning potential social instability since the mid-1990s. In 2001, a report by a Communist Party research organization on mounting public anger concerning inequality, corruption and official aloofness in China, described a spreading pattern of 'collective protests and group incidents' arising from economic, ethnic and religious conflicts. The report cites growing inequality and corruption as major sources of discontent, and warns that even greater social conflicts are likely as China opens its markets to foreign trade and investment (Eckholm 2001). In August 2002, three prominent scholars issued a serious warning about the social crisis in China. In their article, entitled 'The most serious warning: the social crisis behind the economic prosperity', the authors, using a large number of statistics and data, argued that civil discontent in China is growing fast, and society is on the eve of great crisis. If not handled properly, the society will be out of control, and the government will step down. According to the article, the main reasons for social crisis include unemployment, political corruption, the heavy tax burden of the peasants, the increasing gap between the rich and poor, the deterioration of law and order, and so on (Wang et al. 2002).

To maintain social and political stability, some policy adjustments have been made in China since the mid-1990s. To placate peasant discontent, the central government has periodically criticized excess taxes and corruption at the local and grassroots levels of government. Village elections have been promoted as giving more power to the peasants. The government has also pursued a social security policy of setting minimum prices for agricultural commodities and purchasing grain that fails to sell in the market at that price. A new scheme, tax for fee, is being introduced in rural China, aimed at abolishing all taxes levied by township and village councils and replacing them with a national tax that should not exceed more than 5 per cent of household income (Li 2006). To pacify disgruntled workers, more money has been invested in the national minimum living guarantee scheme, a public income maintenance system for laid-off workers and urban poor people (Wong and Ngok 2006).

The first few years of the new century witnessed further policy changes in China. In order to narrow down the regional disparity, the strategic policy of 'Developing the West' was implemented in 2000. One year later, China joined the WTO so as to respond the challenges of the economic globalization. Nevertheless, the worsening development conditions resulted from the unilateral economic growth paradigm in China had not been recognized fully by the policymakers until the outbreak of the SARS epidemic.

The SARS crisis, leadership succession, and the emergence of a new policy paradigm

In early 2003, China was heavily hit by an unprecedented public crisis: Severe Acute Respiratory Syndrome (SARS). The first SARS case appeared in Guangdong in November 2002 but failed to attract attention from either the government or society. In early January 2003, local medical practitioners reported the existence of SARS to Guangdong provincial authorities, and expert teams were sent out to investige. In February, the SARS virus spread to Guangzhou and in March to Beijing, Shanxi, Inner Mongolia and other provinces. Despite the rapid spread of SARS, China's government maintained a news blackout and actively tried to conceal the extent of the outbreak. As two important sessions were held in Beijing in March, it was understandable that the authorities covered up the truth. They worried that the epidemic would create more panic and social unrest, and thus harm economic growth.

Chinese officials' initial response to the SARS crisis reflected the constraints of the old policy paradigm of unilateral economic growth. In order to secure stable social settings for economic growth, paramount priority was given to social stability and all events that could potentially damage that stability were suppressed.

However, in the era of globalization, domestic efforts to keep state secrets were no longer as effective. The SARS epidemic was soon out of control and became an international crisis. In February, SARS spread to Hong Kong, Vietnam, Singapore and Toronto. In March, a rapid and extensive outbreak of SARS occurred in Hong Kong. The Chinese government's efforts to cover up the truth encountered increasing international pressure and internal opposition. In early April, American mass media suggested isolating China. Many countries banned Chinese people from entrance. On 8 April, Jiang Yanyong, a retired PLA doctor, at great personal risk exposed government efforts to cover up the SARS crisis in Beijing's military hospitals to international media. Suddenly, the Chinese government was under unprecedented international pressure. Obviously, the widespread outbreak of SARS in China was a significant policy failure, and such a failure did much to discredit the prevailing policy paradigm. In this sense, the outbreak of SARS triggered the initiation of a policy paradigm shift (Guo et al. 2004).

Under these circumstances, the newly established leadership led by Hu Jintao and Wen Jiabao was determined to push for policy change. A U-turn in government policy occurred in late April 2003 after a Politburo Standing Committee meeting on the SARS outbreak held on 17 April. The policy change was signalled by the announcement of the dismissal of the Minister of Health Zhang Wenkang and Beijing Mayor Meng Xuenong on 20 April. Though the inside story of the political confrontation within the Politburo was not known by outsiders, the outcome of the meeting showed the victory of the new party chief Hu Jintao in the power struggle. Afterwards, other effective measures were adopted. An Anti-SARS Leading Group was formed at national level, with Vice-Premier Wu Yi as its head. The traditional May long holiday was cancelled. All places of entertainments were closed. The government proclaimed the launch of a people's war to fight SARS. During this 'war', top leaders travelled nationwide to inspect local responses to the SARS outbreak; thousands of people were quarantined all over the country; and hospitals encountering mass outbreaks of the epidemic were closed. New Emergency Regulations on Sudden Outbreaks of Public Health Incidents, involving stiff penalties, were drawn up and promulgated. Anybody who knowingly spread SARS could face the death penalty. Cadres who were not effective in fighting SARS were dismissed. Full reporting of the SARS crisis was allowed and encouraged by the government. The Party and the media were ordered to be absolutely transparent regarding the extent and nature of the SARS epidemic in China, mobilizing society into confronting the crisis. A better mechanism of information flow was established. While the central information collecting institutions were strengthened, local governments were required to report the SARS cases in a timely and accurate manner. The government was active not only in mobilizing domestic forces and resources to fight SARS, but also in international cooperation. The government pledged to actively cooperate with the WHO, which played a large role in dealing with the SARS crisis. As a token of China's willingness to cooperate with its neighbours, Premier Wen Jiabao attended the special meeting on SARS in Bangkok on 29–30 April.

All these changes indicate how the Chinese party-state has been adjusting its policy style. After the SARS crisis, we can easily identify the following new developments in Chinese public management and public policy: the increase of transparency brought by the increasing role of mass media; the emergence of public accountability demonstrated by the dismissal of unqualified officials; and the focus on social justice as more attention is directed to socially disadvantaged groups. Meanwhile, the government's public relations management capabilities have improved considerably.

It seems that these changes in Chinese public management and public policy were not only the instinctive reaction to the SARS crisis. In fact, the SARS crisis forced the Chinese policy makers to think about how to strike a balance between economic growth and social development. Taking lessons from the SARS crisis and the worsening developmental conditions, the new leadership sought to formulate a new set of ideas on Chinese development. In October 2003, at the Third Plenary Session of the Sixteenth Central Committee of the CCP, the Chinese leadership put forward a new notion of 'scientific concept of development'. In the light of this new notion, the Communist Party proposed for the first time a people-centred development policy. This was a breakthrough in Chinese development policy. Since then, much new political rhetoric has become fashionable in Chinese political discourse, such as 'people-centredness', 'harmonious society', 'governing capacity', 'environmentally-friendly society' and 'energy-saving society'. Along with the popularity of these new buzzwords, new changes have occurred in Chinese public policy process. Not only were the settings of policy changed but the hierarchy of goals and sets of instruments employed to guide policy also shifted radically. Balance of economic growth and social development replaced the GDP figure and became the pre-eminent concern of policymakers. All these new adjustments mark the fact that the Chinese party-state has started to adapt in quite significant ways to new social and economic realities, and a new paradigm of the development policy is emerging in China.

A thorough analysis of the key policy documents released after the SARS crisis by central government reveals the main components of the shape the policy paradigm was taking in the development policy field. We label this new paradigm 'People-Centred Development' (see Table 2.3). Under this new paradigm, policy problems are redefined from a social equity perspective. Although economic growth is still regarded as the important policy goal, the same priority is given to social development and environmental protection; at least, we can see this change in the official policy statements. People rather than materials are seen as the basis of policy choice. In terms of policy

Table 2.3 Paradigmatic phase III: people-centred development (2003–) (in progress)

Policy paradigm	People-centred development
Problem definition	Social inequality leads to conflicting society
Policy goal	People-centred: • Striking a balance between economic growth, environmental protection and social equality • Maintaining economic growth without ignoring social equity • Building a harmonious and environmentally-friendly society
Policy orientation	Mix of state, market and civil society: • Enhancing partnership among state, market and civil society • Providing more benefits to unprivileged social groups • A shift from economic policy to social policy
Policy instrument	Mixed instruments: • Regulatory state • Citizen participation • Consensus building • Responsive governance
Policy-making style	State–society partnership: • More participation of the public in policy process • Combination of science and democracy in policy-making • Transparency and accountability • A learning Politburo
Policy language	Green language: • Common prosperity • Energy-saving society • Environmentally-friendly society • Sustainable development • Social justice and equity • Full development of both socio-economy and human being • Partnership, fraternity and harmony

orientation, the wellbeing of the people, especially socially disadvantaged groups, has drawn much of the policy-makers' attention. In choosing policy instruments, the government has given more weight to the role of civil society and business. Bottom-up perspectives and public participation are emphasized in policy-making processes. Even the Politburo of CCP, the top policy-making body in China, is seeking to gain more policy-related knowledge from academia and so improve the quality of public policy. This new paradigm, though it is still in its early stage of construction, has become the framework of the policy actions taken by the Chinese leaders.

Take the making of the Eleventh Five-Year Plan as an example. In October

2005, the Fifth Plenary Meeting of the Sixteenth Central Committee of CCP approved a series of recommendations for the Eleventh Five-Year Plan. Unlike the previous five-year plans, which focused on economic growth, the Party's recommendations place social development and people's livelihood as the foremost priority, and aim to achieve balanced and sustainable development. Though economic construction is still highly important, social justice and people's wellbeing are given the same attention. The new plan calls for building up a harmonious, energy-saving and environmentally-friendly society. It is expected that future policy options will focus on the reduction of poverty, and the elimination of social conflict (Wang 2005). In fact, top Chinese policy-makers positioned 2006 as the 'Year of Retracking' (*zhuangui nian*), in which the direction of Chinese public policies would shift from the well-entrenched GDPism paradigm to a 'people-centred development' paradigm. That is to say, 2006 would be the first year of 'paradigmatic shift' to 'people-centred development'. See Table 2.3.

In reviewing the paradigm shift process, we can see that widening income inequality among social groups, the urban–rural gap, regional disparity, urban poverty and ecological degradation were threatening to the unilateral economic growth (GDP) policy. In other words, they were 'anomalies' in the Kuhnian sense. The outbreak of SARS functioned as a triggering event, intensifying all these problems. As Hall (1993: 280) put it, a policy paradigm can be threatened by the appearance of anomalies, namely by developments that are not fully compatible, even as puzzles, with the terms of the paradigm. Efforts to deal with such anomalies may entail experiments to adjust existing lines of policy, but if the paradigm is genuinely incapable of dealing with anomalous developments, these experiments will result in policy failures that gradually undermine the authority of the existing paradigm and its advocates even further.

The completion of the leadership transition and the formation of the new administration under the leadership of Hu Jintao and Wen Jiabao are key components of the shift. Hu and Wen played a key role in institutionalizing the new policy paradigm. The locus of authority in relation to policy making shifted towards the Hu-Wen Administration after the policy failure during the early stage of the SARS crisis. Following the SARS crisis, the Hu-Wen leadership realized that the overemphasis on the GDP figure often conceals, justifies and even worsens inequality between income groups and between regions. Although policy paradigms did not become the object of open political contestation in the Chinese political context, the outcome of the political 'black box' reflects the shift in policy paradigm, which we can see from the policy documents produced by the Chinese authorities from 2003 onwards.

Conclusion

This chapter outlines the paradigmatic stages of development policy in China, with a focus on the paradigm shift taking place after the SARS crisis in 2003. Three policy paradigms in the Chinese development policy arena have been identified in terms of policy problem definition, goals, orientation, instruments, policy-making style and language. In the first paradigmatic phase of catching-up development, policy problem definition centred on the poor situation of the country, and the policy goal was to build up a strong country. In doing so, the state-led policy orientations and the authority-based policy instruments were chosen. With the existence of a totalistic state and a charismatic leader, key leaders dominated the policy-making process. As a reflection of the revolutionary ideology, policy statements were full of 'red' language, such as class struggle and rebellion.

In the second paradigmatic phase of unilateral economic growth policy (GDPism), policy problem definition focused on the poor economic situation of the people, and the policy goal was to develop the economy and give the people enough food so as to increase the legitimacy of the party-state. For this purpose, market-oriented policy orientations and market-driven policy instruments were adopted. With the growth of the market economy and the capitalist class, economic elites began to be heavily involved in policy-making processes and market discourses (desribed in 'yellow' terms: the colour of gold/money) were incorporated into policy contents.

In the third paradigmatic phase of people-centred development, policy problem definition revolves around increasing social inequality resulting from imbalances in economic growth, and the policy goal is to build up a har- monious society to reduce social conflict. For this purpose, people-oriented policy orientations and mixed policy instruments are chosen. Cooperation and partnership between the state and civil society is encouraged in policy- making processes, and the participation of the public in policy making is beginning to be emphasized. In order to realize a balanced development between economy, society and environment, an increasing number of environmental protection elements are included in policy statements. As a result, policy language is becoming much 'greener'.

On the whole, this chapter is a preliminary step in applying the notion of policy paradigms to the context of China. As a result of the lack of transpar- ency in the Chinese political regime, the process of paradigm shift is far from clear. So it is not surprising to find that paradigmatic changes described in this chapter are less clear-cut than Hall allows. Although I argue that a new paradigm has emerged in Chinese public policy in general, and in the devel- opment policy domain in particular, the institutionalization of the new policy paradigm is far from complete. For the time being, the new paradigm is merely an embryo. To a large extent, it is a policy advocacy made by the new leadership represented by Hu Jintao and Wen Jiabao. Given the complex central–local relationship in the Chinese political system and the increasingly powerful and strong localities, it will take a long time for local governments to shift from the well-entrenched GDPism paradigm to the people-centred approach. As Hall points out, the power of existing institutions to channel forces of change requires the presence of a powerful exogenous shock (or shocks) sufficient to undermine a well-entrenched policy paradigm. Without substantial reform in the existing authoritarian political system, the realization of the shift to the people-centred paradigm will be a tough task facing the Chinese ruling elite. The completion of the paradigm shift may or may not decisively impact China's future. Nevertheless, it is safe to say that current Chinese policy-makers are moving in the right direction.

References

Central Committee of Chinese Communist Party (CCCCP) (2003) *The Communiqué of the Third Plenary Session of the Sixteenth Central Committee of the Chinese Communist Party*, Beijing: Central Committee of the Chinese Communist Party.

Campbell, J.L. (1998) Institutional analysis and the role of ideas in political economy, *Theory and Society*, 27(5): 377–409.

Cheng, J. and Ngok, K.L. (2004) The potential for civil unrest in China, in A. Heijmans, N. Simmonds and H. van de Veen (eds), *Searching for Peace in Asia Pacific*, Boulder and London: Lynne Rienner, 166–180.

Eckholm, E. (2001) Chinese warn of civil unrest across country, *International Herald Tribune*, 2–3 June, p. 1.

Guo W.Q., Zhu Y.P. and Li, L. (2004) Zainangzhong xuexi: SARS weiji yingdui [Learning from disasters: coping with the SARS crisis], in CSSA Public Policy Research Center and Governance in Asia Research Center, City University of Hong Kong (eds), *Public Policy Analysis in China 2004*, Beijing: Zhongguoshehui kexue chubanshe.

Hall, P.A. (1993) Policy paradigms, social learning and the state: the case of economic policy-making in Britain, *Comparative Politics*, 25(3): 275–296.

Howlett, M. and Ramesh, M. (2003) *Studying Public Policy: Policy Cycles and Policy Subsystems*, Toronto: Oxford University Press.

Hu A.G., Zou, P. and Li, C.P. (2001) The regional disparity in economic and social development in China between 1978 to 2000, in X. Ru, X. Lu and T. Shan (eds), *Zhongguo Shehui Xingshi Fenxi Yu Yuce [Analysis and Forecast of Social Conditions in China, 2002]*, Beijing: Social Science Documentation Publishing House.

Hu, J. (2005) *Speech at the Opening Ceremony of Fortune Global Forum in Beijing*, 16 May.

Kuhn, T. (1970) *The Structure of Scientific Revolutions*, second edition, Chicago, IL: University of Chicago Press.

Li, L.C.L. (2006) Embedded institutionalization: sustaining the rural tax reform in China, *Pacific Review*, 19(1): 63–84.

Lin, Y.F., Cai, F. and Li, Z. (1994) *Zhongguo de Qiji: Fazhanzhanlue yu Jingji Gaige [China's Miracle: Development Strategy and the Economic Reform]*, Shanghai: Sanlian Bookstore and Shanghai Renmin Chubanshe.

Liou, K.T. (2000) State–society relations in post-Mao Chinese economic reforms: changes and challenges, *International Journal of Economic Development*, 2(1): 1–17.

Oliver, M.J. and Pemberton, H. (2003) Learning and change in 20th century British economic policy, paper read at the British Study Group, Centre for European Studies, Harvard University, 3 December.

United Nations Development Programme (UNDP) (2005) *The National Human*

Development Reports for China, at: hdr.undp.org/docs/reports/national/ CPRy_China/China_2005_en.pdf.

Wang, J. (2005) The theme of the Fifth Plenary Session of the Sixteenth Central Committee of CCP is to build a harmonious society, *The Mirror*, 11: 27–29.

Wang, S.G., Hu, A.G. and Ding, Y.Z. (2002) The social crisis behind the economic prosperity [Jingji fanrong beihou de shehui weiji], *Zhanglue yu Guanli* [*Strategy and Management*], 3: 26–33.

Wong, L. and Ngok, K.L. (2006) Social policy between plan and market: xiagang (off-duty employment) and the policy of the re-employment service centres in China, *Social Policy and Administration*, 40(2): 158–173.

Yang, Y.Y. and Xin, X.B. (2002) The current pattern of income distribution and its development trend in China, in X. Ru, X. Lu and T. Shan (eds), *Zhongguo Shehui Xingshi Fenxi Yu Yuce* [*Analysis and Forecast of Social Conditions in China 2002*], Beijing: Social Science Documentation Publishing House.

3 Empowering the public and the policy science of democracy from a post-modernist perspective

Weiqing Guo

Reorientation in the name of 'post-'

'All are agreed that there is and ought to be a move away from descriptions of processes (i.e. from what is) to recommendations of outcomes (i.e. to what ought to be). Integrating the normative, value dimension into policy analysis is their common task' (Wildavsky 1992: 21). This statement is from Aaron Wildavsky's chapter in the edited volume *Advances in Policy Studies Since 1950*. Later, in 1993, the term 'argumentative turn' (Fisher and Forester 1993: 2) was brought to policy studies to further explain and develop Wildavsky's thoughts on the role of norms and values. It provides simple but invaluable insights – the nature of policy studies and planning is substantially argumentative in practical policy-making contexts (ibid.). In John Dryzek's words, both policy analysis and policy planning are experiencing a significant shift, 'from Science to Argument' (1993: 213).

Three distinctive features lie in this 'argumentative turn'. First, it challenges the epistemology and paradigm grounded on Positivism, and digs out new theories beyond Positivism and Empiricism and therefore it rebuilds the fundamental policy studies framework. A wide range of studies can be seen as a relevant endeavour for this 'dig-out', including analysis of daily life languages in Britain, post-structuralism in France, critical theory advanced by the Frankfurt School and the reframing of American pragmatism. Narrative analysis and other research methods are also developed from these efforts.

Second, it shakes the technocratic policy regime established by professional experts and bureaucratic elites, and re-stresses the 'Policy Science of Democracy' in the Lasswellian tradition. Its purpose is twofold. On the one hand, it calls for the democratization of the policy process, which attempts to re-balance power among government, experts and public. Institutions must also be redesigned so as to re-balance the knowledge structure between universal and local knowledge. More public participation and local knowledge constitute the core of advocacy. 'Deliberative democracy' is the term used to describe this new institutional design, in which the public participate in important policy decision making and programme planning. It also advocates the democratization of policy studies. As an academic discipline, this should be demonstrated by paradigm shift and re-conceptualization, including re-emphasis on policy formulation, policy evaluation and policy learning, and so on.

Third, it opposes the isolation from and disinterest in social sciences from real-life contexts, and stresses the need to address individual plights and social issues. However, any policy resolutions should not be misunderstood as specific assignments of welfare to vulnerable people, but as empowerments that enable the public to decide on appropriate ways of sharing interest, with dignity and intelligence. 'Empowerment of the public' therefore becomes a core concept in the argumentative turn. It focuses on the public's action-ability, as well as their powers of decision making in the policy process. Correspondingly, it has seen development on a technical level in order to address the means of empowerments and the ways, procedures and criteria to assess the effects of empowerment.

In short, these three characteristics can be seen as three key nodal points in the argumentative turn of public policy studies, namely: a theoretical shift to post-positivism; an institutionalization of democracy through participation; and a practical empowerment of the public. It should also be noted that all three changes are closely related to the trend of post-modernist thought in social science theories, as well as that in political sciences. Therefore, the above-mentioned post-positivism, together with later post-empiricism and post-structuralism, have been featured as the most important theoretical foundations and weapons for critiques in the argumentative turn of public policy studies. Since the second half of the twentieth century, terms with 'post-' as their prefix have increasingly become buzzwords in academic circles. Some of them even spread beyond the academic boundary and emerge in the public sphere through mass media. It is widely acknowledged that the term 'post-modernism' is hard to define, but it is given a clear direction in policy studies. It has triggered substantive developments for self-inquiry and self-critiques. In short, this trend can be called 'reorientation in the name of post-'.

The following sections in this chapter will first critically review three features of the argumentative turn in policy studies, with a focus on logical relations between post-modernism and the policy science of democracy. Second, it will place their relationship in the Chinese policy context and bring in some brief discussions. It attempts to demonstrate that both argumentative turn and policy science of democracy can and should become one important direction of policy studies: normative inquiry and policy practices.

Meanwhile, it is noteworthy that due to the differences in language structures and ways of thinking in Chinese linguistic contexts, Chinese readers regard many 'post-' conceptions as merely fashionable or even odd words. Policy studies are therefore often confined to providing purely practical resolutions for policy problems. Unsurprisingly, those who advocate 'post-' terms in China are criticized for chasing superficial and whimsical fashion.

However, post-modernism has close connections with critical epistemology and creative democratic arrangements. Nevertheless, two stereotypes decouple their relations. First, post-modernism is nothing but something produced by high technologies in highly affluent societies. Those relative theories are therefore labelled as odd thoughts. Second, 'democracy' is subordinated to 'science', while 'science' is simply equal to positivism. To break down these two stereotypes, policy studies are required to explore social realities and start with individual experiences. Post-modernism has been understood from worldwide policy cases of 'science–positivism–elite–democracy–administrations'. This rigid but common approach in the policy-making process frequently causes policy failures and demolishes the foundations of democracy. Researchers' interests in post-modernism have thus grown out of reflections upon policy failures, rather than of accidents. In conclusion, the occurrence of policy failures is attributed to the incapability of 'understanding in otherness' or policy targets, but not to the less scientific nature of the policy-making process. To reach this understanding, it requires us to raise policy dialogues and debates from the perspective of 'otherness'.

This perspective allows 'others' that have long been oppressed and marginalized, to voice and to talk to the 'centre'. It is in this sense that public policy studies are turning to post-modernism. The core in this fundamental turn is about how to empower the public and how to encourage the individual's presence in every critical moment throughout the policy-making process that affects their life chances, by enhancing their decision-making powers, avoiding information asymmetry and improving their abilities to chart life courses.

Policy failures and the breakthrough in methodology

As discussed above, the argumentative turn in policy studies is as starting with the critique of policy failures. Criticism is twofold, related to (a) philosophical methodology in a theoretical vein, and (b) directly connected to political institutions and policy practice in the real world. Critics focus on social risks, crises and policy failures. These critiques also drive us to inquire as to the underlying causes argued to be inbuilt in our traditional conceptual, institutional and practical structures.

Christopher Hood and failures in public management

Christopher Hood (1998) identifies four types of failure in public management. They occur due to different factors, namely, hierarchical order, egalitarianism, individualism and fatalism, respectively (pp. 27–48). He also reveals how the weakness of human nature inbuilt in organizational procedures results in massive management tragedies and policy failures. Citing David Collingridge et al.'s (1992) research findings, Hood (1998: 38) points out that,

Excessive faith and trust in organizational competence have been identified by David Collingridge (1992) as lying at the heart of what he calls
'inflexible technologies' like nuclear power and large-scale transport
projects. The paradox of such technologies resembles the well-known
problem of 'groupthink' screening out critical judgement in top-level
policy or management groups (Janis 1972). A high degree of trust has to
develop among the key participants (contractors, public bureaucracies,
professional experts) for such projects to be developed at all; but that
high-trust relationship tends to make the whole process impervious to
what may be only too well-founded doubts and questions coming from
outside the charmed circle. The result of unchallenged faith in particular
'technological fixes' include the fiascos stemming from post-World War
II beliefs that nuclear energy could produce clean and cheap power
(William 1980) or the beguiling but often disappointed hope that expensive new computer systems can save money, improve accuracy, and
increase efficiency.

(Margetts 1991)

Furthermore, organizations not only frequently experience failures, but also
rarely learn from the lessons. Hood (ibid.: 39) cites Norman Dixon:

Why the recurring failure to learn from experience in this type of organization? Dixon claims the learning problem comes from the social psychology lying behind the conventional military structure. He argues that,
'It is a sad feature of authoritarian organizations that their nature inevitably militates against the possibility of learning from experience through
the apportioning of blame. The reason is not hard to find. Since authoritarianism is itself the product of psychological defences, authoritarian
organizations are past masters at deflecting blame. They do so by denial,
by rationalization, by making scapegoats, or by some mixtures of the
three. . . . However it is achieved, the net result is that no real admission of
failure or incompetence is ever made by those who are really responsible;
hence nothing can be done about preventing a recurrence.'

Grounded within his four type theories, Hoods stresses that modernized
rhetoric in the public management sphere should be dealt with highly cautiously. In his view, 'it is far from certain that public management at the turn
of the century is headed everywhere towards the same "modern" paradigm,
unless "paradigm" (admittedly a vague and elusive word) means no more
than a set of ambiguous catchwords in common linguistic usage' (p. 220).
Not only is it less plausible, such an ultimate 'modern' resolution also exposes
the world to more risks. Because 'different approaches to organization can
have a "self-disequilibrating" character as much as a self-reinforcing one',
'each of those polar approaches to organisational design in public management may have a propensity to achieve exactly the opposite of the goals

intended through the various reverse-effect mechanisms' (op. cit.). Close attention, therefore, needs to be given to Hood's inspirational study of the connections between cultures, organizations and consequences. He notices that every style of organisation inclines to devoting itself to endless organizational re-shaping processes for seeking cardinal recipes; however, such over-commitment to management sometimes worsens further substantial problems and causes policy failures (Dunleavy and Hood 1994). Hood's analysis, however, does not provide a clear approach for avoiding policy failures.

James Scott and large scheme failures

Approaching from the perspective of knowledge and power, researchers advocate more pungent and radical critiques. Scott (2004) reveals various forms of dystopia caused by highly modernized schemes in the last century. Based on the observation on 'scientific forestry' in Germany, compulsory villagization in Tanzania and urban planning projects in Brasilia, he argues that bureaucratic urban planners and policy-makers often prefer to create grand schemes, which are on such a large scale that common people's lives and human environments are entirely disregarded. Even when destructive consequences occur, those projects are still temerariously continued.

Scott further elaborates the underlying causes. He points out that those large projects and programmes end up as massive disasters because of combinations of four factors, namely: the administrative ordering of nature and society; high-modernist ideology; the authoritarian state; and prostrate civil society (pp. 4–5). The combination of these four creates a 'knowledge–power' structure, which ruins policy efforts, causes policy failures and even massive disasters. Scott's analysis provides another valuable insight on possible causes of policy failure. His specific 'knowledge–power' structure tends to be based on rationalism, instead of 'cultures', as Hoods argues.

The main characteristics of the 'knowledge–power' structure can be well demonstrated in two examples. Scott takes scientific forestry in eighteenth-century Prussia and Sachsen as a fable, and concludes that 'the carriers of high modernism tend to see rational order in remarkably visual aesthetic terms' (p. 4). Scott calls this type of knowledge 'state simplifications', because

> ... high modernism was about 'interests' as well as faith. Its carriers, even when they were capitalist entrepreneurs, required state action to realize their plans. In most cases, they were powerful officials and heads of state. They tended to prefer certain forms of planning and social organization (such as huge dams, centralized communication and transportation hubs, large factories and farms, and grid cities), because these forms fit snugly into a high-modernist view and also answered their political interests as state officials. There was, to put it mildly, an elective affinity between high modernism and the interests of many state officials.
>
> (p. 4)

Yet, 'facts' filtered from this device are characterized by five features, namely: interested utilitarian (more precisely, state interest-oriented), documentary, static, aggregate and standardized (p. 80). These key features show that the filter for simplification of knowledge in fact excludes local/practical knowledge possessed by those on-the-spot and accumulated from people's daily life, because the social nature of facts – dynamic and individually characteristic – often goes against the state's interests. Therefore the political filter is virtually an exclusive device, which monopolizes the classification of knowledge.

This feature is also exemplified in Brasilia's new town planning. Declaring war on the corrupt, undeveloped and ignorant Brasilia in the old days, architects built up a grandiose new capital surrounding the city axis. However, this magnificent and overarching regeneration plan did not involve and consult those stakeholders holding property rights to the land. As a result, the intervention created a 'dead city', which was disconnected from traditional cultures and demolished social relationships in the old daily life. A delicate planned forest has no diversity of species; a well-planned modern capital crowded out the vitality of city life. In this sense, it incurred many criticisms of huge waste and failure (pp. 103–146).

Scott, however, also considers the factors that help human society overcome policy failures and sustain its development. He emphasizes the role of 'metis', a word introduced from ancient Hellenic. Scott sees it as another influential force outside a 'simplified' structure. It represents local knowledge originating from individual life experiences and passed down through the generations. The key point here is that public policies fail to address social problems if policy-makers only follow simple and centrally driven resolutions and do not include local knowledge, which is always characterized by practical and experiential insights (ibid.). The significance of local knowledge in the analysis of policy failures and democratic policy studies deserves greater attention. Further discussion will be provided later.

Further analysis of policy failures

As one important issue in public policy science, policy failure has attracted wide discussion and study. Drawing on the twentieth century's eight policy programmes of the US Federal Government as good examples of policy failure, May (1992) concludes that policy failure undoubtedly widely exists. Such occurrences should promote enormous policy learning in the US, yet some chief features of US politics hinder this development. If 'political learning' is launched in the top political circle, the status quo can be changed.

In the same vein, deLeon (1988) argues that the development of US policy studies is influenced by several grand political decisions, including the declaration of war in the Second World War, the Great Society (war on poverty), the Vietnam War and the energy crisis in the 1970s. In his view, most of these political occurrences show that sophisticated policy analysis should be responsible for the consequent policy failures. Those participants, decision-makers and policy analysts should feel great shame.

From a perspective similar to Scott's, Fischer (1995) also focuses on the 'knowledge–power' structure in contemporary society. Policy failures suggest that social sciences, unlike what people believe, can neither address most social issues and political problems, nor predict the future trends in a fast-changing policy environment. We have arrived at a time to reflect upon the fundamental nature of social sciences (Fischer 2003).

Starting with the observation of the Great Society, Fischer goes on to reveal the complicated connections between the booming development of policy studies and changes in political environments since the second half of the twentieth century. He points out that under the coverage of 'science', policy studies is inherently political, given that it is influenced by political ideologies. Despite different political positions, governments use policy analysis to serve their political ends. It is against this backdrop that policy studies have boomed since the Second World War. A 'new class' (Fischer and Forester 1993: 21–38), which mainly refers to policy analysts with professional expertise in specific policy fields, has also emerged. These highly political policy analysts have established close connections with their clients (i.e. the government departments that are required to make decisions and produce policy packages) through providing their expertise, thereby monopolizing the policy-making process.

In conclusion, policy-analytic enterprises have not yet assumed the roles set up by their founder, Harold Lasswell. They are limited to providing techniques in a narrow sense, instead of enhancing democracy significantly. Policy studies has contributed to society far less than it promised (Fischer 2003). Not only have specific policies failed, so has the whole discipline.

Reflection upon policy studies: seeking what we lost

Policy analysis constitutes a key part of policy development, as policy evaluation often determines whether a policy or a programme should continue or be terminated. However, based on the above analysis of policy failures, it is believed that critiques are mainly related to reflections on a macro level, but not upon individual policy programmes. Explicit here is recognition that policy analysis has failed to describe what exactly happens in real life and to capture the substantial conflicts and changes in social structures, though policy adjustment is made. In contrast, it drives us away from the real issue and exposes us to a more risky and uncertain policy environment. This creates a basis for the criticism that the whole academic discipline underpinning policy-making processes has failed.

This perspective goes further than simply criticism by exploring another approach to policy studies. Some commentators (Hajer 2003; Stone 2001; Torgerson 2003; Yanow 2003) attempt to employ a 'criticism–reflection–learning' approach to roll back policy studies to the Lasswellian tradition: the

Policy Science of Democracy. 'Criticism' stresses the need to go beyond both positivist and empiricist paradigms in methodology so as to discover the fundamental causes of policy failure. 'Reflection' calls for a reconsideration of the relationships between governments, policy experts and the public throughout the policy process. The question here is: can we reshape this structure through re-empowerment? The aim of 'learning' is twofold, i.e. promoting new policy goals and policy tools, and establishing a new comprehensive conceptual framework.

In contrast to the highlighting of policy experts and decision makers in technical and pragmatic approaches, democratic policy science proposes a method of stressing the role of public participation in the policy process. Yet, policy processes operating on a highly pragmatic and technical level often marginalize the public. As a result, the voice of the public, the foundation of democratic governance, as Robert Dahl (1989) noted, is neglected in the policy process. In Fischer and Forester's (1993) view, the most important lesson is that citizens' rights should be reasserted in the policy-making circle. This is a challenge that democratic theories and practices cannot avoid. However, how can the public participate in and influence the decision-making process? The question becomes the core issue of democratization of policy process.

This issue leads us to a discussion on why and how we should bring the public back into the policy process. Discourse analysis in post-Positivism lends support in terms of methodology, while policy practices advocated by deliberative democracy or public deliberation can provide some insights into institutional arrangements. The argument is that good policy can only be made in a condition in which all stakeholders participate in a deliberative policy debate. Argumentative turn thus distinguishes itself from Positivism policy analysis by emphasizing equal participation in policy debate throughout a deliberative process, instead of exclusive consultation with professionals.

Discursive policy analysis and democratization of policy process

It has been said that a post-modernism driven approach in policy making and analysis is widely acknowledged as a more appropriate way to democratize policy process than the traditional technical and pragmatic one (Schram 1993). It provides policy alternatives grounded in post-positivism, post-empiricism and post-structuralism in the post-modernist camp. Fischer (2003) further points out that, in policy science, the core of post-modernism lies in 'discursive policy analysis' and 'deliberative policymaking practices'. Both of them are based on policy discourse. This is an entirely new light in which policy analysis and practices can challenge the monopoly of the technical and empiricist approach. At this point, policy science can be reshaped, as described in the following three sections.

A post-modernism based theoretical perspective

Three important points need to be further clarified below. Firstly, post-modernism can be understood as an epistemology that stresses the significance of discourse and rhetorical expression in human recognition and social behaviour. Our recognition of objective reality is not independent, but virtually constituted within communicative systems, i.e. telling others and being told by others. Common understanding is built up among social members and provides the basis for collective action. This is how people understand reality and participate in social activities. All these rely on communication and discourse.

Secondly, it claims that rhetoric and discourse not only enable us to understand objective reality, but also to shape the ways in which we think and know. Understanding and consensus are produced within discursive systems through rhetoric and communication. Yet, their social meaning is pre-constituted within wider social contexts and reality is never purely objective. This means that every individual takes part in communication and constructs reality simultaneously.

Thirdly, as post-modernists argue, discourse and rhetoric actually represent an influential force, because they articulate specific cultural and behavioural rules. This explains why they underpin social consensus and develop collective action. More precisely, they guide and confine people's behaviours. Thus, battles in the political field are virtually fights for the dominance of discourse, because power/interest structures can be changed once policy discourse is rebuilt.

Post-modernism is obviously a big camp. The above discussions have not yet fully distinguished each stance from every other. Nevertheless, its significance to the democratizing policy process can be demonstrated through three main features.

Firstly, because reality is socially constructed within discursive systems, as post-modernism argues, policy issues are inherently social. They are either pre-constituted or open to be constituted. Therefore, the same policy issue/problem may have different explanations, which lead to different policy responses. One of the main responsibilities for policy studies thus is to analyse the policy paradigm or policy discourse behind a specific policy.

Secondly, it further points out that every explanation is equal. In fact, the flaw of positivism does not lie in the deployment of various technologies but in granting them a monopolized role. Breaking down this monopolization calls for discursive deliberation in order to facilate public participation and to acknowledge other knowledge and values; a deliberative policy process will be open to different stakeholders who have various experiences, knowledge, values and social norms. As a result, through discursive analysis and democratic deliberation, workable policy resolutions and consensus can be produced.

Thirdly, it highlights the role of policy debate and deliberation in developing recognition. Rather than being limited to expert and policy-making circles, policy deliberation and policy arguments should be open to public participation. To achieve this, policy-makers and experts must act as facilitators to provide stakeholders with access to information, thereby increasing citizens' capacity for analysis.

Re-conceptualization in policy science

The re-conceptualization process has close linkage with three issues, namely: critiques of policy failures and traditional Positivism; embracing of post-modernist thoughts; and reflections upon Lasswell's Policy Science of Democracy. These three extend the boundary of policy science by reshaping theoretical frameworks and re-conceptualizing notions. The development of policy science as an academic discipline is demonstrated following two main directions. One involves embracing various theories for re-considering the policy process. The purpose of reconsideration is to offer comprehensive knowledge and a value structure (Howlett and Ramesh 2003). The other is the discursive policy analytical framework proposed by Fischer (2003).

Studies on public policy widely employ the so-called 'stage approach' to investigate policy processes in real policy arenas, which see policy process theoretically constituted by several stages. From a post-modernist standpoint, reflections on this approach are twofold.

First, it points out the key stage in democratizing the policy process, which is by changing the focus of the policy arena. Based on Positivism, the stage approach focuses on the decision-making stage because, according to the rational choice model in Positivism, policy issues are the objective reality and remain unchanged. Therefore, the main priority is to employ various techniques and expertise to seek out optimal resolutions. In contrast, according to post-modernism, more attention needs to be paid to the pre-decision making stage, namely agenda-setting and policy formation. Because policy issues are open to debate and are also socially constituted, questions regarding what the main issue actually is and what should be dealt with first are fiercely contested. Policy agenda is therefore subjective in deciding which issues should be included and how they should be prioritized. Thus, policy formation is also constituted and the underlying logic might have already pre-excluded other alternatives before moving into the decision-making stage. Moreover, such re-conception helps us recognize the key for democratizing the policy process – to involve public deliberation in the pre-decision making stage, so as to establish consensus on policy issues and policy resolutions.

Second, it identifies potential solutions for promoting democratization of the policy process by re-shaping understanding on the nature of that policy process. Policy process should not be understood as a linear developmental progression, which is supposed to unfold through several stages. Instead, as post-modernism suggests, it is a cyclical system, in which each stage can be the end point and generate another policy cycle. The linear progression view leads us to top-down control and management, while the cyclical view stresses policy learning within each sub-cycle, in which all policy issues/ problems, policy resolutions, policy goals and evaluation criteria are to be re-assessed. It is in this sense that democratization of the policy process can be developed by generating policy learning and innovations within sub-cycles, once multiple policy actors, diverse values and explanations are actively involved. Policy learning is likely to be promoted by increasing stakeholders' access to the policy process, thus enhancing interdependence among policy participants, and developing policy transfer through frequent communication.

Regarding the discursive policy analytical framework, it offers another valuable insight into re-conceptualization. In a stage approach grounded in Positivism, policy evaluation is simply seen as one stage in which all kinds of techniques are used to evaluate policy performance. The evaluation is based on whether or not the policy has achieved the policy goal. However, technical-driven evaluation fails to confront the real debate in policy studies. For example, experts are barely concerned with whether or not a nuclear power plant should be built and where. Technical issues are all that they bear in mind.

Beyond both positive evaluation and normative evaluation, Fischer suggests that both approaches should be referred to and integrated into one policy evaluation framework. To achieve this end, he suggests discursive policy analysis, which entails two levels. The first is to assess whether the policy goal is fulfilled and the second is to place the policy goal within the wider social context to see if the policy fits social norms and values. Lastly, policy evaluation is subject to the question of whether social norms and ideologies provide a reasonable basis for solving social conflicts. It is called 'social choice'.

Three key features characterize the logic of policy deliberation. Firstly, policy evaluation relates closely to policy debate. Except for 'programme verification', which depends on rigorously defined technical criteria, the other three steps (situational validation, societal-level vindication and social choice) concern normative values. Citing the Times Square Redevelopment and Disability Policy as examples, policy debates and contests on a normative level play a positive role. Secondly, the logic of policy deliberation is fundamentally discursive. The purpose of discursive policy is to increase the public's capacity for debating policies. Thirdly, it also suggests that deliberation and debate can better inform policies by producing insightful knowledge and information. This policy analysis framework can thus be understood as a 'policy learning' process, as policy evaluation enriches understanding and builds up consensus on policy goals, policy issues and policy problems. Public participation in policy debates and consequent learning through policy evaluation are more significant than enhancing policy performance because they provide practice and help promote democratization of public policy.

Deliberative policy practice to empower the public

Wider public participation can better inform public policy and governance in complicated social contexts. As Beck (1992) observes, risks are actually generated by the expert circle, which holds an exclusive right to explain and interpret risks, because policy experts are inclined to cover risks. However, they do not possess sufficient knowledge to understand risks (pp. 98–100). Public participation in policy-making is necessary to address risks and crises. Concerning the same issue but from a different perspective, Hajer and Wagenaar (2003) point out that the 'network society' has imposed five challenges on modern politics and call for a reshaping of politics and policy-making processes in order to produce policies accepted by all stakeholders. Drawing on the Netherland's experience, Hajer and Wagenaar demonstrate that in contrast with 'political elites deciding policy-making' in representative democracy, the network society creates new political action and political demands from the bottom for rebuilding policy consensus.

However, how and to what extent should the public participate in the policy process? Is democratization relevant to policy performance? Although these questions are still open to debate, so-called deliberative policy practices attract increasing concern.

The notion of deliberative democracy has prevailed since the 1990s. It stresses the public's equal opportunities, rights and capabilities in relation to participation in policy deliberation. Deliberative policy-making requires that: collective decision-making rights be distributed equally; all participants have equal and valid participatory opportunities; the influence of individual wealth/power on decision making should be minimized; communicative and debating methods should defend participants' real thoughts; and the outcome of deliberation should be demonstrated in policy implementation.

Deliberative policy practices in the US suggest that the strength of deliberative democracy is twofold. The first lies in enhancing the public's capability for understanding and analysing public policies. The second lies in increasing their influence in policy decision making. Fishkin and Ackerman (2004) further points out that collective deliberation effectively advances individual apperception. It also enables participants to cope with different viewpoints from various backgrounds. Finally, group discussion decreases pressure imposed on participants and promotes individual presentation.

From the perspective of empowerment, deliberative policy making could also fulfill the aim of empowering the public. Fishkin's study suggests that citizens can offer systematic and insightful suggestions, if sufficient data and background information are given. It also shows that participants might change their views after communication with others. Interviews also prove that those participating in policy deliberation can maintain responsible attitudes and enthusiasm regarding public affairs for longer periods.

Unlike traditional participative democracy, which is limited to political election and public vote, deliberative democracy advocates the need to debate policies in the light of careful consideration and reflection. On the one hand, this is highly dependent on citizens' communicative and analytical abilities. On the other hand, it could promote citizens' abilities in return. Deliberative democracy also distinguishes itself from social movements in two ways. Firstly, it does not impose substantial pressure and limitations on governmental policy making. Secondly, it has not yet created innovation, either concerning policy resolutions or policy paradigms. In the policy science of democracy, there is still a long way to go in terms of both theories and practices.

References

Beck, U. (1992) From industrial society to risk society: questions of survival, social structure and ecological enlightenment, *Theory, Culture and Society*, 9(1): 91–124.

Collingridge, D. (1992) *The Management of Scale: Big Organizations, Big Decisions, Big Mistakes*, London: Routledge.

Dahl, R.A. (1989) *Democracy and Its Critics*, New Haven: Yale University Press.

deLeon, P. (1988) *Advice and Consent: The Development of the Policy Science*, New York: Russell Sage Foundation.

Dryzek, J.S. (1993) Policy analysis and planning: from science to argument, in F. Fisher and J. Forester (eds), *The Argumentative Turn in Policy Analysis and Planning*, Durham and London: Duke University Press.

Dunleavy, P. and Hood, C. (1994) From old public administration to new public management, *Public Money and Management*, 14(3): 9–16.

Fischer, F. (1995) *Evaluating Public Policy*, Chicago, IL: Nelson-Hall.

Fischer, F. (2003) *Reframing Public Policy: Discourse Politics and Deliberative Practices*, New York: Oxford University Press.

Fischer, F. and Forester, J. (eds) (1993) *The Argumentative Turn in Policy Analysis and Planning*. Durham and London: Duke University Press, 21–38.

Fishkin, S. and Ackerman, B. (2004) *Deliberation Day*, New Haven, CT: Yale University Press.

Hajer M.A. (2003) A frame in the fields: policymaking and the reinvention of politics, in M. A. Hajer and H. Wagenaar (eds), *Deliberation Policy Analysis: Understanding Governance in the Network Society*, Cambridge: Cambridge University Press.

Hajer, M.A. and Wagenaar, H. (eds) (2003) *Deliberation Policy Analysis: Understanding Governance in the Network Society*, Cambridge: Cambridge University Press.

Hood, C. (1998) *The Art of the State: Culture, Rhetoric and Public Management*, Oxford: Clarendon Press.

Howlett, M. and Ramesh, M. (2003) *Studying Public Policy: Policy Cycles and Policy Subsystems*, second edition, Toronto: Oxford University Press.

May, P.J. (1992) Policy learning and failure, *Journal of Public Policy*, 12(4): 342–343.

Schram, S.F. (1993) Postmodern policy analysis: discourse and identity in welfare policy, *Policy Science*, 26: 249–270.

Scott, J.C. (2004) *Seeing Like A State: How Certain Schemes to Improve the Human Condition Have Failed*, New Haven; London: Yale University Press.

Stone, D. (2001) *Policy Paradox: The Art of Political Decision Making*, third edition, London: W. W. Norton.

Torgerson, D. (2003) Democracy through policy discourse, in M. A. Hajer and

H. Wagenaar (eds), *Deliberation Policy Analysis: Understanding Governance in the Network Society*, Cambridge: Cambridge University Press.

Wildavsky, A. (1992) Speaking truth to different subjectivities, in W. N. Dunn and R. M. Kelly (eds), *Advances in Policy Studies Since 1950*, New Brunswick, NJ: Transaction Publishers.

Yanow, D. (2003) Accessing local knowledge, in M. A. Hajer and H. Wagenaar (eds), *Deliberation Policy Analysis: Understanding Governance in the Network Society*, Cambridge: Cambridge University Press, 228–246.

4 Japan's changing domestic governance and its impact on foreign policy

Ito Go

Introduction

Two decades ago, G. John Ruggie, a professor at Harvard University, proposed the idea that the post-war international system had been predicated on the linkage between the international demands for free trade and domestic requests for welfare policies. So-called 'embedded liberalism' was a legacy of the post-war international order. The wealth of each country stemming from the free exchange of goods and services led to the development of comprehensive social policies, and conversely, the liberal ideas involved in implementing domestic welfare reflected the international norms supporting abandonment of the international protectionist movement (Ruggie 1982).

Six decades later, Japan is now facing a dilemma between its willingness to cultivate security ties with the United States, and its need to deepen economic relations with China. First, the incremental changes in the post-war security policy of the Japanese government indicate that the US–Japan relationship has altered into a more equal partnership in which security contributions are demanded by the US government. Japan's dispatch of peacekeeping operations, the establishment of US–Japan security guidelines, and counter-terrorism operations in Afghanistan and Iraq are examples of a more global security partnership with the US.

Second, an increasingly ageing society has pushed Japan to look for an economic market that can absorb exports, and in this process, China's rapid growth has attracted much attention. Japan has advocated the concept of an East Asian Community, and both the Foreign Ministry and the Ministry of Economy, Trade and Industry (METI) have been quite eager to tap the Chinese market so that both countries can enjoy the benefits of rapidly rising intra-regional trade.

This chapter argues that issues of domestic governance in Japan have had an increasing influence on its foreign relations, and seeks to examine in historical context what kind of domestic–international nexus has arisen. It is assumed that the fundamental structure of 'embedded liberalism' was created during Japan's rapid economic growth in the 1960s, and also that this 'embedded liberalism' survived even during the 1970s. The system started to be questioned after the end of the Cold War, and Prime Minister Koizumi Junichiro raised the issue of whether the underpinnings of Japan's 'embedded liberalism' could last given that China was rising for the first time in post-war history.

Japan at the crossroads: the '1970s system' and the new century

Thanks to the US provision of security and access to international markets during the 1960s, the Japanese public was able to prosper economically. Those enjoying the rapid economic growth also received social welfare benefits, since the expansion of the entire economy at the national level increased the welfare budget as well. The government planned fundamental social policies, such as those related to pensions, health insurance and child allowance, as the economy grew, and implemented them starting around the year 1970.

It was also during the 1960s that the entire decision-making process was consolidated. The Liberal Democratic Party (LDP) had dominated the Diet since 1955, and with a stable hold on power in the legislature, those in the party were generally most concerned not about the substance of public policy but rather about continuously being elected. Thus, bureaucracy came to be the major player in policy making. The focus was on economic growth even during the Cold War period, and the US provision of security to Asia's 'springboard' against Communism enabled the Japanese government to pay less attention to security than the nation's prosperity.

The '1970s system'

High economic growth did not last long. In October 1973, the oil shock occurred, starkly highlighting Japanese oil-dependency. Facing the fear of an end to the 'export-led' economy, officials in the government responded in two ways. One was to increase the budget for various public works. 'Public works' here implies the government-led construction business. In order to activate local economies, Diet members became quite closely involved in leading various construction works, such as building highways, bullet trains, bridges, roads, and so forth, in their constituencies.

Prime Minister Tanaka Kakuei was the political leader who established Japan as a construction country. The Ministry of Construction created the public housing loan system in the late 1960s, and Tanaka tried to develop the system so that it would not only be used by general construction companies but also by the general public for individual houses.

The other way in which the government responded was to develop various kinds of energy-saving technologies. The government initiated a 'Save Energy' campaign, at the same time providing subsidies so that private companies could create energy-saving technologies. In short, the general urban public became preoccupied with advanced technologies, while those in local areas focused on what level of subsidies the central government could provide for public works.

Budgetary deficits increased in line with measures to address the 'oil shock' focusing on government-led 'public works'. Discussions on 'governability' became popular at the time, which sought to reduce the government's burden, since the worldwide recession due to the oil crisis caused the government to view its own budget as the most important 'built-in-stabilizer' of economic policy.

Looking back on history, it can be said that the basis for today's regional order in East Asia was stipulated during the 1970s. President Nixon's initiative to open China announced in 1971, and his visit to Shanghai in 1972, led to the normalization of Sino–Japanese relations in late 1972. US–China relations were normalized in 1978, and US–Taiwan relations repudiated in 1978.

In relation to security in the Taiwan Strait, the US Congress enacted the Taiwan Relations Act so that the US government, regardless of which branch, would be able to maintain its commitment to stability between the PRC and Taiwan. Article 3 of the Act states that in response to non-peaceful Chinese actions against Taiwan, the US president is obligated to maintain US military capability such that Taiwan may 'maintain a sufficient self-defence capability', and that the President and Congress should collaborate on 'appropriate action(s)' to accomplish this goal (Bush 2004: 2005).

As for the US relationship with Japan, 1972 was the year that Okinawa was returned to Japan. From today's vantage point, the Okinawa reversion can be seen as important primarily for the overall change it brought to the nature of the US–Japan relationship. During the 1950s, the alliance rested on a reciprocity in which the US provided security for Japan and Japan provided territories for the US military. In the 1970s, Japan's provision of economic assistance to Southeast Asia after the end of the Vietnam War was newly included as part of Japan's contribution in exchange for the continued US provision of Japanese security. The entire security and political relationship with Japan was more important for the US government than the use of Japanese territories as such. That is, the 1970s provide the foundation of today's bilateral alliance (Go 2002).

My term 'the 1970s system' stems from my own conception of the détente period that has characterized the international order in East Asia until today. In the cases of both China and Japan, US policy determined their reactions and behaviour, and the triangular configurations among the three countries, borne as a result of the end of ideological confrontations between the US and the PRC, have defined the dynamics of regional security (Go 2004).

The 'bubble economy' and after

During the 1980s, Prime Minister Nakasone Yasuhiro sought to resolve the issue of the government's economic burden. He first pursued the privatization of national corporations, such as railways, telephone and tobacco, all of which were privatized in the late 1980s. Although the privatization was expected to promote economic competition among private companies instead of harmonization, the emergence of the 'bubble economy' weakened the 'competition' concept in the economic arena.

A more serious image of 'competition' arose after the bubble burst. Koizumi became convinced that the structure of the LDP was rotten as a result of major factions within it. Due to the accidental end of the Cold War, the US government's priorities altered, and Japan's economic rise became a target of friction until the turn of the century.

This '1970s system' is now close to becoming outdated in the new century. With regard to relations with Japan, the US government now seems to envision a much more equal sharing with the Japanese government of security responsibilities in the Asia-Pacific region. The US criticism of Japan's Gulf War cooperation as being 'too little, too late' signaled the beginning of this new era in which the US government expects and demands direct Japanese cooperation in military operations overseas.

Moreover, the new National Defence Program Outline, announced in December 2004, assumed that Japan's primary goal was to address 'new threats' like international terrorism or weapons of mass destruction, seeking to create a stable international environment. Given that fact, it paid more attention to the international dispatch of Japan's Self-Defence Forces (SDF) along with an increase in its transportation capabilities. Compared with the 1970's conception of a 'Basic Defence Force' that stemmed from the international environment of growing détente, the new outline indicated Japan's readiness to prepare for a more active role in international security. The outline also underscored Japan's concern about North Korea's development of nuclear weapons and the rise of China's military capabilities, a clear indication of which was mentioned for the first time since the Japanese government issued the initial defence programme outline in 1976.

With regard to Sino–American relations, the '1970s system', which stipulated both US engagement with the PRC and its security commitment to Taiwan, has also become outdated. First, China and Taiwan were divided political regimes, and they were supposed to bolster the legitimacy of the 'one China' principle. Given that, there was no middle ground between the 'unification' of China and independence for Taiwan. Second, the way Beijing sought to incorporate Taiwan into China was to be via use of force. Depending on how Beijing thinks of possible paths to unification, the dialogue may maintain the status quo stalemate, with no possible solution for either side. Finally, both the US and Chinese governments have maintained the stability of East Asia by making use of the balance of power idea in Taiwan. While evincing ambiguous attitudes, the US government sought to deter China's belligerent posturing while at the same time restrain Taiwan's voice for independence.

However, these three premises were beginning to collapse around 2000 when Chen Shui Bain became president of Taiwan. First, while economic interdependence between China and Taiwan has diluted the zero-sum nature of the stalemate in cross-strait issues, Chen's victory has led the former ruling KMT to cultivate ties with mainland China's Communist Party. Taiwanese working on the mainland favour the more stable cross-strait policies of Chen, and the KMT has sought to make use of those people benefiting from China's economic growth.

Second, given President George W. Bush's clear statement of intent in April 2001 to defend Taiwan, it would be of no use for Beijing to use force because such an action would invite US intervention. Since the current Bush administration's strategy hinges on unilateral commitments in various hotspots including Taiwan, it is natural that Beijing seeks to make use of multilateral diplomacy to soften criticisms regarding the 'Chinese threat'.

Finally, China's new conception of security has eroded the traditional stance of maintaining the balance of power between the US and China for stability in East Asia. The lack of a multilateral framework, along with the US penchant for unilateralism, has produced an advantageous environment for Chinese foreign policy, since the establishment of various institutions in East Asia, such as the Shanghai Cooperation Organization, the ASEAN+3 Framework and free trade agreements, have provided the Chinese government with a political space for their activities.

Given the changing international order in East Asia, Japan now stands at the intersection between US demands for a more equal US–Japan balance in international security matters and China's solicitation of Japan's participation in the economic community of East Asia. With a rapidly ageing society, the Japanese began to look to China and its role in the East Asian community as a factor that could invigorate Japan's economy. By applying Ruggie's argument about maintaining the balance between international free trade and domestic welfare, I will argue that Japan now stands at the threshold of a re-conceptualization of the basis for its economic prosperity.

Koizumi's 'structural reform'

Koizumi's political as well as economic slogan was: 'No structural reform, no economic growth.' He prioritized private companies' economic activities, and the 'transfer from the public to the private' sector. Public health policy was revamped, and such areas as pensions, health insurance and university tuition became targets in a campaign to reduce government spending.

Koizumi was also critical of the 'construction-centred' distribution of public money to local regions. Every time general elections were held, Koizumi's faction (the Mori faction) increased their seats little by little, and the 11 September 2005 election dramatically reduced the number of Diet seats held by the other major factions.

Unfortunately, the Koizumi reforms were also the end of the 'embedded economy' system in Japan. Before Koizumi became premier, the major factions sought to spend a large amount of public money on construction, while at the same time leftist political parties, such as the Japan Socialist Party and the Japan Communist Party, pursued fractional modifications of LDP plans by asking for revisions related to social policy matters. However, the end of public money for construction not only weakened the major factions within the LDP, but also dramatically reduced the presence of left-wing parties.

Koizumi pursued reforms at three levels – the local, the national and the international. At the local level, central government was about to abandon the 'national minimum' of public money under the banner of local auton-omy. Local governments had more autonomy, but less direct transfer of public money from central government, which lead to a rise in fees for educa-tion, poverty-saving programmes and social security.

Second, at the national level, Japan finally stopped being a 'developmental state' as the government sought to gradually reduce the tremendous budget-ary deficits that were undermining the standing of Japan's credit in the inter-national community. Public administration started to focus on new methods of public management, a development that would lead to the integration of various ministries at the national level.

Finally, at the international level, the 11 September 2001 terror attacks marked the beginning of a new century for security issues. Watchers of Japa-nese politics witnessed the decisiveness with which Koizumi acted to lend Japanese support to the US war on terrorism. While Japan's response to the 1991 Gulf War was condemned as 'too little, too late', the Bush administra-tion has praised Japan's swift cooperation since 2001, including the dispatch of SDF personnel to Iraq.

During the late 1990s, Japan's approach toward redefining its security rela-tionship with the US took the form of creating security guidelines. After the end of the Cold War, the decline of the Soviet threat, combined with existing regional fears of strife in East Asia, was given as one of the reasons for the formulation of the new guidelines. The parties to the deliberations on the future of the US–Japan alliance were concerned with the lingering potential for strife in the region, while at the same time trying to develop a structure better suited to the less hostile post-Cold War global environment.

During the Cold War, the existence of the enemy was clear, as was the objective of forming an alliance with the US. By contrast, after the fall of the Soviet Union, security alliances, including the US–Japan alliance, could not be justified simply in terms of containment. Instead, both Japan and the US had to interpret national security interests from a wider perspective and define as their new goal the pursuit of an institutional means to form and maintain a stable geopolitical environment through which to build confidence and promote mutual exchange among alliance members.

The US–Japan new guidelines

With the April 1996 US–Japan Joint Declaration on Security, both govern-ments started to seek new roles for the alliance. The new US–Japan security guidelines, announced in September 1997, tried to apply the joint declaration to post-Cold War East Asia in two ways. First, an item on 'Various Types of Security Cooperation' notes that the 'bilateral [US–Japan] cooperation to promote regional and global activities in the field of security contributes to the creation of a more stable international security environment' (MOFA 1997). In other words, it is the new global role of the alliance and its complex functions within the region that are of particular importance. These functions include UN peacekeeping, international humanitarian relief operations, and emergency relief activities in major disasters. They also include encouraging security dialogue, defence exchange, regional confidence building, as well as arms control and reduction – alternatives to focusing on the containment of an adversary.

Second, the US–Japan security guidelines expanded the geographical breadth and reach of the alliance. The guidelines sought to incorporate neighbouring areas under US–Japan political and economic cooperative relationships. Under Article 6 of the Japan–US Security Treaty, US forces are granted the use of facilities and areas in Japan for the purpose of contributing to not only Japan's security but also the Far East region. Given this Article, the guidelines sought to announce a need for US–Japan joint cooperation in areas surrounding the Japanese territory. For the Japanese government, this implies the enlargement of areas in which Japanese SDF members conduct military operations with US personnel. That is, if a military conflict happens in the areas surrounding Japan, it is lawful that the Japanese government dispatches SDF personnel for joint military action led by the US military, although Japan's support should be limited to support-oriented logistics.

Ironically, however, one of the greatest sources of anxiety regarding the enlargement of joint defence areas was the fear that it could dilute the alliance's ability to ensure security for Japan. According to Stuart and Tow (1990: 3–20), the following issues are of concern when an alliance is modified to enlarge its functions:

1 How the responsibility for rear-area support and frontline battles, as well as burdens associated with military action, are to be distributed between the member countries?
2 To what extent can a threat be recognized jointly by the alliance members?
3 Will collective multilateral action result in a loss of autonomy for a member country's foreign policies?

With regard to the above issues, there were two critical conceptual questions. The first related to the extent to which the 'areas surrounding Japan' were defined and what was included and not included. Since the late 1960s, it has been agreed in the Diet that the area north of the Philippines belonged to what was called the 'Far East'. With the inclusion of the wording 'areas surrounding Japan' in the guidelines, it is now possible for Japan to dispatch to more distant 'neighbouring areas' for the purpose of supporting US military operations. However, because the Cabinet Legislative Bureau has prohibited the use of collective self-defence rights, it is questionable whether the new guidelines can operate within the parameters of Article 9 of the Constitution (Sase 2001, Chapter 4).

The second question concerned the division of labour within the re-conceptualized US–Japan alliance. During the 1950s, the alliance rested on the exchange of US provision of security for Japan and Japan's provision of territories for US military use. In the 1970s, Japan's provision of economic assistance to Southeast Asia was newly included as part of Japan's share in exchange for continued US provision of Japanese security. Now, in the new century after the end of the Cold War, the US government seems to envision a much more equal sharing of the responsibilities for security in the Asia-Pacific region with the Japanese government. The US condemning Japan for 'too little, too late' cooperation and assistance during the Gulf War signaled the beginning of this new era when the US government expected and demanded direct Japanese cooperation in military operations overseas (Lake 1999: 261).

Japan's new defence programme outlines

With regard to defence capabilities, the year 2004 can be considered as marking decisive changes. Koizumi created a new Council on Security and Defence Capabilities in April 2004, and the Council issued a report in October of the same year on their vision for the future.

'Integrated Security Strategy' is the key term in this vision, and has two goals. The first is to prevent a direct threat from reaching Japan to minimize any damage, while the second focuses more on creating a stable international environment, pointing out the importance of '[reducing] the chances of threats arising in various parts of the world . . . affecting the interests of Japanese expatriates and corporations overseas.' The strategy is pursued via three methods: Japan's own efforts, cooperation with an alliance partner, and cooperation with the international community. The two goals and three methods imply the 'integration' of Japan's security strategy, and the report argues that there is a need for the government to apply an 'integrated decision-making mechanism'. It also emphasizes the role of the government Security Council, which is supposed to coordinate the six constituents of the strategy (Security Council 2004).

Along with the overreaching plan, the report also sets out the role of the defence forces in supporting the new security strategy as a 'multi-functional flexible defence force'. The pivotal requirement is the ability to collect and analyse information. Encompassing defence roles from (1) responding to emergency situations, (2) strengthening intelligence capabilities, (3) reforming the defence industrial and technological base, and (4) emphasizing international peacekeeping roles, the report envisioned a more 'global' role for Japan in international security issues.[1]

Following the 2004 report to the prime minister, Japan's Defence Agency issued a new outline of the defence programme that attempts to foresee the upcoming decade. It assumed a more global role for Japan, reaching from East Asia toward the Middle East. That is, the role of the SDF is not limited to domestic defence issues within Japanese territory, but rather focuses on its international aspect. The internationalized role corresponds to the collabourative work with the US military, and the outline emphasizes the importance of Japan's alliance with the US government, while at the same time seeks to enlarge both allies' security tasks geographically.

While the budget aspects of the new programme seek to restrain spending under the banner of the 'administrative reform', the programme also aims to advance the substantial functions and transportation capabilities of the SDF. The Defence Agency outlined a plan for reducing the number of SDF officials, although the current shortage of personnel will result in the maintenance of the number of uniformed people in the near future.

The outline also indicates a need to re-examine the principle of banning the export of arms, at least to the United States. In the current joint technological research on ballistic missile defence by Japan and the US, it assumes the philosophy of the ban ought to be upheld while pursuing the enhancement of procurement and R&D defence capabilities. From the above modifications of Japan's defence policy initiated by the Council on Security and Defence Capabilities and the defence programme outline, three policy implications can be pointed out. First, the main focus of policy has become the global agenda representing counter-terrorism, with little attention being paid to regional security issues. Given that East Asia is a region with lingering sources of conflict, the defence programme outline should have paid some attention to the reconciliation between Japan's advocacy of its global roles, together with the US government, and its regional roles concerning, for instance, the Korean peninsula and China.

Second, the Chinese government criticized the defence programme outline, since it included the possibility of the 'China threat'. While arguments surrounding the topic of the China threat have long been debated within the Japanese government, it was the first time that central government decided to clearly articulate the matter in a security policy document. China considered the phrase unacceptable, and saw it as a sign that the Japanese government may view China as a threat, or even worse, as an enemy. Thus, an important task from now for the development of the US–Japan security relationship is to keep the architecture open to China as well, although the means by which China can be included in the US–Japan security framework remains a key issue, which I will discuss later.

Finally, the globalization of Japan's security role widens the concept of 'Asia', which will make it possible for Asian countries including Japan to discuss the security roles of individual governments in promoting international stability. After the Second World War, Japan saw only China, Taiwan, the two Koreas, and Southeast Asian countries as its 'neighbours', all of which had profoundly negative memories of Japanese war crimes. The legacies of imperialism and colonialism have prevented Japan's relationships with other Asian countries from developing and maturing. Although Japanese war crimes are unforgivable historical facts, it is also true that there has been excessive emphasis on the issue for political purposes by Japan and its neighbours alike.

Now, in the post-September 11 period, Japan's conceptualization of 'Asia' includes India, Russia, Afghanistan, Iran, Uzbekistan and other central Asian countries. The conceptual widening of 'Asia' should be able to dilute the excessive focus on Japan's war crimes by neighbouring countries, which will make it possible for all concerned parties to discuss the history issue in a way that promotes mutual understanding.[2]

The impact of Koizumi's reforms on foreign relations: China-Japan bilateral relations and the 'nationalism spiral'

Japan's national interests and the 'nationalism spiral'

A set of bilateral relations can develop in three phases. In the first phase, both sides refrain from making drastic demands so that they can 'get to know each other' through exchanging opinions and demands incrementally. In most cases, the side that presses its demands more forcefully in this stage makes greater gains. The second phase is one of more forceful demands in which the mutual restraint fades away, and the side that has been less insistent begins to become more so. If either side fails to respect the other's ideas, bilateral ties may be severed. The third phase is the one in which both sides come to understand each other fully, and most of the demands pressed by one side will be addressed properly or discussed to achieve a degree of mutual understanding. From this perspective, China–Japan relations are currently in transition from phase one to phase two.

There is a clear sense among the Japanese general public that, until now, China–Japan relations have been dominated by the pressing of demands by China, with Japan having to respond on problems such as unresolved historical issues, maritime territorial rights and the Japan–China intermediate line in the East China Sea,[3] the handling of Chinese survey vessels, and so forth. The terms 'a masochistic view of history (toward China)' and 'a resolute attitude (against China)', that are often used in Japan reflect this fact. The former has recently been used to criticize Japan's conciliatory post-war attitude as too placatory to Chinese demands, while the latter has been applied not only to China's assertiveness but also to North Korea's reluctance to resolve the abduction issues.

There is also a clear sense that three decades after the normalization of relations, the Japanese government is willing for the first time to press demands with China. From the perspective of national interests, Japan has repeatedly made apologies, as in the 1972 China–Japan joint communiqué, the 1978 China–Japan Peace Treaty, the 1995 Murayama talks, and so forth. China, on the other hand, has never apologized for its 1979 incursion into Vietnam.[4]

The compensation issue has been resolved legally, but trillions of yen in aid has also been provided. China has ignored the Japan–China intermediate line by entering exclusive maritime economic zones, and has treated Japan's resulting objections as mere 'requests'. But if Japan were to cross the same line, the Chinese government would certainly not remain silent on the matter. If Japan says nothing, Chinese submarines appear likely to pass through the waters around Japan without identifying themselves.

And if Japan does complain, it is immediately criticized as returning to 'old imperialism'. It is therefore only natural for the Japanese government to come to the conclusion that historical issues are thus being exploited to current political ends.

The result is the current 'nationalism spiral', in which China seeks apologies for Japanese atrocities committed during the Second World War. Japan, for its part, seeks apologies for crimes committed by the Chinese during recent anti-Japan demonstrations – these appear to involve mainly young people in their twenties who have no memories of events six decades ago. So we appear to have finally arrived at the second phase of bilateral relations.

However, virtually no one denies that China–Japan relations are crucial to the future of Asia, which is a good indication that this is a bilateral relationship that must not be allowed to end at the second phase of development. How can we address such 'ambivalent' feelings among various strata of the Japanese public?

Improving China–Japan relations

If developing relations further is to be achieved, then it is through the verbal wrangling of the second phase that the path to the third phase must be sought. More than three decades since the normalization of Chinese–Japanese diplomatic ties, Japan's China policy has developed the aim of assimilating China into the regional order in Asia, as well as into the international community as a whole. This effort has manifested itself in areas such as the handling of historical issues and the provision of ODA. Since China itself understands that its current economic growth largely depends on foreign direct investment, it is aware that allowing relations with either the United States or Japan to deteriorate would have far-reaching implications domestically.

But that does not mean that silence must be maintained, as it has until now, with respect to Chinese demands, many of which appear unreasonable to Japanese in the twenty-first century. If governments of both countries end up being a mouthpiece for respective anti-Japanese or anti-Chinese voices, I believe it would be more productive for the people on each side to endeavour to build the relationships they feel are mutually necessary.

To be specific, the Sasakawa Peace Foundation is likely providing funding for the School of International Studies at Beijing University. Rather than via Japanese government ODA, there is nothing wrong with recommending improvements in curriculums based on private funding. The best option is for the beneficiary of the funding to voluntarily decide whether or not to concur with Sasakawa's principles.

Also, Japanese companies are investing directly in China, although most Chinese companies are not yet at the multinational level of development where they can pursue business independently in Japan. If opportunities for joint business projects by Japanese and Chinese companies are actively sought using special economic zones in Japan to make it easier for Chinese companies to enter, Chinese business people will experience in ever greater numbers what it means to live in a society with a free economy. This will also lead to increasing reforms within China itself. Of course, Japan should open its economy more and invite Chinese investments.[5]

China–Japan undergraduate-level exchanges have become well known. But more mid-level exchange between the generations that will have the responsibility for leading their societies could include a broader base of participants than just scholars researching historical issues issues (something that was agreed at the foreign minister summit in April 2007, and has been jointly conducted since then). Ample resources are available for effectively increasing the exchange of know-how through technical experts and non-profit organization group personnel, who have been building friendly personal relationships with their Chinese counterparts for years.

Bilateral relations in the new age

In that sense, the period of government-to-government diplomacy in China–Japan relations is over. As long as the relationship is between governments, no matter how useful the dialogue is said to be, it cannot rise to a level beyond social formality. In addition, if China were to repeatedly insist, in the name of dialogue and friendly relations, that history and politics be treated as an undifferentiated package, there will be no other choices for Japan than to either fall silent and remain as it has in the past at the first stage of relations, or stall at the second stage, where it is now, by continuing to criticize its counterpart.

One major difference between China–Japan relations and US–Japan relations is the interchange of a wide range of business operations and other projects among industry, NPOs, various specialists and students, and so forth. In the development of relationships between nations, it is necessary to rely on the support that numerous concerned actors provide for diplomatic efforts. This corresponds to the ideas put forward by Henry Kissinger in *Diplomacy* (1995).

When the crisis on the Korean Peninsula came to a head in the early 1990s, for instance, former President Jimmy Carter visited Pyongyang, relieving the crisis. Actors of comparable capabilities must certainly exist among Japanese political and business leaders. And making effective use of their personal relationships and specialized knowledge can be expected to be of great benefit.

Regional order-making in East Asia

China's behaviour: China's hierarchy versus China among equals

China has its intrinsic presence in the East Asian regional order. Geographically speaking, China is the only country in the region that has made a tremendous impact on its neighbours. For neighbouring countries, there seems a hierarchy centred round China, and those who have learned Chinese history tend to emphasize this point. China achieved stability along its borders and gained the upper hand vis-à-vis domestic contenders because it monopolized legitimacy while benefiting from trade–tribute relations.

The opposite notion is that China has acted like France, that is, it has been always mindful of power games related to emerging and threatening powers within China and adjacent areas. It has thus been first among equals. From this perspective, any stability based on a Chinese hierarchy would be fragile and temporary. China's potentially massive military forces are prone to intervene in domestic matters, or to be the object of political intervention, especially when a new leader finds it necessary to demonstrate superiority.

Japanese (and American) behaviour: balancing versus bandwagoning

In response to the economic and political rise of China, there have been two different approaches in the realist school. One is to counterbalance the rise of China (Goldstein 2000), and the other is to join forces and lend support to the (peaceful) rise of China (Ross 1997). The former approach assumes that given the overwhelming potential and actual threat China poses, it is natural that countries join forces to counter the prospect of regional hegemon emerging. The latter predicts that given the defensive realist nature of the Chinese strategy for the foreseeable future, lending support to China is a safe bet.

For Japan, the choice depends on US influence. Its globally hegemonic character makes the latter bandwagoning idea sound less convincing, as countries adjacent to China are often part of the American hegemonic umbrella. At least, China perceives the US–Japan security cooperation as an action aimed at balancing Chinese power.

However, not to be dismissed is the bandwagoning influence of economic interdependence. As if lured by the ever-expanding Chinese market, a huge number of business firms, especially those from neighbouring countries, pour direct investment into China. It is important here to distinguish between the language of business and that of power. Business is uniformly referent to itself, whereas power involves uniquely characteristic expressions of meaning each time it is exercised. Sometimes 'business speak' is convergent with 'power speak', but not always. Rather, the flow of foreign trade and direct investment into China might not be interpreted directly and singularly as lending credence to the growth of a regional hegemony (Tucker 2002).

American commitment: alignment versus distance

As stated above, the US hegemonic character makes the bandwagoning school sound slightly strange as countries adjacent to China are often part of the American hegemonic umbrella. Similarly, the nature of global hegemony makes the balancing school sound slightly strange as the act of balancing vis-à-vis China is bound to be conducted along with the United States. That is, China may say that the US ally's action is jumping on the US bandwagon, an action triggered by the emergence of the Chinese threat.

On the other hand, the maritime orientation of US hegemony often leads Washington to adopt the policy of offshore balancing, rather than getting deeply involved with Continental power politics. Thus when the US adopts an isolationist stance, it temporarily ceases to be a power that counts in the Chinese sphere.

All things considered, the US is able to gain advantage through having distance from Japan and China and detaching its own commitment to East Asian security. Along with the above policy options of balancing and bandwagoning, the US provision of a security umbrella would be a source of US leverage if it comes to have a penchant for isolationist tendencies. See Table 4.1.

Conclusion: Japan's map in domestic governance and its foreign relations

I have argued that the respective sides of the domestic–international nexus have become more difficult to distinguish the closer we get to the present. The impact of Koizumi's reforms on Japan's foreign relations has been clear, and the post-war axiom is unlikely to survive anywhere on the political map in the future.

Now, we come back to Ruggie's 'embedded liberalism'. How long can the system be maintained in the future? With a rapidly ageing society, the entire

Table 4.1 US methods of maintaining leverage

Distance	Alignment	
Off-shore Balancing	Containment (Balancing)	Engagement (Bandwagoning)

Japanese social structure is in flux. The government now depends on women's labour to sustain various kinds of social welfare programmes, and has to spend more money on the young and aged. It is not the case that economic growth automatically leads to the development of a national public welfare policy.

That is, during the 1960s and 1970s, the provision of resources to the social welfare of the general public was the product of nationwide economic growth. However, the ageing society in Japan has made it difficult to expand domestic markets, while at the same time more elderly will cause costly redistribution of social welfare to those who in the past supported Japan's high economic growth.

Koizumi's reforms temporarily stopped the system of 'embedded liberalism', since he predicated economic growth on dramatic structural reforms. At this stage, it is difficult to argue that the gradual, but continuous economic growth for the past several years has been the product of the Koizumi reforms, but growth without redistribution to the aged and young will weaken Japanese society as a whole. It is time for us to think of another type of 'embedded liberalism' so that we can distribute society's resources to the general public as a whole, while at the same time further develop Japan's foreign relations with China.

Given the situation, is it possible that Japan could act as a trans-Pacific bridge that links the security alliance with the United States to the economic power of Asia?

Notes

1 The report also touched upon the need to re-examine Japan's constitution in the future. It says there is a need to discuss the exercise of the right of collective self-defence rights with an eye to clarifying what Japan should and can do for the international roles outlined in the report (*National Defence Program Guideline, FY 2005* 2004).

2 The political use of history was argued in the 2002 article written by the author (see Go 2002).

3 Things become more complicated if one has to include issues on continental shelves into the intermediate line. The Chinese government argues that the continental shelf on the Chinese side can expand far to the east, which naturally gives the Chinese an advantageous position. If one does not include issues on continental shelves, and instead focuses only on economic zones over the sea, both China and Japan will be able to stand on an equal footing.

4 Brad Glosserman has counted the number in Japan, and concluded that the Japanese government has delivered apologies at least 17 times (for instance, see Glosserman 2005).

5 Japan's Foreign Ministry recently started to advocate the idea of 'Invest Japan', which tries to invite foreign firms' investment into Japan. Interestingly enough, the Japanese government did not try to keep themselves open to foreign firms even during the period of bubble economy. In this sense, Japan's Foreign Ministry and other parts of the bureaucracy came to understand various types of 'symmetric' interdependence.

References

Bush, R.C. (2004) *At Cross Purposes: US–Taiwan Relations since 1942*, New York: M. E. Sharpe.

Glosserman, B. (2005) Blame enough to go around, *PacNet*, 20 April, p. 18.

Go, I. (2002) Redefining security roles: Japan's policy toward the September 11 terrorism, *Journal of East Asian Studies*, 2(1): 285–305.

Go, I. (2004) Leadership in bandwagon: a historical sketch of Japan's security policy, *Policy and Society*, 23 (1): 21–37.

Goldstein, A. (2000) *Deterrence and Security in the 21st Century: China, Britain, France, and the Enduring Legacy of the Nuclear Revolution*, Stanford, CT: Stanford University Press.

Kissinger, H. (1995) *Diplomacy*, New York: Touchtone.

Lake, D.A. (1999) *Entangling Relations: American Foreign Policy in Its Century*, Princeton, NJ: Princeton University Press.

Ministry of Foreign Affairs (MOFA) (1997) Guidelines for Japan–US defense cooperation, at: http://www.mofa.go.jp/region/n-america/us/security/ guideline2.html.

National Defence Programme Guideline, FY 2005 (2004), at: http://www.kantei.go.jp/ foreign/policy/2004/1210taikou_e.html.

Ross, R. (1997) *Negotiating Cooperation: The United States and China, 1969–1989*, Stanford, CT: Stanford University Press.

Ruggie, J.G. (1982) International regimes, transactions, and change: embedded liberalism in the post-war economic order, *International Organization*, 36(2): 379–416.

Sase, M. (2001) *Shudanteki Jieiken: Ronso no Tameni [Collective Self-defence Rights]*, Tokyo: PHP.

Security Council (2004) Final report submitted by the Council on Security and Defence Capabilities, October.

Stuart, D. and Tow, W. (1990) *The Limits of Alliance: NATO Out-of Area Problems since 1949*, Baltimore, PA: Johns Hopkins University Press.

Tucker, N.B. (2002) If Taiwan chooses unification, should the United States care?, *Washington Quarterly*, 25(3): 15–28.

Part II

Changing policy instruments and regulatory regimes

5 Competition and control in public hospital reforms in Hong Kong and Singapore

M. Ramesh

The city-states of Hong Kong and Singapore are unusual among high-income societies in combining fine healthcare status with modest spending. The achievements have been built on many similar and as many different policy measures. The objective of this chapter is to assess public hospital reforms in Hong Kong and Singapore, with the goal of drawing conclusions about the efficacy of different management strategies in the hospital care sector and drawing lessons for other countries contemplating reform.

The chapter will start by providing a brief profile of the healthcare system in Hong Kong and Singapore, which will show that both spend less than the OECD average, but yet enjoy healthcare status superior to their western counterparts. It will argue that the dominance of public sector hospitals in inpatient care in both places is one of the main reasons for the city-states' superior performance. Centralized coordination and planning afforded by public ownership allows the government to correct many failures in the healthcare market. Efforts to promote competition among hospitals in Singapore have had the added benefit of making hospitals responsive to consumer demand, though this may have worsened access for those unable to pay. Besides, the case of Hong Kong shows that competition is not as central to efficient management of hospitals as suggested by the New Public Management (NPM) protagonists and mainstream health economists, and accepted by Singaporean policy-makers. The two cases show that a well-crafted and coherent intervention is essential for providing quality services at affordable cost. Indeed coherence and comprehensiveness is more important than the primacy of state or market in provision of healthcare.

Most informed observers of health policy accept that there are characteristics unique to healthcare which make it particularly vulnerable to market failures. This is particularly true for public hospitals which supply services that involve significant externality effects and information asymmetries that make it difficult for governments to design and monitor management contracts, unlike the case of banking and telecommunications, for example (Over and Watanabe 2003: 111). Yet their efficient management is essential as hospitals account for the bulk of public healthcare expenditures. Quite apart from the technical limitations of full privatization, public hospitals are often the only ones to which the poor have access, which makes operating them as commercial enterprises difficult, politically as well as commercially.

International efforts to reform public hospitals have taken numerous forms, which may be broadly classified as autonomization, corporatizaton and privatization. The three may be conceptualized as a spectrum, stretching from autonomization at one end and privatization at the other, with corporatization somewhere in-between. Autonomization involves increasing management autonomy for managers, while privatization in the strict sense involves complete divesture (Preker and Harding 2003: 2). Corporatization, in comparison, entails transforming public hospitals into an autonomous state enterprise with considerable operational autonomy and significant exposure to market competition. The reformers may well prefer privatization but political and technical difficulties in implementing it lead them to accept corporatization as a workable compromise. While reforms in both Hong Kong and Singapore can be broadly described as corporatization, the case of the former veers towards autonomization while the latter verges on privatization.

Inspired by New Public Management, efforts to reform public hospitals target improving internal governance and instilling some degree of market discipline. The measures typically include (ibid.: 43–47):

- Allowing hospitals substantial autonomy in making decisions.
- Allowing hospitals to retain additional resources they raise from users.
- Requiring hospitals to rely to some extent on market earnings rather than entirely on government budget.
- Holding hospitals accountable to the government through contracting and monitoring processes.
- Ensuring that hospitals continue to treat patients who cannot pay for services.

Greater decision rights and ability to retain earnings are intended to encourage managers to focus on efforts that generate revenues (including treating more patients or avoiding high-cost patients), while greater market exposure is intended to pressure them to improve efficiency. Considering that public hospitals are not meant to be a commercial enterprise, accountability mechanisms and government subsidies and regulations are put in place to encourage mangers to provide services to those unable to pay for them. The greatest challenge before reformers is to strike a meaningful balance between commercial orientation and the need to provide services to all in need. Hong Kong and Singapore have addressed the challenges differently, with somewhat different outcomes thus yielding different lessons.

Healthcare in Hong Kong and Singapore: background

The World Health Organization's Word Health Report 2000 (which assessed national health systems in terms of care quality, cost-effectiveness and accessibility) ranked Singapore sixth overall among the 192 countries it evaluated. Hong Kong is likely to be similarly ranked, even though it was not included in the study. The infant mortality rate (IMR) in both countries is less than half the rate found in OECD countries and the average life expectancy at birth is superior (Table 5.1). Even more remarkably, the IMR declined (by over 85 per cent between 1970 and 2003) and life span increased (by over 16 per cent over the same period) much more rapidly than in the OECD countries.

The health systems of the two countries also perform very well when measured for Healthy Life Expectancy (HALE) at birth: 69 for men and 72 for women in Hong Kong and 67 and 69, respectively, in Singapore. These place Hong Kong thirteenth for both men and women and Singapore 27th and 29th, respectively, among 191 countries on the list (Law and Yip 2003). Both countries rank ahead of the USA, the world's largest spender on healthcare.

Their health status looks yet more striking if seen in the context of the comparatively small amount of money that the two societies spend on healthcare (Table 5.2). Hong Kong and Singapore spend modestly on healthcare in terms of both amounts per capita and as share of GDP, especially the latter which spends less than half of what an average OECD country spends. National health expenditures in Hong Kong are 18 per cent below what is predicted by its income level, while Singapore's is 43 per cent lower than the predicted level (Wagstaff 2005: 5).

There is, however, a vast difference between the two in terms of the proportion of total health expenditures accounted for by the government: 57 per cent in Hong Kong and only 30 per cent in Singapore. Moreover, in Singapore the share has remained largely unchanged since 1990, after declining during the late 1980s. Government spending on health forms approximately 3 per cent of GDP in Hong Kong and 1 per cent in Singapore, compared to almost 6 per cent in OECD countries (Table 5.3). Even more remarkably, in the case of Singapore the proportion has remained largely unchanged since the 1980s.

In Hong Kong and Singapore, not only is the majority of total health expenditure from private sources, an overwhelming majority of private payment is

Table 5.1 Health status

	Infant mortality rate (deaths per 1000 registered live births)		Life expectancy at birth (years)	
	1970	*2003*	*1970*	*2003*
Hong Kong	19.4	2.3	70	82
Singapore	19.7	2.9	68	79
OECD average	22.0	5.8	71	78

Source: World Bank (2005).

Table 5.2 National healthcare expenditures

	Current US$		Percentage of GDP	
	1990	*2002*	*1990*	*2002*
OECD average	1,417	1,979	7.1	8.5
Hong Kong	481[2]	1,354[1]	3.7[2]	5.7
Singapore	444	898	3.3	4.3

Notes:
1 Figure in 2000.
2 Not comparable to 2000 data because the latter is based on National Health Accounts (NHA); employing the NHA method for Singapore is also likely to show a higher total as well as public expenditure.

Source: World Bank (2005).

provided out of pocket or by employers: approximately 70 per cent in Hong Kong and 97 per cent in Singapore (World Bank 2005). Out-of-pocket payments form one-third of national health expenditure in Hong Kong and nearly two-thirds in Singapore (Wagstaff 2005: 6). In OECD countries, as well as many developing countries, in contrast, more than half of all healthcare expenditures come from some form of health insurance.

The level of personnel and physical resources devoted to healthcare in Hong Kong and Singapore is consistent with the modest financial resources they devote to it. The ratio of both physicians and hospital beds to population is significantly lower than in the OECD countries. However, not too much should be read into this because both are compact places, allowing intensive use of medical resources. Note also that even OECD countries have experienced a decline in the ratio of hospital beds in recent years.

Another notable fact about the two city-states is the dominance of public hospitals in provision of inpatient and specialist outpatient care. Over 80 per cent of the hospital beds in both places are in the public sector; though only 45 per cent of all physicians in Hong Kong and 49 per cent in Singapore are in the public sector. Specialists in both places are overwhelmingly in the public sector, while general practitioners are largely in the private sector: nearly 72 per cent of ambulatory consultations in Hong Kong and 80 per cent in Singapore take place in private clinics.

Table 5.3 Public health expenditures, percentage of GDP, annual average

	1991–1995	*1996–2000*	*2001–2004*
Hong Kong	2.0	3.3	2.7
Singapore	1.1	1.2	1.1
OECD average	5.6	5.6	5.9

Source: Asian Development Bank (2005).

Table 5.4 Physicians and hospital beds, per 1000 persons

	Physicians			Hospital beds		
	1980	*1990*	*2000*	*1980*	*1990*	*2000*
High income: OECD	1.9	2.4	3.8	8.8	8.0	7.4
Hong Kong	0.8	–	1.3	4.0	3.6	4.9
Singapore	0.9	1.3	1.4	–	3.2	3.5

Source: World Bank (2005).

The conclusion to be drawn from this short description of the performance of the healthcare system in Hong Kong and Singapore is that both have delivered a fine healthcare system at modest cost. One thing both have in common is the overwhelming dominance of public hospitals in inpatient care. Indeed no understanding of their healthcare system is possible without recognizing this salient feature of it. The public hospital systems of the two countries share many similarities, but they have been on divergent reform paths since the late 1980s, a fact that is yet to be fully reflected in aggregate statistics.

Hong Kong

Until the 1950s, state involvement in healthcare in Hong Kong was confined to looking after civil servants and military officials while the general population relied on private providers and charities. The inadequacies of the existing system were exposed with the influx of refugees from the mainland following communist victory. It was estimated that four-fifths of the residents could not afford private healthcare, the only option often open to them at the time. In response, the government began to establish hospitals and clinics providing services nearly free of charge without thinking of the long-term fiscal implications of the arrangement (Gould 2001). Unlike the British National Health Service which had complete government provision and financing as its explicit objective, the Hong Kong authorities believed that public hospitals would be used only by the poor, as those with the means to pay would be turned off by austere services, over-crowded conditions and long waiting times. This did not happen in reality, as public hospitals came to be used not only by the poor but also increasingly by the middle class, which did not mind the inconvenience in return for nearly free services. The result was that public hospitals came to gradually replace private hospitals as the dominant supplier. Improvements in services at public hospitals in the 1990s further undermined private hospitals, which were not only expensive but also viewed as providing inferior clinical services due to the concentration of experienced medical personnel in the public sector.

The resulting rapid increase in government expenditure on hospitals did not raise serious fiscal concerns as the economy grew even more rapidly and generated sufficient public revenues to pay for the increased expenditures. This was reflected in the reform efforts, notably the Scott Report of 1985, which focused on improving management of public hospitals and expanding services rather than on how to finance the services more economically or effectively. However, it was recognized at the time that the existing system of healthcare delivery was inadequate for meeting the growing demand for healthcare and was therefore in need of fundamental reorganization.

Public hospitals in Hong Kong until reorganization in 1991 were owned and operated directly by the Medical and Health Department, which was a large organization employing 13 per cent of the entire civil service and receiving 9 per cent of the government budget (Cheung 2002: 345). Moreover, it indirectly controlled the non-profit private hospitals through grants of subvention. Indeed the public hospital system had grown so large and grown so haphazardly that the government released a White Paper in 1974 calling for regionalization of public hospitals, whereby each region was to have one large hospital supported by a network of smaller hospitals. The result was the growth of large regional hospitals with overcrowded conditions because the population preferred them to smaller hospitals.

Unable to meet the growing demand for hospital care and address the general dissatisfaction with the disparities between regional and non-regional hospitals and between public and subvented hospitals, the government began to explore ways to restructure the entire hospital system. The disparity between aided and public hospitals, which fostered much discontent, was rooted in the lower salaries at the former despite similar responsibilities and workload. An Australian management consultant was commissioned to inquire into the system and the report, popularly known as the Scott Report, was published in 1985.

The Scott Report was surprisingly ahead of its time and featured a line of thinking which came to be later described as NPM. It recommended corporatizaton of public hospitals under an autonomous entity run by professional managers. The organization was to be outside the civil service but directly accountable to the government through a government-appointed board and funded largely by the government. It was to have three organizational levels: a central board, regional boards and individual hospitals. The Report proposed giving wide autonomy to each hospital under the coordination of regional boards, with the central board and government setting broad policy directions only. It also recommended that non-medical staff assume greater management responsibilities in hospital administration.

There was little legislative or public support for the reforms proposed by the Scott Report because it dealt with management issues outside their area of interest or comprehension. Doctors and nurses at public hospitals opposed the proposal because they thought they might lose out by being outside the civil service. Only subvented hospital staff were strongly in support of the proposal to put them on the same footing as their public hospital counterparts (ibid.). To build support for the proposed reforms, the government offered public hospital staff salaries and conditions similar to the civil service.

The Hospital Board (HA), which began functioning in 1991, was given complete freedom in personnel and resource allocation matters. Individual hospitals, in turn, were given considerable autonomy in routine personnel and purchasing matters. The most immediate objective of establishing the HA was to free public hospitals from rigid civil service rules. The HA was expected to use its autonomy to increase the supply of healthcare services and improve quality. 'Professional management of hospitals to provide adequate and better quality service was the objective of establishing HA – not reducing government expenditure. [. . .] HA was never meant to be run like a commercial organization,' said one Legislative Councilor (personal interview with Joseph Lee, 17 May 2006).

Soon after its establishment, HA indicated that it would gradually increase fees to recover 15–20 per cent of the cost, which, if implemented, would have been a massive increase over the existing arrangement. There was a public outcry at the proposal and the government was forced to retract and reaffirm the status quo, which meant continuing to maintain negligible fees for patients. Without additional revenues, the HA continued to be entirely reliant on the government for funding and its objective to be autonomous remained elusive. Correspondingly, there was to be no competition among hospitals for patients. Moreover, instead of establishing regional boards with clear management responsibilities as suggested by the Scott Report, the HA established purely advisory regional bodies. The public hospital system that emerged was thus highly centralized, with the HA head office firmly controlling individual hospitals (ibid.: 353).

Only minor changes in financing followed the establishment of HA. Instead of the MHD allocating money directly to hospitals, the government began to allocate funds to HA, which in turn allocated the funds to hospitals. Historical precedence was for the most part the only determinant of the size of funding. In recent years the system has changed somewhat: funds are now given to HA, which apportions them among clusters, which in turn allocate them to hospitals. The funding formula is based on population size in the catchment area adjusted for age – this is to reflect changes in habitation and age patterns.

Corporatizaton opened new opportunities for medical professionals with management aptitude to assert control over traditional medical professionals. As a result, doctors remained dominant in the management of hospitals, contrary to earlier expectations that HA would be dominated by business managers (ibid.). The continued dominance of doctors, albeit of those with flare for management, arguably had the effect of muting profit motives characteristic of those trained in business management.

In terms of autonomy, while HA started as a highly centralized organization with most significant decision authority concentrated at the headquarters level, over time hospitals were accorded considerable autonomy in personnel and financial matters. A significant recent development is the emergence of regional hospital cluster administration as a key management link in the HA organization. Clusters first emerged in the mid-1990s, with the purpose of coordinating delivery of hospital services at the regional level and eliminating duplications and redundancies; they lacked substantive power, however, and had to work through HA headquarters or hospital managers. In 2000, CEOs were appointed to head the clusters and were given real line agency powers with responsibility for allocating budgets to hospitals within their clusters. There are currently seven clusters and they have taken over many functions that used to be handled at the hospital level. 'Clusters are the key management nodes in the new hospital management system. Their main function is allocation of resources and coordination of services' (interview with Dr Hong Fung, Cluster Chief Executive, New Territories East Cluster, Hong Kong, 17 May 2006). However, the clusters are not health trusts purchasing services from providers, as is the case in the UK.

The appointment of Shane Solomon, who is not a medical professional, as the head of HA indicates the government's renewed interest in improving the organization's management capability. In a speech to the Hospital Authority Convention in 2006, he highlighted the importance of more professional management of hospitals and the need for reforms to make high-income earners pay a greater percentage of the costs. He may have had in mind the Australian system where high-income earners are induced to buy private insurance despite the availability of universal access to public hospitals. The Secretary of Health Bureau at the same HA convention hinted at establishing private clinics in public hospitals to complement the other private services.

The government and the HA have long recognized that government funding alone is insufficient for the growing healthcare needs of an ageing population. The report of the Harvard Team (1999) appointed by the government concurred and proposed radical reforms. It recommended establishment of an insurance scheme (Health Security Plan) and a savings scheme funded by employer and employee (Medisage). However, the Harvard Report found little public or political support: the public was opposed to contributing to HSP and Medisage, private doctors were opposed to central purchase by the government and the HA was opposed to the erosion of its role.

The HA offered a counter-proposal to the Harvard Report whereby the government was to fully subsidize only essential healthcare services, with the costs of other services to be partially or fully recovered through user charges. There was to be a medical savings scheme to help patients pay for non-subsidized services. It was also in favour of expanding its services into primary care provided through its network of hospitals and clinics and funded on a capitation basis. HA's thinking was subsequently reflected in the consultation document 'Lifelong Investment in Health', issued by the Health and Welfare

Bureau in 2000. Economic recession and weak government made adoption of deep reforms nearly impossible. The public was opposed to increased user charges or contributory insurance or savings schemes (Cheung 2002: 361). At the same time, the proposal to expand HA's services to primary care was opposed by the medical association and private doctors who saw it as a plan to reduce their business. While the Harvard proposal itself is dead, the idea of insurance and raising private payments for healthcare is unlikely to disappear from policy debates.

In recent years the government has turned its attention to reforming the system of providing healthcare, including inpatient services. The consultation document *Building a Healthy Tomorrow* recommends deep changes in the delivery of healthcare. It recommends that the HA hospitals concentrate only on: (1) acute and emergency care; (2) services for low-income and under-privileged groups; (3) illnesses that entail high cost, advanced technology and multidisciplinary teamwork; and (4) training of healthcare professionals. The implication of the change would be, if put into effect, that all non-emergency and non-acute cases will be shifted to general practitioners, who are and will be predominantly in the private sector (Health and Medical Development Advisory Committee, Health, Welfare and Food Bureau 2005). The pro-posals look fine on paper but are likely to raise intense opposition from certain quarters when concrete measures are announced.

HA currently operates 41 hospitals, of which 14 provide acute care, and 74 general and 45 specialist outpatient clinics. Each acute care hospital is stra-tegically located in a densely populated area and is joined by a network of non-acute hospitals in neighbouring areas. Total admission to public hos-pitals increased from 0.64 million in 1990 to 1.1 million in 2004. All 14 acute care hospitals provide a comprehensive range of services, even though the use of some specialities is low in some hospitals. The government has begun to rationalize acute care by removing duplications and matching facilities to local needs.

Singapore

Singapore was the first country in the world to introduce public hospital reforms featuring a prominent role for market-based performance pressures (Preker and Harding 2003: 15). The reforms were designed to promote increased autonomy as well as cost consciousness among both managers and consumers. Mechanisms were put in place to encourage managers to reduce costs and to recover a greater proportion of operating expenses from users while still delivering on their social mandate. Parallel reforms were made in the financing system to make consumers pay a larger proportion of the hos-pital costs. But marketizing hospital care while still keeping it accessible and without imposing an additional fiscal burden on the state is a challenging task and the government has had to constantly tinker with the arrangements to make the reforms work.

The process of reforming public hospitals began in 1983 with the publication of the National Health Plan (NHP), which proposed the shift of the financial burden of healthcare from the government to individuals. In the following year, Medisave was established as an individual compulsory savings account arrangement (also called Medical Savings Accounts or MSAs). Under the scheme, individuals compulsorily save a portion of their income (currently 6–8 per cent, depending on age), which they can only use for specified hospital services. There also exist other healthcare financing schemes, such as Medishield (voluntary catastrophic health insurance) and Medifund (means tested), but even together they form an insignificant proportion of total health expenditures.

Direct reform of public hospitals began with the announcement of a plan to 'restructure' public hospitals in 1984, soon after the Medisave scheme came into effect. The plan proposed a higher degree of professional management, private sector accounting practices, and enhanced competition among hospitals.

A holding company called Health Corporation of Singapore Private Limited (HCS) was incorporated in 1985 to own and manage restructured public hospitals, which were to be its subsidiaries. The HCS and its subsidiaries were technically private companies, but they were fully owned by the government. The government appointed their board of directors, which enabled it to monitor and direct the hospitals' performance. The first restructured hospital to be launched was the National University Hospital in 1985. Considering public scepticism and even antipathy towards privatization of healthcare, the government moved slowly, taking 15 years to gradually restructure all hospitals.

By the end of the 1980s, however, the government was uneasy with developments suggesting that the managers of the corporatized hospitals were concentrating unduly on revenue-maximizing activities and thereby possibly limiting services to those without the capacity to pay. In 1993, it published a White Paper called *Affordable Healthcare*, which clearly espoused a case for heightened government intervention in the functioning of public hospitals. In the following years, the government intervened to regulate the introduction of technology and specialist disciplines in public hospitals, the number of doctors and hospital beds and, most significantly, the charges imposed by hospitals to control undesirable developments (Hanvoravongchai 2002).

In 1999, the government announced the creation of two 'clusters' of public hospitals and clinics to replace the HCS: National Healthcare Group (NHG) and Singapore Health Group (SingHealth). NHG and Singhealth are separate private companies owned entirely by the Ministry of Health Holdings Private Limited, which in turn is owned entirely by the government. Each public hospital (except Alexandra Hospital and Institute of Health) in turn is a separate private company owned entirely by either an NHG or Singhealth cluster. The two clusters also own and operate outpatient 'polyclinics', which prior to 1999 were run directly by the Ministry of Health.

NHG and Singhealth, as autonomous private firms, enjoy complete operational autonomy but the government, as the sole owner, appoints the board of directors and continues to monitor them closely and issue directives as necessary. Each hospital, similarly, is an autonomous private entity but subject to direct control of its parent group and ultimately the Ministry of Health. In most routine and operational matters, the hospitals enjoy broad autonomy in areas of recruitment, remuneration, purchase, and user charges. However, the government intervenes through numerous formal and informal means as it deems fit. The hospitals are entitled to retain any additional revenues they raise: the revenue after costs that they collect from Class A and B1 wards. For C and B2 wards, the government pays for the gap between what patients are billed and what they actually pay, i.e. the government covers the deficit. The financing arrangement promotes competition to particularly attract non-subsidized patients while not turning away the subsidized patients.

The formula by which the government funds hospitals has been constantly tweaked over the years. Until the restructuring, hospitals were funded by a block grant that formed a global annual budget within which hospitals had to stay. This changed with the adoption of an output-based formula that paid hospitals according to the services they actually provided. After it was suspected that the hospitals were inflating the quantity of services they were providing in order to maximize revenues, the government adopted a casemix (also referred to as Diagnostic Related Group or DRG) funding formula, which pays a set fee for standard services. The casemix formula creates incentives for hospitals to make better use of resources by providing only the necessary services because they are allowed to keep any surplus. The government recently moved to a hybrid system involving both block funding and fee for service funding on a casemix basis. There are also provisions to claw back a portion of revenues beyond an agreed level to prevent over-servicing or over-charging of unsuspecting patients.

The government also intervenes heavily in matters related to physicians' remuneration, user charges for patients and acquisition of expensive equipment by hospitals. Physicians' salaries became a matter of major concern after the restructured public hospitals began to offer salaries comparable to private hospitals, which put pressure on the latter to offer yet higher salaries, which in turn triggered a wage escalation spiral. The government has taken a variety of measures in recent years to increase the number of doctors with the objective of dampening pressures for salary increases (Balaji 2004).

To take advantage of modern information technologies available for hospital management, the government has encouraged hospital clusters to harmonize their financial, clinical, administrative and diagnostic processes through integrated information systems. An innovative measure the government has employed to improve service quality and lower prices is to increase the information on hospital charges and clinical outcomes available to customers. Since 2003, public hospitals have been required to publish their average bill sizes (which include ward charges, daily treatment fees, surgery costs, laboratory costs, etc.) for different common conditions and procedures. The collated data is subsequently published on the Ministry of Health's web page (MOH 2007). In 2006, the government turned its attention to clinical outcomes, starting with cataract surgery, which is a standard procedure performed in large volume. The government plans to expand the list of conditions for which it collects and publishes data, moving gradually from simple to more complex procedures.

Comparison of the reforms

The healthcare systems in Hong Kong and Singapore have a lot in common, including provision of inpatient care overwhelmingly in the public sector. This is unsurprising given their common British colonial past. Yet there are significant differences between the two. The roots of the variations lie in the different reform objectives they have pursued since the 1980s. The primary objective of hospital reforms in Hong Kong was to increase supply of hospital care and improve delivery through better coordination. In contrast, the primary objective in Singapore was to slow down, and preferably reduce, growth of government healthcare expenditures.

To meet its objective, HA's immediate task at the time of its establishment was to reduce overcrowding in government hospitals and bring some coherence to the fragmented governance of public hospitals due to the existence of separately managed public and government-aided hospitals. Beyond the minimum, it was tasked to improve the quality of services to patients. However, the establishment of HA was not accompanied by any new incentive to encourage managers to do a better job. Nor was there effort to expose hospitals to greater competition. Indeed its establishment reduced competition because there remained one large organization controlling most of the beds and employing most of the medical staff in the colony, and providing a comprehensive range of services nearly free of charge. Its establishment was also not accompanied by any change in funding mechanism, as the government continued to fund it through block grants as before. The amount the government allocated to HA and the amount the latter, in turn, allocated to individual hospitals was still determined by historical precedence and there was no explicit link between funding and performance. The only accountability mechanism was, and is, annual review of performance with respect to 'inputs such as number of beds, implementation of clinical protocols, developing cost information system, rather than outcome or output' (Yip and Hsiao 2003:405). There was no reward for higher productivity or consumer satisfaction and indeed there was no penalty for not meeting performance targets (Preker and Harding 2003: 14–15).

The establishment of HA was, in essence, a simple transfer of management functions from the government's health department to the HA. Instead of a government department, it was the Authority that was to henceforth manage and fund individual public hospitals – management at the level of individual hospitals remained unchanged. The objective of improving quality without competition was achieved through alternative mechanisms in the forms of elaborate planning, coordination and consultation. HA's annual reports are replete with mentions of 'seamless coordination' among hospitals, which is understandable given the absence of competition or market to perform these functions. There are elaborate 'patients' charters', quality service standards, and 'professional codes of practice' for public hospitals to improve their services to the public. Each hospital has its own community advisory body and considerable effort is spent on making them work. Similar arrangements are unnecessary in Singapore because public hospitals compete among themselves for patients and how they fare in the competition provides a constant commentary on the hospitals' performance.

Notwithstanding its near total reliance on the government for funding, HA is a corporate organization with significant decision autonomy. It takes its corporate mission seriously, setting explicit output targets and linking them to budgetary allocations. The professionalization of HA, coupled with extra government funding allocated to it through much of the 1990s, enabled it to meet Hong Kong's growing demand for more and better healthcare. While public hospitals do not seek international accreditation, they do have internal quality standards and audits of clinical and management outputs. Internal audits show that Hong Kong hospitals perform well by world standards (interview with Dr Fung, ibid.). The absence of market competition means fewer management staff, and lower marketing and management costs, which are reflected in public hospitals' relatively low administration costs in Hong Kong.

Planning and coordination featured less prominently in Singapore's reforms, as these were intended to be achieved through competition among hospitals. It did not turn out as intended, however, as shortcomings of the arrangement became increasingly apparent in the late 1980s and early 1990s. Notwithstanding the hospitals' autonomy, the Singapore government had to intervene extensively in organizational, personnel and budgeting matters, in addition to establishing the broad policy framework. Establishing two large hospital clusters, monitoring hospitals' billing practices, and requiring them to publish data on bill size and clinical outcomes indicate the extent of its intervention.

Notwithstanding government ownership of public hospitals in both countries, they are funded on an entirely different basis. In Hong Kong, nearly all of public hospitals' funds come from the government, whereas in Singapore patients themselves provide the majority of the funding.

In fact, not only does the Hong Kong government provide nearly all of HA's funds, the funding is in the form of an annual block grant with few strings attached. The HA allocates funds to the regional clusters on the basis of population adjusted for age and the clusters, in turn, allocate funds on the same basis to individual hospitals. The sum allocated to each level forms an overall ceiling within which managers must remain. Even though there is no cap on demand, it effectively forces managers to limit supply, which in effect rations demand for elective surgery. While in principle hospital managers have broad autonomy on how they spend their money, in practice ongoing commitments leave little room for discretionary spending.

In contrast, public hospital managers in Singapore are funded by a hybrid casemix formula combining block grants and fee for service. The government, in its role as a purchaser, plays a vital role. The combination of two formulas plus significant charges they collect from users allows Singapore managers much more substantive autonomy in running their hospitals. In Hong Kong, tying funding to population rather than actual service provided does not offer incentives to hospitals to increase productivity or improve quality. Singapore public hospitals' need to win customers and negotiate with the government makes them more responsive to different stakeholders.

In the area of staffing, medical personnel in both countries are on fixed salaries, which reduces the incentive to over-service or over-charge. Medical professionals in Hong Kong are well paid but nevertheless resemble trad-itional civil servants in that they are on standard salary package with little room for performance-based rewards. In Singapore, however, there are provi-sions for performance bonuses for hospital employees to encourage them to work harder.

Another apparent similarity that conceals substantive differences between the two is the use of 'clusters' as an organizational form. In Hong Kong, clustering began as a vehicle for pooling medical resources whereby smaller hospitals in a regional area act as a supporting hospital for a major hos-pital. Only recently have clusters become a key layer in the hospital system with substantial management responsibilities, though the nature of the funding system allows only limited room for discretion. In Singapore, the two clusters are autonomous vertically integrated medical firms tasked to compete on a national basis. The clustering of individual hospitals under the umbrella of two cluster firms was intended to rationalize resources internally while making them of similar size so that they can compete on even grounds.

The weak private hospital sector in Hong Kong compared to its southern counterpart has significant policy implications. Public hospitals in Hong Kong offering quality service nearly free of charge means that private hos-pitals have no realistic chance of competing against them, except in some niche segments. In Singapore, on the other hand, only half of the public hospitals' revenues come from the government, which leads them to compete aggressively for patients. Indeed their unsubsidized wards compete head on with private hospitals. As a result, public hospitals compete among them-selves as well as with private hospitals. Although private hospitals find it hard to compete with their public counterparts, they remain viable. Indeed the government is committed to maintaining a viable private hospital sector because of the enhanced competition they offer. It is also significant that private hospitals are the main vehicle through which the government is promoting health tourism in Singapore.

HA has a mixed performance record over the period of its existence. It no doubt replaced camp beds that were common in the 1980s but waiting times are still long and consumers report dissatisfaction with hospitals' responsiveness. Between 1992 and 1996, while the cost per *discharge* for in-patient services fell, the cost *per day* increased (Yip and Hsiao 2003: 416). This is possibly because hospitalization has in many instances been replaced by day surgery, which has reduced the average cost of discharge but increased the cost of treating those who are hospitalized because such patients tend to be sicker.

Singapore's hospital reforms were ambitious in that they sought to actually reduce government expenditure on health while improving quality and without diminishing access and, as such, required tremendous and constant efforts. The hefty rise in user charges at public hospitals raised their share of total costs from 15 per cent in the pre-reform period to 55 per cent of costs (Phua 2003: 460). The result has been a noticeable reduction in the government's share of total expenditure, which is rather unique worldwide as governments' shares tend to rise with economic growth.

In Singapore, there is a significant degree of competition among public hospitals, as well as between them and private hospitals in the premium market segment. The public hospitals' efforts to attract patients, especially non-subsidized patients from outside the country, have raised the standards at all hospitals, so much so that private hospitals find it difficult to compete with them. Competition for patients, coupled with incentives to provide services in the form of retained revenues from user charges, explain the near absence of patient backlogs waiting for elective surgery in Singapore, in contrast to most other countries with an extensive system of public hospitals, for instance Hong Kong and the UK. User surveys show a high degree of satisfaction with services – evidence of positive effects of competition.

But competition among public hospitals also has had adverse effects, as it is believed that they are more likely to concentrate on services that generate additional revenues and neglect subsidized patients. The government has therefore had to constantly monitor what hospitals charge and the volume of service they provide, and instigate changes to curb emerging undesirable practices. The efforts in this regard include adjustment of funding formula, including clawing back the 'excess' revenues generated by public hospitals.

Conclusion

This chapter shows that healthcare systems in Hong Kong and Singapore share much in common, but are also characterized by significant differences. One of the key commonalties between them includes the fact that both have achieved excellent healthcare outcomes at modest cost. Not coincidentally, they both rely overwhelmingly on public hospitals for providing inpatient care.

Beyond this very significant commonality, the two are quite different systems, which have become particularly divergent since the mid-1980s.

In 1984, Singapore embarked on efforts to reform the way public hospitals were managed, followed by Hong Kong in 1990. The objective of Hong Kong's reforms was to more efficiently provide inpatient care through better planning and coordination. In contrast, Singapore's reforms sought to reduce government expenditure on healthcare through greater competition among providers while maintaining the public sector's lead role and without compromising its social welfare obligations. Both reforms were largely successful in achieving the objectives they set out to achieve, but were accomplished through very different means.

Hong Kong relied mainly on centralized planning and community consultation to achieve its objectives. Its public hospitals provide adequate and good, if somewhat austere, clinical services at highly subsidized prices that nearly everyone can afford. This makes for a highly equitable healthcare system, which, while open to all, is used heavily by low-income households. Remarkably, the comprehensive provision of equitable and accessible hospital services does not impose undue burden on the state, as Hong Kong's hospital care expenditures are still lower than most countries at similar income levels. The long waiting lists for elective services, while resented by those affected, are an integral part of a public hospital system working under the constraint of a global budget which unavoidably involves rationing of services.

The lack of competition in the healthcare sector is thus not as disastrous as argued by mainstream health economists and New Public Management protagonists because good planning and professional management can substitute for the market. The lack of profit motive is well suited to markets with significant externality effects and information asymmetries.

Singapore's reforms were more ambitious and, as such, required tremendous efforts to make them work. While the objectives of marketization and corporatization were avowedly to reduce the government's role, the case of Singapore shows that this requires more rather than less state intervention. The government had to maintain a close watch on all macro-level developments in the hospital sector and intervene as often and as intrusively as it considered necessary. Its complete ownership of what were technically private hospitals allowed the government to control their operations without intervening in the operational details.

Retaining the provision and financing of hospital care in the public sector has advantages of resource planning and, most significantly, equity. Expansion of private provision and financing reduces the burden on the government and improves responsiveness to consumers, but increases overall costs and compromises equity.

Hong Kong offers more useful lessons for developing countries than Singapore. The constant monitoring and improvements necessary to correct undesirable developments show that greater reliance on the market in the healthcare sector can only be achieved if it is accompanied by a high level of bureaucratic capability and willingness on the part of the government to use it. Therefore the counsel that weak governments should shed functions to markets because they lack capacity is misguided because reliance on markets to achieve social objectives requires more rather than less capacity. Without a strong state that can intervene to protect public interests, profit motives are likely to overwhelm social objectives; weak governments will be better off directly providing the service. As such, Hong Kong rather than Singapore provides a better template for reforming public hospitals in developing countries.

References

Asian Development Bank (2005) *Key Indicator 2005: Labour Markets in Asia: Promoting Full, Productive, and Decent Employment*, Manila: Asian Development Bank.

Balaji, S. (2004) *MOH Budget Speech* (Part 3), at: http://www.moh.gov.sg/corp/about/newsroom/speeches.

Cheung A.B.L. (2002) Modernizing public healthcare in Hong Kong, *Public Management Review*, 4(3): 343–365.

Gould, D.B. (2001) The reform of healthcare funding, *Hong Kong Medical Journal*, 7: 150–154.

Hanvoravongchai, P. (2002) Medical Savings Accounts: lessons learned from limited international experience, Discussion Paper Number 3, EIP/FER/DP.02.3, Geneva: World Health Organization.

Harvard Team (1999) *Improving Hong Kong's Health Care System Why and for Whom?*, Hong Kong: Health and Welfare Bureau, Government of Hong Kong.

Health and Medical Development Advisory Committee, Health, Welfare and Food Bureau (2005) *Building a Healthy Tomorrow – Discussion Paper on the Future Service Delivery Model for our Healthcare System*, Hong Kong: Health and Medical Development Advisory Committee, Health, Welfare and Food Bureau.

Law, C.K. and Yip, P.S.F. (2003) Healthy life expectancy in Hong Kong Special Administrative Region of China, *Bulletin of the World Health Organization*, 81(1): 43–47.

Ministry of Health (MOH) (2007) Hospital bill size, at: http://www.moh.gov.sg/mohcorp/billsize.aspx?id=302.

Over, M. and Watanabe, N. (2003) Evaluating the impact of organizational reforms in hospitals, in A. S. Preker and A. Harding (eds), *Innovations in Health Service Delivery: The Corporatization of Public Hospitals*, Washington, DC: World Bank.

Phua Khai Hong (2003) Attacking hospital performance on two fronts: network corporatization and financing reforms in Singapore, in A. S. Preker and A. Harding (eds), *Innovations in Health Service Delivery: The Corporatization of Public Hospitals*, Washington, DC: World Bank.

Preker, A.S. and Harding A. (eds) (2003) *Innovations in Health Service Delivery: The Corporatization of Public Hospitals*, Washington, DC: World Bank.

Wagstaff, A. (2005) *Health Systems in East Asia: What Can Developing Countries Learn from Japan and the Asian Tigers?*, Washington, DC: World Bank.

World Bank (2005) *World Development Indicators 2005*, Washington, DC: World Bank.

Yip W.C. and Hsiao, W.C. (2003) Autonomizing a hospital system: corporate control by central authorities in Hong Kong, in A. S. Preker and A. Harding (eds), *Innovations in Health Service Delivery: The Corporatization of Public Hospitals*, Washington, DC: World Bank.

6 Pro-competition policy tools and state capacity

The corporatization of public universities in Hong Kong and Singapore and the implications for Asia[1]

Ka Ho Mok

Introduction

Being two major East Asian Tiger economies, Hong Kong and Singapore are very keen to position themselves as world cities in East Asia. As such, they have been improving and reforming their higher education systems in order to establish themselves as regional hubs of higher education. The major objectives of this chapter are to analyse how governments in Hong Kong and Singapore have adopted indirect policy instruments along the line of 'corporatization' to reform higher education governance and to discuss policy implications when more pro-competition policy instruments are adopted. This chapter will examine whether these 'state-guided' regimes are no longer relevant, particularly when 'liberalizing and marketizing trends' are more globally driving their policy instruments.

Emerging new forms of governance

Despite the disagreements and diverse interpretations of globalization impacts on state capacity in governance, the growing impact of globalization has caused a number of modern states to rethink their governance strategies in coping with rapid social and economic changes. New forms of governance and new governance philosophies have emerged in order to maintain the competitiveness of modern states in recent years. Theories of 'new governance' propose that modern governments are adapting to radical changes in their environments by turning to new forms of governance which are 'more society-centred' and focus on 'co-ordination and self-governance' (Peters 1995; Pierre 2000: 2–6). Instead of relying solely upon government bureaucracy in terms of delivery of goods or services, there has been a massive proliferation of tools and policy instruments, such as a dizzying array of loans, loan guarantees, grants, contracts, insurance, vouchers, etc. to address public problems. Diversified policy tools and instruments may render the conventional governance model inappropriate. It is particularly true when many of these tools are highly indirect. More states rely heavily on a wide assortment of 'third parties' such as commercial banks, private hospitals, industrial corporations, universities, social service agencies and other social organizations (Salamon 2002).

Therefore, networks and partnerships supplant hierarchical command and control (Rhodes 1997, 2000); in the delivery of services, public authority is shared between governments and non-government actors – what Salamon (2002: 2) calls 'third-party government'; services are decentralized and in some cases privatized; and the role of governments in managing the economy is more sharply delineated and circumscribed by new arm's length (from government) market-supporting instruments, in some cases relying on self-regulation (Gamble 2000: 130–131; Jayasuriya 2001). Many possible causes have been highlighted: ideological changes such as the discrediting of 'statist' models; fiscal and bureaucratic 'overload' problems; the growth in supra-national bodies that undermine a government's control; and economic globalization eroding state 'steering capacities'.

Like countries in their western counterparts, Asian states have launched public policy and public management reforms along the lines of ideas and practices of marketization, privatization, corporatization and commercialization. Privatization has been a common theme in evolving patterns of government–business relations in some countries (for example, Malaysia and South Korea) (Gouri et al. 1991; World Bank 1995). Pressures for broad governance changes have been strong, coming to a head in the financial crisis of 1997 in Asia. A feature of these pressures is the presence of influential international agencies such as the IMF and World Bank. Their preferred models of governance reflect many of the same tendencies noted above: a less interventionist and arbitrary state; a strengthening of juridical 'forms of regulation (often associated with fundamental legal reform), more disaggregated and decentralized forms of government, including partnerships and a stronger "co-production" role for civil society groups; and a preference for market-like mechanisms over bureaucratic methods of service delivery' (World Bank 1995). Hence, it is not surprising that strategies, measures and policy instruments in line with the global neo-liberal orthodoxy of pro-competition are introduced and adopted by Asian states to transform the way the public sector is managed (Cheung and Scott 2003; Mok and Welch 2003).

Searching for new governance and educational restructuring

Education policy, management and governance, like other public policy domains, are not immune from the growing pressures for improving service delivery and better governance. In order to make individual nation-states more competitive, schools and universities across the globe have been under tremendous pressures from government and the general public to restructure/reinvent education systems in order to adapt to the ever-changing socio-economic and socio-political environments. Governments across different parts of the globe have had to expand higher education but they are facing increasing financial constraints in meeting people's pressing demands for higher education. In order to create more higher education opportunities, modern universities have started to change their paradigm in governance by adopting the doctrine of monetarism, which is characterized by freedom and markets to replace Keynesianism (known as static options) (Apple 2000). Like their western counterparts, revitalizing the role of family and individuals and involving the private sector, the market and other non-state sectors in education service delivery are becoming increasingly popular in East Asia (Mok 2006). Once education meets market forces, especially in the context of globalization, 'its effects in education are largely a product of that financially driven, free-market ideology' (Carnoy 2000: 50), while most recent education reforms in East Asia could be characterized by a finance-driven reform emphasizing decentralization, privatization and better performance (Mok 2003a; 2006).

Such changes are accelerated when more governments are exploring additional resources from the civil society or the third sector. One seminal work shows that an increasing number of countries have started to revitalize the non-state sectors, including the market, the community, the third sector and the civil society to engage in education (Meyer and Boyd 2001). Scholars who support the diversification of education services point out the problems associated with state action in education. Reconsidering the society-based tradition of education as represented by writers such as Humboldt, Jefferson, de Tocqueville or Mill seems timely and appropriate under the conditions of cultural pluralism (Meyer 2001). The myriad social ties that connect actors in a community – in the case of education, students, parents and teachers – and neighbours could generate rich social resources as 'social capital' that modern education systems could tap into/use (Coleman 1990). In short, the diversification of education service and funding providers, coupled with the revitalization of the third sector or the civil society involvement in education, open new venues and arenas for modern states to reconsider the way education governance activities are to be managed.

The trends discussed earlier in the realm of education are consistent with other public policy domains where notions such as 'co-production', 'bringing society back in' and 'coordinative relations' between state, society and other non-state sectors are stressed. Not surprisingly, the non-state sectors now share more power of control and influence in governing education policy and educational development. 'Co-arrangement', 'co-production' and 'co-management' relationships between the state and the non-state sectors (including the market, the community, the family, individuals and other social forces) are experiencing changes; hence the evolution of new coordination efforts and governance modes is urgently needed. As Salamon (2002) has rightly suggested, the proliferation of policy tools and instruments requires 'an elaborate system of third-party government in which crucial elements of public authority are shared with a host of nongovernmental or other-governmental actors, frequently in complex collaborative systems that sometimes defy comprehension' (p. 2). Therefore, public–private partnerships in running the public sector or in delivering social services have started to take shape in different countries (Broadbent et al. 2003; Klijn and Teizman 2003; Reeves 2003).

During such a restructuring process, the role of the government has shown signs of fundamental change from a 'provider of welfare benefits' to a 'builder of market' role, whereby the state actively builds markets, shapes them in different ways and regulates them (Sbragia 2000). Some major tools, which modern states could adopt in education delivery and financing, range from direct government delivery to loan guarantees delivered by commercial banks. The proliferation of policy actors in general and diversification of policy instruments in particular has suggested that the relationship between the state and other non-state actors in education delivery and financing has changed from a 'hierarchical' to a 'network' relationship; thereby the conventional governance mode of 'command and control' has shifted to a 'negotiation and persuasion' model (Salamon 2002: 9). Such a critical and reflective analysis could throw more light on changing roles and relationships between the state and other non-state sectors /actors in education governance activities. Such fundamental changes have therefore led us to call for new governance approaches and regulatory frameworks in education.

In this theoretical/policy context, this chapter examines how Hong Kong and Singapore have responded to the popularity of new governance by adopting indirect policy instruments along the lines of 'corporatization' in improving higher education governance. A few major issues to be discussed are: Do the selected Asian states lose their control in governing/managing higher education after the adoption of indirect policy instruments? Do these Asian states intend to devise new regulatory frameworks in higher education governance? If so, what regulatory framework(s) are they trying to develop? If these Asian states have tried to follow 'global liberalizing trends', would it mean that the conventionally 'state-guided' Asian states are no longer relevant? Let us now turn to the corporatization of universities in Hong Kong and Singapore.

The corporatization of public universities in Hong Kong

Policy background

Recent reforms and transformations in Hong Kong higher education are closely related to the wider context of public sector reform that began in the city-state in 1989. Since the early 1990s, the Hong Kong government has adopted different strategies along the lines of managerialism, neo-liberalism and economic rationalism to reform its public management and policies, such as those relating to housing and health services (Cheung and Lee 2001; Mok

2000). Hoping to make the public sector more responsive and sensitive to the public, different reform strategies such as 'quasi-marketization' (in the health sector) and 'privatization' (in the housing sector) have been proposed and/or implemented in recent years (Gauld and Gould 2002). Education, and particularly higher education in Hong Kong, has also been affected by the current trend of managerialism-oriented reforms (Mok and Lau 2002).

In addition to the impact of the managerialism-oriented reforms on education policy and development, the globalization challenges have indeed accelerated structural transformations and critical changes in the higher education sector. When Tung Chee Hwa came to office as the first Chief Executive of the Government of the HKSAR, he commissioned the Education Commission (EC) to conduct a comprehensive review of Hong Kong's education system. After the review, the EC published the Review of Education System Proposal in 2000, making it very clear that the political, economic and cultural changes taking place in Hong Kong and around the world signalled a trend towards globalization, a knowledge-based economy and cultural diversity. To meet the challenges ahead, there was an urgent need to provide opportunities and an environment for the people of Hong Kong to develop their potential and to build a culturally diverse, democratic and civilized society with a global outlook in order to strengthen Hong Kong's competitive edge (EC 2000). In response to the EC's recommendations, the Chief Executive directly addressed the issue raised by the EC in his 2000 policy address, asserting that 'Hong Kong is ready for the global economic competition' and that a 'holistic reform of education for the challenge is needed' (Tung 2000). On the higher education front, the government believed that more graduates with higher education training would foster the HKSAR's future social and economic development. In order to maintain the competitiveness of higher education, the Education and Manpower Bureau (EMB) commissioned the University Grants Committee (UGC) to conduct a review on higher education in May 2001. The review report was published in March 2002, recommending that the government adopt different reform measures to restructure the higher education system.

In addition to the external factors outlined above, higher education transformations in Hong Kong have also been driven by the massification of university education since the late 1980s. The rapid expansion of higher education enrolments has raised social concern about how higher education quality can be assured and maintained, particularly when an elitist system has rapidly been turned into a massified system of higher education (UGC 1996). It is in a wider policy context that the Hong Kong government has initiated reforms and transformations of higher education. Central to the higher education reforms is the adoption of the principles and practices of managerialism, neo-liberalism and economic rationalism to improve the performance and efficiency of the higher education sector.

Corporatizing strategies and questing for entrepreneurial universities

As mentioned above, the University Grant Committee (UGC) was commissioned by the EMB to launch another comprehensive review of the higher education system in Hong Kong. A Steering Committee chaired by Lord Sutherland, formerly Principal and Vice-Chancellor of the University of Edinburgh in the United Kingdom, was appointed by the UGC to carry out the review. The review report, entitled Higher Education in Hong Kong, was released in March 2002. Central to the report was a major rethinking of the way that higher education is managed and governed. Believing that the introduction of market principles and practices could promote competition and improve performance and efficiency in the higher education sector, the review report recommended that a small number of institutions be strategically identified as the focus of public and private sector support in order to create universities capable of competing at the highest international level. The UGC further recommended that the government decouple the salary scale of university academics from that of civil servants to allow more flexibility and freedom to universities to determine remuneration and terms of service for academic staff. Linking resource allocation with performance in teaching, research and management, the UGC was keen to increase the proportion of public funding that is distributed according to performance and mission. In addition, the review team recommended reviewing the existing Research Assessment Exercise (RAE) by sharpening the assessment methodology and identifying areas of research excellence for further development (UGC 2002).

In order to make Hong Kong higher education more competitive internationally, the UGC openly acknowledges that depending on the state/government resources alone is insufficient to enable all eight UGC-funded universities to become world-class institutions. In order to boost up a few universities in Hong Kong to become competitive within the international community, the UGC believes 'the higher education sector will need to diversify its income from private and public resources, and then focus its resources to attain the highest quality of teaching and research. Because resources are always limited, it will be necessary to selectively identify outstanding performance where that occurs in institutions, teachers, learners and researchers, to ensure they receive the support to achieve international excellence in the application of their expertise' (UGC 2002: vii). In light of the opening statement of the Higher Education Review, it is clear that the higher education sector in Hong Kong will face keener competition, especially when resource allocation is very much driven and determined by outstanding performance. With these general directions in mind, the UGC (2002: viii–ix) recommends that:

- A small number of institutions be strategically identified as the focus of public and private sector support, with the explicit intention of creating institutions capable of competing at the highest international levels.

- As the new landscape of the post-secondary sector is defined, the UGC conduct an internal review of its procedures, and publish a clear statement of its responsibilities in the light of new challenges, emphasizing an enhanced strategic role for steering the higher education sector.
- The governing body of each university carries out a review of the fitness for purpose of its governance and management structures. Such an exercise will necessarily include a review of the relevant ordinances and, where appropriate, proposals for legislative changes should be made.
- In consultation with the institutions, the UGC build on the success of the RAE in allocating research funds on the basis of research performance, and devise means to sharpen the RAE so that the highest levels of research excellence can be identified and funded accordingly.

In view of all these key higher education reform recommendations, it can be argued that the universities in Hong Kong will experience additional pressures to perform even better in order to secure resources from the government. It is clear that the HKSAR government is keen to select a small number of institutions to be strategically identified as the focus of public and private sector support with the clear intention of making the selected ones competitive institutions globally. Stressing outstanding performance and calling for role differentiation among all universities in Hong Kong, the UGC has recently conducted a role differentiation exercise to drive the universities to reflect upon their missions, visions and roles. After the role differentiation exercise, the UGC published a roadmap document entitled *Hong Kong Higher Education: To Make a Difference, To Move with the Times* in January 2004, stressing the importance of division of labour and clearer roles and missions to be differentiated among the local universities. When developing their academic development plans for the triennium 2005–2008, all local universities must be sensitive to their newly designated roles and missions. The UGC also announced that future activities taking place in universities will be assessed in terms of their 'role consistency', and that future funding will tie closely with their fulfilment of roles and missions.

In March 2004, the UGC announced another report entitled *Hong Kong Higher Education: Integration Matters*, encouraging universities to engage in deeper collaboration. All these new initiatives adopted by the UGC are to promote Hong Kong as a regional hub of higher education and to enhance the 'international competitiveness' of the HKSAR in the global marketplace (UGC 2004a; 2004b), hence taking a strategic approach to developing an interlocking system where the whole of Hong Kong's higher education sector can be *integrated as one force, with each institution fulfilling a unique role, based on its strengths* (UGC 2004a: 1, italics added). In addition, the UGC is very much concerned with better integration among all UGC-funded institutions. The UGC makes its position very clear, that it:

... values a role-driven yet deeply collaborative system of higher education where each institution has its own role and purpose, while at the same time being committed to extensive collaboration with other institutions in order that the system can sustain a greater variety of offerings at a high level of quality and with improved efficiency.

(2004a: 1)

By positioning Hong Kong as the hub of higher education in the region, together with the strong motivation to strengthen the academic collaboration with mainland higher education institutions, the UGC openly declares the importance of taking up the challenge of the mutually beneficial relationship between Hong Kong and the Pearl River Delta and mainland China. In response to the Chief Executive's Policy Address in 2004, and to the Closer Economic Partnership Arrangement (CEPA) signed between the HKSAR and the Guangdong Government in mainland China in 2004, the UGC urges all higher education institutions to explore the possibilities of deeper collaboration with local and overseas institutions (UGC 2004a).

In mid-March 2004, the UGC sent letters to all presidents/vice-chancellors to inform them that some HK$203 million has been set aside by the UGC as a 'Restructuring and Collaboration Fund' for 2004/2005 to encourage institutions to engage in deeper collaboration. The newly set up fund is for better focusing of resources in accordance with institutions' defined roles or in response to the changes brought about by the *Higher Education Review* and the roadmap document *To Make a Difference, To Move with the Times*. In addition, the fund aims to build strong, purposeful and cost-effective collaboration, locally and internationally, for delivery of UGC-funded programmes or administrative arrangements in accordance with the roadmap document and Integration Matters Report (UGC 2004c). All in all, the reform strategies outlined above indicate that the UGC is keen to adopt the principle of 'selectivity' in funding/rewarding local higher education institutions with outstanding performance in terms of research, teaching and management. More importantly, public universities in Hong Kong are run like business corporations and university presidents or vice-chancellors act like CEOs in business firms. Fund raising and diversifying financial sources from the industry, the business sector, the community and alumni are becoming increasingly popular practices in the Hong Kong higher education sector (Mok 2005).

The corporatization of public universities in Singapore

Policy background

As in the case of Hong Kong, higher education policy and development in Singapore has been affected by the socio-economic changes generated from the external and internal environments. Being a small city-state and an open economy, Singapore has never isolated itself from changes resulting from globalization challenges. The ruling People's Action Party (PAP) has consistently made the whole society well aware of potential challenges and threats in both the regional and global contexts (Quah 1999).

In 1999, the Singapore government published a report entitled *Singapore 21: Together, We Make the Difference*, highlighting how the island-state might cope with the emergence of the knowledge economy in the twenty-first century. In the borderless knowledge economy, knowledge and information are changing fast. A lot more brain than brawn is required for work, and lifelong learning is essential for human resources (Singapore Government 1999: 9–10). The Singapore government has identified globalization and the information technology revolution as the two driving forces behind the changes in the new century. Besides the increased flows of trade and investment, globalization is also about the flows of people, ideas and knowledge. Globalization is not a choice but a necessity. It means new markets, increased investments and opportunities. Education plays an important role in preparing citizens to manage the impact of globalization. At the same time, the government envisages the need to prepare workers and the next generation for lifelong learning and employability (Goh 1999). On the other hand, the forces of globalization challenge the powers of government, as civic groups and non-governmental organizations will want to play a bigger role in governance. With the advent of the knowledge economy, skills, creativity and entrepreneurship will command a premium. Education has to be relevant to the needs of society by bestowing on the younger generation their culture and heritage in addition to their capacity to understand the complexities and the potential of globalization in order to compete and live in the global village (Goh 2000).

Apart from the globalization impacts and the potential pressures generated by the regional environment, Singapore's higher education developments have been affected by the wider public sector management reforms taking place in the city-state. The government has initiated the PS21 Project, a reform package aimed at reinventing the public administration of Singapore, to pursue total organizational excellence in public service, to foster a culture of innovation and enterprise, and to cultivate a spirit of openness, responsiveness and involvement (PS21 Office 2001). The most current theme of this project is to cultivate a culture of entrepreneurialism among civil servants by making them aware of the importance of creativity and innovation (ibid.). In addition, the Quality Movement in the city-state increasingly shapes higher education development in Singapore. SPRING Singapore, an institution responsible for promoting high-quality services in Singapore, has been adopting market principles and practices to assure a high quality of services offered by both the private and public sectors. Organizations that can reach a certain quality benchmark will have their achievements recognized and certified by SPRING Singapore in the form of Singapore Quality Class awards (Mok 2003b). Hence, the latest higher education reforms and governance changes should be connected to the wider public sector reform and Quality Movement taking place in Singapore.

Corporatization of public universities

The corporatization of national universities in Singapore is closely related to the University Governance and Funding (UGF) Review, embarked upon in 2000 by the Ministry of Education (MOE), Singapore. The purpose of such a review was to ensure that systems and structures in relation to talent management, organizational processes and resource allocation within the universities were properly linked up to their mission and objectives of development in the long run. After the UGF Review, under which NUS and NTU were granted some operational autonomy, especially in terms of staff remuneration and a block budget for recurrent expenditure, the internal governance structures of the universities were also strengthened, with university councils encouraged to play a role by providing input on strategic planning, ensuring that the university is progressing according to its strategic plans and stipulated objectives, and overseeing the internal quality assurance systems. However, as statutory boards, NUS and NTU still have to refer to the government for approval each time they want to make an important decision, for example changing their core admission requirements or investing in capital projects. Having reflected upon the changing university governance models and evaluated the recent experiences of SMU, coupled with the recommendations from the Steering Committee of the University Autonomy, Governance and Funding Review (UAGF), the Singapore government decided to reform the governance style of the existing public universities.

In January 2005, the MOE in Singapore made a press release in which it accepted the recommendations of the Steering Committee of the UAGF to make NUS and NTU more autonomous by being corporatized as not-for-profit companies, similar to how SMI is currently run. According to the MOE, Singapore,

> ... as autonomous universities, NUS, NTU and SMU will be given greater flexibility to decide on matters such as their internal governance, budget utilization, tuition fees and admission requirements. These flexibilities given to our universities will enable them to differentiate themselves and pursue their own strategies to bring about the most optimal outcomes for their stakeholders.
>
> (2005a: 1)

By incorporatizing these state universities, the Singapore government hopes that universities on the island state will become more entrepreneurial. When public universities are 'incorporatized', key governance changes mean they will become:

- Free from the operational regulations and constraints imposed on statutory boards.
- More administratively and financially autonomous.

- More accountable to different stakeholders in the local community.
- More responsible for the key decisions affecting university directions and strategic developments.
- More rigorous in terms of internal quality assurance systems.
- More flexible in student admissions and tuition fee policies.
- More resourceful since the government will continue investing in public universities (MOE 2005a).

More power will also be decentralized to deans, department heads and faculty members; and more performance-driven assessments will be developed which will inform government funding decisions.

The belief is that once public universities in Singapore are incorporatized, a greater sense of ownership among the larger university community will be cultivated. As the MOE of Singapore suggested, 'the contributions and support of this larger community, building on the strong government support, will go a long way towards helping our universities achieve peaks of excellence' (2005a: 1). One point that deserves particular attention here is that the proposed corporatization project in Singapore's public universities does not mean that these universities, when incorporatized, will become entirely independent from the state. The MOE makes its relationship with incorporatized universities very clear in the UAGF Review report,

> Even as we seek to devolve greater autonomy to NUS, NTU and SMU, we remain mindful that our universities are vital national institutions and they have a public obligation to fulfil. **They contribute to Singapore's progress and development through providing quality education, and knowledge creation. Hence, we need to ensure that our universities' missions remain firmly aligned with our national strategic objectives.** At the same time, our Steering Committee proposes that the Minister for Education appoint the university Council members. In addition, the Steering Committee recommends that an enhanced accountability framework for universities be introduced, comprising the existing Quality Assurance Framework for Universities (QAFU), and the proposed Policy and Performance Agreements between MOE and each university.
>
> (MOE 2005a: 1, bold in original)

In short, the above paragraph clearly demonstrates that even when public universities in Singapore become 'corporatized' they will never become entirely autonomous. Judging from the future relationship between the government and the universities spelt out in the above quotation, public universities will certainly enjoy far more operational autonomy but the government will still control/influence their strategic directions and major development plans through the appointments of Council members. Corporatization strategies, seen in this light, are adopted as policy tools to partially reduce government's burden in financing higher education and to introduce further forces for making public universities more productive and proactive.

Comparing corporatization projects in Hong Kong and Singapore

Table 6.1 compares and contrasts corporatization of public universities in Hong Kong and Singapore, indicating similarities and differences between the two city-states. In terms of policy objectives and motives, the corporatization project in Hong Kong is deepened in order to cope with economic downturn and fundamental economic restructuring. Despite the fact that the HKSAR government is very keen to create greater higher education opportunities to enhance its citizens' global competence in general and to improve the global competitiveness of its universities in particular, the government realizes the financial constraints resulting from relying on state funding alone. The introduction and implementation of corporatizing strategies in higher education governance are to serve both management and financial purposes. After funding channels diversify and education providers proliferate, the HKSAR government cannot only reduce its financial burden but also steer higher education development in a more efficient and effective manner.

Comparing Hong Kong with Singapore, we may argue that the latter is a latecomer in terms of marketizing and corporatizing public universities. Since the Singapore government has long been 'monopolizing' national universities, higher education could be interpreted as one of the government's policy tools in regulating social mobility and as a means for social control.

Table 6.1 Comparing the corporatization projects of Hong Kong and Singapore

Areas for comparison	Hong Kong	Singapore
Government managerial approach	Hard managerialist state	Soft managerialist state
Policy objectives and motives	Strong financial reasons Strong managerial reasons	Moderate financial reasons Strong managerial reasons
Change of university status	Remain as independent statutory bodies	Become independent legal bodies, incorporated as non-profit corporation
The market in higher education	Already developed and becoming more prominent	Starting to evolve
Higher education governance model	Societal-market governance	De-regulated governance

Source: Table developed by the author.

Only when the Singapore government realized that its national universities would not be competitive enough to cope with rapid changes did it introduce a new governance model in line with 'corporatization'. Believing that corporatizing strategies would make its national universities more flexible and responsive to external changes, the newly introduced governance changes were more concerned with managerial purposes than financial drives, especially when the government openly declared its commitment to further investment in higher education (see MOE 2005b). In addition, corporatizing strategies introduced in national universities are certainly in line with the 'quest for entrepreneurialism', one of the major national agendas of the city-state in recent years (Mok 2005).

Comparing Hong Kong with Singapore, we believe the educational marketization and corporatization projects in Hong Kong have already driven the education sector to follow the market-led model, especially in the case of higher education, at a time when the HKSAR government has to expand higher education within the context of budgetary constraints. The diversification of educational providers and the revitalization of non-state sectors in educational financing will eventually lead the sector to shift towards 'societal-market governance', whereby transformations and changes along the line of marketization, privatization and societal regulation will become more popular. Like other policy areas in the HKSAR, market forces and practices are becoming increasingly prominent. Educational changes and transformations should be connected to the wider context of public sector restructuring in the city-state. When analysing the most recent higher education governance changes in Hong Kong from a macro public policy and public management reform perspective, we can argue that the corporatization of public universities in Hong Kong is an ongoing and extended process of public sector reform along with the ideas and practices of New Public Management and new governance. Although public universities in Hong Kong have been experiencing corporatization processes, they have maintained their own statutory status, remaining as independent bodies, and their autonomy is well protected by ordinance as statutory organizations. Unlike Hong Kong, the corporatization project in Singapore has changed the status of national universities, turning them into independent legal entities and they are now run as non-profit making corporations.

Compared to Singapore, the HKSAR government is a genuine believer in neo-liberalist doctrine, trusting the adoption of market principles and strategies to promote better service delivery and good governance in the public sector; while the Singapore government may be more cautious when adopting neo-liberalist ideas and practices. Unlike Hong Kong, the Singapore government will not allow the rise of a genuine education market since the government does not want to see education being primarily led and guided by the market. The Singapore government has adopted marketization strategies only as a means to improve the management of the education sector instead of moving towards genuine deregulation. Analysing the ways in which these

Asian states have utilized indirect policy instruments, the HKSAR government is a believer in hard managerialism while the Singapore government could be categorized as a soft managerialist, as Trow (1994) suggested. Through the adoption of special measures in unique times, Singapore has successfully maintained its effective developmental state role. Selectively adopting the so-called 'global agendas' and 'global practices' in restructuring its higher education system, the Singapore government has strengthened its governance over the university sector instead of weakening its controls. As Gopinathan (2005) has rightly suggested, the education reforms and governance changes in Singapore are not those of a state pushed to the wall by globalization; they are the responses of a strong state acting with a view to strengthening the local and the national in order to deal better with the regional and international. Singapore is not a case of a weakened post-colonial state and its current reforms in a number of areas promise a toughened model for tougher times.

Discussion: policy implications for Asia

The search for new governance and new regulatory regimes

In an age of governance, two central features of modern pro-competition regulatory regimes exist. First, 'pro-competitive' regulations prefer removing regulation from the realm of politics and establishing independent regulatory agencies. Second, interactions based on interdependence between public and private actors have grown in importance (Scott 2004). As Painter and Wong (2005: 1) argue, 'the global neo-liberal orthodoxy of pro-competitive regulation in an era of liberalization promotes regulatory regimes that place less emphasis on direct, political intervention through state authority and more on indirect, neutral policy instruments.' A more flexible regulatory environment could characterize such a restructuring; thereby public policy formulation is reoriented towards a smaller and more business-oriented state machine. This paradigm shift, manifested by a more individualistic, competitive and entrepreneurial approach, has become increasingly prominent in public management. In short, the nature of the 'pro-competitive' regulatory regime is changing from 'setting down rules and powers' to 'mega-regulation'; that is, a steering role that includes 'legal underpinning for indirect control over internal normative systems' where '. . . ends are ultimately set and determined by the sovereign state' (Scott 2004: 167–168).

The ongoing processes of corporatization of public universities in Asia, coupled with the trends of decentralization, deregulation, privatization, marketization and administrative reforms in higher education (Mok 2003a), should have rendered the conventional state–higher education relationship inappropriate. When education financing and provision is no longer monopolized by the state, the conventional 'interventionist regulation' framework (implying a hierarchical intervention of the state in imposing micro control of every aspect of education delivery) is found to be problematic. With diversification of actors/coordination, institutions in education financing and provision, coupled with growing patterns in 'co-production', 'co-arrangements' and 'co-management' in education services, we anticipate a new regulatory model: *Regulated Self-regulation* will evolve. Through 'regulated self-regulation', 'the state plays a central and active role and disposes of powers and resources which are not available to societal actors' (Knill and Lehmkuhl 2002: 50). Although the state is held responsible for promoting quality education and meeting heightened expectations of education, the state cannot adopt the same interventionist regulatory framework to govern the relationship between the state and the non-state/private actors, especially when education provision and financing is diversified. Special arrangements are to be made in allowing private/non-state actors to participate in policy making and implementation. One method is delegating power to these non-state actors, particularly when they play increasingly important roles in education. A self-regulatory framework should be established to govern these newly emerging private/non-state education coordination institutions, providing that these participative institutions still follow the overarching framework or directions set out by the state.

Table 6.2 shows a *regulated self-regulatory* framework, which could be further developed in conceptualizing the relationship between the state and professional bodies. Unlike other private goods, it is believed that overall quality assurance responsibility for education still lies with the state. But state intervention somehow is filtered by the professional influences. Taking professional qualifications, for instance, it is not the state that sets detailed requirements for approving professional credentials. Instead, professional bodies have a very important role to play in governing professional standards. Similar to Painter and Wong's (2005) case studies regarding telecommunication regulatory regimes in Hong Kong and Singapore, the governments of

Table 6.2 Different modes of governance

Mode of governance	Bureaucratic governance	Deregulated governance	Societal-market governance
Policy trend and style	Centralization State dominance	Decentralization Diversification Mobilization	Marketization Privatization Various social sources
Form of regulation	Interventionist regulation	Interfering regulation	Regulated self-regulation
Means of regulation	Government's direct rules and regulations	Procedural framework, rules and contracts	Monitoring by benchmarking/best practice models

Source: Table developed by the author.

Hong Kong and Singapore have begun to draw on new regulatory modes of 'self-regulation' and 'standardization' informed by benchmarking/best practice models. To maintain high quality education the state has to liaise with those professional organizations concerned or refer to international benchmarks to assure quality instead of specifying detailed requirements. Establishing new 'regulated self-regulation' frameworks (with more emphasis given to 'negotiated regulation') should be developed, especially when cooperative patterns of interaction between private and public actors in education delivery and 'cooperative contracting' are becoming increasingly common in education provision and financing.

After introducing corporatizing strategies, higher education governance in Hong Kong and Singapore has changed from the traditional 'state control model' to the 'state supervision model'. 'Bureaucratic governance' (that is, centralization and state dominance) has been transformed into 'deregulated governance', as characterized by decentralization, diversification and mobilization. If the private sector (or the market) and civil society (or the third sector) continue to play increasingly important roles in education, I believe the 'market-led model', whereby market governance takes the lead in shaping policy, will shape the education governance of Hong Kong and Singapore. Policy strategies along the lines of marketization, privatization and a societal sources-led approach will become more prominent and popular in shaping future directions and developments of education in these two Tiger economies.

The search for new governance and the rise of a market accelerationist state in Asia

In order to enhance their global competitiveness, governments in different parts of the world have started to conduct comprehensive reviews of and implement plans to restructure their higher education systems (Mok and Welch 2003). In response to the growing pressures generated by globalization forces, modern states have attempted to reinvent themselves by moving beyond the welfare state to become competition states (Gill 1995; Jordana and Levi-Faur 2005; Moran 2002). Governments across different parts of the globe, facing similar competitive pressures, have undertaken regulatory reforms such as privatization or corporatization of state-owned industries or publicly-owned organizations such as post offices and universities, opening up new markets to multiple providers and introducing new regulatory regimes under the control of independent regulators (Drahos and Jospeh 1995; Levi-Faur 1998; Scott 2004). To enhance the efficiency of public policy/public management, modern states may deregulate some areas while enforcing competition in others, hence becoming facilitators or even generators of markets. Thus, it is common to witness the extent and role of reregulation or recentralization in the processes of market restructuring accompanied by the emergence of strong regulatory states and by the entrepreneurial role states play (Chan and Tan 2006; Ng and Chan 2006). Unlike Cerny's (1997) characterization of the competition state as a basically liberal state, Levi-Faur (1998: 676) argues that the state (particularly in the intensified global competitive environment faces a paradox: *'the greater the commitment of the competition state to the promotion of competition, the deeper its regulation will be'* (my emphasis). More importantly, the actions and mission of the competition state do not necessarily result in the retreat of the state from the market but rather in a reassertion of the role of the state under changing social and economic circumstances (op. cit.).

Promoting basic national interests through the creation and enforcement of competition, the developmental states in Asia have taken the opportunity offered by the fundamental economic restructuring processes to transform them into 'market accelerationist states' by proactively shaping the market institutions for the benefits of market creation (Lee 2004; Mok 2006). Unlike the regulatory state in America that evolved within a liberal market economy context, the regulatory state in Asia has emerged from the context of a combined strong state and a free market economy, by which the state ideologically commits to an 'authoritarian mode of liberalism'. As Jayasuriya (2000) has rightly pointed out, 'this authoritarian liberalism presupposes the existence of a strong (or better described as politically illiberal) state with a capacity to regulate the economy' (p. 329). In order to promote competition in the markets against the context of the authoritarian liberalizm, a *market accelerationist state* is forming (Mok 2006). The market accelerationist state has the features of a 'dualistic state' as described by Fraenkel (1941): a strong state combined with a liberal market economy. With this kind of state architecture in place, the success of the markets rests heavily upon the presence of strong regulatory institutions. It is within such a wider socio-political context that far more pro-competition policy instruments are adopted by modern states to transform the way the public sector is governed. Hence, the higher education sector, like other public policy domains, has 'gone private'; while ideas and strategies along the lines of neo-liberalism and economic rationalism are increasingly influencing the way public policy is managed (Deem and Brehony 2005; Neubauer 2006).

Our above discussions regarding higher education governance change in Hong Kong and Singapore seem to suggest that these East Asian states are reduced to the role of the 'night-watchman state' of classical liberalism, that is, taking care only of law and order, protecting the sanctity of contract, maintaining the minimum level of welfare to protect the really poor and vulnerable, and facilitating the free operation of the market, particularly within the tidal wave enacted by a 'pro-competition' regime. In this connection, it seems that the capacity and the role of nation states have changed in the sense that they have become less autonomous and have less exclusive control over the economic, social and cultural processes and distinctiveness of their territories (Giddens 1999). Nonetheless, before we jump to such a conclusion, we must examine how skilful and tactical these Asian states have been in managing to protect their own autonomy when making use of these indirect policy instruments.

Our above discussion has shown that the adoption of 'pro-competition' policy instruments in response to the growing impact of 'liberalizing and marketizing' forces does not necessarily lessen state capacity in the public sector management. As outlined earlier, both Hong Kong and Singapore governments would find it easier to govern their higher education systems by the introduction of corporatizing strategies to drive institutions and academics to enhance their productivity. The quality assurance movements institutionalized in these Asian higher education systems and their reference to international benchmarking and good practices should have strengthened nation-states' ability to steer higher education developments rather than weakened state capacity. Lee's (2004) research on university corporatization in Malaysia has also indicated that the role of the state is strengthened rather than weakened. According to Lee, 'the restructuring of higher education in Malaysia is taking place in the context of a strong interventionist state' (p. 15). My recent comparative research on educational decentralization in mainland China, Taiwan and Japan has also suggested that a 'centralized decentralization' trend is evolving in education governance, further suggesting that these Asian states still maintain a significant level of control over higher education policy formulation, management and governance (Mok 2003c, 2006).

Contrary to Castells' (1997) argument regarding the demise of the developmental states in East Asia, the above case studies have shown that East Asian states remain robust and dynamic in pursuing their nation building projects despite globalization pressures and crises. It is particularly true that when we analyse the current education developments in these societies from a public policy perspective, we may find that the higher education reforms in these East Asian societies are pursued within the context of managing state building (or government capacity) and economic growth within the paradigm of governance rather than de-powering the state/government. In addition, the adoption of new governance in higher education in these Asian states can be interpreted as the strategies adopted by the government to cope with problems of political and bureaucratic governance instead of purely problems of severe economic and social difficulties. Even so, our above discussions have suggested the presence of diverse national and local agendas that have given different meanings to common management jargons and statements. Even though similar strategies are adopted by different countries in response to the so-called tidal wave of policy instruments reform, different governments may use similar strategies to serve their own political purposes. As Hallak (2000) rightly suggested, modern states may tactically make use of the globalization discourse to justify their own political agendas or legitimize their inaction.

Conclusion

This chapter has reviewed how Hong Kong and Singapore have attempted to adopt pro-competition policy instruments to promote the global competitiveness of their higher education systems without significantly undercutting the state capacity in educational governance. The comparative studies above have clearly shown that in the era of growing pro-competitive regulation, states still exhibit distinctively different regulatory regimes due to the need to formulate strategies to suit their own traditions, capacities and goals. Such observations are confirmed by the findings from other comparative studies related to policy instruments and governance in East Asia, repeatedly reporting that adopting 'pro-competition' policy instruments may not necessarily weaken the capacity of nation-states. Instead, the adoption of 'pro-competition' and indirect policy tools may have strengthened the state capacity in steering public sector management more effectively. Taking the case of mainland China, for example, the government has skilfully and tactically made use of the 'globalization discourse' to justify its reform programmes originally grounded locally; while other Asian states like Malaysia and Thailand can guard against the growing impact of globalization by creatively developing policies matching local needs instead of blindly following the global trends (Moore 2005; Yeoh et al. 2004). Similarly, 'pro-competition' tools for managing the health sector in Singapore are adopted within a strong interventionist state context (Ramesh 2005). We must also note that the choice of policy tools is highly political (Peters 2002; Salamon 2002) and therefore we must be sensitive about the political culture, the nature of the state and the unique socio-economic and socio-historical contexts in which policy tools are chosen by different Asian states, despite the fact that they are not entirely immune from the growing impact of globalization. In conclusion, the comparative studies above have clearly indicated that the role of government in East Asia is still important, especially when there is a strong need for government to set up appropriate regulations, and social protection and welfare systems. Governments in East Asia are thus very much perceived as a complement to the markets (Stiglitz 2005).

Note

1 This chapter is based upon a paper published in *Policy and Society*, 24(3): 1–26. The research findings reported in the chapter were generated from a research project funded by the Research Grants Council of the Hong Kong Special Administrative Region, China (Project No. CityU 1276/03H). The author expresses his gratitude to the grant offering body.

References

Apple, M. (2000) Between neoliberalism and neoconservatism: education and conservatism in a global context, in N. C. Burbules and C. A. Torres (eds), *Globalization and Education: Critical Perspective*, New York: Routledge, 57–78.

136   *Ka Ho Mok*

Broadbent, J., Gray, A. and Jackson, P.M. (2003) [Editorial] Public–private partnerships, *Public Money & Management*, 23(3): 135–136.

Carnoy, M. (2000) *Sustaining the New Economy in the Information Age: Reflections on Our Changing World*, University Park: Pennsylvania State University Press.

Castells, M. (1997) *The Power of Identity: The Information Age: Economy, Society and Culture*, Volume II, Oxford: Blackwell.

Cerny, P. (1997) Paradoxes of the competition state: The dynamics of political globalization, *Government and Opposition*, 32: 251–274.

Chan, D. and Tan, J. (2006) Privatization and the rise of direct subsidy scheme schools and independent schools in Hong Kong and Singapore, paper presented at the Asia Pacific Educational Research Association International Conference, 28–30 November, Hong Kong.

Cheung, A. and Lee, J. (eds) (2001) *Public Sector Reform in Hong Kong in the 21st Century*, Hong Kong: Chinese University Press.

Cheung, A.B.L. and Scott, I. (eds) (2003) *Governance and Public Sector Reform in Asia*, London and New York: RoutledgeCurzon.

Coleman, J.S. (1990) *Foundations of Social Theory*, Cambridge, MA: Harvard University Press.

Deem, R. and Brehony, K.J. (2005). Challenging the post-Fordist/flexible organization thesis: The case of reformed educational organizations, *British Journal of Sociology of Education*, 26(3): 395–414.

Drahos, P. and Jospeh, R. (1995) The telecommunications and investment in the great supranational regulatory game, *Telecommunications Policy*, 188: 619–635.

Education Commission (EC) (2000) *Review of Education System: Reform Proposal*, Hong Kong: Government Printer.

Fraenkel, E. (1941) *The Dual State*, translation from the German by E. A. Shils, in collaboration with E. Lowenstein and K. Knorr, Oxford: Oxford University Press.

Gamble, A. (2000) Economic governance, in J. Pierre (ed.), *Debating Governance*, Oxford: Oxford University Press.

Gauld, R. and Gould, D. (2002) *The Hong Kong Health Sector: Development and Change*, Hong Kong: Chinese University Press.

Giddens, A. (1999) *Runaway World*, London: Profile Books.

Gill, S. (1995). Globalization, market civilization and disciplinary neoliberalism, *Millennium*, 24(3): 399–423.

Goh, C.T. (1999) Making globalisation work with social accountability, keynote address by Singapore Prime Minister Goh Chok Tong at the Commonwealth Business Forum on 11 November, Singapore: Ministry of Information and the Arts.

Goh, C.T. (2000) Education: meeting the challenge of globalization, opening address by Prime Minister Goh Chok Tong at the APEC Education Ministers Meeting on 6 April, Singapore: Ministry of Education.

Gopinathan, S. (2005) Globalization, the Singapore developmental state and education policy: a thesis revisited, working paper, National Institute of Education, Singapore.

Gouri, G., Shankar, T.K., Reddy, Y.V. and Shams, K. (1991) Imperatives and perspectives, in G. Gouri (ed.), *Privatisation and Public Enterprise*, New Delhi: Oxford and IBH Publishing.

Hallak, J. (2000) Globalization and its impact on education, in T. Mebrahtu, M. Crossley and D. Johnson (eds), *Globalization, Educational Transformation and Societies in Transition*, Oxford: Symposium Books.

Jayasuriya, K. (2000) Authoritarian liberalism, governance and the emergence of the regulatory state in post-crisis East Asia, in R. Robinson, M. Beeson, K. Jayasuriya and H. R. Kim (eds), *Politics and Markets in the Wake of the Asian Crisis*, London: Routledge, 315–330.

Jayasuriya, K. (2001) Globalization and the changing architecture of the state: the regulatory state and the politics of negative coordination, *Journal of European Public Policy*, 8(1): 101–123.

Jordana, J. and Levi-Faur, D. (2005) Preface: the making of a new regulatory order, *Annals of the American Academy of Political and Social Science*, 598, March: 1–6.

Klijn, E.H. and Teisman, G.R. (2003) Institutional and strategic barriers to public–private partnership: an analysis of Dutch cases, *Public Money & Management*, 23(3): 137–146.

Knill, C. and Lehmkuhl, D. (2002) Private actors and the state: internationalization and changing patterns of governance, *Governance*, 15(1): 41–63.

Lee, M.N.N. (2004) *Restructuring Higher Education in Malaysia*, Penang: School of Educational Studies, Universiti Sains Malaysia.

Levi-Faur, D. (1998) The competition state as a neo-mercantalist state: understanding the restructuring of national and global telecommunications, *Journal of Socio-Economics*, 27(6): 655–686.

Meyer, H.-D. (2001) Civil society and education: the return of an idea, in H.-D. Meyer and W. L. Boyd (eds), *Education between States, Markets and Civil Society: Comparative Perspectives*, Hillsdale, NJ: Lawerence Erlbaum, 13–34.

Meyer, H.-D. and Boyd, W.L. (eds) (2001) *Education between States, Markets and Civil Society: Comparative Perspectives*, Hillsdale, NJ: Lawerence Erlbaum.

Ministry of Education, Singapore (MOE) (2005a) Autonomous universities: towards peaks of excellence, press release 6 January.

MOE (2005b) Autonomous universities: towards peaks of excellence. Preliminary report, Singapore: Ministry of Education.

Mok, K.H. (2000) Impact of globalization: a study of quality assurance systems of higher education in Hong Kong and Singapore, *Comparative Education Review*, 44(2): 148–174.

Mok, K.H. (2003a) Similar trends, diverse agendas: higher education reforms in East Asia, *Globalization, Societies and Education*, 1(2): 201–221.

Mok, K.H. (2003b) Decentralization and marketization of education in Singapore: a case study of the School Excellence Model, *International Journal of Educational Administration*, 41(4): 348–366.

Mok, K.H. (ed.) (2003c) *Centralization and Decentralization: Educational Reforms and Changing Governance in Chinese Societies*, Dordrecht: Kluwer Academic.

Mok, K.H. (2005) Fostering entrepreneurship: changing role of government and higher education governance in Hong Kong, *Research Policy*, 34(4): 537–554.

Mok, K.H. (2006) *Education Reform and Education Policy in East Asia*, London, Routledge.

Mok, K.H. and Lau, M. (2002) Changing government role for socio-economic development in Hong Kong in the twenty-first century, *Policy Studies*, 23(2): 107–124.

Mok, K.H. and Welch, A. (eds) (2003) *Globalization and Educational Restructuring in the Asia Pacific Region*, Basingstoke: Palgrave Macmillan.

Moore, T.G. (2005) Chinese foreign policy in the age of globalization, in Y. Deng and F. L. Wang (eds), *China's Rising: Power and Motivation in Chinese Foreign Policy*, Lanham, MD: Rowman & Littlefield.

Moran, M. (2002) [Review article] Understanding the regulatory state, *British Journal of Political Science*, 32: 391–413.

Neubauer, D. (2006) On the public good, paper presented at the senior seminar, Education for 2020 Project of East–West Center, 6–12 September, Hawaii.

Ng, P.T. and Chan, D. (2006) A comparative study of Singapore's school excellence model with Hong Kong's school-based management, paper presented at the Asia Pacific Educational Research Association International Conference, 28–30 November, Hong Kong.

Painter, M. and Wong, S.F. (2005) Telecommunications regulatory regimes in Hong Kong and Singapore: when direct state intervention meets indirect policy instruments, unpublished paper.

Peters, G. (1995) *The Future of Governing*, Lawrence: University Press of Kansas.

Peters, G. (2002) The politics of tool choice, in L. Salamon and O. Elliott (eds), *The Tools of Government: A Guide to the New Governance*, Oxford: Oxford University Press.

Pierre, J. (ed.) (2000) *Debating Governance*, Oxford: Oxford University Press.

PS21 Office (2001) *Public Service for the Twenty-first Century*, Singapore: PS21 Office.

Quah, S.T. (1999) Learning from Singapore's development, *International Journal of Technical Cooperation*, 4(1): 54–68.

Ramesh, M. (2005) Public sector reforms in health care administration in Hong Kong and Singapore, paper presented to the Second Congress of the Asian Political and International Studies Association, 14–16 November, Hong Kong.

Reeves, E. (2003) Public–private partnership in Ireland: policy and practice, *Public Money & Management*, 23(3): 163–170.

Rhodes, R.A.W. (1997) *Understanding Governance*, Buckingham: Open University Press.

Rhodes, R.A.W. (2000) Governance and public administration, in J. Pierre (ed.), *Debating Governance*, Oxford: Oxford University Press.

Salamon, L.M. (ed.) (2002) *The Tools of Government: A Guide to the New Governance*, Oxford: Oxford University Press.

Sbragia, A.M. (2000) Governance, the state, and the market: what is going on?, *Governance*, 13(2): 243–250.

Scott, C. (2004) Regulation in the age of governance: the rise of the post-regulatory state, in J. Jordana and D. Levi-Faur (eds), *The Politics of Regulation: Institutions and Regulatory Reforms for the Age of Governance*, Cheltenham: Edward Elgar.

Singapore Government (1999) *Singapore 21: Together, We Make the Difference*, Singapore: Singapore 21 Committee.

Stiglitz, J.E. (2005) More instruments and broader goals: moving toward the post-Washington consensus, in A. B. Atkinson et al. (eds), *Wider Perspectives on Global Development*, Basingstoke: Palgrave Macmillan.

Trow, M. (1994) Managerialism and the academic profession: the case of England, *Higher Education Policy*, 7(2): 11–18.

Tung, C.H. (2000) *Policy Address 2000*, Hong Kong: Government Printer.

University Grants Committee (UGC) (1996) *Higher Education in Hong Kong*, Hong Kong: Government Printer.

UGC (2002) *Higher Education in Hong Kong: Report of the University Grants Committee*, Hong Kong: Government Printer.

UGC (2004a) *Higher Education in Hong Kong: To Make a Difference, To Move with Times*, Hong Kong: Government Printer.

UGC (2004b) *Higher Education in Hong Kong: Integration Matters*, Hong Kong: Government Printer.

UGC (2004c) *UGC letter to Universities in Hong Kong*, 7 March, Hong Kong: UGC.

World Bank (1995) *Higher Education: The Lessons of Experience*, Washington, DC: World Bank.

Yeoh, M. et al. (2004) *Globalisation and its Impact on Asia*, Kuala Lumpur: Pelanduk Publications.

7 Comparative welfare policy instruments in East Asia

Embedding trust in policy[1]

Yeun Wen Ku

... there can be no higher priority for any democratic government than maintaining the trust of its citizens. ... This is especially important in today's globalized world where effective and efficient public governance is more important than ever in order to ensure economic and social development.

(Alexander Pechtold, Netherlandish Chairman, speaking in OECD Ministerial Meeting, 28 November 2005)

Introduction

East Asian economies have long benefited from state-led developmental strategies, but that approach is now under critical scrutiny. The core assumption of this strategy is that the state has the capacity to maintain and pursue an effective economic production and political reproduction strategy within its territory. This capacity, however, has been eroded by two important, but contradictory, changes. The first is the development of globalization with an increasingly competitive world order, putting constraints on the pursuit of goals other than performance competitiveness. The second is the process of democratization in East Asia that leads to pressures for more provision of public services for the population as a whole. To respond to these two changes, East Asian countries stepped forward with diversified responses that involve varied welfare policy instruments. For example, Korea and Taiwan have developed their social insurance programmes, while Singapore and Hong Kong have gone down the provident fund road.

However, this is not the end of the story. Social insurance schemes in Korea and Taiwan now face the decline of state capacity to pool risks across gender, class, the life cycle, and across generations. Provident funds, especially in Singapore, often simply assume that the accumulated capital and interest should guarantee a comfortable standard of living in retirement. This scenario is, however, not always the case. To fill the gap, some insurance programmes and social services were introduced and developed around provident funds (Ku 2003).

The argument of this chapter is that, whatever the welfare policy instruments adopted, we should not overlook the new importance of trust in policy development. The success of a policy is determined not only by carefully designed policy making but also by the people's trust in such a policy. Given the fact that social programmes affect the lives of so many people of different socio-economic status, age and gender, it is particularly important to have people's trust in what is being attempted in the chosen policy and also in the public accountability of the state. A pure market-led welfare model is not likely to generate such trust.

Under the pressures of democratic politics, governments have to reshape public sector leadership in terms of both substantive policy and in terms of policy style to cope with new challenges. Some new roles are required for public sector leaders, including roles as change agents, promoters of enhanced performance, coordinators of government policies and keepers of public service values, through which a more trust-creating policy environment will evolve.

Policy instruments: from single instruments to a policy mix

Since the pursuit of welfare is no longer simply a private activity but a field in which the state is deeply involved in relation to both policy formation and delivery, social policy making has become an important window into understanding welfare in the modern era. The term 'policy' is widely used in the analysis of processes of governmental decision making, explaining and legitimating the actions taken by policy-makers and related practitioners (Colebatch 1998: 13). Furthermore, 'policy' also refers to an activity involving leaders, aides, followers, executives, interested parties and knowledge workers (pp. 90–99). Such talk implies a series of policy instruments that can be mobilized by government to systematically implement and institutionalize policy statements. Policy does not necessarily translate directly into social action if policy-makers and practitioners cannot mobilize sufficient and consistent capacity to accomplish the task. The development of the instrument-choice perspective was designed to highlight this issue, defining the approach as follows:

> At its (the instrument-choice perspective) core, it is rooted in a commitment to understanding policy formulation and implementation, as well as the policy-making process itself, by focusing on instruments of government action rather than on policies and programs.
>
> (Eliadis et al. 2005: 4)

Governments may mobilize many instruments for their purposes, which are closely linked to the rise of the modern state. This rise began with the absolutist state in the sixteenth and seventeenth centuries, was followed by the liberal and bureaucratic state in the nineteenth century, and culminated in a gradual transition to democracy (liberal or social) in the twentieth century (Bresser-Pereira 2005). The tools for collective violence – military forces and the levying of compulsory taxes – have long been recognized as two basic elements of the nation-state in the claim for sovereignty, as well as the means of imposing necessary duties upon their people. The transition to democracy implies more constraints on the arbitrary operation of state violence and taxation but does not change their nature as instruments employed only by the state (Giddens 1987). The expansion of policy instruments, spanning law and regulation, subsidies and grants, organization and bureaucracy and information dissemination, endows governments with more regulatory powers to define the legal system, the system of rights and obligations, and the rules for social life (Bresser-Pereira 2005; Eliadis et al. 2005). However, this expansion also presents a challenge to governments struggling to evaluate which instruments are more likely to achieve their ends, and the effects vary depending on which instrument is used to address a given problem or issue (Eliadis et al. 2005).

The choice is not simplicity itself because of two reasons. The first is the complexity of targeted problems or issues that often require instrument-choice in poorly defined, ambiguous, decision-making circumstances and information asymmetries (Howlett 2005: 40). This complexity is particularly true as national governments enter into the heart of debates concerning diversified requirements that are not generated only from within their own societies. In the era of globalization, as Axford (1995: 27) notes, an ever-evolving pattern of interconnectedness and interdependence between states has been developing. For many countries, it is not just a theoretical issue but has a real impact on their political and social development. The Asian financial crisis was witness to just how powerful a force rapid global capital flows could be and in spheres far beyond the simply economic. Rather, it is a politico-economic problem, bringing together global economic competition, domestic democratic politics and expectations for social reform. Such pressures present a very difficult challenge to the role and function of the state, and its policy-making capacity in particular.

The second reason is internal, regarding the level of state capacity (Howlett 2005: 41–2). There is an uneven distribution of power and resource across every state in the world. The stronger states may impose their rules upon the others and further seek to construct the world order according to their own interests, so attracting radical criticism; for example, the charge that the WTO has facilitated economic colonialism of the countries in the South (Adams et al. 1999). On the other hand, governments may have varied capacity to carry out their policies due to different executive–parliament relationships, the strength and ethos of the civil service, and tax revenues and budgets, as well as varied social situations. Bressers and O'Toole (2005: 150) comment, 'Instruments are not simply tools to be selected and applied with no eye toward the political and other constraints operating in the relevant social settings.' In the process of instrument choice, four questions are, therefore, often posed (Ringeling 2005: 187):

- In terms of effectiveness, does it work?
- In terms of feasibility, does it suit?
- In terms of acceptability, is it normatively correct?
- In terms of legality, is it permitted?

These four questions formulate a complicated context in which governments are not likely to deal with varied problems or issues with exactly the same, or even with a single, instrument. Moreover, the most effective instrument does not mean the fairest one because of reasons of feasibility, acceptability and legality. Beyond the simplistic, cleaver-like recommendations for instrument choice that overemphasize the direct relation between certain means and ends, Howlett identifies the 'second-generation' scholars of instrument choice attempting to address the issues of influence of policy context and nature of instrument mixes. 'In most cases, however, in practice policy-makers use a mix of instruments in seeking to achieve their desired ends,' he argues (2005: 34). Governments are not making their choices from among all available individual policy instruments but are thinking about the integration and operation of various policy instruments in achieving, even, a single end that may better fit with the four questions raised by Ringeling.

The concept of instrument mixes exerts an influence in different fields of policy study. For example, the sectoral perspective of welfare provision involving the statutory, the commercial, the voluntary and the informal (e.g. Johnson 1987), the so-called mixed economy of welfare, has become a widely accepted analytical framework for comparing welfare systems in different countries. Esping-Andersen's (1990) analysis of welfare regimes, namely liberal, conservative and social democracy, also reveals varied mixes of welfare instruments having, therefore, different impacts on decommodification, stratification, class coalitions and historical institutions. In this sense, the concept of instrument mixes is not only an analytical tool that can be used to explain governmental policy making in a specific context; it can also be valuable in comparative analysis to present the trends and styles of policy making across country cases.

Instrument mixes in East Asian welfare

Many scholars have argued that East Asian governments are reluctant to become involved in welfare issues. The various characterizations of welfare in East Asia whether in terms of 'Oikonomic' or 'Confucian welfare states' (Jones 1990, 1993), 'productivist welfare capitalism' (Holliday 2000) or 'conservative welfare state systems' (Aspalter 2001; Ramesh 2004) all stress a limited state involvement. However, we also witness the significant development of modern welfare measures in East Asia going well beyond the traditional welfare provisions of kinship and charity. Although the welfare role of the state in East Asia is still lagging behind the level in European welfare states, in terms of governmental expenditure or social programmes, the

state's involvement in the establishment of some institutional welfare programmes has been developed even earlier than the economic take-off in
East Asia; for example, the Central Provident Fund in Singapore in 1953,
the labour insurance scheme in Taiwan in 1950, and compensation for
work injury in Hong Kong and Korea in 1953. In particular, there has
been a gradual but important expansion of state welfare in East Asia in the
most recent decade following the upheaval of the Asian financial crisis (Ku
2003; Kwon 2005). This constitutes a very different image of East Asian
welfare.

Against the theoretical accounts of welfare development in terms of capitalist requirements or democratization, Walker and Wong insist that:

> In fact, neither capitalism nor democracy are necessary conditions for
> constituting a welfare state or explaining its development. Non-capitalist
> and authoritarian states such as the former Soviet bloc countries and pre-
> reform Maoist China had established many essential social policies on a
> par with those in the West. . . . a 'state-led' or 'top-down' theory seems
> more likely to explain welfare system development in those societies
> where capitalism or democracy is either absent or rudimentary.
>
> (2005: 4–5)

We return to this issue in the next section. Here, there are indeed varied
welfare instrument mixes in East Asia, implying different choices have been
made by governments during the process of instrument selection. Table 7.1
sets out the distinctive characteristics of the main welfare instruments chosen.
Briefly, assistance and allowance systems require more state involvement in
their financing and regulation, though both are generally regarded as welfare
instruments with an emphasis on selectivity. This is particularly true if the
coverage and benefit level of assistance and allowance schemes do not constitute a basic safety net for people in need. Clearly, the state is the major,
sometimes even the only, agency to guarantee basic wellbeing for the people,
especially when other private and informal provisions are insufficient or
absent. Insurance and provident fund systems would need statutory laws and
rules to regulate their establishment and operation, but governments would
not necessarily bear financial responsibility. The contributions for insurance
and provident funds may be mainly shared, if not equally, by employers and
employees, and the benefits assigned to meet certain needs defined by previous regulation. Since the provident fund is an individual savings account
where financial resources are accumulated and redistributed during an individual's personal lifetime, it assumes more individual responsibility than
insurance, where risks are pooled across individuals and, even, generations.
Employers' liabilities imply a feudalist relationship between employers and
employees, requiring loyalty and labour responsibility upwards and gratitude and care downwards. However, in the modern era the state has also
been involved in the redefinition and formation of such old and primary

Table 7.1 Welfare instruments and their characteristics

Characteristics	Instruments				
	Assistance	Insurance	Allowance	Provident fund	Employers' liability
Purpose	Poverty alleviation	Poverty prevention	Social compensation	Poverty prevention	Poverty prevention
Funding	Taxes	Contributions	Taxes	Contributions	Employers
Eligibility	Means test	Contribution record	Some social or demographic category	Contribution record	Current employment
Benefits	Flat-rate cash and in-kind, up to poverty line	Earnings- and (or) contributions-related cash	Flat-rate cash	Contributions refund	Earnings-related cash
Focus	Persons in need	Persons suffering interruption of earnings	Persons with additional income need	Persons suffering interruption of earnings	Persons suffering interruption of earnings
State role	Regulatory and funding	Regulatory	Regulatory and funding	Regulatory	Regulatory
Responsibility	Social responsibility	Social and individual responsibility mixed	Social responsibility	Individual responsibility	Employers' responsibility
Redistribution	Interpersonal	Lifetime and interpersonal mixed	Interpersonal	Lifetime	Gratitude

Sources: Adapted from Dixon and Chow (1992) and Jacobs (1998: 12).

relationships. Some forms of employers' liability have been transformed and become a kind of insurance and provident fund like the contribution borne by employers, but some welfare provisions, like retirement and severance payments for lay-off, remain the employers' responsibility.

In this sense, each welfare instrument chosen by governments also implies what kinds of action should be taken with which method, regulation or financing, or both. As instrument mixes have acquired more elaborations in policy studies, we may actually find that different welfare instruments are mobilized together to target the same problem faced by governments. Table 7.2 shows how East Asian governments mix different welfare instruments when coping with contingencies.

In the four East Asian countries, assistance is popularly used as the basic safety net against poverty, showing the importance of government in guaranteeing people's ultimate economic security. However, significant differences exist in the way they address the following issues. Taiwan and Korea choose national health insurance to meet the rising demand for healthcare, while the Hong Kong government controls and finances around 90 per cent of health provision in the secondary sector through a statutory hospital authority, as well as approximately 20 per cent of primary care. Healthcare in Singapore is mainly paid from health savings accounts, which are part of its central provident fund (CPF). Insurance remains the major instrument in Taiwan

Table 7.2 Welfare instruments by country and contingency

	Country			
Contingency	*Taiwan*	*South Korea*	*Hong Kong*	*Singapore*
Poverty	Assistance	Assistance	Assistance	Assistance
Health	National Health Insurance	National Health Insurance	Public provision	Medical saving account
Old age	Insurance Assistance Employer liability Allowances	Insurance Assistance Employer liability	Employer liability MPF Assistance Allowances	CPF Insurance Assistance
Unemployment	Insurance Assistance	Insurance Assistance	Employer liability Assistance	Employer liability
Disability, death and survivor	Insurance Allowances	Insurance Assistance	Assistance Allowances	CPF Life insurance
Occupational injury	Insurance Employer liability	Insurance Employer liability	Employer liability	Employer liability

Source: Adapted from Jacobs (1998: 27).

and Korea against the contingencies of old age, unemployment, disability, death and occupational injury, and secondary help comes from assistance, allowances and employers' liability. Hong Kong's chosen instrument is assistance and employers' liability, but the newly established provident fund (MPF) providing for the elderly will become more important. Singapore relies on its CPF as the most important pillar in its welfare system and other instruments are relatively weak.

A further question addresses the implications of Tables 7.1 and 7.2. Two criteria are used to examine the possible East Asian models of welfare instrument mix. The first focuses on the degrees of state involvement. If the perspective of a reluctant state in East Asian welfare is right, governmental policy instrument choice should not become too involved with welfare. Governments would sooner leave welfare as a field mainly for private and informal provision rather than pursue welfare outcomes with public and formal regulation. The second criterion emerges from the networked nature of instrument choice, suggested by Bressers and O'Toole (2005), meaning that action taken by governments does not depend only on government. They insist:

> The multiplicity of instruments and their resulting collective impact involve several dimensions, all of which deserve consideration for anticipating and perhaps improving the results of instrument selection in practice. . . . policy action develops in and through a networked social context.
>
> (p. 150)

Given this reason, various welfare instruments and their mixes also demonstrate degrees of networking across sectors like the labour market, individual lifetimes, formal and informal systems, different groups of the population, and so on. The degrees of networking will, therefore, affect the capacity of the state to mobilize and manage possible instruments for policy action.

Table 7.3 shows the ideal models of welfare instrument mixes in East Asia. Taiwan and Korea come together as a group, in which they are both more deeply involved in welfare provision than Hong Kong or Singapore, and

Table 7.3 Welfare instrument mixes in East Asia

	Networking	
State involvement	*High*	*Low*
High	Taiwan Korea	Social democracy
Low	Hong Kong	Singapore

multiple instruments are mobilized to cope with this development. In contrast, Singapore has low scores on both criteria because it is heavily dependent on the CPF, the most important pillar of welfare policy, and employers and employees mainly share contributions. Hong Kong has low state involvement and high networking. Government merely acts as the guardian of the basic safety net through assistance, but it also mobilizes and integrates other resources and instruments under regulation. It seems that no East Asian country, at least of those from our chosen group, fits into the category of high state involvement and low networking, which implies the state's important and even sole role in welfare provision. If, however, we take examples from outside East Asia, social democratic welfare states could probably fit in this category because governments acquire the major share of welfare responsibilities.

The models are helpful for understanding the welfare instrument mixes in East Asia, and show that some East Asian countries, especially Taiwan and Korea, are moving away from the reluctant state of welfare provision. Even if we agree with Walker and Wong's argument that neither capitalism nor democracy necessarily leads to or explains welfare development, this by no means constitutes an explanation of welfare expansion in East Asia. In comparison with Hong Kong and Singapore, many analysts do observe more significant welfare development in Taiwan and Korea (e.g. Holliday 2005; Kwon 2005). Why? The reason must relate to the social and political setting as governments make their instrument choice and therefore alter their welfare instrument mixes.

The implications of democratization for policy instruments

Even with the hostility towards state welfare, some welfare schemes have been expanded, some remarkably, in East Asia. Midgley (1986) sees the incrementalist style of social policy making as the explanation, but, more specifically, this expansion is due to declining state legitimacy in the wake of democratization. This explanation is particularly important as we examine welfare expansion in Taiwan (e.g. Ku 1997) and Korea (e.g. Kwon 1999) over the 1990s. Tang (2000) also concludes, 'The experiences of Korea and Taiwan have shown that democratization could be a crucial factor which influences social welfare development' (p. 60). Furthermore, Gough extends this explanation to new welfare states in Southeast Asia,

> ... democracy is belatedly emerging in East Asia, at least in the form of opposition parties and contested elections. Korea and Taiwan both witnessed democratic contestation in 1987; the result was a significant shift towards state responsibility in social welfare in the 1990s. It is not too optimistic to expect similar transformations in Southeast Asia.

(2004: 201)

Beyond the state-led and top-down process of policy making in authoritarian regimes, the importance of democratization lies in the way it changes the policy context: expanding access to ideas and interests and allowing actors to participate in policy processes previously dominated by the state and its servants. Moreover, and secondly, democratization means a change in the relationship between the state and the people, from control and loyalty to accountability and political rights. Both, in turn, have a critical impact, or act as a constraint, to use Bresser-Pereira's (2005) term, on the policy process of instrument choice because policy-makers cannot ignore the voters' will.

Let us further elaborate this point. Differing from authoritarian regimes, democratic policy making should involve many actors and activists and not just those from the state sector. They may have different ideals and thus would like to pursue goals other than those of the state, and, more importantly, they must be able to bargain with, and even act against, the state's previous policy orientation. In his study of health policy in Taiwan and Korea, Wong (2004) provides a good example, concentrating his analysis on the impact of democratic change on social *policy making*. This change involves a dynamic and continuing process of democratization, altering all important elements of policy making in respect to agenda setting, interests and idea formation, and actors and networks involved. It also provides specific opportunities for policy change (ibid.). In other words, no one can now single-handedly set up a policy agenda and make decisions in a democratic political system. The new openness of the political setting also implies that advocates with their different, and even conflicting, policies are able to confront and debate with one another. There is not likely to be a single voice and a pluralistic approach will be the normal pattern in democratic policy making. This constitutes the most significant difference between authoritarian and democratic regimes.

On the other hand, democratization also alters the vertical relationship between the state and the people by endowing the people with more powers and rights against the dominance of the state and its agents. The top-down requirement of loyalty is no longer a necessary issue in defining citizenship within a specific territory. On the contrary, those who exercise public power should be answerable to those on whose behalf they exercise it. This does not only mean that those who control public institutions should be required to give an account to the public of their exercise of power, but also that there should be a means for the public to hold themselves accountable. For this reason, duration and election are both important and connected mechanisms for governments and policy-makers to use to make good their accountability to the people. Therefore, success in mobilizing maximum accountability and support determines the legitimacy of governments and governmental options and capacities in policy making and implementation. Rather than the top-down order and regulation in authoritarian regimes, governments and policy-makers maximize their accountability in democratic politics by processes of persuasion and discussion, through direct and indirect networks.

This provides support to Immergut's (1992) argument: 'Political institutions do not predetermine any specific policy outcome; rather, they construct a strategic context in which political actors make their choices' (p. 239). Democratization does not mean that welfare development is mandatory. Rather, it opens opportunities for policy-makers, stakeholders and people to rethink the welfare they would like to have and ways in which it can be provided.

By understanding this, we may now draw up a list of some important implications of democratization for policy instrument choice. First, as we discussed above, multiplicity of policy instruments is very likely to appear in a democracy and influence welfare instrument mixes, because instrument choice cannot be isolated from social and political settings where pluralism is usual. Second, as a result of the change of relationship between the state and the people and the multiplicity of policy instruments, 'vertical instruments' (e.g. command and control) will give way to 'horizontal instruments' (partnership and coordinated policy planning), in Ringeling's (2005) terms. More networking is essential to formulate and manage multiple instrument mixes.

Third, the challenge for governments and policy-makers lies not in merely choosing an effective instrument or mix of instruments but in choosing a *just* instrument, one that is both accountable to the people and accepted by them. Such an instrument is necessary for implementing policy in a pluralist and varied social setting. Here, our discussion moves on to the issue of governance, meaning the degree to which governments and policy-makers construct a reliable and tolerant context in which power can be shared, differences respected and discussed, interests coordinated, participation encouraged and an interest in the public good motivated. Crucial here is that the people should not fear the abuse of power and policy instruments in the pursuit of personal interests. The link between policy instrument and governance has been noted by some 'second-generation' scholars in relation to the instrument choice perspective, arguing: '. . . it is impossible to think analytically or sensibly about governance without also thinking about the tools or instruments that make it a practical reality. The reverse is true as well' (Eliadis et al. 2005: 5). However, how can such a context be created? It is not simply an instrument issue but depends on some kind of collective awareness of social solidarity beneath democratic politics. It depends essentially on relationships of trust.

Trust in social policy: theoretical considerations

In a plural and even more complicated society involving so many cultures, ideas, interests, actors, and networks, locally as well as globally, how to maintain and further promote social solidarity is now an issue pre-occupying contemporary governments and thinkers. Giddens (1998a) has long emphasized the importance of trust in the fractional post-modern society, arguing, for example, that trust is necessary to a solidaristic society in which interdependence and reciprocity together contribute to people's sense of community and security. Many scholars have addressed trust as a key element in policy making, though the themes they explore are not all the same.

Social capital theory

By emphasizing the social networks extending beyond individual families, social capital theory regards such networks as one of the factors, differing from both financial capital and human capital, facilitating successful action. To a certain extent, the concept has grown in importance in line with the understanding that a fractionized society requires more bonding, partnership and coordination across its various sectors. Trust remains important as an aspect of social capital for at least two reasons. The first is to bond individuals together within a society thus allowing that society to function successfully. According to Putnam (1995: 67) this involves: '. . . networks, norms and social trust that facilitate coordination and cooperation for mutual benefit.' The second reason is the ability of trust to erase doubts and uncertainties in a society and therefore decrease the potentially destructive impacts of pluralism. Rahn and Transue (1998: 545) define trust as, 'a standing decision to give most people – even those whom one does not know from direct experience – the benefit of the doubt.' In this sense, trust does not exist only within established relationships and social networks, but also extends to strangers. This is generalized or social trust, which relates to that placed in the formal institutions of governance (Baum and Ziersch 2003: 321).

Governance and trust

Trust is an aspect of governance, especially good governance, which functions to remedy the inevitable limitations of formal institutional arrangements. Although a healthy financial balance, an efficient and honest civil service and properly contested elections are often identified by international organizations as the key pillars of good governance, we should not overlook some more informal factors behind the process through which individuals and officials may interact to express their interests, exercise their rights and obligations, work out their differences, and cooperate to produce public goods and services. Even certain client-oriented measures, usually thought of as negative and destructive, may have hidden positive functions, such as giving poor people access to resources (Brinkerhoff and Goldsmith 1999). The distinction between good or bad governance can be determined by whether real democratic principles, such as transparency, pluralism, citizen involvement in decision making, representation and accountability, can be widely accepted and implemented, so the voices of the poorest and the most vulnerable are heard and understood. Giddens (1990) develops the concept of 'active trust' to mean 'on a personal level, decisions must be taken and policies forged. . . . No one can be completely outside' (pp. 148–149). Trust will be helpful in reducing the complexity of a globalizing and fractionalized world, and good governance is more likely to be secured if trust can be fostered and maintained.

Social exclusion/inclusion and trust

As no one should be left completely outside society and its production and distribution of public goods and services, the debate about social exclusion and inclusion pays much attention to the question of how people may trust each other in a community, even though there are so many differences between genders, classes, lifestyles and lifetimes. Based on the European experiences, promoting social inclusion requires collective efforts to achieve structural shifts measured by the four criteria of socio-economic security, social cohesion, social inclusion and social empowerment (Beck et al. 1997). Similarity implies a certain degree of assimilation and dominance and thus is not appropriate for combating social exclusion. Rather, combating social exclusion encompasses both objective and subjective interpretations. The former means a given standard of economic security and material welfare. The latter refers to the interaction between the individual's self-realization as a social being and the formation of collective identity, expressing cohesion and leading to collective empowerment. People have many differences, but their sense of inclusion and the ability to trust derive from a belief that there should not be institutional and systematic discrimination between people.

The third way

Leaving behind the left-wing approach, the third way aims to provide a new bridge between equality and meritocracy. As a key element of socialist thought, equality has long been accused of reducing people's competitive drive and motivation. In an ideal society of the new right, the distribution of income, wealth and opportunity will be according to individual talents and efforts and should never be equal. For Giddens, the founding father of the third way, this vision makes it difficult to work out a new approach between left and right. Blair (1998) argues that, 'Talent and efforts should be encouraged to flourish in all quarters, and governments must act decisively to end discrimination and prejudice' (p. 3). Giddens has recently taken a more positive view of meritocracy, one that he avoided in his previous work (1998b). He claims, 'a meritocratic approach to equality is inevitable . . . we should want a society that is more egalitarian than it is today, but which is meritocratic and pluralistic' (2002: 38). Giddens's own answer to the possible resulting problems lies in trust in the fairness of the social order. This enables people to feel more secure, believing that there is not always a downward course in their life. Without trust in the fairness of the system and a sense of underlying security, meritocracy will create a state of relative deprivation in which no one will really feel satisfied, no matter how open the society or how equal the outcomes.

Economic developmentalism and trust

In contrast to liberalist explanations of economic development in terms of relying on market mechanisms, the developmentalist strategy focuses on those elements in society seen as crucial for economic development. Several of the elements have been generally identified, including educational levels, physical infrastructure, corporate governance, competition and economic openness, political stability, and flexible labour markets. There are also other elements that might be better defined as social capital in particular, such as inter-personal trust, social cohesion, association and cooperation (Mkandawire 2004: 9). However, some scholars especially note the importance of trust. For example, in his study of economic success in the US, Germany and Japan, Fukuyama (1995) shows the success to be predicated on reservoirs of social trust, which, in turn, depend on some kind of associational infrastructure. Because of its important impact on the formation of trust and trust-creating social conditions, developmentalist scholars no longer regard social policy as pure consumption. As Kwon (2005) argues, for example, 'economic development requires social policy' (p. 5).

Can government promote trust?

We have discovered the importance of trust in many theoretical considerations for social policy. They all demonstrate that trust has been taken into account in policy making. However, whether governments can, and should, seek to promote trust in society remains a disputed question. If trust is purely a subjective state based on moral claims, it will most likely be an act of faith that cannot be rationally proven or objectively known. Given that trust is naturally determined by personal faith, a vast array of regulations and policies may destroy it because such measures are fundamentally contradicting its nature. Planned action by the state to create and enforce particular norms is not a new development, but the approach does make goals and policies unpopular. For instance, I would not change my favourite flavour of ice cream just because a new governmentally-approved flavour exists; I may eat the new ice cream, but this does not mean I like it. Similarly, it is very difficult to make a person feel trust through governmental exhortation, regulations and policies. For this reason, government cannot enforce trust.

However, our trust or distrust of a stranger is also a socially created situation or state which may be influenced by associations or groups, the characteristics and values of the society in which we are living and growing up, our past experiences with other people, and the historical legacy of our country. This implies that trust, especially social trust, can be promoted in a way that is somehow more indirect and generalized – it is some kind of social atmosphere and culture. It may be true that we cannot directly regulate and intervene in the formation of trust by public means but trust can be motivated and encouraged – and discouraged. Participation in voluntary associations has long been regarded as an important factor in fostering trust in society, and this, in turn, better enables society to create and maintain a real democracy, particularly from the social capital perspective. If civic participation is the mechanism to promote trust, governments could make an effort to provide secure settings in which people can join together, and organize and manage their associations freely and openly; rather than questioning people's participation in certain activities. In this case, governments and public policies are the ultimate guardians of the basic circumstance required for trust.

Therefore, governments and their policies cannot and should not ignore the aim of fostering trust. This is particularly important in the modern world where higher degrees of fraction, isolation, complexity, uncertainty and risk occur, challenging and shaking our existing primary inter-personal contacts and relationships. Moreover, the market is not a good mechanism to promote trust because it is itself a source of risk and uncertainty, dependent on competition, which is directly at odds with trust. In his study of trust in pension policy, Ring discovered the destructive impact of governments reluctant to play the role of securing financial market stability, leaving the people to take all the risks inherent in an uncertain pension future. He says:

> Trust is a key issue for financial services consumers. It expresses confidence in the ability of a person or system to help secure financial outcomes. Eventual outcomes are always contingent and uncertain, and trust does not provide a guarantee; but it allows individuals to 'manage' circumstances and complexities that might otherwise become overwhelming. Loss of trust in the financial service sector is therefore an important issue.

> (2005: 69)

Furthermore, Ring calls for governmental policies and actions to attempt to restore trust in the structures of private pension provision and even to accept a greater role for government as provider. Trust is even more important during the restructuring of existing welfare provision when people's benefits and wellbeing are threatened; this, in turn, could considerably damage trust-based public order. Governments must secure people's trust as policies are put forward for implementation. Ultimately, governments'accountability will be subjected to public scrutiny.

In the context of East Asia, the financial crisis has proved that the market is unable to provide a foundation of stability and people's economic security is critically threatened both nationally and globally. However, policy responses are different across countries. As we have discussed, Taiwan and Korea are moving towards larger degrees of welfare instrument mixes and state involvement, in accordance with democratization that requires more coordination between different sectors, more public participation in policy making, and more trust in governmental accountability and governance. The restructuring of the existing welfare system is a remarkable task of social engineering, but new welfare instrument mixes cannot on their own guarantee its success. Trust is crucial and the question of whether trust can be maintained and even promoted will largely determine the final outcome of welfare restructuring in Taiwan and Korea.

Though the situation is not the same, the Hong Kong government still provides a basic safety net, which operates mainly through social assistance and public provision and funding of medical care. Communities, associations and charities are still encouraged to become involved with welfare. In Hong Kong, people place their trust mostly in traditional networks at the community level, rather than in policy issues. In the case of Singapore, the government's reluctance to provide welfare is still significant; the CPF remains its single and most important pillar and use of welfare instrument mixes is less significant than in the other three societies. So far, government commitments to economic growth and full employment are the major areas of accountability. Trust, especially social trust, has not been systematically promoted in Singapore since the operation of the CPF is more an individual matter than an issue of public policy.

Concluding remarks: embedding trust in social policy

Instrument choice in policy making is moving discussion away from an overly simplistic analysis of means-and-ends relationships to analysis of instrument mixes and governance. More attention is now paid to the requirements of increased coordination, partnership, civil participation and network development in a more fractionalized and pluralised world. Trust is noted in many theoretical discussions as an important and necessary element in determining a just society, good governance and real democracy. We also argue that governments can, and should, promote trust in society by way of securing a context in which trust can grow and flourish, rather than by directly seeking to promote it.

In the East Asian cases, we also witness the emergence of welfare instrument mixes together with democratization particularly in Taiwan and Korea; Singapore, meanwhile, relies on its single CPF pillar. Welfare instrument mixes cannot guarantee policies working or not working. Whether governments can acquire trust from people is a key issue for policy-makers in East Asia. Beyond the basic choice of policy instruments, governments must work to embed the promotion of trust as an aim of the social order, as well as a step towards the construction of a trust-based politico-economic order.

Note

1 This chapter was first presented at the 'Changing Governance and Public Policy Paradigms: Asian Perspectives' international conference, Guangzhou, China, 19–20 November 2005. I appreciate the comments at the conference, as well as the supporting facilities available when I visited IR/PS, University of California, San Diego. Thanks are especially due to Paul Wilding, for his very helpful suggestions and revises on the earlier version of this chapter.

References

Adams, F., Gupta, S.D. and Mengisteab, K. (1999) 'Globalization and the developing world: an introduction', in F. Adams, S. D. Gupta and K. Mengisteab (eds), *Globalization and the Dilemmas of the State in the South*, Basingstoke: Macmillan.

Aspalter, C. (2001) *Conservative Welfare State Systems in East Asia*, Westport, CT: Praeger.

Axford, B. (1995) *The Global System: Economics, Politics and Culture*, Cambridge: Polity Press.

Baum, F.E. and Ziersch, A.M. (2003) Social capital, *Journal of Epidemiology and Community Health*, 57(5): 320–323.

Beck, W., Maesen, L. and Walker, A. (1997) *The Social Quality of Europe*, Bristol: Policy Press.

Blair, T. (1998) *The Third Way: New Politics for the New Century*, London: Fabian Society.

Bresser-Pereira, L.C. (2005) *Democracy and Public Management Reform: Building the Republican State*, Oxford: Oxford University Press.

Bressers, H.T. and O'Toole, L.J. (2005) Instrument selection and implementation in a networked context, in P. Eliadis, M. M. Hill, and M. Howlett (eds), *Designing Government: From Instruments to Governance*, Montreal & Kingston: McGill-Queen's University Press.

Brinkerhoff, D.W. and Goldsmith, A.A. (2005) Institutional dualism and international development: a revisionist interpretation of good governance, *Administration and Society*, 37(2): 199–224.

Colebatch, H.K. (1998) *Policy*, Minneapolis: University of Minnesota Press.

Dixon, J. and Chow, N.W.S. (1992) Social security in the Asian Pacific region, *Journal of International and Comparative Social Welfare*, 5(1): 1–29.

Eliadis, P., Hill, M.M. and Howlett, M. (2005) Introduction, in P. Eliadis, M. M. Hill and M. Howlett (eds), *Designing Government: From Instruments to Governance*, Montreal & Kingston: McGill-Queen's University Press.

Esping-Andersen, G. (1990) *The Three Worlds of Welfare Capitalism*, Cambridge: Polity Press.

Fukuyama, F. (1995) *Trust: The Social Virtues and the Creation of Prosperity*, London: Hamish Hamilton.

Giddens, A. (1987) *The Nation-state and Violence*, Cambridge: Polity Press.

Giddens, A. (1990) *The Consequences of Modernity*, Cambridge: Polity Press.

Giddens, A. (1998a) Post-traditional civil society and the radical center, *New Perspectives Quarterly*, 15(2): 14–20.

Giddens, A. (1998b) *The Third Way: The Renewal of Social Democracy*, Cambridge: Polity Press.

Giddens, A. (2002) *Where Now for New Labour?*, Cambridge: Polity Press.

Gough, I. (2004) East Asia: the limits of productivist regimes, in I. Gough and G. Wood (eds), *Insecurity and Welfare Regimes in Asia, Africa and Latin America: Social Policy in Development Contexts*, Cambridge: Cambridge University Press.

Holliday, I. (2000) Productivist welfare capitalism: social policy in East Asia, *Political Studies*, 48(4): 706–723.

Holliday, I. (2005) East Asian social policy in the wake of the financial crisis: farewell to productivism?, *Policy and Politics*, 33(1): 145–162.

Howlett, M. (2005) What is a policy instrument? Tools, mixes, and implementation styles, in P. Eliadis, M. M. Hill and M. Howlett (eds), *Designing Government: From Instruments to Governance*, Montreal & Kingston: McGill-Queen's University Press.

Immergut, E.M. (1992) *Health Politics: Interests and Institutions in Western Europe*, Cambridge: Cambridge University Press.

Jacobs, D. (1998) *Social Welfare Systems in East Asia: A Comparative Analysis Including Private Welfare*, CASEpaper 10, London: London School of Economics.

Johnson, N. (1987) *Welfare State in Transition: The Theory and Practice of Welfare Pluralism*, London: Prentice Hall.

Jones, C. (1990) Hong Kong, Singapore, South Korea and Taiwan: Oikonomic welfare states, *Government and Opposition*, 25(3): 446–462.

Jones, C. (1993) The Pacific challenge: Confucian welfare states, in C. Jones (ed), *New Perspectives on the Welfare State in Europe*, London: Routledge.

Ku, Y.W. (1997) *Welfare Capitalism in Taiwan: State, Economy and Social Policy*, Basingstoke: Macmillan.

Ku, Y.W. (2003) Social security, in I. Holliday and P. Wilding (eds), *Welfare Capitalism in East Asia: Social Policy in the Tiger Economies*, Basingstoke: Palgrave Macmillan.

Kwon, H.J. (1999) *The Welfare State in Korea: The Politics of Legitimation*, Basingstoke: Macmillan.

Kwon, H.J. (2005) An overview of the study: the developmental welfare state and policy reforms in East Asia, in H. J. Kwon (ed.), *Transforming the Developmental Welfare state in East Asia*, Basingstoke: Palgrave Macmillan.

Midgley, J. (1986) Industrialization and welfare: the case of the four little tigers, *Social Policy and Administration*, 20(3): 225–238.

Mkandawire, T. (2004) Social policy in a development context: introduction, in T. Mkandawire (ed.), *Social Policy in a Development Context*, Basingstoke: Palgrave Macmillan.

Putnam, R.D. (1995) Bowling alone: America's declining social capital, *Journal of Democracy*, 6(1): 65–78.

Rahn, W.M. and Transue, J.E. (1998) Social trust and value change: the decline of social capital in American youth, 1976–1995, *Political Psychology*, 19(3): 545–565.

Ramesh, M. (2004) *Social Policy in East and Southeast Asia: Education, Health, Housing, and Income Maintenance*, London: Routledge.

Ring, P.J. (2005) Trust in UK pension policy: a different approach?, *Policy and Politics*, 33(1): 55–74.

Ringeling, A.B. (2005) Instruments in four: the elements of policy design, in P. Eliadis, M. M. Hill and M. Howlett (eds), *Designing Government: From Instruments to Governance*, Montreal & Kingston: McGill-Queen's University Press.

Tang, K.L. (2000) *Social Welfare Development in East Asia*, Basingstoke: Palgrave Macmillan.

Walker, A. and Wong, C.K. (2005) Introduction: East Asian welfare regimes, in A. Walker and C. K. Wong (eds), *East Asian Welfare Regimes in Transition: From Confucianism to Globalization*, Bristol: Policy Press.

Wong, J. (2004) *Healthy Democracies: Welfare Politics in Taiwan and South Korea*, Ithaca: Cornell University Press.

8   Regulatory reform and private sector development in China

A case study of downsizing administrative licences[1]

Bill Chou

In China, ideological suspicion against private sector development has been dissipating. It is a consensus that a healthy private sector can contribute to poverty reduction and job creation, as well as private consumption and economic growth. Further private sector development requires a reform of regulatory regime to improve the business environment and encourage business people to invest. Reforms of regulatory regime encompass many measures. This chapter focuses on administrative licence downsizing, and is structured in the following way: it introduces the background and impact of administrative licensing systems on private sector development.

The chapter then outlines the contours of downsizing measures. Administrative Licensing Law, a major downsizing instrument, is comprehensively discussed. In the end, the outcome of the implementation of downsizing measures will be evaluated. It is found that many measures of administrative licence downsizing have not been implemented. Based on an institutional analysis, this chapter argues that the institutional features of China's bureaucracy have shaped the incentive system in such a way that local public officials have a greater incentive to maintain burdensome licensing systems for pursuing local economic growth than to reduce business activities requiring licences. The barriers involved in policy coordination and monitoring enable local public officials to hide their activities from their principals' scrutiny and ignore those central directives which conflict with local agendas. The institutional weaknesses in the mechanisms for reining in local public officials have given them high discretionary power to distort many national policies going against their interests, the policy of administrative licence downsizing included.

Regulatory reform in China: background

Regulatory reforms are widely used for resolving economic problems because of the reforms' potential in encouraging private investment and boosting GDP without incurring government expenditure and debt. Two models of regulatory reform have been identified. One is an Anglo-American tradition and increasingly European trend of correcting market failure. Behind the model are mistrust of government and worship of market: the government should refrain from intervening in the market to reduce inefficiency. Government's primary function is to ensure smooth market functioning and deal with market failure such as protection of public health and safety. A desirable regulatory reform is one seeking to reduce the regulatory costs for firms (such as the costs of adapting business processes to meet regulatory requirements, licensing fees, delays in obtaining regulatory approval, costs of time, and bribery used for dealing with officials) to a level no higher than necessary to tackle market failure. The advocacy of anti-trust, transparency and competition is largely based on this model. The second model is a developmental state model represented by Japan, Korea and Taiwan. The advocates of this model display a high trust in government. They believe that public officials should actively foster technological development and designate particular industries and businesses for government support. This model is characterized by government's extensive use of licences to influence economic development. For the purposes of protecting these industries from 'excessive' competition, accumulating a technological foundation for quick modernization, and facilitating 'late developers' being able to catch up with those countries which industrialized early, no companies are able to alter their mode of production, or import particular products without appropriate licences (Carlile and Tilton 1998).

China's regulatory reform exhibits similar models and characteristics shared with many transition and developing economies. China's regulatory reform is a mix of corporatization, privatization, deregulation and re-regulation. It is a response to the de-nationalization of public *ownership* (such as telecommunications), rise of new economic activities (such as insurance and the stock exchange), emergence of market failure (such as coalmine accidents, shoddy product quality and environmental pollution), and the perceived necessity of protecting domestic enterprises against foreign competition resulting from trade liberalization (such as banking). In contrast to the Anglo-American model – which emerges out of market failure, a mistrust of public officials and a developmental state model that searches means to fast-track modernization through state planning – the regulatory regime of China has been constructed primarily out of the need for filling the regulatory vacuum left by the state's rolling back from the micro-management of the economy (Pearson 2004). A burdensome licensing system forms the basis of a regulatory regime. Like their counterparts in many developing countries, public officials in China often use various administrative and business licences to extract rent. Removing officials' licensing authority and the opportunities for extracting rent by downsizing regulations relating to the private sector has become a major strategy in the latest round of regulatory reform.

In comparison to other developing countries, China's licensing system for regulating businesses on paper is not particularly burdensome (see Table 8.1). However, China's business environment is still far from investor-friendly. The licensing system is arbitrary, cost inflating and inconsistent. Setting up a local

Table 8.1 A comparison of selected indicators of business regulations in eight developing countries in 2003

Business regulation indicators	Countries								World average (countries of low and middle income)
	China	India	Indonesia	Malaysia	Thailand	Philippines	Brazil	Argentina	
Number of start-up procedures	11	10	11	8	9	11	15	15	11
Time to start a business (days)	46	88	168	31	42	59	152	68	65
Employment law index[1]	47	51	57	25	61	60	78	66	55

Note:
1 Employment law index ranges from 0 (less rigid) to 100 (very rigid).

Source: World Bank (2004: 262–264).

Table 8.2 A comparison of the minimum capital requirement in eight developing countries in 2003

	Countries								World average (Countries of low and middle income)
	China	India	Indonesia	Malaysia	Thailand	Philippines	Brazil	Argentina	
Minimum capital requirement (percentage of GNI per capita)	3856	430	303	0	0	10	0	0	118

Source: World Bank (2004: 262–264).

retail business needs 112 licences from different departments. Gaining approval for importing certain types of foreign equipment may require six months or longer (Meng 2004). Moreover, public officials have high discretionary power to revoke licences. The government of an unnamed city may suddenly revoke the business licences of some 100 joint ventures without any prior notice or legal grounds. Beijing municipality once revoked the permission granted to the fast-food chain giant McDonald's for establishing a restaurant in a prime location (Ambler and Witzel 2004: 84). In 2003, the public security bureau of Leqing city of Zhejiang province withdrew 150 business licences of man-powered tricycles auctioned in 1999, and penalized the licence holders who refused to return the licences (Liu 2006). An unnamed city arbitrarily withdrew the operational licences of schools below the government-imposed benchmark without compensation or grace period (Zhao 2006). Moreover, many regulations and policies adhered to by different levels of government were inconsistent with each other. The resultant unpredictable business environment, as the Asian Development Bank pointed out, had put off many private investment projects, especially those involving more than one level of government, because the risk involved in these projects is difficult to calculate and prohibitively high. Licensing barriers also precluded private sector entry to the market sectors dominated, but badly served, by state-owned enterprises. To get things done, many investors had to rely on personal relationships and bribery to transcend the red tape. The consequences were a lower level of private investment, a lower degree of institutionalization of administration, rampant corruption and business cost inflation (Asian Development Bank 2003).

The burdensome regulatory framework has not been created in a vacuum. It was established when the market system was budding and the private sector was insignificant. Many new regulations were targeted at big state-owned companies and reflected a greater emphasis on economic security than efficiency values. Investors were required to put down a large registered capital and undergo strict examinations before starting a business so that the risks for creditors – which were from the state sector – could be minimized. Less resourceful investors from the private sector were then barred from entering markets. Therefore the minimum capital requirement as a percentage of GNI per capita in China is the second highest in the world, following Syria at 5.627 per cent (see Table 8.2). Also, regulators take a highly interventionist approach to market regulation and oblige investors to prove their technical abilities measured against government-imposed standards before they can enter markets. The dynamics of commerce and convenience to private businesses are not regulators' main concern (All-China Federation of Industry and Commerce 2005: 20; Jiao 2005).

The decentralized public finance system is another barrier to the formation of a business-friendly regulatory regime. The Chinese government has decentralized much of its economic authority to local governments in order to motivate them to achieve higher economic growth. This decentralization has turned the Chinese economy into, using the terms of Qian and Weingast (1995), 'market-preserving federalism'. However, local governments are not authorized to adjust the rates of local taxes or to create new taxes. Without adequate tax revenue, many local governments have to rely on extra-budgetary revenue – the government revenue not included from planned revenue. It includes both officially sanctioned and semi-legal (and illegal) levies beyond the narrowly defined formal budget (Breslin 1996: 129; Lü 2000: 218; Wong 1997: 60). Examples of extra-budgetary revenue include various fines and licence fees. Licence fees are huge and provide an important source of extra-budgetary funds. The abolition of 78 business activities requiring licences (or licensing items) in Zhejiang province engendered a loss of licence fee revenue of 120 million *yuan* (US$14.96 million) a year (Luo and Yu 2005: 21).[2] Heilongjiang provincial finance bureau predicted that the downsizing of 152 licensing items in 2006 would reduce its revenue by 300 million *yuan* (Xian and Yu 2006). Between May and September 2003, Yanggang, a medium-sized city in western Guangdong province, had to give up 22.97 million *yuan* due to administrative licence downsizing (Xiao 2004).

The level of licence revenue may also impact the amount of subsidies paid to public officials (a regular monthly income, usually paid in cash but sometimes in kind). In the late 1990s, subsidies accounted for around 70 to 85 per cent of the total income of individual public officials (Chou 2004: 230). In view of the impact of extra-budgetary revenue on their wellbeing, local leaders are highly motivated to create and defend licence revenue.[3] They may assign a quota of extra-budgetary revenue that individual departments must generate. The size of bonuses and penalties paid to public officials (a more irregular cash income) is often linked to the amount of extra-budgetary revenue they generate, even though central government has ruled out this practice. In 1995, Yulin city, in the Guangxi Autonomous Region, imposed a highway fee collection target of RMB 12 million *yuan* (US$1.44 million) on the city's highway management office. The subsidies of the office's employees would be cut back if they missed the target. If they generated more than the target, they could retain 80 per cent of the surplus for subsidies (Qin 1996).

Often, licensing items were created purely for generating revenue but not regulating markets. An entrepreneur of Yanggang city complained that the city labour bureau required him to use 'appointment cards' (*shang gang zhen*) for all his employees. Each appointment card cost him over 100 *yuan*. The fee collected was supposed to finance government-sponsored induction courses for new employees. In the end, no courses were organized. Another agricultural entrepreneur complained that the traffic bureau of the city charged him a 1,000 *yuan* vehicle maintenance fee every year without providing any meaningful maintenance service in return (Xiao 2004).

The implication of licence provision is furthered complicated by the narrow focus of local leaders' performance appraisals in relation to local economic development and the opportunistic behaviour of local leaders resulting from a job rotation system. On the basis of a Soviet practice of industrial management in which factory managers were appraised according to sets of specific production quotas, the CCP introduced a cadre responsibility system in the early 1980s to hold local leaders responsible for specific performance targets that were skewed towards economic growth. The current performance appraisal of local leaders is largely modeled on this system.

Exact performance targets vary across the country, depending on the economic structure of the regions that local leaders oversee. Many of these performance targets are related to economic development, such as industrial and GDP growth, the amount of tax and non-tax revenue generated, and foreign direct investment. The achievement of these targets is linked to cadres' future advancement, the level of their bonus, and punishment (Edin 2003; Zhong 2003). In the meantime, central leaders are often worried that local leaders may establish their own patronage and breed corruption and localism (a tendency of defying central directives for local interests). Thus local leaders are posted to different localities at regular intervals, usually three years for county magistrates and five years for the governors of upper-level governments; shorter periods of time are not uncommon, however. The performance appraisal and job rotation systems shape local leaders' behaviour in such way that they are keen to promote policies benefiting the local economy, regardless of the policies' impact on neighbouring regions and the country as a whole. Their short terms of office encourage them to pursue immediate work achievement at the expense of long-term policies, such as improvement of the business environment and product quality. Therefore, many local leaders rely on regional protectionist measures: through a licensing system, they can raise the barriers of market entry for outside entrepreneurs and products to protect local business interests. The municipalities of Shanghai and Beijing were reported to support their own car industry by instructing the taxi companies in their respective cities to use the sedan cars manufactured by local producers. Shanghai charged non-Shanghai made sedan cars higher licence fees to undermine their competitiveness (Lardy 2002: 29–62). As a result of a high degree of financial autonomy and local leaders' peculiar incentive systems, local governments, especially those with small tax bases, have strong motives for safeguarding and expanding their licensing authority.

Regulatory barriers have not stopped the Chinese economy from growing. Private sector development remains robust. Foreign investment is huge. From the perspective of economic growth, downsizing administrative licences is non-urgent if not unnecessary. The accession to the WTO has made the matter different. China's regulatory framework fails to live up to China's three major commitments:

- *Transparency*: The use of secretive decrees (*hongtou wenjian*) to create new regulations is incompatible with Paragraph 332 of the Report of the Working Party of the Accession of China (hereafter 'the Report of the Working Party'), stating that China would:

... publish in the official journal, by appropriate classification and by service where relevant, a list of all organizations, including those organizations delegated such authority from the national authorities, that were responsible for authorizing, approving or regulating services' activities whether through grant of licence or other approval. Procedures and the conditions for obtaining such licences or approval would also be published.

- *Uniform administration of trade regime*: Inconsistency of regulations among different levels of government contradicts Paragraphs 73, 75 and 68:

  > ... the provisions of the WTO Agreement ... would be applied uniformly throughout its customs territory, including in SEZs [Special Economic Zones] and other areas where special regimes for tariffs, taxes and regulations were established and at all levels of government.
  >
  > (Paragraph 73)

  > All individuals and entities could bring to the attention of central government authorities cases of non-uniform application of China's trade regime ... Such cases would be referred promptly to the responsible government agency, and when non-uniform application was established, the authorities would act promptly to address the situation utilizing the remedies available under China's laws, taking into consideration China's international obligations and the need to provide a meaningful remedy ...
  >
  > (Paragraph 75)

  > ... the central government would undertake in a timely manner to revise or annul administrative regulations or departmental rules if they were inconsistent with China's obligations under the WTO Agreement and Draft Protocol.
  >
  > (Paragraph 68)

- *Licensing issues*: Blocking market access through licences and charging exorbitant licence fees conflict with paragraphs 308 and 308(d), respectively:

  > ... China would ensure that China's licensing procedures and conditions would not act as barriers to market access and would not be more trade restrictive than necessary.
  >
  > (Paragraph 308)

> Any fees charged . . . would be commensurate with the administrative cost of processing an application.
>
> (Paragraph 308(d))

These commitments have profound impacts: the Chinese government is obliged to reform its business regulatory framework as soon as possible. All levels of government in China have to stop using hidden documents to create their licensing authority. Licensing authority must be based on national legislation, which, in turn, has to be kept in line with WTO requirements. Business licences should not cost more than necessary for actually processing a licence application. Setting up regional trade blocs through licensing is prohibited.

Strategies for downsizing administrative licences

Downsizing administrative licences may be construed as the second stage of structural reform since the early 1980s.[4] By the end of the 1990s, the Chinese government had launched several rounds of administrative licence downsizing. In the 1998 administrative reform, most industrial ministries were either transformed into quasi-governmental industrial associations or downgraded and merged with other ministries. Many administrative licences disappeared, together with these industrial ministries. In September 2001, the State Council set up an interdepartmental State Council Leadership Small Group on the Reform of the System of Administrative Licensing (*Guowuyuan xingzheng shenpi zhidu gaige gongzuo lingdao xiaozu*) to improve the coordination of downsizing. Through several rounds of downsizing, the State Council ceded authority on 1,795 licensing items. Some of these abandoned licensing items were annulled altogether, whereas others were handed over to industrial associations and intermediary agencies (Meng 2004). The downsizing campaign soon penetrated into many local governments (see Table 8.3). Licence fee costs, which used to be secret, were now made public. Licence applicants deposited the fees directly into bank accounts under the scrutiny of finance bureaus to prevent the fees from being embezzled. The licensing procedures were streamlined by setting up one-stop service centres. Complaint centres and telephone hotlines were set up to keep rent-seeking behaviour in check (Yang 2004: 154–175).

These rounds of downsizing, however, could not prevent some annulled licensing items from being re-established at a later date. The number of licensing items in Shenzhen city rose to 652 in 2001 after having been slashed from 1091 to 463 in 2000 (*Shizhenfu* 2001: A1). Guangdong province slashed the number to 1,205 in June 2000. Soon afterwards, the number rose to 1,519 (*Guanshe shishi* 2006). To stop licensing items from being re-established, the National People's Congress (hereafter NPC, the national legislature) enacted the Administrative Licensing Law (hereafter 'the Law') and institutionalized the procedures of creating licences through restricting administrative power and increasing the transparency of licensing procedures. The drafting of the

Table 8.3 The number of licensing items in selected governments

Year	Governments	Original items	Items relinquished	Percentage of items relinquished
1999	Heilongjian provincial government	2325	1283	55.18
1999	Henan provincial government	2706	1764	65.19
2000	Zhejiang provincial government	1372	751	54.7
2000	Tianjin city government	935	n.a.	40+
2000	Shenzhen city government	1091	463	42.44
2001	Shenzhen city government	652	277	42.48
2001	Shanghai city government	n.a.	n.a.	40

Sources: Wang (1998), Li (2000: 15), Shizhengfu tisu xiaoguo xianzhu (2001, 15 October, p. A1), Hu and Guo (2002: 245).

Law began in the mid-1990s. It took almost five years to finish the consultation with various stakeholders before the State Council started drafting the Law in 2000. The NPC Standing Committee reviewed the draft law in 2002 and passed it on 27 August 2003. The effective date of the Law was postponed to 1 July 2004 to allow local governments more time for aligning their licence regulations with the Law (*Xingzhen xukefa* 2004).

Several provisions of the Law are noteworthy: Article 12 states that only six broad market sectors require licences for market access.[5] Article 25 removes the licensing authority created by sub-provincial governments. All licensing authority granted to sub-provincial governments must be either based on national laws or delegated from provincial-level governments. Article 15, in turn, restricts provincial-level governments: the licensing items created by provincial-level governments may only be valid for one year, at most. An enactment from provincial people's congresses (legislatures at provincial level) is required to extend the validity of the licensing items. Furthermore, this Article addresses issues of regional protectionism: it prohibits local governments from using licences to restrict market entry and import of products, services and labour. Article 13 signifies state retreat from licensing. It states that government departments should not create licensing items when business activities can be effectively regulated by: (1) citizens, legal entities and 'other organs'; (2) market competition; (3) industrial associations; and (4) post-verification.

Several provisions seek to address rent-seeking. Article 27 prohibits licence-issuing departments from compelling licence applicants to purchase particular products produced by the departments or enterprises linked to them. Article 58 allows departments to charge licence fees only if: (1) the fees are stipulated in laws or administrative decrees, and (2) the public has prior knowledge of the fees. This provision reflects the Law's convergence with Paragraph 308(a) of the Report of the Working Party, stating: 'China's licensing procedures and conditions were published prior to becoming effective'. In contrast to the user charge principle widely used in industrialized countries, Article 58 requires licensing departments to cover administrative cost by their budgets. This requirement is even stricter than the commitment in the Report of the Working Party Paragraph 308(d) discussed above, which permits charging licence fees to cover operating costs.

Transparency issues are addressed in the following provisions. Article 5 states that unless state or business secrets or privacy are involved, *hongtou wenjian* cannot be used as sources of licensing authority. Article 19 states that before introducing new licensing items, provincial-level governments should consult the public through public hearing – a means of consultation increasingly popular in China. Article 42 mandates departments to inform applicants of the result of their licence applications in 60 days. Article 50 reflects the rule of 'silence as consent', stipulating that if departments fail to deal with licence holders' applications for renewing their licences within 30 days, the licences will be automatically renewed. These articles converge with the requirement in Paragraph 308(f) of the Report of the Working Party concerning speedy decisions on licence applications.

As suggested in Paragraph 308(a) of the Report of the Working Party concerning publishing China's licensing procedures and conditions prior to the date they come into effect, the State Council issued Directive No. 412 and published a list of 500 licensing items two days before the Law came into effect. No departments can issue licences on matters beyond these 500 items, down from 4,000 items in 2002 (Meng 2002). Most of the licensing items fall under the jurisdictions of market regulation departmentds, such as the General Administration of Civil Aviation, the Ministry of Information Industry, the China Insurance Regulatory Commission, the China Securities Regulatory Commission, the State Development and Reform Commission and the Ministry of Commerce (see Table 8.4).

Most licensing authority had now been centralized by the State Council. Central bureaucracies are responsible for almost 70 per cent of these items (see Figure 8.1). Centralization has extended to the provincial and sub-provincial branches of some central organs, such as the Securities Regulatory Commission, the Insurance Regulatory Commission, the Banking Regulatory Commission, the Ministry of Railway and the State Environmental Protection Administration, which have now become executive agents of the central organ with no authority for licensing. The provincial branches of the Ministry of Information for Industry and the Bank of China are allowed to keep only two licensing items. Less than 16 per cent of the licensing items have been assigned to sub-provincial governments. This centralization policy

Table 8.4 Surveys of managers on business environments

Ministries and Commissions	No. of items	Organizations directly under the State Council	No. of items
Ministry of Information Industry	21	General Administration of Civil Aviation	44
Ministry of Railways	21	General Administration of Press and Publication	14
State Development and Reform Commission	17	General Administration of Customs	12
Ministry of Commerce	18	State Administration of Radio, Film and Television	11
People's Bank of China	15	State Environmental Protection Administration	8
Ministry of Public Security	9	State Food and Drug Administration	8
Ministry of Finance	7	State Administration for Religious Affairs	7
Ministry of Water Resources	7	General Administration of Quality Supervision, Inspection and Quarantine	7
State Commission of Science, Technology and Industry for National Defence	7	State Forestry Administration	5
Ministry of Health	6	State Administration for Industry and Commerce	4
Ministry of Communications	6	National Tourism Administration	3
Ministry of Education	6	State Administration of Taxation	2
Ministry of Justice	5	State Administration of Work Safety	1
Ministry of Labour and Social Security	5	General Administration of Sport	1
Ministry of Culture	4		
Ministry of Construction	3	**Administrative Offices under the State Council**	**No. of items**
Ministry of Personnel	2	Information Office	2
Ministry of Agriculture	2	Overseas Chinese Affairs Office	1
Ministry of Land and Resources	2	Hong Kong and Macao Affairs Office	1
Ministry of State Security	1		

(*Continued Overleaf*)

Table 8.4 Continued

Ministries and Commissions	No. of items	Organizations directly under the State Council	No. of items
Ministry of Civil Affairs	1	Administrations and Bureaus under the Ministries and Commissions	No. of items
Ministry of Science and Technology	1	State Administration of Foreign Exchange	31
		State Oceanic Administration	6
Institutions Directly under the State Council	No. of items	State Administration of Foreign Experts Affairs	5
China Insurance Regulatory Commission	38	State Bureau of Cultural Relics	6
China Securities Regulatory Commission	23	State Tobacco Monopoly Administration	2
China Banking Regulatory Commission	5	State Bureau of Surveying and Mapping	1
Xinhua News Agency	2	State Post Bureau	1
China Earthquake Administration	1		
China Meteorological Administration	1		
		Total number of licensing items: 419[1]	

Note:

1 The figure is higher than the 386 licensing items stipulated in Directive No. 412. The discrepancy in figure is due to the involvement of more than one department in approving certain licensing items and the consequential double counting.

Source: Zhonghua renmin gongheguo guowuyuan ling di xiyier hao (2004).

is conducive to standardizing commercial practices, implementing trade-related policies uniformly across the country, and tackling the problems of inconsistent regulations.

Evaluation and analysis

Successful cases of administrative licence downsizing have been reported. Central government and Guangdong province declared the previous regulations on chemical industries void and revoked subordinate departments' licensing authority on chemical industries (Yu and Tan 2005). Wuhan city declared that 48 government documents for creating licences were ineffective. Ningxia province annulled 170 items of administrative licensing. Liaoning province annulled almost half of its licensing items. Gulou district of Nanjing city reduced its licensing items from 278 to 53 (Mao and Ming 2005).

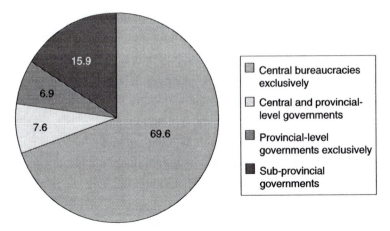

Figure 8.1 Distribution of licensing items among central bureaucracies (%).

Note: The category of 'Sub-Provincial Governments' refers to the licensing items either under the exclusive jurisdiction of sub-provincial governments, or administered jointly with provincial-level governments and/or central bureaucracies.

Source: Zhonghua renmin gongheguo guowuyuan ling di xiyier hao (2004).

Chongqing city planned to reduce the processing time of licence applications for construction projects involving land acquisition from 350 days to between 110 and 150 days. The city government predicted that if the downsizing was successfully implemented, licence fees worth hundreds of thousands of *yuan* could be saved (Lan 2006). Guangdong province annulled the Regulations on Pesticide Management, implying that no licences were necessary for trading pesticides. The province also permitted foreign investors to trade pesticides by the end of 2004 and fertilizers by the end of 2006. Domestic private entrepreneurs were granted equal footing with foreign investors, and may now enter all the markets open to foreign investors (Yu 2005). Caution is necessary when interpreting this success, however. There is no knowing whether the improvement is due to administrative licence downsizing or other measures: an earlier longitudinal survey (see Table 8.5) reported that a number of business managers observed an improvement in government efficiency and business environment before the Law came into effect. Moreover, the most chosen option in the survey was 'unchanged'. This reflected the lack of substantial change in government efficiency.

Other survey data suggest a gloomier picture. A survey of 1,500 citizens in seven cities suggested that the Law failed to live up to its public expectation regarding its ability to improve administrative efficiency. The survey, conducted by Social Survey Institute of China at the end of 2004, revealed that 73 per cent of the respondents did not feel the Law had improved administrative efficiency; 76 per cent of the respondents thought that local government had watered down the effect of the Law; and 49 per cent believed that

Table 8.5 Distribution of licensing items among central bureaucracies

| Answers questions | Year | | | | | |
| | 2003 | | | 2005 | | |
	Improved (%)	Unchanged (%)	Deteriorated (%)	Improved (%)	Unchanged (%)	Deteriorated (%)
Do you think government efficiency has improved?	41.6	47.2	11.2	40.2	46.3	13.5
Do you think the problem of regional protectionism has improved?	25.4	59.7	14.9	31.8	60.0	8.2

Source: Centre of Human Resources Research and Training, Development and Research Centre of the State Council (2002, 2005).

individual public officials had circumvented the Law (Jin 2004). With regard to creating a pro-competition business environment, this policy has achieved only limited success. A survey of business managers in 2005 revealed that 34, 58.1 and 7.9 per cent of the respondents, respectively, thought the problems associated with barriers to market entry had been alleviated, unchanged and worsened. Discriminatory administrative licensing procedures remained the most cited factor impeding business expansion, with 42.9 per cent of the respondents thinking so, followed by discriminatory quality inspection standard (38.2 per cent), exorbitant fees and unpredictable taxation policies (27.8 per cent), restrictions on import and sale (23.5 per cent) and discrimin-atory price restriction (17.3 per cent) (Centre of Human Resources Research and Training, Development Research Centre of the State Council 2006). It has to be emphasized that over 17 per cent of the respondents in the survey worked in state-owned enterprises. State-owned enterprises are better pro-tected by local governments and are therefore able to bypass administrative barriers more easily. If respondents from state-owned enterprises had been excluded and only private entrepreneurs had been interviewed, the percentage of respondents expressing negative opinions about licensing issues would have been higher.

In addition, implementation of the Administrative Licensing Law has been watered down by old licensing practices. According to the State Council Dir-ective Number 412, provincial governments are permitted to keep 144 licens-ing items. However, Sichuan province kept 383 items (Gao 2005) and Fujian province kept 445 (*Fujian sheng* 2006). Selective implementation occurs in the form of substantial delays. Private business people are allowed to trade agricultural factor inputs – such as seeds, fertilizers and pesticides – according to the Article 12 of the Law. By the end of 2005, the trade was still under state monopoly in Guangdong province. Private entrepreneurs in Guangzhou city were denied licences to run businesses selling agricultural factor inputs because the agriculture bureau in charge of agricultural licences ran a company in this business (Yang 2005; Yu 2005; Yu and Tan 2005).

Certain localities violated Article 58 of the Law prohibiting licences fees. Foreign-invested enterprises in Lianyungan city of Jiangsu province with a registered capitalization of US$3 million or above have to obtain at least 11 licences and pay a licence fee of 15,000 *yuan* before starting any business. The city also violated Article 26; it failed to designate one department to handle licence applications involving more than one department. Only the urban management department, of 50 departments with licensing authority, followed this Article. Also the city government did not annul all of its illegal licensing items: 109 out of its 428 illegal licensing items remained in force (Chen 2005: 75; Yan 2005: 44). Efforts to alleviate legislative inconsistency and create a uniform trade regime have been compromised. Some depart-ments of Guangzhou city broke Article 5 of the Law by maintaining the practice of referring to *hongtou wenjian* or even department directors' per-sonal opinions in the creation of licensing items. The city's industry and commerce bureau justified some of its licensing authority by quoting the *hongtou wenjian* 'State Council Directive Number 68' issued in 1988 (Yang 2006; Yu and Tan 2005).

It may take several years before the impact of administrative licence downsizing become more obvious. At this stage, it can be concluded that the success of administrative licence downsizing is mixed. In fact, the CCP has several means of leverage to apply to sub-national governments to ensure their subservience, such as the control of the appointment of the leadership of provincial-level and prefectural-level governments (the level of governments immediately below provincial level), interlocking positions between the CCP and state apparatus, the job rotation system, and the establishment of leading party members' groups (*dangzu*) in Party and state apparatus. Why are local governments under strict political control able to defy central policies in downsizing administrative licences? Lü (1999) characterized the phenomenon that policy executors in communist countries distort national policies as communist neo-traditionalism, a concept first used by Walder in his analysis of bureaucratic behaviour in the Chinese communist regime. Lü stated that public officials in communist regimes often refused to adapt themselves to the 'modern' (such as rational, empirical and impersonal) bureaucratic structures imposed by political elites. Instead they reshaped the processes behind the structures so that traditional (or patrimonial) modes of operation could be reinforced and elaborated. The concept of communist neo-traditionalism can be illustrated through an analysis of the institutional features of the local political landscape. Institutional features here refer to both the formal rules and informal practices that regularize individuals' behaviour and structure the relationships among individuals in polities and economies (Hall 1992: 96). The interactions between central policy-makers and local leaders can be considered principal–agent relationships. From a principal–agent perspective, agents have incentives to hide information or falsify reports to their principals because the information may provide clues for their fault-finding principals and expose their wrongdoings. Also, the role of agents in information gate-keeping turned them into veto points of policy implementation. The consequential informational asymmetry increases principals' monitoring costs. Informational asymmetry is especially obvious when the implementation of principals' tasks entails many actors, and each actor monopolizes certain information that affects implementation outcomes. The more actors are involved, the more information will be hidden, and higher monitoring and coordination costs will result in order to solicit agents' compliance (Huang 2002).

With regard to administrative licence downsizing, various levels of government and their departments wield some sort of licensing authority and are involved in administrative licence downsizing. The implementation of downsizing is contingent on the concerted actions of numerous local actors with diverse interests. Local actors' defiance is difficult to detect and correct. Over-reporting of the number of annulled licensing items is possible. Consequently, since the late 1990s, central government has been partially centralizing authority from sub-provincial to provincial-level governments. The 31 provincial-level governments have been given more authority in monitoring sub-provincial governments and aligning local regulations with national and provincial legislation. The bureaucracies of administrative regulation, financial regulation and commodities management such as the bureaus for industry and commerce, quality technology supervision bureaus, pharmaceutical supervision bureaus, and securities supervision commissions have been removed from the control of sub-provincial governments. These bureaucracies have been made to report to superior functional agencies which, in turn, are responsible to provincial-level governments. Central government can then narrow its attention to provincial-level governments and monitoring of policy execution can be made easier (Mertha 2005).

A recent evaluative study suggests that this partial centralization cannot help central bureaucracies tap into more information. In his case study of financial industry, Heilmann (2005) pointed out that the securities regulators in Shanghai city previously under the Shanghai Municipal Government were incorporated into a central government regulatory commission. Due to geographical distance, communications between central and Shanghai regulators were based on ad hoc meetings and unsystematic data transfers. Consultations and coordination were inadequate. Moreover, many local public officials reportedly resisted the partial centralization, which removed much of their decision-making power and downgraded them to mere agencies of a far-away central body. Being managed by a central body following a much stricter policy for dispensing subsidies and approving overseas business trips, these local officials saw their salaries and overseas travel opportunities cut (ibid.). Some bureau directors believed that if their bureaus remained accountable to local governments at corresponding levels, they had more opportunities to be appointed to people's congresses or people's political consultative conferences and thus to retain political influence after their retirement (Yang 2004: 100–101).

Owing to the difficulties inherent in soliciting compliance through a top-down command-and-control approach, O'Toole argued that policy-makers should use a bottom-up model to implement their policies and align policy executors' interests with policy objectives and broader collective benefits in order to succeed in policy implementation. Policy-makers should either modify the incentive systems in bureaucracies or involve policy executors in policy-making processes to encourage appropriate behaviour on the part of policy executors (O'Toole 1989: 313–339). The implementation of licence downsizing follows a top-down model. The inputs from local actors in policy-making processes are not actively solicited. Local governments' incentive systems, characterized by a linkage between extra-budgetary revenue with levels of subsidy and bonus, remain largely unreformed. Some local governments have tried to sever the link to reduce the incentive of individual departments and public officials to defend their licensing authority and the associated extra-budgetary revenue. In 2003, Beijing municipality decreed to level out the subsidies to its public officials. Individual public officials at the same rank were paid equally, regardless of the level of extra-budgetary revenue individual departments generated (Chou forthcoming). Nevertheless, the model cannot be widely practised because the tax bases of many local governments are much narrower. Some of them are so short of funds that they cannot cover the expenditure of basic public services and pay their employees on time. To balance their financial needs and the obligation of carrying out administrative licence downsizing, some local governments may annul only the items with limited potential of revenue generation and maintain others illegally (Chen 2005: 75; Yan 2005: 44).

Furthermore, local leaders' performance appraisal still places heavy emphasis on their ability to develop the local economy and links the appraisal result with career advancement and punishment. This system compels local leaders to narrow their focus to local economic growth and to downplay collective interests. Licensing authority can help local leaders to develop the local economy and to form a stable source of revenue by creating local-invested monopolies, fending off the competition from more competitive outsiders, and protecting the monopolies' profits. Undoubtedly, administrative licence downsizing can help to improve the local business environment, attract more investment, enlarge tax bases, create more job opportunities and fuel economic growth in the long run. But regular job rotation discourages local leaders from committing to policies that cannot achieve immediate results.

Two more institutional features entrench local leaders' incentives to promote short-term local economic growth at the expense of the Administrative Licensing Law. The first is a lack of pro-reform interest groups or a strong functional bureaucracy representing the societal actors who benefit from the downsizing of the licensing regime. After investigating the regulatory reforms of the telecommunications industry in 50 countries, Li et al. (2005) argued that successful regulatory reforms are more likely in countries with strong pro-reform interest groups that help to maintain reforms' momentum and overcome resistance from vested interests. Within the telecommunications industry, the financial sector and urban consumers are frequent users of telecommunication service and are beneficiaries of a reformed telecommunication industry that holds the potential of improving the telecommunications infrastructure and providing cheaper services. The major opponents are the incumbent telecommunication operators who have vested interests in old regulatory systems. Those countries trying to implement reforms without powerful officials who would benefit from them are less successful (ibid.). The major beneficiaries of administrative licence downsizing are private entrepreneurs, whilst the bureaucracies with licensing authority are major opponents. The institutional position of Chinese private entrepreneurs is very weak. China denies autonomous interest groups access to institutional positions within the policy process. The strict control on association formation makes it difficult for private entrepreneurs to organize collective action. The

All-China Federation of Industry and Commerce, the state-sanctioned national association representing private enterprise, resembles a government's executive arm more than their Anglo-American counterparts, which pro-actively advocate the interests of their members. Without beneficiaries having strong institutionalized positions, administrative licence downsizing can easily lose momentum in the face of bureaucratic resistance.

The second feature is the ineffectiveness of the legislation review mechanism. The Law of Legislation promulgated in 2000 is the major legal foundation of legislative review to align local regulations with national legislation. This Law identifies a hierarchy of Chinese laws, with the Constitution as supreme. The laws enacted by the NPC should prevail over the State Council's administrative decrees, which, in turn, prevail over provincial legislation. Local administrative decrees are placed at the bottom of the hierarchy (Articles 78–80). The NPC Standing Committee is responsible for reviewing and striking down lower-level legislation contradictory to Constitution and NPC laws (Article 88).[6] Under its Law Committee, the NPC Standing Committee set up the Judicial Review Office (*Fagui shencha bi an bangongshi*) to provide the Law Committee with expert advice on legislative review. Review of consistency among administrative regulations and local people's congress regulations was left to the State Council, its ministries, and local-level administrative agencies (Article 86). Since the promulgation of the Law of Legislation, the NPC Standing Committee has received some 20 requests for legislation review. But the NPC Standing Committee could not take any action in response because it had no idea about how to operationalize review procedures. The Judicial Review Office had a staff of less than 30 officers – far to few to review all legislation and decrees (Wen and Chang 2004).

Conclusion

Administrative licence downsizing has the potential to improve the business environment on the basis of China's WTO commitments. This downsizing can also contribute to a change in public officials' behaviour towards private businesses. By removing the licensing authority of local public officials, the downsizing can reduce the use of an overly complicated licensing system for rent-seeking and creating market barriers. The Chinese government has slashed most licensing items and issued laws and regulations to prevent annulled licensing items from being re-established. Sub-provincial governments are now obliged to refer to national laws and regulations before making decisions on licensing issues.

The mixed success of administrative licence downsizing demonstrates that the masterminds behind the policy have not adequately considered local institutional features when designing the downsizing policy. Since the policy entails numerous ill-coordinated implementers with diverse interests, a top-down downsizing approach neither solicits voluntary compliance from implementers nor provides adequate information for policy-makers to supervise policy implementation and exercise sanctions. Also, the incentive systems operated by local governance militate against downsizing: the performance appraisal systems applied to local leaders encourage them to focus on the short-term economic growth of small localities but to ignore the collective benefits of investment environment improvement for the wider region. Licensing authority conducive to achieving the immediate result of economic growth by fending off competition against local enterprises and their products is much sought after. Local governments are also required to be financially self-sufficient. Accordingly, the potential for licensing authority to form an important source of revenue provides a strong incentive for local governments to thwart administrative licence downsizing.

Notes

1 This chapter is a revised version of the author's occasional paper for the Asian Development Bank Institute, entitled 'Downsizing administrative licensing system and private sector development in China: a preliminary assessment', at: http://www.adbi.org/discussion-paper/2006/08/23/1958.admin.licensing.prc.
2 In February 2007, US$1 = 7.77 *yuan*.
3 In this chapter, 'local leaders' refers to CCP secretaries and governors of local governments, as well as their deputies.
4 The first stage of reform, characterized by de-bureaucratization, de-nationalization and greater use of market principles, comprises the strategies of bureaucracy downsizing, departments merging, reform of state-owned enterprises, transformation of government departments into quasi-governmental organizations and civil service reform. Control on business opportunities was relaxed. Monopolies of foreign trade were broken up. Industrial ministries were either transformed into economic entities or industrial associations, or absorbed into other ministries. Market forces were phased in to replace bureaucracy in directing economic production and resource distribution. Bureaucracy was trimmed. New ministries and departments were set up to take charge of economic and social regulatory functions, such as the environment, food safety, work safety, financial services, telecommunications and intellectual property.
5 These six sectors are: (1) industries involving 'national security, public safety, macro-economic management, environmental protection, public health, personal safety and property protection'; (2) industries involving scarce natural resource exploitation and public resource allocation; (3) professions involving public interest and service provision to the public (such as legal and accounting professions); (4) sale of equipment, facilities, products involving public safety, public health, and personal safety and property; 5) restricted industries; (6) other industries covered by other laws promulgated by the National People's Congress and its Standing Committee and administrative decrees by the State Council. The definition of the six sectors is so unclear that individual bureaucrats are left with much discretionary power in creating licenses.
6 In reality, this provision can be applied in different ways. In 2005, the Standing Committee of the NPC received a petition from a peasant in Hebei province protesting that the provincial regulations on land management violated the national Law of Land Management. Before the State Committee of NPC took action, Hebei provincial people's congresses amended the provincial regulations to make them consistent with the Law (for details, see Yang 2006).

References

All-China Federation of Industry and Commerce (2005) *Zhongguo minyin jingji fazhan baogao No.2* [*The Development Report of Non-State-wwned Economy in China, No. 2*], Beijing: Social Sciences Academic Press.

Ambler, T. and Witzel, M. (2004) *Doing Business in China*, London and New York: RoutledgeCurzon.

Asian Development Bank (2003) *Private Sector Assessment: People's Republic of China*, Manila: Asian Development Bank.

Breslin, S.G. (1996) *China in the 1980s: Centre–Province Relations in a Reforming Socialist State*, London: Macmillan.

Carlile, L. and Tilton, M.C. (1998) Regulatory reform and developmental states, in L. Carlile and M. C. Tilton (eds), *Is Japan Really Changing Its Ways? Regulatory Reform and the Japanese Economy*, Washington, DC: Brookings Institution Press, 1–15.

Centre of Human Resources Research and Training, Development and Research Centre of the State Council (2002) *Qiye Jingyingzhe dui Hongguan Jingji Xingxi ji Gaige Redian he Panduan* [*The Opinions and Suggestions of Entrepreneurs towards the Economy*], at: http://www.drc.gov.cn/view.asp?doc_ID=030466.

Centre of Human Resources Research and Training, Development and Research Centre of the State Council (2005) *Qiye jingyingzhe dui jingji huanjing he gaige redian de panduan – 2005 zhongguo qiye jingyingzhe wenquan diaocha baogao* [*The Opinions of Entrepreneurs towards the Context and Hot Issues of Economics*], at: http://www.drc.gov.cn/view.asp?doc_ID=032802.

Centre of Human Resources Research and Training, Development Research Centre of the State Council (2006) *Qiye jingyingzhe dui jingji huanjing he gaige redian de panduan – 2005 zhongguo qiye jingyingzhe wenquan diaocha baogao* [*The Opinions of Entrepreneurs towards the Hot Issues of Economy*], at: http://www.drc.gov.cn/view.asp?doc_ID=032802.

Chen, Z. (2005) Jian xi xingzheng xuke fa shishi zhong chuxian de jige wenti' (Several problems in implementing administrative licensing law), *Heihe xuekan* [*Journal of Heihe*], 116: 74–76.

Chou, B.K.P. (2004) Civil service reform in China, 1993–2001: a case implementation failure, *China: An International Journal*, 2(2): 210–234.

Chou, B.K.P. (forthcoming) Does governance matter? Civil service reform in China, *International Journal of Public Administration*.

Edin, M. (2003) State capacity and local agent control in China: CCP cadre management from a township perspective, *China Quarterly*, 173: 35–52.

Fujian sheng gongbu 445 xian xingzheng shenpi xianmu [Fujian province announced 445 administrative licensing items] (2006) *Fujian zhi chuang* [*The Windom of Fujian*], at: http://www.66163.com/Fujian_w/bdxw/20060329/fj148889.html.

Gao, Y.J. (2005) Xingzheng xukefa shishi yinian, 'mingaoguan' anjian dafu shangsheng [The cases of 'citizens suing officials' increases substantially after the implementation of administrative licensing law for one year]) *Sina xinwen zhongxin* [*Sina News Centre*], at: http://news.sina.com.cn/c/2005-07-04/11587125969.shtml.

Guanshe shishi xingzheng xukefa, Guangdong dafu xiaojian xingzheng shenpi shixian [Guangdong has substantially reduced licensing items in the implementation of administrative licensing law] (2006) *Jinyangwang* [*Golden Goat Net*], at: http://www.ycwb.com/gb/content/2006-03/05/content_108015.htm.

Hall, P.A. (1992) The movement from Keynesianism to monetarism: institutional analysis and British economic policy in the 1970s, in S. Steinmo, K. Thelen and F. Longstreth (eds), *Structuring Politics: Historical Institutionalism in Comparative Analysis*, Cambridge: Cambridge University Press.

Heilmann, S. (2005) Policy-making and political supervision in Shanghai's financial industry, *Journal of Contemporary China*, 14(45): 643–668.

Hu, A. and Guo, Y. (2002) Zhuanxingqi fangzhi fubai de zhonghe zhanlue yu zhidu sheji [Corruption prevention strategies in transition period], in Hu Angang (ed.), *Zhongguo zhanlue [The Strategies of China]*, Hangzhou: Zhejiang People's Press.

Huang, Y.S. (2002) Managing Chinese bureaucrats: an institutional economics perspective, *Political Studies*, 50(1): 61–79.

Jiao, X.Y. (2005) Ease of incorporating open doors, *China Daily*, 2 March.

Jin, L. (2004) Xingzheng xukefa shishi qingkuang qicheng beifangzhe buman [70 per cent of the respondents are dissatisfied with the implementation of the administrative licensing law], *Jinyangwang [Golden Goat Net]*, at: http://www.ycwb.com/gb/content/2004-11/26/content_801758.htm.

Lan, X.B. (2006) Qiye banshi fudan jianqin yiban [The burdens on enterprises were cut by a half], *Zhongguo jinji shibao [China Economics Time]*, 9 January.

Lardy, N (2002) *Integrating China into the Global Economy*, Washington, DC: Brookings Institution Press.

Li Gan, Difang jigou gaige jinrui shishi jieduan [Administrative reform in local governments is in implementation stage] (2005) *Zhongguo gongwuyuan [Chinese Public Servants]*, 4: 15.

Li, W., Qiang, C.Z.W and Xu, L.X.C. (2005) Regulatory reforms in the telecommunications sector in developing countries: the role of democracy and private interests, *World Development*, 33(8): 1307–1324.

Liu, X. (2006) Renli sanlunche paizhao shiyongquan ruci bi shouwei – dui yiqi xingzheng xuke anjian de falu fengshi [A case study on administrative licensing recalling business licenses of man-powered tricycles], *Zhongguo wang [ChinaNet]*, at: http://www.china.org.cn/chinese /law/603503.htm.

Lü, X.B. (1999) From rank-seeking to rent-seeking: changing administrative ethos and corruption in reform China, *Crime, Law and Social Change*, 32(4): 347–370.

Lü, X.B. (2000) *Cadres and Corruption*, Stanford: Stanford University Press.

Luo, J. and Yu, G.H. (2005) Xingzheng xukefa dailai 'guanli zhenkong' [Has administrative licensing law resulted in a 'management in vacuum'], *Zhejiang rendai [Zhejiang People's Congress]*, 6: 21–22.

Mao, Q. and Ming, L.P. (2005) Xingzheng xukefa ke yianjiedu la [Case studies of administrative licensing law are available], *Sina xinwen zhongxin [Sina News Centre]*, at: http://news.sina.com.cn/o/2005-11-03/07047347027s.shtml.

Meng, Y. (2002) Administrative license under scrutiny, *China Daily*, 29 August.

Meng, Y. (2004) New licensing law streamlines bureaucracy, *China Daily*, 1 July.

Mertha, A.C. (2005) China's 'soft' centralization: shifting tiao/kuai authority relations, *China Quarterly*, 184: 791–810.

O'Toole, L.J. (1989) Alternative mechanisms for multiorganizational implementation: the case of wastewater management, *Administration and Society*, 21(3): 313–339.

Pearson, M.M. (2004) China's WTO implementation in comparative perspective: lessons from the literatures on trade policy and regulation, *Review of International Affairs*, 3(4): 567–583.

Qian, Y.Y. and Weingast, B.R. (1995) *China's Transition to Markets: Market-*

preserving Federalism, Chinese Style, Stanford, CA: Hoover Institution on War, Revolution and Peace, Stanford University.

Qin, J. (1996) Guangxi, Henan officials disciplined for corruption, Beijing *XINHUA*, in Chinese, translation by the Foreign Broadcast Information Service, FBIS Daily Report – China, 2 May.

Shizhengfu tisu xiaoguo xianzhu [City government made progress in improving administrative efficiency] (2001) *Shenzhen tequ bao* [*Shenzhen Special Zone Daily*], 15 October, p. A1.

Wang L. (1998) Reform of Party and government organizations advances steadily, Beijing *Xinhua* in Chinese, translation by the Foreign Broadcast Information Service, FBIS Daily Report – China, 7 May.

Wen, H. and Chang, Y.X. (2004) Weixian shencha haizai yunchu [Constitutional review is still looming], *Zhongguo xinwen zhoukan* [*China News Weekly*], 185: 28–32.

Wong, C.P.W. (1997) Overview of issues in local public finance in the PRC, in C. P. W. Wong (ed.), *Financing Local Government in the People's Republic of China*, New York: Oxford University Press.

World Bank (2004) *World Development Indicators 2004*, Washington, DC: World Bank.

Xian, W. and Yuan J.Y. (2006) Yinian jianfu san yi yuan, luoshi xingzheng xukefa quanshen 138 xian xingzheng shoufei suxiao [The implementation of administrative licensing law and the downsizing of 138 administrative licensing items reduces revenue of 300 million a year]) *Sina xinwen zhongxin* [*Sina News Centre*], at: http://news.sina.com.cn/o/2006-01017/12108007248s.shtml.

Xiao, H. (2004) Yanggang shi xingzheng xing shoufei xianmu taidou taigui yao zhengtun [Yanggang city has to reduce the burdensome and expensive licensing items], *Jinyangwang* [*Golden Goat Net*], at: http://www.ycwb.com/gb/content/2004-11/05/content_789516.htm.

Xingzhen xukefa shisih, zhengfu zishou bude niansheng [Government cannot arbitrarily intervene in daily lives of the people after administration licensing law coming into effect] (2004) *Tom.Com*, at: http://news.tom.com/1002/20040630-1045934.htm.

Yan, B.J. (2005) Shixian cong guanzhi dao fuwu de zhuanbian: xingzheng xukefa shishi hou de daolu yunshu xingzheng shenpi gaige linian [A transformation from regulation to service: reform of licensing in road transportation after administrative licensing law is effective], *Tongling Xueyuan Xuebao* [*Journal of Tongling College*], 1: 44.

Yang, D.L. (2004) *Remaking the Chinese Leviathan: Market Transition and the Politics of Governance in China*, Stanford: Stanford University Press, 154–175.

Yang, G. (2005) Guangzhou gongshang dao kushui: geng bieren de di, huang jizi de tian [The grievance of Guangzhou City Bureau of Industry and Commerce: tender the fields of other people but give up their own], *Nanfang wang* [*NanfangNet*], at: http://www.southcn.com/news/dishi/guangzhou/shizheng/200512170093.htm.

Yang, S.R. (2006) Putong nongmin shangshu quanguo rendai, difang tudi fagui huode xiuzheng [Local regulations have been amended because of a written appeal by a peasant to National People's Congress], *Jinyangwang* [*Golden Goat Net*], at: http://www.ycwb.com/gb/content/2005-06/07/content_916874.htm.

Yu, X.M. (2005) Wo sheng nongzi zhuanying zhi sida guaizhuang [Four strange issues in the monopoly of agricultural input], *Nanfang wang* [*NanfangNet*], at: http://www.southcn.com/nflr/nydkt/kandian/200512280247.htm.

Yu, X.M. and Tan, Y.F. (2005) Huizhen nongzi zhuanying zhi liubi [Collectively finding out the roots of monopoly of agricultural inputs], *Nanfang Wang* [*Nanfang-Net*], at: http://www.southcn.com/nflr/nydkt/kandian/200512280248.htm.

Zhao, Y.L. (2006) Rang xinzheng xukefa yingqilai [Enforcing administrative licensing law with vigor], *Zhongguo wang* [*ChinaNet*], at: http://www.china.org.cn/chinese/law/650395.htm.

Zhong, Y. (2003) *Local Government and Politics in China: Challenges from Below*, Armonk, NY: London: M. E. Sharpe.

Zhonghua Renmin Gongheguo Guowuyuan Ling di Xiyier Hao (2004) *Directive No. 412 of the State Council of the People's Republic of China*, at: http://www.gov.cn/zwgk/2005-06/20/content_7908.htm.

Part III

The changing role of the private sector in public policy

9 Accommodating business interests in China and Hong Kong

Two systems – one way out

Ray Yep

Introduction

The concept of 'one-country two systems' is premised on the possibility of institutional osmosis between mainland China and Hong Kong. However, the time dimension of the notion has always been overlooked. The guarantee of the Hong Kong lifestyle remaining unchanged for 50 years implies the transient nature of the one-country, two-system formula. It assumes a gradual integration and mutual imitation of practices, arrangements and values across the border. While the mainland may maintain its dominance in the political realm, there exists a genuine possibility of peripheral Hong Kong asserting its influence on the trajectory of the economic integration process. Behind the facade of rhetoric lies the Party leadership's enthusiasm for the market economy. Hong Kong provides the motherland with an opportunity to observe and understand the operation, strength and limitations of capitalism at close range. Central to the political economy of capitalism is the issue of accommodation of business interests. A vibrant market economy is simply inconceivable without the full blossom of capitalist entrepreneurial spirit. Yet, over-dominance of capitalists can be detrimental to capitalism: monopoly may replace competition, and privileges and cronyism may take precedence over efficiency in determining economic survival. The search for a balance between inclusion of business interests in the policy process and state autonomy is thus a fundamental task for political leaders in the market economy. Neither Hong Kong nor mainland China is immune to this challenge. The quest for synchronized political–economic order has a much wider implication. The Asian financial crisis revealed the obsolescence of the economy-centred perspective in understanding the dynamics of economic growth. And, as rightly pointed out by Krugman,

> the biggest lesson from Asia's [recent] troubles is not about economics, it is about government. When the Asian economies delivered nothing but good news, it was possible to convince yourself that the alleged planners

of these knew what they were doing. Now the truth is revealed, they do not have a clue.

(1997: 27)

China and Hong Kong are hardly immune to the imperative of political reform and it is necessary to reconsider their respective political strategies of business engagement. Examination of this pair is thus revealing not only for scholars specializing in studying China, but it also helps shed new light on the common concern of students of political economy.

This chapter attempts to evaluate the limitations of the current political strategies deployed in China and Hong Kong. The analysis is confined, however, to the role played by indigenous capital. There are two reasons for this strategy. Foreign and domestic capital access different resources and means of leveraging influence; consequently their choices of strategy are likely to be distinct. It is thus unrealistic to try to include both sets of player in a single chapter. More importantly, despite the advent of market reform in the mainland, there remain numerous fundamental differences in the business habitat for overseas investors in Hong Kong and China. The former presents a much more open economy in terms of foreign exchange control, freedom of inflow and outflow of capital, and a regime for foreign investment regulation.

The main argument put forward here is that political leaders in both systems are constrained by their institutional legacy and some form of political reform is imperative. The post-1997 Hong Kong Special Administration Region inherits from its colonial predecessor a strong bias towards business interests in her political system and this is the main reason for rising tension within the local population, which shows a growing appetite for political equality. In the case of China, the legacy of economic planning leaves its mark on the pattern of state–business interface. Non-state economic actors simply did not exist in Mao's China. Obsolescence of the pre-reform mode of economic representation that was organized along a bureaucratic divide is vividly exposed in the age of marketization, when the contours of the Chinese economy are now characterized by the rapid ascendancy of non-state sectors. Re-enfranchisement in the policy process is imperative in both settings if effective governance is to be maintained. For both China and Hong Kong, political reform is the only way out.

Hong Kong

Many depicted colonial Hong Kong as an administrative state. Painter (2005) described its governance style as 'a close parallel to a traditional Asian form of governance that placed a heavy reliance on a meritocratic, centralized, more or less autonomous, paternalistic bureaucracy.' The team of professional civil servants, particularly the so-called 'administrative officers', maintained a monopolistic control of political power until the development of 'representative government' in the late 1980s. Nonetheless, the legitimacy of the colony was premised on its ability to deliver economic prosperity and stability and public administrators are only one side of the governing formula. Coexistent with the powerful bureaucracy was a thriving capitalist economy. The colonial administration took pride in its approach of 'positive non-interventionism' in regulating the economy. As the *Hong Kong Yearbook 1991* proudly stated:

> the government considers that, except where social considerations are over-riding, the allocation of resources in the economy is best left to market forces with minimal government intervention in the private sector. This basically free-enterprise, market disciplined system has contributed to Hong Kong's economic success ... the primary role of the government is to provide the necessary infrastructure and a sound legal and administrative framework conducive to economic growth and prosperity.
> (Miners 1991: 47)

In essence, such a position implied limited regulation, minimal welfare and low taxation and it certainly endeared the colonial administration to the local business community. This entente cordiale was further consolidated by the inclusion of business interests in the policy process.

Synarchy between colonial officials and business elites

Colonial governance was defined by a close state–business alliance. Constitutionally speaking, the Governor was the representative of the Crown and his power was constrained only by the *Letters Patent, Royal Instructions and Colonial Regulations*, or specific directives from the Foreign and Commonwealth Office. In principle, the Governor was immune to local influence. This was, of course, hardly an accurate description of the British tradition of colonial rule. Promotion of some kind of 'synarchy' between colonial officials and non-British local leaders was, however, the rule rather than an exception (King 1981: 130). Business leaders, in particular, were heavily absorbed into the governing machinery. Goodstadt provides a colonial perspective for such integration:

> To the colonial administration, the business and professional classes seemed the group most firmly rooted in Hong Kong, with the biggest personal stake in its survival because of their investments and ownership of local assets. They also appeared entitled to a special voice in the conduct of public affairs because when Mainland or local political developments threatened British rule, they could be relied on to cooperate in keeping revolution and anarchy at a distance. Thus, the leaders of business and the professions were seen by the British as the best qualified to be involved in the colonial power system.
> (2005: 10)

Consequently, leaders in the local business community mostly occupied unofficial positions in the Executive Council – the chief advisory body to the Governor – and the Legislative Council – the law-making body of the colony. Beneath this privileged access to the decision-making process was an extensive network of advisory committees. By the end of British rule in 1997, the number of advisory committees had increased from 50 in the 1950s to more than 300. As Cheung and Wong argued,

> under colonial rule, the co-optation of elites to advisory committees helped the Hong Kong Government secure political consent and given an impression of government by consultation. This approach formed a key pillar of stability for British colonial rule.
>
> (2004: 878)

Most noteworthy is the business-bias of the advisory committee membership. There was a clear preference for people from the trade, business, finance and industry sectors, with more than one-quarter of the total membership of major advisory committees coming from these sectors.

The commencement of the Sino–British negotiation over the future of Hong Kong triggered off waves of political challenge to the local polity. The mutual distrust and altercations between Beijing and London did lead to a more fundamental change in the pattern of business representation. Local Chinese capitalists took a gamble in allying with Beijing and their 'loyalty' was handsomely rewarded. The political uncertainty over the post-1997 Hong Kong led to a confidence crisis in the colony, which was followed by an exodus of capital, especially among the leading British companies (Feng 1996). Beijing was determined to stop this flight of capital to preserve the economic vitality of Hong Kong after 1997, and one of the chief tasks of the Chinese officials in Hong Kong since the mid-1980s was to delay the flight of capital and maintain the confidence of the capitalists (Xu 1993). Local Chinese businessmen, who had been living under the shadow of British capital, seized the opportunity and launched a number of major investments in Hong Kong during this period. To Beijing, this helped send a welcoming signal of confidence and commitment to Hong Kong society, and in reward some of these Chinese capitalists also secured lucrative contracts from the colonial administration with help from Beijing (Feng 1997). The struggle over democratization also reinforced the bonding of the 'unholy alliance' between Beijing and local businessmen (So 2000). Local capitalists feared that continued democratization would threaten their vested interests, and the grassroot politicians would drive Hong Kong towards a welfare state and bring in heavy taxation. While Beijing shared this fear, she was also alarmed by the role played by the Hong Kong democrats during the 1989 Beijing democracy movement. During the 1989 movement, democrats in Hong Kong were at the forefront of the Hong Kong support movement, subsidizing the mainland students and dissidents with money and other material resources, and helping to smuggle dissidents out of China after the crackdown. The Chinese government was worried that rapid democratization in Hong Kong would bring the democrats to power, and was reluctant to grant full-fledged democracy in Hong Kong.

Business leaders: new allies for post-1997 rule

The Chinese government quickly found the politically conservative business sector in Hong Kong a convenient ally in balancing the democrats' progressive demands for democracy. She also needed the support of the local business class in her crafting of the post-colonial elite in Hong Kong. The business sector therefore formed the cornerstone of the 'united front' of the Chinese government in the transition era from 1984–97, and they were well represented in most of the Beijing-appointed bodies related to the political transition (Goodstadt 2000). For example, they made up about half of the Hong Kong membership of the Basic Law Drafting Committee, and business and professional representatives were also the largest single group in the Basic Law Consultative Committee. The Basic Law instituted a corporatist design by which business representation was well guaranteed. From 1997 to 2007, half of the seats in the Hong Kong legislature are returned by the so-called 'functional constituencies', which only represent the major business and professional groups in the territory, covering a total franchise of about only 200,000 electors. The Chief Executive of Hong Kong, whose constitutional power rivals that of the colonial Governor, was not popularly elected but only elected by an 800-member Election Committee (EC). Representatives from business and professional groups each make up 25 per cent of the EC, with other pro-Beijing politicians also well represented through other social and political sectors. The business sector was thus granted the power of both king-making (i.e. electing the Chief Executive) and the privilege of exclusive representation in the legislature.

The privileged access of business interests to the policy process is further consolidated by the growing economic integration between Hong Kong and the mainland. Even before the sovereignty handover, Hong Kong's economy benefited from China's open-door policy and became increasingly integrated with the mainland. The coincidence of the handover and the onset of the Asian financial crisis ensured the continuation of the trend under the SAR. On the one hand, Hong Kong's stalled economy made it more desperate for external economic stimuli. On the other, the phenomenal growth of China's economy and the rapid opening up of its market made it the obvious place to turn. At the same time, China's presence in the Hong Kong economy also expanded considerably, and by 2001 China was the largest investor in the territory, with a total accumulated investment of US$122.8 billion, or nearly 30 per cent of total inward investment. Over 2,000 mainland enterprises currently operate in Hong Kong and account for about 25 per cent of the market shares in banking insurance, shopping and tourism businesses in the territory (*Hong Kong Yearbook 2003*, Chapter 3).

Hong Kong's financial links with the mainland have also been expanded significantly over the last decade. The Bank of China (Hong Kong) Limited is now the second largest banking group in Hong Kong and one of the three note-issuing banks in Hong Kong. And since 1995, three other state-owned banks, namely the China Construction Bank, the Agricultural Bank of China, and the Industrial and Commercial Bank of China have started their operations in the territory. And, in the face of growing cross-border banking transactions, joint cheque-clearing facilities have been further extended. In 2003, about 250,000 cheques, totaling HK$22 billion, were cleared through the two-way joint clearing facilities. A major breakthrough came in November 2003 with the People's Bank of China's agreement to provide clearing arrangements for personal RMB business in Hong Kong, thus allowing selected banks in Hong Kong to be involved in RMB business, including deposit-taking, exchange, remittances and RMB cards (*Hong Kong Yearbook 2003*, Chapter 4). Nonetheless, the role of Hong Kong as a leading international financial centre appears to be the major catalyst for growing financial linkages between the two economies. Hong Kong has been serving as a major funding centre for mainland enterprises. A total of 64 state-owned mainland enterprises had been listed on the Main Board of Hong Kong's stock market by the end of 2003, raising total equity capital of HK$191 billion. In addition, another 72 non-state owned mainland enterprises had also been listed by the end of 2003, raising a total of HK$590 billion (*Hong Kong Yearbook 2003*, Chapter 3). And apart from the equity market, mainland enterprises also raise capital in Hong Kong by issuance of bonds, project financing and loan syndication.

Such economic intimacy coincides with further co-optation of local business leaders into the power hierarchy of the sovereign state. Major business leaders or their associates are mostly 'elected' to the People's Congress at national or provincial levels, or appointed to the leading advisory body to the Party, the People's Political Consultative Conference. Business tycoons are thus guaranteed direct access to top leaders and their exclusive passage was vividly reflected in the three-day visit of Zeng Qinghong, the Vice-President of the People's Republic in September 2005. While most local dignitaries including legislators and senior officials were largely confined to handshaking or photo opportunities with the Vice-President, private meetings with selected super tycoons were arranged. The symbolic scenes epitomise the unprecedented intimacy between local capitalists and the sovereign state. The authority of the colonial Governor was partly derived from his immunity from local influence. Not only was his authority attributed to the lack of transparency and openness of the selection process of the Governor, but it was also related to the lack of rapport between London and the local business community under colonial rule. Goodstadt (2005) goes further to argue that there was even a certain degree of mutual distrust between British firms in Hong Kong and London (p. 53). Regardless of the validity of this observation, one thing is certain: local business leaders had never enjoyed the same level of cordiality with the sovereign state before 1997 as they do now. The undeniable fact of being under alien rule may account for its half-hearted effort in creating links between London and local elites, and the economic relationship between Britain and Hong Kong was also evidently dwarfed by the monumental pace of integration between Hong Kong and mainland economies since the 1980s. The relatively limited interaction thus affected the value of policy inputs from local business leaders. As a result, London remained by and large indifferent to local opinion in making policy concerning Hong Kong. London, for example, stood firm behind Chris Patten during the stormy discussion over political reform with Beijing, despite strong voices from local business requesting a change of Governor (Patten 1999: 97).

The restricted access to the sovereign state was a blessing for the Crown's agent in the colony. The colonial Governor could thus personify the will and interest of London and no one in the territory could legitimately challenge his interpretation of the sovereign's intent. The post-1997 SAR Chief Executive can hardly contemplate this enviable position. Eminent business leaders now all enjoy some form of direct access to top Chinese leaders, and they can always bypass the SAR government in making claims or even complaints directly to Beijing. Reference to private conversation with senior Chinese officials is a common tactic to undermine the Chief Executive's authority when business leaders see their interests affected by policies of the SAR government. Business leaders are, in short, emboldened by their access to sympathetic ears at the very top level in Beijing and have become more assertive in the public policy process.

Thus growing assertiveness is further reinforced by a gradual change in the governing philosophy of the government. Many commentators have pointed out the gradual erosion of the cornerstone of government–business alliance – positive non-interventionism – since the late 1980s. Ngo (2000) argues that the approach of positive non-interventionism is more than a 'small government' approach of economic management; it also implies a 'substantive consent' among the ruling elite under colonial rule. He argues,

> This meant that the government refrained from using public resources to assist or protect individual business sectors and enterprises. This avoided rent-seeking by individual elite groups, ensuring that policy outcomes were acceptable to the less powerful and to the wider population of players.
>
> (pp. 31–32)

Nonetheless, business leaders feel tempted to stake their claims on public resources once they realize that the non-interventionist approach no longer prevails. Tang (1999) argues that, 'with the growing sophistication of the Hong Kong economy, rising protectionism and the intensification of competition from neighbouring countries, the liberal economic ideology of the administration has been eroded over the past two decades' (p. 283). Cheung (2000) nevertheless attributes this change to the 'decolonization syndrome' accompanying the transfer of sovereignty. The anxiety of the 'takeover elites' to prove that there is life after the departure of the British explains the new 'visions' and 'blueprints', like Tung Chee Hwa's infamous programme of providing 85,000 public housing units every year. The government's role in macro-economic management has become more and more visible. The Tung administration is also renowned for its commitment and determination to improve the competitiveness of the economy. In financial terms, this means that the government no longer shies away from giving direct subsidies to selected sectors – a direct contradiction to the 'substantive consent' in colonial times. The Tourism Board, Science Park at Pak Shek Kok and Film Service Office are only a few of the many examples of Tung's giveaways to specific sectors. No one wants to be left behind in this scramble for favours.

Business leaders, however, feel that they are not only pulled by the opportunity unleashed by ambitious administrators, but also pushed by other worrying signs in local scenes. There has been growing demand for better and more public services over the last two decades, and different social interests have become more organized and politicized in articulating their views (Lee 1999). The new interventionism has created a similar effect – encouraging public expectations for better and more public services (Lau 2002). Business elites find little comfort in the rise of electoral politics and the persistent call for democratization as they dismiss these developments as nothing more than leverages for populist demands of welfare and higher taxation. For them, the renewed enthusiasm in engaging in public policy, or Beijing in particular, is a logical way to 'defend' their privileges.

Nonetheless, the coexistence of a proactive government, the business bias in the power structure, limited democracy and a vibrant civil society could only breed suspicion and tension; any government's initiative is now seen by more and more people as proof of government–business collusion. The case of the Cyberport development is illustrative. Motivated by the desire to enhance competitiveness of the local economy in the aftermath of the Asian financial crisis, the government accepted the proposal of the Pacific Century Group to build a Cyberport – avant-garde office premises for enticing leading players in the field to invest in Hong Kong. In return for its shouldering of the construction cost, the developer was rewarded with a generous land grant and the right to include a residential property project on the site. The government's explanations of the urgency of the project and the financial advantages inherent in this public–private partnership carried little persuasive power in the face of a suspicious public. In fact, during the two years of the second term of the Tung administration, almost none of the government's initiatives went unscathed; most were accused of favouring business interests. From a capitalist haven, Hong Kong has witnessed a rising scepticism towards business domination in the political scene. While tycoons and the super-rich remain idols for people of the territory, more and more people are becoming wary of the imbalance between business interests and other legitimate concerns in society. Debate in the legislature has become more and more polemical, with class-based voting emerging as a trend (SynergyNet 2005). The conditions for the old mode of governance have simply disappeared and now public authority dependent solely on the basis of business support is no longer tenable.

China

Post-Mao China has witnessed a paradigmatic shift in economic management. The Leninist approach of central planning has been replaced by decentralization and the profit motive. Long gone is the policy of splendid isolation, with China emerging as a leading trader on the global scene. The scope and progress of the market reforms have been well documented and thus need no repetition here. It is, however, necessary to reiterate the relevance of one distinctive feature of the reform trajectory: the socialist legacy. Despite her embrace of the market, the notion of 'socialism with Chinese characteristics' is more than rhetoric, though it would be more accurate to describe the reality as 'capitalism with Chinese characteristics'. Two 'characteristics' are particularly noteworthy: the lingering of the state sector and the dominance of the Communist Party. Both factors continue to shape the policy process of China and contribute to a dysfunctional representational framework that fails to accommodate the growing economic diversities in today's China.

Preserving the state sector

China distinguishes herself from other socialist countries in her gradual approach towards reform. Unlike the 'shock therapy' approach cherished by Russia or Poland (Boycko et al. 1996; Murrel 1997), Chinese reformers are guided more by their pragmatism and political instincts than a blueprint of a market nirvana. More specifically, though post-Mao reforms were primarily triggered off by the general inefficiency of the state sector two decades ago, massive privatization of state enterprises has never been an official goal. While public listing of state enterprises has provided leverage for the mobilization of capital, the Chinese government's reluctance to relinquish her control over these assets is illustrated vividly by the generally high proportion of state shares in most of these listed companies. Bankruptcy and the sale of state enterprises have been few and far between, with most cases confined to smaller scale enterprises. The spirit is subsumed in the latest policy of 'grasping the large and letting go of the small' (*zhuadai fangxiao*). However, the policy denotes not only a reluctance to privatize but also, more significantly, a faith in the state sector. More than 100 leading state enterprises have been selected and are urged to develop into gigantic enterprise groups (*qiye jituan*) through mergers and takeovers. In return, preferential treatment and policy support, including subsidized credit, technological support and the clearance of debts, have been provided. These 'command heights' of the national economy are seen as engines of national growth and Chinese ambassadors in global competition (Smyth 2000; Smyth and Zhai 2003; Sutherland 2003). Large state enterprises are thus not seen as liabilities but as possible leverages for economic success. In sum, the state sector continues to play a significant role in the national economy despite the accelerated drive for reforms over the last two decades. The data shown in Table 9.1 speak volumes about its impact.

The same old mode of business representation

This chapter argues that the strong presence of the state sector explains the lingering of the pre-reform approach of economic representation.[1] As in Mao's China, the interests of state enterprises are transmitted via the intermediaries of bureaucratic supervisors. Despite their 'all-people ownership' (*quanmin suoyou*) nature, the majority of state enterprises are assigned to a specific ministry, department or other bureaucratic unit instead of the State Council. Such jurisdictional divide defines the distribution of power and control over resources, revenue, employment opportunities and political capital. Reforms of corporate governance and ownership structure in the post-Mao era may have created a different style of supervision and entailed a new form of presence of officials in enterprise management, but the symbiosis between interests of the supervising unit and the enterprises concerned remains intact. However, the interest divide is not only framed along a vertical division between ministries and departments (*tiao tiao*); local governments also have their interests at stake here (*kuai kuai*). Firstly, some state enterprises have been assigned to provincial government supervision, a legacy of Mao's emphasis on decentralization in the pre-reform era. Secondly, prospering state enterprises within the administrative boundary can certainly

Table 9.1 Shares of state sector in China's economy in 1985 and 2000

	1985	2000
GDP (%)	56[1]	29
Industrial assets (%)	74	67
Labour force (%)	41	38
Industrial output value (%)	64	47

Note:
1 Figures recorded in 1979.

Source: Guo (2003: 558).

bring more benefits than harm to the local economy, irrespective of the formal linkage between the enterprise concerned and the local administration. It is simply in the self-interest of the respective unit or officials to defend and promote the interests of state enterprises under their purview in the policy process.

This overlapping of bureaucratic and enterprise interests guarantees the enthusiasm of ministries and departments in advancing the concerns of the state sector in the policy process. Their bureaucratic patrons ensure enterprises' access to different important avenues of consensus building and bargaining. These include:

1   Meetings held by various coordinating units such as the Ministry of Finance.
2   Work meetings held by different department and ministries.
3   The People's Congress system.
4   The annual budgeting process.

Interaction and deliberation between agencies and units in these bodies define and shape the policy outcomes (Lieberthal and Oksenberg 1988).

In addition to these avenues, the Chinese Enterprise Management Association (*zhongguo qiye guanli xiehui*) was also founded in 1979 to serve as an agency for medium and large state-owned industrial enterprise under the approval of the State Council. Renamed as the China Enterprise Confederation (*zhongguo qiye lianhehui*), it has a national office and branches in every province and many major cities.

Under-representation of the non-state sector

Such representation of the state sector is, however, in sharp contrast to the limited access enjoyed by non-state enterprise. Post-Mao China witnesses a dramatic proliferation of the non-state sector. Two new players are particularly noteworthy: private enterprise and rural enterprise.

The rise of private enterprise in the post-Mao era is phenomenal. Originally seen as a stop-gap measure to accommodate millions of sent-down youths who returned to the cities at the end of the Cultural Revolution, the pace of growth of private enterprise soon surpassed the wildest imagination of Chinese officials. In approximately 20 years, the private sector has transformed into a significant component, providing more than 27 million jobs in the cities and 90 billion *yuan* in annual tax payments to the national economy (Table 9.2).

Nevertheless, the rise of private enterprise is dwarfed by the even more spectacular impact exerted by another new player: rural enterprise (Table 9.3). The origin of rural enterprise can be traced back to Mao's era. Mao emphasized the importance of developing factories in rural areas as part of his 'walking on two legs' industrialization strategy. Millions of enterprises

Table 9.2 Growth of private enterprises in selected years

	Number of enterprises (million)	Number of workers employed (million persons)	Tax contribution (100 million yuan)	Volume of registered capita (billion yuan)
1992	0.14	2.32	4.55	22.1
2000	1.76	24.1	414.4	1330.8
2001	2.03	27.1	917.6	1821.2

Note:
Private enterprises here refer to xiying qiye only, i.e. enterprises employing more than eight people.

Source: *Zhongguo Xiying Qiye Fazhan Baogao* (2002: 2–5).

were set up focusing predominantly on agriculture-related products: cement, small electricity plants, fertilizers, building materials and machinery (Byrd and Lin 1990; Sigurdson 1977). These ventures, though inefficient and nothing more than backyard workshops, did, through the experience of non-farming activities and enterprise operation, sow the seeds of entrepreneurism among the Chinese peasantry. Many of those peasants who had been involved in the commune-bridge enterprises in the days of the People's Commune became the first generation of rural enterprise managers in the early 1980s. Decollectivization also guarantees an abundant supply of cheap labour from individuals who now have to be responsible for their own wellbeing under the household responsibility system and the rise in peasant income in general also implies sufficient demand for the products of rural enterprise. It is also in the interest of local government to promote these enterprises. For local government, these are new sources of employment, growth and, most important, revenues (Oi 1992).

Table 9.3 Growth of rural enterprises in selected years

Year	No. of enterprises (million)	No. of workers employed (million workers)	Tax contribution (billion RMB yuan)	Fixed asset value (billion RMB yuan)
1978	1.52 (1.52)	28.3 (28.3)	2.2 (2.2)	23.0 (23.0)
1980	1.42 (1.42)	30.0 (30.0)	2.6 (2.6)	32.6 (32.6)
1990	18.7 (1.45)	92.7 (45.9)	28.8 (19.6)	285.7 (220.2)
2000	20.9 (0.80)	128.2 (38.33)	199.6 (93.1)	2622.4 (1368.5)
2001	21.2 (0.67)	130.9 (33.72)	230.8 (97.3)	2905.2 (1351.4)
2002	21.3 (0.73)	132.9 (38.01)	269.4 (142.4)	3569.8 (1774.7)

Note:
Figures in parentheses = collective enterprise.

Source: *Zhongguo Xiangzhen Qiye Tongji Jiliu 1978–2002* (2002: 3–18).

Who speaks for non-state enterprises?

The rapid growth of these non-state enterprises does lead to a different interest configuration in the Chinese economy. With so much at stake now, these players feel compelled to articulate their concerns and views in the policy process. And their gradual expansion of scale of production also entails a different approach to participation. Yep's (2003a) previous research on the interest articulation of rural enterprises confirms this argument. The concerns of rural enterprises had changed from the need for survival during the infancy stage in the 1980s into more policy-related demands when they reached the stage of consolidation in the 1990s. While the concerns about fiscal predation and unfair treatment by administrative units and demands for greater support have continued unabated, calls for reasonable rewards for managers, necessary legal and administrative reforms to facilitate the growth of rural enterprises and the intensification of market reform appeared to be the dominant views in the 1990s. Changes in concerns probably also imply a different pattern of interaction between state and business. The intensification of horizontal market exchanges on a national or global scale requires a new type of administrative support that in many cases cannot be provided by local administrations alone. Cordiality with the local bureaucracy may still make life easier, but managers are also aware that township or even county administrations alone can no longer solve all their problems. For many ambitious enterprises, with targets focusing on the nationwide and overseas market and more resources at their disposal, only the higher authorities can address their concerns.

Unfortunately, there simply exists no effective formal channel to accommodate the views of these significant economic players. Unlike their counterparts in the state sector, their contribution to the national economy does not guarantee an official representation of their interests in the policy process. While ministries and departments at the central level are highly motivated to defend the interests of state enterprises under their nomenclatural jurisdiction, the guardianship of non-state sectors is assigned to two junior-rank units. The Industry and Commerce Administration (*gongshang guanliju*) is in charge of the management and regulation of private enterprises and the Rural Enterprise Administration (*xiangzhen qiyeju*), under the Ministry of Agriculture, performs a similar role for rural enterprises. Both units have national networks of offices extending from national to township levels and play a significant role in the administration of today's economy. Nevertheless, both are bureau-level (*juji*) units under the Chinese bureaucratic hierarchies. Their sub-ministry level ranking implies their limitation in access to the policy process and, unlike the ministerial level patrons of state enterprises, their opportunities to have a direct presence in top level coordinating meetings are far and few between.

The relative plurality of post-Mao society may offer up the possibility of an alternative mode of business representation: business organizations. Evidently, there has been a steady growth in the number of business organizations over the last two decades. According to Dickson (2003), toleration of the proliferation of these bodies may help enhance the legitimacy of the Party:

> the Party relies less on coercion and propaganda to control society and develops links with other organizations, either new ones that it sanctions or old ones it revives, such as united front organizations, labour unions or professional associations. These corporate groups allow the party to organize interests emerging in the course of reform. Links between the Party and the organizations allow both the articulation of those interests and the preservation of the Party's role as the arbiter of competing interests.
>
> (2003: 57–58)

The Party, however, always views the rise of spontaneous business organizations with caution. Stringent administrative measures have been imposed to deter the rapid proliferation of such entities. First, all these organizations must be sponsored by a government or party organization. Application for registration can only be forwarded by the sponsoring organization (*yewu zhuguan bumen*). There is also an informal policy of representational monopoly for sectional interests. That is, only one organization is allowed for any industry in any administrative jurisdiction. In reality, most of the 'quota' has been taken up by 'social' organizations with official sponsorship.

Parallel to such spontaneous development is the expansion of government-sponsored bodies. Several official organizational efforts have been made to accommodate the interests of non-state enterprises. At present, there are three main bodies 'representing' the interests of the private sector. A nationwide network of the Self-Employed Labourer Association (SELA) (*geti laodongzhe Xiehui*), with a constituency of private businesses with a small scale of operation and limited staff, was established under the auspices of the Industry and Commerce Administration (ICA) in the 1980s. Businessmen of larger enterprises who do not want to be confused with *getihu* are invited to join the Private Entreprenuers' Association (PEA), another business body under the guidance of the ICA. While these two bodies are organizational innovations in the reform era, the Party has also made use of its institutional inventory to strengthen the creditability of its business representation framework. As a result, the Industrial and Commercial Federation (ICF) (*gong-shang lian*) was restored in the 1980s. Founded before 1949, the ICF was utilized as a tool of the Party's united front policy (*tongyi zhanxian*) towards compatriot capitalists in Mao's time. It was, however, closed down during the turbulent years in the 1950s when private ownership was under severe attack from radicals. The pragmatic leadership in the post-Mao era saw the necessity of its revival. With its status equivalent to one of the eight so-called democratic parties, the ICF has been promoted as the most prestigious organization representing the interests of private business in today's China.

It is, however, widely off the mark to conceive China as moving towards a corporatist model of business representation. The facade of organizational representation should not obscure the top-down nature of these linkages (Foster 2002; Pearson 1994; Unger and Chan 1994; White et al. 1997). Both SELA and PEA are primarily administrative extensions of the ICA. In many cases, local branches of these organizations are financially dependent on the official budget and ICA officials seldom shy away from direct control of the daily operation of these 'unofficial' organizations. In reality, these bodies perform a conventional 'transmission belt' function of a mass organization sponsored by the communist regime. In a similar vein, the ICF is also under the close supervision of the United Front Department of the Party and overlapping membership is common. And despite the state-sponsorship of these bodies, the Party remains cautious about their subversive potential. Accordingly, all local units of these organizations are forbidden to establish formal vertical or horizontal connections with sister units of the same name. There is no leadership relationship between business bodies at different levels and, most importantly, their 'national network' should stay loose and nominal (Wank 1999; Yep 2000).

Private initiative

The Party's uneasiness towards collective representation explains why many businessmen prefer the more individualistic approach of interest articulation. Central to this approach is the possession of political titles and recognition. At local level, officials embrace business leaders enthusiastically. Oi's (1999) notion of 'local state corporatism' – a definitive perspective for understanding government–business relationship in rural China – highlights the symbiotic relationship between local government and business leaders. Economic influence is a licence to political power. Yep (2003b) conceptualizes this as a process of 'manager empowerment' in which economic elites are co-opted into the local policy process on the basis of their management expertise, ability to deliver prosperity and fiscal health. In many localities, it has become routine to appoint successful businessmen as deputy mayors or to recommend welcoming them into the People's Congress or the people's political consultative conference. Some successful private businessmen go further and manage to achieve a kind of iconic status of the 'new rich' on the national scene as well (*Ming Pao* 2005: A26). The relatively small size of non-state enterprises in general, when compared with their state counterparts, however, still hinders the reach of the former into the policy process. Most private and rural enterprises remain dwarfed by state enterprises in terms of asset values and staff strength, though neither of these measures would necessarily imply economic efficiency. Individual firms' relative economic lightweight, nonetheless, may deprive these non-state enterprises of the attention or response of policy-makers occasionally.

Lobbying on the part of non-state sector firms could be suffocated by changes in the political climate. Political endorsement does not always come naturally. Worse still, private entrepreneurs remain an easy target during a reversal of the political tide. They were singled out as 'spiritual pollutants' in the early 1980s and as major culprits of tax evasion in the 1990s. However, when compared with the attack in the aftermath of the events occurring on 2 June 1989, these harassments appear trivial and irrelevant. Private entrepreneurs were seen as one of the many 'black hands' behind the student movement (Black and Munro 1993). The active involvement of a few private businessmen like Wan Yunnan of the Beijing Stone Group (*xitong jituan*) certainly provided ammunition for the dogmatic who felt uncomfortable with these non-state elements. One punitive measure is the exclusion of private entrepreneurs from Party membership. Despite the advent of marketization, Party membership still maintains its appeal to aspirants in Chinese society. In addition to the romantic few who still share the Party's rhetoric of egalitarianism and idealism, many private businessmen do appreciate the Party connection for practical reasons. For many, a facade of official sponsorship is crucial for survival. The prevalence of this sentiment is reflected in the tendency of 'fake collective' (*jia jitie*) registration during the early years of reform, when many private enterprises tried to obtain a collective enterprise business license. They believed such 'redness' would make their business look more legitimate and acceptable in the sceptical eyes of the Party ideologues. Party membership should perform a similar function. Unfortunately, the door was shut until very recently, when the Jiang Zemin introduced the 'three presentation theory' (*sange daibiao lilun*) into the Party Constitution, which in essence cherishes the contribution of the private sector.

Non-state business leaders are not the only victims of their marginalization from the policy process. Such exclusion may further alienate the decision-makers from reality. And under-representation of non-state sectors results in irrational policies and economic dislocations. Economic policies that only accommodate the concerns of the state sector in many cases cause damage to the national interest. Take banking policy, for example. Non-state sectors appear to have out-competed their state sector counterparts in terms of efficiency in recent years. Despite the trend of gradual decline in the share of total losses, state enterprises still contributed more than half of the total losses in the country. Ironically, it is the more efficient non-state sector that suffers from paucity of credit supply. State banks are, in general, reluctant to provide loans and credit facilities for private enterprise in particular. There appears little connection between efficiency and credit decisions (Lardy 1998; Tsai 2002). Such dramatic discrepancy between economic performance and the distribution of credit uncovers the possible damage caused by the over-representation of the state sector in the policy process.

State enterprises remain well protected and continue to enjoy preferential treatment that they may not deserve in economic terms. This may be attributed to the gradual approach of the Chinese reforms: unlike the advocates of 'shock therapy', the Chinese Communist Party has never envisaged a full privatization of state enterprise in the foreseeable future. Yet, the mismatch between the economic landscape and interest representation may amplify the possible dislocation in economic policy. Marginalized from the decision-making process, the non-state economic actors could possibly be deprived of a level-playing field with their competitors in the state sector. Nevertheless, the consequent policy bias towards the state sector can simply defeat the whole purpose of economic reforms: the hardening of budgetary constraints (Kornai 1992). If efficiency is no longer the imperative for survival, and avail-ability of resources is determined more by political or other non-economic reasons, why should state enterprise care about improvement in performance? And if this is the case, the damage is not confined to non-state enterprises which are squeezed out of competition because of their marginalization in the policy process: the national economy suffers as well.

Conclusion

Chinese leaders never hide their admiration of the success achieved by the dragon economies in East Asia. For the communist leaders, the synthesis of the developmental state approach and authoritarianism provides the best blueprint for China, a country obsessed with hyper-growth but which remains reticent on political liberalization. Economic growth always comes first. Such preoccupation with growth applies not only to China's understanding of the nature of post-Mao governance, but is also relevant to her perception of the developmental trajectory of the post-1997 Hong Kong. The fundamental value of Hong Kong lies in the economic realm. At minimum, Hong Kong must show to the world that there is life after British colonial rule and pros-perity is possible after China's resumption of sovereignty. In a more positive light, Hong Kong should serve as a conduit facilitating China's integration with global capitalism and the world financial market. Hong Kong is nothing but an economic city. Such preoccupation with economic growth precludes the idea of political reform as the prerequisite for sustained development. Political liberalization, the sharing of power or ultimately democratization can wait. This is the case for the motherland; this is the case for Hong Kong. Zhao Ziyang's notion of neo-authoritarianism (*xinquanwei zhuyi*) in the 1980s, or Hu Jintao's catchphrase of 'harmonious society' (*hexie shehui*) in the twenty-first century, share the same logic of economy first (Diamond 2003; Pan 2003; Pei 2000).

Academic rethinking on the notion of the developmental state should have provoked serious reflection among the Chinese leaders. The focus has now shifted to the contribution of non-state actors to the success of state devel-opmentalism (Stiglitz and Shahid 2001). According to the 'revisionist' view, the developmental state is no longer seen as 'an imperious entity lording it over society but a partner with the business sector in a historical compact of industrial transformation' (Woo-Cumings 1999: 16). The limitations of the state in promoting development should not be overlooked (Doner 1992;

Okimoto 1989). According to the new logic, the state derives its strength not from its alienation but from social embeddedness – the ability to engage key economic players (Migdal 2001) – and the developmental state entails both autonomy and embeddedness (Evans 1995). Synchronicity between political structure and economic landscape is thus mandatory and the sequential view of economic-political changes finds no place in this revised paradigm. Changes in political institutions are thus necessary in Hong Kong and China, not because of the pressure of the international community, or the appetite for the western way of life cherished by the educated few. As seen from the above analysis, the current arrangement of interest representation in both administrations has brought unnecessary strain to their respective political order. In the case of Hong Kong, the naked bias favouring local business has bred suspicion and tension in the local society and the unceasing accusations of government–business collusion has also weakened the legitimacy of the Special Administration Region Government. Certain forms of concession to the growing demand for acceleration of democratization are unavoidable if the local administration is to retain the trust and respect of the local population, and to convince the public of its capacity for autonomous decision making *vis-a-vis* the capitalist class. The current debate over the electoral reforms concerning the Chief Executive and the legislature could have been a good opportunity for addressing public concern.

In the same vein, the obsolete decision-making structure characterized by an over-representation of the state sector exerts a similar negative impact on the mainland's political economy. The marginalization of non-state enterprises in the policy process restricts state access to invaluable information, support and feedback on its policies. By alienating itself from a significant constituency for further reform, the Chinese state makes itself vulnerable to the narrow concerns of the state sector that has strong incentive to prolong its privileged position. Some form of political liberalization or institutional plurality may help unleash the voices of non-state business. Universal suffrage or national-level electoral reforms certainly remain taboo for the current leadership, yet a more inclusive approach of business representation is possible in spite of the Party's resistance to experimentation with western style democracy. Greater respect of and tolerance towards a spontaneous move of interest articulation, more self-restraint in intervening in the administration of social organizations, and a pragmatic approach in the political co-optation of the business elite could help address the dislocation of business articulation and representation without fundamental challenge to the supreme position of the Party.

The pro-growth orientation witnessed in both the mainland and Hong Kong has not only led to a convergence in favouritism towards business and the institutional configurations of business representation in both settings, but also also reveals a high degree of path dependence that further consolidates the inherent bias of their respective systems. Though different trajectories and genesis are discernable in these two cases, both systems are confronted with the same challenge: how to strike a proper balance between political privilege and socio-economic change. And despite their many differences in social and political landscapes, they share the same way out. The common lesson revealed from the analysis here is that, without some form of inclusionary effort and re-enfranchisement in policy process that shows accord with the changing outlook of the social and economic structures, long-term sustainability of economic growth is doubtful.

Note

1 It is, however, important to reiterate the caveat in inferring from such a broad-stroke depiction the current stage of state–business relationship in China. Countries do not just have one political economy, but multiple political economies (Kennedy 2005), factors such as economic characteristics of firms, sectoral uniqueness and configuration of the business environment can all affect the pattern of interaction between policy-makers and business actors.

References

Black, G. and Munro, R. (1993) *Black Hands of Beijing*, New York: Wiley.

Boycko, M., Shleifer, A. and Vishny, R. (1996) *Privatizing Russia*, Cambridge, MA: MIT Press.

Byrd, W. and Lin Q. (1990) *China's Rural Industry: Structure, Development and Reform*, Oxford: Oxford University Press.

Cheung, A. (2000) New interventionism in the making: interpreting state interventions in Hong Kong after the change of sovereignty, *Journal of Contemporary China*, 9(24): 291–308.

Cheung, A. and Wong, P. (2004) Who advised the Hong Kong government? The politics of absorption before and after 1991, *Asian Survey*, 44(6): 874–894.

Diamond, L. (2003) The rule of law as transition to democracy in China, *Journal of Contemporary China*, 12(35): 319–332.

Dickson, B. (2003) *Red Capitalists in China*, New York: Cambridge University Press.

Doner, R. (1992) Limits of state strength: toward an institutionalist view of economic development, *World Politics*, 44: 398–431.

Evans, P. (1995) *Embedded Autonomy*, Princeton, NJ: Princeton University Press.

Feng, B. (1996) *Xiang Gang Ying Zi Cai Tuan 1841–1996* [*British Conglomerates in Hong Kong 1841–1997*], Hong Kong: Joint Publishing.

Feng, B. (1997) *Xiang Gang Ying Zi Cai Tuan 1841–1997* [*British Conglomerates in Hong Kong, 1841–1997*], Hong Kong: Joint Publishing.

Foster, K. (2002) Embedded within state agencies: business associations in Yantai, *China Journal*, 47: 41–65.

Goodstadt, L. (2000) China and the selection of Hong Kong's post-colonial elite, *China Quarterly*, 163: 721–741.

Goodstadt, L. (2005) *Uneasy Partners: The Conflict between Public Interest and Private Profit in Hong Kong*, Hong Kong: Oxford University Press.

Guo S. (2003) The ownership reform in China: what direction and how far?, *Journal of Contemporary China*, 12(36): 553–573.

Hong Kong Yearbook (various years) http://www.yearbook.gov.hk/2003/english/hkfact/hkfact.html.

Kennedy, S. (2005) *The Business of Lobbying in China*, Cambridge, MA: Harvard University Press.

King, A. (1981) Administrative absorption of politics in Hong Kong: emphasis on grass roots level, in A. King and R. Lee (eds), *Social Life and Development in Hong Kong*, Hong Kong: Chinese University Press.

Kornai, J. (1992) *The Socialist System*, Princeton, NJ: Princeton University Press.

Krugman, P. (1997) What ever happened to the Asian miracle?, *Fortune*, 18 August.

Lardy, N. (1998) *China's Unfinished Economic Revolution*, Washington, DC: Brookings Institution.

Lau, S.K. (2002) Tung Chee-hwa's governing strategy: the shortfall in politics, in S. K. Lau (ed.), *The First Tung Chee-hwa Administration*, Hong Kong: Chinese University Press.

Lee, E. (1999) Governing post-colonial Hong Kong, *Asian Survey*, 39(6): 940–959.

Lieberthal, K. and Oksenberg, M. (1988) *Policy Making in China: Leaders, Structures and Processes*, Princeton, NJ: Princeton University Press.

Migdal, J. (2001) *State in Society*, New York and Cambridge: Cambridge University Press.

Miners, N. (1991) *The Government and Politics of Hong Kong*, fifth edition, Hong Kong: Oxford University Press.

Ming Pao (2005) Rong Jijie maintains his position as the richest in China, 4 November, p. A26.

Murrell, P. (1997) What is shock therapy? What did it do in Poland and Russia?, in P. Hare and J. R. Davis (eds), *Transition to the Market Economy: Critical Perspectives on the World Economy*, Volume I, London: Routledge.

Ngo, T.W. (2000) Changing government–business relations and the governance of Hong Kong, in R. Ash et al. (eds), *Hong Kong in Transition: The Handover Years*, London, Macmillan.

Oi, J. (1992) Fiscal reform and the economic foundations of local state corporatism in China, *World Politics*, 45: 99–126.

Oi, J. (1999) *Rural China Takes off*, Berkeley: University of California Press.

Okimoto, D. (1989) *Between MITI and the Market*, Stanford, CT: Stanford University Press.

Painter, M. (2005) Transforming the administrative state: reform in Hong Kong and the future of the developmental state, *Public Administration Review*, 6(3): 335–346.

Pan, W. (2003) Towards a consultative rule of law regime in China, *Journal of Contemporary China*, 12(34): 3–30.

Patten, C. (1999) *East and West: The Last Governor of Hong Kong on Power, Freedom and the Future*, London: Macmillan.

Pearson, M. (1994) The Janus face of business associations in China: socialist corporatism in foreign enterprises, *Australian Journal of Chinese Affairs*, 31: 25–41.

Pei, M. (2000) China's evolution toward soft authoritarianism, in E. Friedman and B. McCormick (eds), *What if China Doesn't Democratize? Implications for War and Peace*, New York: M. E. Sharpe.

Sigurdson, J. (1977) *Rural Industrialization in China*, Cambridge, MA: Harvard University Press.

Smyth, R. (2000) Should China be promoting large-scale enterprises and enterprise groups?, *World Development*, 28(4): 721–737.

Smyth, R. and Zhai, Q. (2003) Economic restructuring in China's large and medium-sized state-owned enterprises: evidence from Liaoning, *Journal of Contemporary China*, 12(34): 173–205.

So, A. (2000) Hong Kong's problematic democratic transition: power dependence or business hegemony?, *Journal of Asian Studies*, 59(2): 359–381.

Stiglitz, J. and Shahid, Y. (2001) *Rethinking the East Asian Miracle*, Oxford: Oxford University Press.

Sutherland, D. (2003) *China's Large Enterprises and the Challenge of Late Industrialization*, London and New York: RoutledgeCurzon.

SynergyNet (2005) *Review of the Performance of Legislative Councillors, 2004–2005*, Hong Kong: SynergyNet.

Tang, J. (1999) Business as usual: the dynamics of government–business relations in the Hong Kong Special Administrative Region, *Journal of Contemporary China*, 8(21): 275–295.

Tsai, K. (2002) *Back-alley Banking*, Ithaca and London: Cornell University Press.

Unger, J. and Chan, A. (1995) China, corporatism and the East Asian model, *Australian Journal of Chinese Affairs*, 33: 29–53.

Wank, D. (1999) *Commodifying Communism*, New York: Cambridge University Press.

White, G., Howell, J. and Shang, X. (1997) *In Search of Civil Society*, Oxford: Clarendon Press.

Woo-Cumings, M. (1999) Introduction: Chalmers Johnson and the politics of nationalism and development, in M. Woo-Cumings (ed.), *The Developmental State*, Ithaca and London: Cornell University Press.

Xu J. (1993) *Xu Jiatun Xianggang Huiyilu* [*Xu Jiatun's Memoir on Hong Kong*], Taipei, Lianhebao.

Yep, R. (2000) The limitations of corporatism for understanding reforming China: an empirical analysis in a rural county, *Journal of Contemporary China*, 9(25): 547–566.

Yep, R. (2003a) Articulating business interests in rural China: trends, prospects and political implications, in J. Cheng (ed.), *China's Challenge in the Twenty-first Century*, Hong Kong: City University Press.

Yep, R. (2003b) *Manager Empowerment in China*, New York and London: RoutledgeCurzon.

Zhongguo Xiangzhen Qiye Tongji Jiliu 1978–2002 [*China's Rural Enterprise Statistics 1978–2002*], Beijing: Zhongguo Nongye Chubanshe.

Zhongguo Xiying Qiye Fazhan Baogao [*Report on China's Private Enterprises*] (2002) Beijing: Shehui Kexue Wenxian Chubanshe.

10 From developmental regimes to post-developmental regimes

Business and pension reforms in Japan, South Korea and Taiwan

Young Jun Choi

The role and power of business appear to have regained academic interest in welfare state literature under the influence of globalization in the western world. In East Asia, however, the literature on welfare regimes has paid fairly limited attention to business until now. It tends to be discussed within the relationship of the state as its subordinate rather than recognizing it as an independent actor, as seen in the literature on the developmental state. Globalization and democratization have unshackled business from the state; however, the influence of the independent sector within the developmental state discourse remains ambiguous. In this chapter, changes in the state–business relationship and also business influences on pension development in Japan, South Korea (hereafter Korea) and Taiwan will be analysed and discussed in the context of the shift from developmental regimes to post-developmental regimes.

Legacies of the developmental regimes (–1980s)

Developmental states and business

The main characteristic of the relationship between the state and business in this period was institutional symbiosis or collusion. Finance was the 'nerve' of the developmental regimes that bound states and business (Woo-Cumings 1999: 10–11). Instead of being a passive actor, business was an essential partner for the governments during this period.

In Japan, the state's financial capacity and regulation played a critical role in defining the relationship with business. After defeat in the Second World War, the private financial sector had poor capacity for providing a long-term fund for business. By contrast, the state had a massive public fund accrued from the postal saving system and pension funds. The government tightly regulated the financial market and channeled funds into strategic industries (Kuwayama 2000; Pempel 1999). Yet, arguably, business, to a large extent, also played a significant role in shaping economic policy along different routes, including formal and informal policy coordination with government ministries and massive financial contributions to the Liberal Democratic

Party (LDP) (Khosla 2000; Yoshimatsu 1997). Business could present a unified voice to the government through the Federation of Economic Organizations (FEO), *Keidanren* (Babb 2002: 325). Kienzle and Shadur (1997: 24) note that the relationship between the LDP and business underwent a process of institutionalization from the late 1950s to the 1960s. With regards to business structure, it is important to understand Japan's horizontally and vertically integrated conglomerate-style business structure, *keiretsu* (Feenstra et al. 1999; Johnson 1987). For example, in 1986, the largest 100 non-financial corporations had 3,899 subsidiary companies, of which over 50 per cent of issued stocks were owned by the parent corporation, and 9,519 affiliate companies, of which 10 to 50 per cent of issued stocks were owned by the parent company (Hiroshi 1991: 223). Also, the MITI reports that 81.6 per cent of small firms have never changed their main contractors (Cowling and Tomlinson 2001: 13).

The authoritative Korean government also directed and promoted business activities through financial and industrial policy. Provided that private sectors were nearly incapable of generating or borrowing capital either domestically or internationally, they needed to rely heavily on the government, who also did not have adequate capital in hand but could get massive long-term loans from abroad with very low interest rates under the favourable international circumstances (Johnson 1987). With tight control of the financial sector, the government controlled the direction of capital to desired sectors according to its developmental plan. Businesses, particularly the conglomerates, *chaebol*, promoted by strategic industrial policy by the Economic Planning Board (EPB), were regarded as quasi-state organisations. The hugely diversified and family-run conglomerates enjoyed all kinds of preferential policies and their risky investments were guaranteed by the state, which made their oligopolistic status possible in the market (Kahal 2001; Wad 2002). As a result, the Korean economy was largely dependent on *chaebol* because a large number of SMEs were connected or subservient to them in one way or another. However, this structure necessarily led to a very high debt–equity ratio, mostly 3:1 or 4:1, as found in *keiretsu*. In return, *chaebol* were the source of political funds for political leaders, which made it possible for them to access ruling elites and influence government policy decision making (Kang 2002). Korean business, like Japanese business, established a head organization, the Federation of Korean Industries (FKI).

The Taiwanese government was also authoritative, exercising firm control over financial institutions and businesses weakened during the post-war era. Yet, the pattern of the state's interaction in financing and industrial policy was very different from that adopted in Japan and Korea. The Taiwanese government adopted monetary policies rather than fiscal policies, i.e. tax breaks and high-depreciation allowances rather than outright loans to encourage investment in particular sectors (Johnson 1987: 149). While financial institutions gave preferential treatment to state-owned enterprises (SOEs) and party-owned enterprises (POEs), small and medium scale enterprises

(SMEs) were funded largely internally through family, equity and informal curb market loans (Johnson 1987; Pempel 1999). Tu (1991: 124) notes that, 'Between 1982 and 1986, the average percentage of capital formation contributed by family members was over 90 per cent and even in manufacturing industries it was over 85 per cent. As a result, there was a clear division of business structure between them (Chung 1999: 19; Evans 1995: 56; Whitley 1996). SOEs and POEs performed several important functions for the KMT: as a source of political funding, patronage outlets, propaganda organs, developmental agents and market regulators (Fields 2002: 126–130). They were not export-oriented like conglomerates in Japan and Korea, and produced intermediate goods that were sold domestically (Feenstra et al. 1999: 76). Instead, a large number of SMEs in the private sector led the export industry. Under these circumstances business organizations did not develop well. Although some large ones existed, including the National Council of Industry and Commerce (Chu 1994: 118–119), their autonomy was much weaker than those in Korea and Japan.

Pension legacies: business influences

In the developmental regimes, pension schemes were formulated and developed. In Japan, although a public pension for employees was introduced in 1942 during the Second World War, it was not until 1954 that the current structure of the Employees Pension Insurance (EPI) was established. During the 1960s and 1970s, Japanese public pension schemes were quickly expanded. The National Pension covering non-employees was introduced in 1961 and the benefit level considerably increased during this period. In addition, in line with remarkable economic growth, occupational retirement benefits, including retirement allowance and corporate pensions, were solidified and dramatically expanded during this period.

In Korea, for private sector employees, there had been no public pension programme until 1988 when the National Pension (NP) was introduced. Before the NP, private sector employees mainly received retirement allowance, particularly those working in medium to large size firms. The Taiwanese government introduced the current Labour Insurance (LI) in 1958, of which a component is the old-age lump-sum benefit. In 1985, when the government introduced the Labour Standard Law (LSL), it also introduced the retirement allowance. All three countries demonstrate productivist welfare development (Holiday 2000; Kwon 2005), but specific forms of pension development varied. There were two notable differences in pension development between Japan/Korea and Taiwan.

The first crucial difference was their preference for funded social insurance pension schemes. In Japan, the EPI as a funded scheme could accumulate a large sum of funds. In the 1950s, the funds were heavily invested in the 'industry/technology' area, but as industrialization and democratization progressed, the funds were used to improve housing and living environments

(Park 2004: 552–553). With the funds, the LDP and the government could steer Japanese politics and the economy by way of honouring election pledges and distributing the funds in different business sectors. In Korea, the one serious innovation before the introduction of the NP was the National Welfare Pension Act in 1973. The Park government also intended to mobilize the large sum of pension funds for the success of the heavy-chemical industrial plan, launched with the Declaration of Heavy Chemical Industrialization (HCI) by President Park in January 1973 (Kwon 1998: 108; Shin 2003: 85, 94–95). In the mid-1980s, when the NP was being prepared, there was also a strong motive to mobilize capital through the NP fund. As Korea came under the increasing international pressure of the open economy, as will be discussed later, the government needed to have a substantial amount of funds to push forward economic and industrial policy (Hwang 2005; Shin 2003: 132).

While the large pension fund was highly attractive to the Korean developmental regime, in which the government provided huge, risky long-term loans to the export-oriented *chaebol* for developing the plans of the HCI, there was no imminent need for that in Taiwan. The politically tied and more-domestically oriented big firms in the countries did not necessarily require funded pension schemes. Exported-oriented SMEs in which efficiency and flexibility were the key to their success did not need huge funds either. In that sense, it seems to be easily understandable that there had been no serious attempt to introduce a fully-funded pension scheme for the purpose of mobilizing capital in Taiwan.

The second important difference is found in the arrangement of occupational retirement benefits. Japanese business had developed advanced retirement packages and different schemes and Korean business also developed the retirement allowance. It is interesting to note that occupational benefits had been developed and expanded, not in a coercive way by the developmental states, but in a voluntary way by business. As a facilitator, the governments encouraged business to introduce occupational benefits by way of providing various tax-related incentives (MHLW, Japan 2004: 127; Shinkawa 2005: 163). In effect, the funds for retirement benefits, either internally or externally managed, were regarded as a source of working capital. Even when externally managed, the fund was managed by a financial institution inside *keiretsu*, or by an institution that invested the fund in the commissioning corporation (Park 2004: 556).

In contrast, there was only very limited development and expansion of occupational retirement benefits in Taiwan. In Taiwan, old-age benefit in the LI had a few things in common with the retirement benefits available in Japan and Korea, e.g. offering a lump-sum benefit and being mostly available to large enterprise employees until the 1980s. However, there are significant differences between them. Initially, the intention was different in that the development of the LI was more obviously politically motivated as the KMT consolidated its power. The one characteristic that reflected this difference is that the LI was transferable between different firms. In relation to this, another difference was that the LI was directly regulated and provided by the government, while business remained an intermediate actor. Therefore, the patron–client relationship was formulated between the state and employees, whereas the benefits in Japan and Korea helped the creation of the patron–client relationship between employers and employees while the governments remained intermediate players. This argument can be strengthened when considering the tripartite contribution of the LI, which was not found in Japan and Korea.

One of the important explanations behind this crucial difference seems to be the varying business structures in these countries. Most SMEs did not seem to have enough financial capacity to develop occupational benefits. Also, in many cases, since SMEs were run and managed by families, they did not need to institutionalize occupational benefits. Occupational retirement benefits in Taiwan were much less developed as a result. In 1985, when the government introduced non-transferable retirement benefit, unsurprisingly many firms did not adopt it and the government had to consider alternative substitutes from 1991 onwards (Cheng and Wu 1997: 8). As a result, Taiwan developed a clearly different policy approach to Japan and Korea.

From developmental regimes to post-developmental regimes (1980s–)

Driving forces

From circa 1980, the developmental regimes began to suffer from internal and external pressures. Interestingly, some of these were to a large extent caused by the success of developmental strategies – what can be labelled 'the paradox of the developmental regimes'. Here I will explain three driving forces causing the transformation of the developmental regimes.

First of all, there have been significant changes in the *international political economy* in the East Asia region, particularly related to the US. During the period of the Cold War and the Bretton Woods system, their *dirigisme* – selling at low prices abroad while keeping domestic markets protected and closed – had been benignly neglected by the US. However, at the end of this period, the US and European countries increasingly pressurized these countries to open their markets, including financial markets, and to fix 'unfair trade practices', e.g. tariff barriers, regulations on foreign capital and financial subsidiaries for business (Schaede 2004: 285). They could not ignore these demands, not least because their exports highly relied on the US. As a result, the governments could not help but abandon their long-established industrial and fiscal policies step-by-step (Chu 1994: 121; Minns 2001: 1032). This development involved currency re-appreciation of the US dollar, which was intended to remove the cost advantage, and liberalization of trade and financial policies. In these circumstances, the export-oriented firms had to find a totally new way to cope with the new international environment (Noh 2005: 123; Schaede 2004: 286).

There were also important *domestic changes* impacting on business. In Japan, big conglomerates could secure large cash flow from their successful exports, which resulted in their diminishing reliance on domestic credits controlled by the government. By the 1980s, it was obvious that they were relying more heavily on retained earnings and equity financing rather than debt financing (Pempel 1999: 150). Also, following the change in the Foreign Exchange Law in 1980, businesses could supply capital from abroad without a great deal of government intervention. As a result, the business establishment began to distance itself from the LDP (Babb 2002: 325). In Korea, by 1979 *chaebol* were growing so fast as a result of their close relationships with the Park regime that they became 'too big to fail' in this 'mutual hostage' situation. The new military government in 1980 desperately sought legitimacy from the people by sacrificing *chaebol* for their 'illicit wealth accumulation' (Moon 1994: 147). Although *chaebol* were indeed forced to sell off 166 subsidiaries upon the arrival of the Chun regime, they then acquired another 120 within the next four years. Financial deregulation also provided more leverage and autonomy for *chaebol* as they moved aggressively into the newly opened financial market. As a result, *chaebol* expanded their scope and power during the 1980s (Kim 1991).

In Taiwan, efforts were made to enhance the state's steering capacity in the development of high-tech sectors and in upgrading conventional export sectors (Chu 1994: 122). In this process, the state used state research laboratories and SOEs/POEs in policy financing, implementation and support. For instance, the Central Finance Committee, one of the major players in this process, created a new commercial entity, a tripartite joint venture linking the SOEs, the KMT and private firms. These innovative hybrids were technically 'private companies' but the combined share of the government and the KMT was typically higher than 50 per cent (ibid.: 124). Since most SMEs were eager to have a political connection with the KMT, the hierarchical relationship between the Taiwanese government and business was largely maintained intact.

Among domestic factors, *democratization* had an important impact on business power in Korea and Taiwan. Again, there were clear differences in its effects between Korea and Taiwan. Democratization in Korea ignited visible conflicts between business and the government. From the mid-1980s the FKI started to publicly criticize the government's policies. In return, the government intimidated *chaebol* by way of dismissing the seventh largest *chaebol*, Kukje, after it refused to make a 'voluntary donation' to the Ilhae foundation linked to President Chun (Kang 2002: 188). After Roh won the presidential election in 1987, however, defiant *chaebol* declared that the FKI would henceforth provide donations only to politicians willing to support and protect business freedom (Moon 1994: 155). Later, the Roh government investigated tax evasion on the part of defiant Hyundai, the largest *chaebol*, and ordered it to pay US$180 million (ibid.: 159). However, the president of Hyundai, Chung Joo Young openly defied this order and even established his own political party for the next presidential election in 1992. Despite his defeat against Kim Young Sam, Roh's successor, it provided a clear indication that *chaebol* were out of the government's hands. In contrast, in Taiwan, SMEs and private capital were still politically weak. Not least because of the financial independence of the KMT from business, democratization could not significantly undermine the state's dominance over business and society. Nevertheless, the KMT needed to carefully listen and respond to the demands of SMEs as these organizations, mainly run by the Taiwanese, significantly increased their importance in the Taiwanese economy over time (Iwasaki 2002).

Moving towards the post-developmental regimes

Due to the above pressures it is obvious that the developmental regimes have been transformed into post-developmental regimes. Yet, again, Japan/Korea and Taiwan have shown different transforming patterns. In Japan, after the appreciation of the yen, the government set interest rates to almost zero in order to permit Japanese industry to relocate its low-wage manufacturing overseas and create new higher-value added enterprises to re-employ displaced workers (Babb 2002: 333). Around this time, mature export-oriented businesses significantly decreased their dependence on bank credit, and the role of main banks inside the *keiretsu* was considerably reduced as a result of selling their stocks; *keiretsu* increasingly depend on the stock market. Meanwhile, the proportion of total manufacturing output produced overseas between 1985 and 1999 had risen almost five-fold, from 7 to 35 per cent, and outsourcing accounted for 31.1 per cent of the total corporate output of Japan's trans-nationals, which represented a more than 350 per cent increase on the 1985 level (Cowling and Tomlinson 2001: 12).

Mighty big businesses led by the FEO forced the government to fully deregulate and liberalize the Japanese economy, as demonstrated by statements made by the FEO leaders during the 1990s. The temporary tumble of the LDP in 1993 made the political sphere more vulnerable to business interests. At the same time, the FEO announced that it would no longer act as a conduit for campaign contributions to political parties from its member corporations (Babb 2002: 334). Although its position was reversed as the LDP resumed power again, it was generally seen that the financial contributions of big business and the FEO to politicians and parties reduced considerably thereafter (Mulgan 1999: 1). Yet, it seems obvious that the Japanese economy still largely relies on the performance of these *keiretsu*.[1] Thus, Cowling and Tomlinson (2001) note that, 'strategic decision-making affecting the level of investment, employment and output in the Japanese economy are concentrated within the corporate hierarchies of Japan's trans-nationals' (p.1).

In Korea, as some *chaebol* have been trying to trans-nationalize themselves, they have also become stronger. From 1993, the Kim Young Sam government initially endeavoured to curb the unlimited growth of *chaebol* in various ways, e.g. by limiting the quantity of bank loans granted to them, by regulating cross-subsidization and cross-payment or by implementing a 'specialization' policy to limit their diversification (Shin 2003: 137–140). However, these were not successful because the government did not actively enforce these policies on *chaebol*. Moreover, in 1995, as the Kim government removed all bank credit system regulations, bank loans were increasingly in the hands of *chaebol* (ibid.: 141; Kang 2002: 199). After substantial financial liberalization and deregulation during the Kim government (Shin 2003: 145–146), it is needless to say that releasing the core of its power markedly eroded state power over business.

Although the state weakened, it still had various means to check business by way of tax audits, rejected loan applications, investigations into cross-subsidization, and so on. Therefore, despite their increasing power *chaebol* still made enormous donations to political parties. As a result, the Asian financial crisis in 1997 severely impacted *chaebol* and, equally, the government who had poorly regulated business and financial markets. The myth of *chaebol*, as being 'too big to fail', was completely shattered. Starting with Hanbo and Kia in 1997, more *chaebol* became insolvent after the crisis, including Daewoo, the fourth largest *chaebol*. In the process of economic recovery, under the influence of the IMF and World Bank, the Kim Dae Jung government, relatively less linked to *chaebol*, drove *chaebol* reforms in 1998 and 1999 (Haggard 2000: 103; Kahal 2001: 175). However, this government drive was far from signalling the return of the developmental regime. Through this process, the government liberalized and deregulated many laws related to foreign capital and business in order to attract them to taking over a few faltering *chaebol* and even banks.

As the economy quickly recovered from the serious loss incurred by the financial crisis, surviving *chaebol* became even stronger than before. With the partial success of corporate restructuring, survivors could be more financially and structurally sound and the dependence of the economy on fewer *chaebol* was stronger. Also, conglomerates like Samsung and Hyundai Motor have succeeded in the international market and are regarded as national champions. As a result, it is widely accepted that the *chaebol*-dominated economy, involving vertically-integrated SMEs, still persists without the developmental state, and their power over and decisions on investment and employment are crucial in determining the performance of the Korean economy.

It is not surprising that Taiwan was not a victim of the Asian crisis, because the SMEs, the core of the Taiwanese economy, have generally been based on more prudent financial bases. Although the Taiwanese government also introduced several measures for financial liberalization, it has cautiously and partially implemented these under the strict supervision of the government. Its main purpose was to finance the rising 'New Economy': information and communication technology, and the semi-conductor industry (Lue 2004: 17). Although the developmentalism was weaker than in the pre-1990s, this 'soft' developmental state still enjoyed high autonomy to direct and regulate industrial and financial policy compared to the other countries. Nonetheless, Taiwan was not completely free from the economic crisis. Since 1990, many SMEs have moved out of Taiwan looking for cheap production sites, mainly to China (ibid.: 20–21). In addition to the dramatic fall in Taiwan's exports to Asian countries after the crisis, the unemployment rate has risen to a historical record and a slowdown in productivity has been apparent since 1999.

However, there has been no sign of changing power configurations between the state and business. In spite of strong demands from employers to deregulate foreign direct investment (FDI) to China, the government still regulates the stream of FDI and the rising of the New Economy has been largely linked to the SOEs/POEs in the form of joint ventures or financial relationships. In fact, the assets of POEs alone, 'KMT Inc.', were around US$42 billion and the profit from them was valued at US$500 million in 1996, which undoubtedly made the KMT the richest political party in the world (Fields 2002: 127). In this situation, the KMT's most important mission was to maintain its political status in order to hang on to the privileged position of the main party as the DPP became stronger throughout the 1990s. The DPP, relatively free from business interests, took the anti-business and pro-welfare/environment stance (Tang 2000: 86). When the DPP seized power in 2000, however, this stance was abandoned and they declared: 'Economic development is the top priority' (Hill and Hwang 2005: 157; Tang 2000: 86). As the economic recession deepens, it appears that the DPP has no alternative but to inherit the technocrats recruited and sponsored by the KMT because the DPP is composed of people who are outside the traditional intellectual mainstream (*Taiwan Business Topics* September 2002).

As a result of current transformations in these post-developmental regimes, the overall structural power of business over the state since 1990 has been considerably transformed.

Pension reforms in Japan, Korea and Taiwan

From the previous sections, it is clear that there are still significant differences in business structure evident in Japan, Korea and Taiwan in the era of post-developmental regimes. Much stronger business power coupled with weakening developmental states have resulted in a fundamental change in developmental regime in Japan and Korea; in contrast, that of Taiwan is still fragmented. This section will discuss how the variability of business influences has affected pension reforms in each country and a short comparative discussion will follow.

Japan

Within the fast-changing internal and external environment, discussion about pension downsizing started from around 1980, though pension expenditure was still very low. In 1985, when the current public pension mix was structured, the National Pension was changed into the Basic Pension (BP) by way of integrating the first tiers of the EPI and the NP. Following the 1985 reform, there has been a series of pension retrenchment reforms increasing contribution rates and years, increasing pensionable age, lowering benefit levels, and tightening benefit entitlement. In this downsizing process, it is noticeable how a turbulent political sphere and labour unions have acquiesced and maintained silence about these changes, whereas the vigorous business sector has imposed pressure on the political sphere[2] (McLellan 2004: 11; Takegawa 2005a: 73), calling for further reforms. Together with economic recession and a rapidly ageing population, it seems that the demise of the left-wing Japan Socialist Party and the rise of another right-wing party, the Democratic Party of Japan (DPJ), as the main opposition have helped create the situation.

Even after the 1994 reform, when the government increased the pensionable age of the BP from 60 to 65 and changed benefit indexation in a more conservative way, business demanded further reforms including corporate pension schemes.[3] Before the 1999 reform, the FEO stressed the sustainability of public pensions and the enlargement of private pensions in tandem with fiscal and tax reform (FEO 1998). The Economic Strategy Council, organized by the government in order to create new guidelines for policies, echoes FEO's arguments in its report to the prime minister in 1999, recommending that public pensions be limited to the level of the national minimum, and the supplementary (earnings-related) pensions be completely privatized within 30 years (Kono 2005: 133). Accordingly, in the 1999 reform, the government introduced several changes including benefit reduction, contribution and pensionable age (EPI) increases, and benefit indexation change.

From around this point, the FEO proposed, somewhat surprisingly, the introduction of the tax-based basic pension financed as a solution to increasing contribution evasion/exemption/non-participation in the BP, which eventually would undermine old-age security for many people. This basic pension would be financed by an estimated 3.2 per cent increase in consumption tax – an indirect tax (FEO 1998). Instead of employers and employees bearing the rising cost of increased contribution rates, the FEO seemed to transfer the cost to consumers, including pensioners.[4] This proposal was rejected in the 1999 and 2004 reforms, even though many economists and pension experts supported it before the 2004 reform (Shinkawa 2005: 177). The MHLW argued that the increase in tax revenue to finance the policy was politically unfeasible.

Before the 2004 reform, business favoured limiting increases in contribution rates (a 15 per cent ceiling) and a benefit cut, and again asked for the promotion of private pensions (FEO 2003). Government shared the business sectors' basic idea regarding possible pension reform, as expressed in the report from the Council on Economic and Fiscal Policy (CEFP 2002), noting that: 'Social security will be restructured to harmonize with the economy.' Consequently, five years after the 1999 reform, in the 2004 reform aimed to reduce pension benefit by 50 per cent, including workers' 40-year contribution pension benefits and the spouses' basic pension. Although the MHLW suggested an increase in the contribution rate to 20 per cent, it eventually lowered this to 18.35 per cent following pressure from business and the MOF (Takegawa 2005a: 97). While the government adhered to the contributory BP, it submitted to the minimum benefit level of the BP. In other words, it became impossible to meet the national minimum living standards with only BP benefit despite 40 years of contributions (Shizume 2005). Furthermore, in 2005, both parties, the LDP and the DPJ, suggested an increase in the consumption tax from 5 to 10 per cent (LDP) and 8 per cent (DPJ) to fund welfare programmes (*Japan Times* 25 October 2005), which almost entirely accords with the argument of the FEO.

Another important change occurring in this period was the moving of the management of public pension funds from the TFB supervised by the MOF to the Government Pension Investment Fund (GPIF) supervised by the MHLW in 2001. As argued earlier, pension funds have tended to play a role as industrial funds, social overhead capital or 'price-keeping operations', without little concern for the poor returns (Manow 2001: 20). As the population is ageing rapidly, however, the main concern for the pension funds is not to help the economy but to maximize investment return because under the TFB it had been inadequate and indeed often incurred losses. Also, the MHLW argues that, 'the government should not be a direct investor in private companies' and 'the GPIF would serve as an intermediary and help avoid any potential conflicts of interest' (Park 2004: 565).

The reform of corporate pensions has also been carried out as a result of long-standing business protests that the merit of corporate pensions as working capital is disappearing, coupled with the rise of an ageing populace. Along with the economic downturn, a serious issue of pension underfunding for corporate pensions emerged (McLellan 2004: 8). Although the dissolution of corporate pensions was prohibited in principle except in special cases, many firms attempted to alleviate the financial burdens generated by them (Shinkawa 2005: 172). The number of employees covered by the corporate pension schemes considerably decreased, from 22.89 million in 1996 to 20.04 million in 2002. According to the 1997 FEO report, its basic ideas were to reduce the financial burden, to minimize government intervention and to promote private pensions. Also, it is worth mentioning that the FEO (ibid.) requested means to 'ensure portability' in order to increase flexibility in the labour market, which seemed to declare the end of the 'life-long employment' practice.

The government responded to the voice of business and in 2001 overhauled the whole existing system by introducing two laws: the Defined-Benefit (DB) Corporate Pension Law and the Defined-Contribution (DC) Corporate Pension Law. Obviously, the DC plan would contribute to a considerable reduction of the financial burden for business by transferring the risk of pension fund management from employers to employees. Furthermore, contributions are fully tax-deductible within the maximum limit of contributions and investment earnings are tax-deferred (Takayama 2004: 12). The DB plan was also designed to be acceptable to employers. It allows business more freedom to dissolve and to return the substitute component to the EPI and introduced the 'hybrid/cash balance model', in which 'the benefits employees will receive in the future will vary according to the performance of the investment, but the employer must guarantee a minimum standard of benefit' (Shinkawa 2005: 173). As a result, business in Japan can partly curb the cost generated by pension schemes.

Korea

Korea, with a similar set of pension schemes, has confronted a comparable situation to Japan, particularly since the late 1990s, but in a much more compressed way. After the introduction of the NP, business was mostly silent on the extension of its coverage (from workplaces with ten or more employees to those with five or more employees in 1992, and to agricultural and fishery sector workers in 1995). Most significantly, the 3 per cent contribution rate divided between employers and employees was believed not to undermine business activities. Also, major economic think-tanks, e.g. the Korea Development Institute (KDI), suggested that the funded-style pension scheme could help the national economy (Hwang 2005: 12). In fact, the large sum accrued by the NP fund had been used by the government as social overhead capital for building industrial infrastructure, e.g. road construction based on the Public Fund Management Act (PFMA), until the Act was revised in 1998. Thus, business was rather an indirect beneficiary of this practice.

However, the favourable or silent stance towards the NP began to change from the mid-1990s. There were two reasons behind this. With the NP financial projection report by the KDI arguing that the fund would be depleted in 2033, it seemed that pro-business sides began to turn against the NP and strongly demand pension reform. Also, as the Korean economy began to open and the financial sector was liberalised, those businesses who wanted to diversify their financing sources developed an interest in the NP fund, which was quickly accumulating without being spent and was expected to reach 13 per cent of GDP in 2000 (Kim and Kim 2005: 235). In December 1996, while criticism of government appropriation of public funds, including the NP fund, was increasing, the FKI argued for decreasing public borrowing from the fund and increasing investment in the financial markets (*Seikeiilbo* 3 December 1996). Civic and labour groups also demand transparency of NP fund management. Meanwhile, the National Pension Reform Board (NPRB) where neo-liberal economists and technocrats from the MOF were appointed as key members, started to discuss pension reform, aiming at its sustainability from 1997 onwards.[5]

Circa 1998 and 1999, because they were being squeezed by the government for corporate restructuring after the financial crisis, businesses did not have enough leverage to address pension issues. Nevertheless, it is interesting to note that pension reforms in 1998 and 1999 were more in accord with business demands than against them. First of all, with the reform of the PFMA in 1998, the pension fund began to invest much more in the private sector rather than the public sector.[6] Secondly, although a bi-pillar option suggested by the NPRB and the World Bank was discarded by the pro-welfare coalition, downsizing measures for a more financially sustainable NP in the 1999 reform, even before the full old-age benefit of the NP is paid (scheduled in 2008), were introduced, which was one of the business demands. In fact, substantial expansion of coverage to the self-employed seemed not to undermine business interests since the contribution for the self-employed was borne totally by the insured. Afterwards, as corporate restructuring was virtually finished, the FKI again asked the government to substantially reform the existing NP and the RA in a more sustainable way.

According to the FKI report in 2001 (FKI 2001), it supported the three-tier pension scheme with the basic pension and the suggestion of making it earnings-related. Also, like the FEO in Japan, increase the contribution rate was the last thing it wanted to do because it would cause a rise in labour costs. As it was projected that the NP contribution rate would inevitably need to increase twofold in order to maintain the current structure, it proposed the tax-based basic pension as the first pillar, the strict earnings-related pension as the second, and the corporate pension, replacing the RA, as the third. It estimated that a business usually spends around 8.33 per cent of a worker's monthly salary on RA contributions, resulting in approximately a 12.83 per cent contribution including the NP contribution and excluding the employees' contribution. Thus, it argued that the RA should be replaced by the tax-qualified corporate pension and the earnings-related portion of the NP should decrease accordingly.

In fact, reform of the RA had been demanded by business since the late 1980s. As a result, introducing the NP in 1988, the government agreed to phase out the RA, and to make the NP contribution consist of a one-third contribution from employee, employer and the RA fund, respectively. However, it was not feasible to abolish the RA since the full NP old-age benefit would not be paid until 2008. Instead, business asked government to replace the RA with a flexible corporate pension, which was expected to diminish the employer's burden and also boost the financial market. Together with changing environments in the labour market[7] and business influence, the government finally passed the Corporate Pension Act in December 2004 and implemented it in 2006. The new system is quite like the Japanese one equipping both the DB and the DC plan.

Taiwan

In Taiwan, despite democratization, the influence of business on the social policy-making process has not been apparent. There are several plausible explanations for this in relation to the Taiwanese business structure. Firstly, the underdevelopment of an independent top business organization has been a major obstacle to the establishment of business demands. Secondly, there has been little distinction between the political sphere, particularly the KMT, and large enterprises. Finally, a SMEs-centred business structure has considerably hampered the rise of visible business demands directed against the strong government. Further, SMEs were subjected to very little pressure regarding pension schemes since the cost of LI or retirement benefits was still low and the KMT government did not push them to strictly implement the retirement benefit under the Labour Standard Law (Cheng and Wu 1997: 12).

During the 1990s when tax-based old-age allowance programmes were discussed, introduced (locally in 1993 and the Old-age Peasants' Welfare Allowance (OPWA) in 1995), and extended (the OPWA to fishermen in 1997), enterprises hardly made their voices heard, neither for nor against the programmes. One possible reason for their silence regarding tax-based programmes was the low tax rate applied to SMEs.[8] Tax-based programmes are likely to have less impact on SMEs, but more on large businesses affiliated with the KMT and the government. Assuming that large enterprises were not happy with tax-based old-age allowance schemes, it is not surprising that the KMT initiated the contributory national pension plan instead.

However, the KMT suffered as a result of its inconsistent policy on old-age income programmes. At first, the KMT criticized tax-based allowance schemes and proposed the National Pension (NP) scheme as 'insurance' not 'welfare'. The first proposal by the Council for Economic Planning and Development in 1995 ruled out the government's contribution to the premium in order to avoid the fiscal burden. However, it could not help increasing the financial commitment of the government in the course of highly competitive electoral political battles with the Democratic Progressive Party (DPP). In fact, it was not a desirable option for SMEs, which were keen to avoid an increase in labour costs in the increasingly competitive market. Although SMEs could not access the KMT, they did have political voting power. Yet, one of the obvious problems was funding, given the rising budget deficit and the political difficulty of raising taxes (*Taipei Times* 6 October 1999). As a result, the contributory NP plan was not implemented and kept being postponed during the KMT era, even when the KMT dominated the Executive Yuan and the Legislative Yuan. Also, the NP plan intended to cover every citizen was changed to cover only those who were not covered by the LI, e.g. students and homemakers.

Since the DPP came to power in 2000, the situation has changed. Most importantly, influence has shifted from the KMT, the amalgam of politics and business, to the DPP, which is distant from business. While the DPP seemed to advocate and push the tax-based plan, the KMT, desperate to regain power, suffered from their inconsistent policies on pensions (Chen and Chen 2003). Although the KMT and the People First Party (PFP) maintained their opposition to the DPP proposals, the DPP, a minority in the Legislative Yuan, successfully promoted the NP plan. Finally, the DPP succeeded in implementing the almost universal old-age allowance schemes in 2002: the Old-age Citizens' Welfare Allowance and the Old-age Indigenous Welfare Allowance. As a result, over 71 per cent of those over 65 received one of the allowances in 2003 (BLI 2004). In this process, it skilfully circumvented the issue of funding and business opposition as it introduced old-age allowances as welfare in order to 'respect the elderly in Taiwan'. The DPP, from a stance of political and political superiority to the KMT and the PFP, and in the light of increasing awareness of issues relating to an ageing population, introduced the schemes without significant difficulty.[9]

The retirement benefit under the LSL has recently been an important topic, particularly for the business sector because it directly incurs the cost. Following a 1990 survey suggesting that many employers had not implemented the benefit schemes, the need for a revision to the policy began to be discussed. Also, from the initial discussion of the NP plan, the need for reform had always been recognised. However, as the NP was not introduced, the idea of transforming the benefit into the Labour Pension (LP) was discussed separately from 2000 onwards. At this time, large businesses and business confederations needed to exercise their instrumental power since they were separate from political power. In 2001, the Council of Labour Affairs (CLA) was ready to propose two ideas to change the benefit into a pension scheme at the Economic Development Advisory Conference (EDAC) (*Taipei Times* 23 August 2001). The first one was a defined-contribution individual retirement account, into which employers would be required to deposit 6 per cent of their workers' monthly salary. The other proposal, called an annuity, was more radical in that all the participants in the programme would be paid the same monthly benefit regardless of how much they contributed to the fund over their lifetime.

The employment panel of the EDAC decided to adopt the first proposal and changed the second one into an earnings-related defined-benefit scheme. It also decided to gradually raise the LP contribution from 2 to 6 per cent, favouring business interests. However, the CLA changed its position by increasing employers' contributions to 6 per cent right from the start. Although the proposed scheme was a defined-contribution scheme, there were many points for business to complain about. In addition to opposing the 6 per cent initial contribution rate, business maintained that employees who have worked less than five years at a single company should not be entitled to the pension reserves in their accounts. Furthermore, it lobbied the government to allow businesses to set up their own asset funds through which a part of the employees' pension accounts would be managed. Despite the fierce lobby from businesses, including the insurance industry (*Taipei Times* 8 June 2004; *China Post* 11 June 2004), the final LP bill in 2004 did not accept the three important points that business had forcefully asked for. The only concession was that the government allowed enterprises with 200 or more employees to set up their own LP fund.[10]

Comparative discussion

In contrast to the pre-1990s, there have been remarkable pension reforms in all three countries and there are some noticeable differences between them. Firstly, business demands have been well accepted by political parties in Japan and Korea where business power is strong, but not in Taiwan. In Japan, business has vehemently exercised instrumental power over the political parties. Also, the series of retrenchment reforms of public pensions and corporate pension schemes received in silence by the labourforce and civil society reflects the high structural power of business over the state and society. Although pension issues have been politicized since around the 2004 pension reform (Takegawa 2005a, 2005b), pension proposals by the LDP and the DPJ are neither progressive nor radical. In Korea, although the NP was immature, a similar pattern to Japan is found. From the mid-1990s, business publicly demanded pension reforms, including the NP and the RA. In 2006, the most important issue for the FKI was to curb a further increase in the NP contribution rate. In this sense, the bi-pillar proposal of the main opposition party for an increase in consumption tax exactly reflects the business position. However, the proposal of the main party is not exactly against the business interest either, i.e. a considerable decrease in the benefit and a moderate increase in the contribution rate. In contrast, in Taiwan, during the KMT era large enterprises never publicly expressed conflicting opinions in relation to the inconsistent pension policy of the KMT government since they were closely connected with the KMT in one way or another. With the arrival of the progressive DPP government, large businesses started to exercise instrumental power to further their political desires before the 2004 reform, but the government accepted very few of their recommendations.

Secondly, with economic and political changes, business preference and power have also changed. For example, although occupational benefits had been developed by the business sector voluntarily, in the light of an ageing population and the end of the full employment labour market these benefits became a burden. In addition, as seen in Korea, as business becomes more independent and autonomous from the state, this sector wants the government to invest more pension funds in the financial market rather than to channel them to strategic sectors. Conversely, although tax-based pension schemes have long been excluded even from the policy agenda, business in Japan and Korea has recently started to ask for the introduction of a tax-based pension scheme, with the rise of consumption tax, thus transferring the financial burden to consumers. Although non-contributory old-age allowance schemes were comprehensively introduced in Taiwan, its context is highly different from Japan and Korea in that it was not because of business demands but largely because of the fierce political competition between the KMT and the DPP. The shift of pension fund management from finance ministries to welfare ministries in Japan and Korea thus largely reflects the changing power relation between the state and business and also the transformation from the developmental to the post-developmental regimes.

Last but not least, it is important to consider the other influences that impact on business structure and the balance of power: institutional characteristics, electoral politics and socio-economic structures. For instance, in Japan and Korea, the rapidly ageing population and economic recession provided strong incentives for business to demand downsizing pension reforms. With a young population demographic, both the business sector and the developmental states regarded pension funds as working capital; as the number of pension beneficiaries increased, however, they changed their attitude. Pension politics became significant in Korea much earlier than in Japan and Korea. Although the persistence of existing pension schemes can be explained by the discourse of path-dependence, business influence is still important in relation to these other issues. The absence of pension politics as an area for dispute between political parties in Japan and Korea, unlike in Taiwan, can be to some extent explained by business power.

Conclusion

This chapter illustrates the importance of business influence and structure in understanding pension reforms in Japan, Korea and Taiwan. National business structure has not been changed a great deal. An export-oriented and conglomerate-centred business structure has persisted in Japan and Korea, whereas an SME-centred business structure with a small number of domestic-oriented large enterprises has remained in Taiwan. Yet, it is found that business influence depends on relations with other actors, particularly the state, and can shift over time. As the developmental regimes have been transformed to post-developmental regimes under the influences of democratization and globalization, conglomerates in Japan and Korea have extended their instrumental power over the state and society; fragmented business in Taiwan, however, has not overridden state power.

In this context, it is argued that pension developments and reforms have been largely influenced by national business structure and business influence. Before the 1990s, the development of enterprise welfare and retirement allowances and the preference for funded social insurance pensions in Japan and Korea are well explained by the export-oriented *keiretsu* and *chaebol* oriented business structures. Since around 1990, surging business power has been illustrated by the consecutive retrenchment pension reforms in Japan. Also, different business structures and power provide the explanation for the different trajectories of Korean and Taiwanese pension development in recent years, regardless of their similar political institutions and experiences. Yet, it is far from the end of the story in that socio-economic, demographic and political transformations have only just begun.

Acknowledgement

An earlier version of this chapter was published in the *Journal of Social Policy and Labor Studies in Japan* (Vol. 19: 91–117).

Notes

1 *Japan Times* (27 April 2004) reports that: 'In 2002, donations from corporations and other organizations, including industry and labour associations, to political parties dwindled to 2.6 billion yen from 3.2 billion yen from a year earlier. . . . Contributions to local party chapters, usually headed by individual law-makers, dropped 15 per cent to 13.7 billion yen in the same year. . . . Hajime Yamazaki, chief consultant of UFJ Institute Ltd.'s investment consulting department, [said] "But the fact is that the economy depends on Japan's biggest exporters. They don't need to make (huge) donations; they are getting their way anyway." '

2 The FEO asked members to donate based on its evaluations of LDP and Democratic Party of Japan performance on ten topics, including deregulation, free-trade agreements and tax and pension reform (*Japan Times* 24 April 2004).

3 McLellan (2004) notes that the former chairman of the FEO lamented: 'Out of all the various cost-cutting measures available to management, benefit costs, including the premiums for the social security and the national health care, are the one aspect out of the company's control' (p. 11).

4 The consumption tax is deemed to be less harmful for the economy since it is 'not a direct levy on the saving and investment that powers the economy' (Takayama 2004: 24), whereas it was predicted to expand intra-generational income disparity (NLI Research Institute 2003: 7).

5 Shin (2003) argues that, 'the Kim (Young Sam) government was increasingly taking into account the imperative of competitiveness in the formation of social security policy' (p. 160).

6 From this point, the responsibility to manage the NP pension fund was shifted from the Ministry of Finance to the Ministry of Health and Social Welfare, like in Japan.

7 Labour had gradually lost its grounds for opposing the corporate pension. Crucially, as the labour market became more flexible following the crisis, except for those who had been in life-long employment – a diminishing number – the non-portable RA was not very helpful for preparing for old-age life. However, the government maintained the RA option in the new Act, leaving the final decision as to whether to stick to the RA or switch to corporate pensions to be made by employers and employees.

8 In 1999/2000, Taiwan was subject to the following corporate tax rates: on total taxable income (TTI) of NT$0–50,000, zero; on TTI of NT$50,001–100,000, 15 per cent; and on TTI over NT$100,000, 25 per cent. These very low tax rates compared to those in Japan and Korea derived from its developmental strategy. Instead of strategic policy loans, the Taiwanese government encouraged the self-development of enterprises with favourable taxation policy. In Korea, the corporate tax rate is 16 per cent on taxable income up to 1,000,000 won and 28 per cent for income in excess of 1,000,000 won. In Japan, the tax rate is 34.5 per cent on both retained earnings and dividends (25 per cent for the first 8,000,000 Yen in

income for smaller corporations, with paid-in capital of 100 million Yen or less (Pricewaterhousecoopers 2000).

9 KMT opposed the scheme at first, arguing that, 'We're very worried that the spending will come at the expense of national infrastructure and economic development projects' (*Taipei Times* 27 July 2001). In response, before the local council election in December 2002, the DPP named 15 opposition MPs as having an anti-welfare stance in their election campaign advertisement, which was blamed for the defeat of some MPs. Subsequently, reluctant to lose the support of the elderly, the KMT has put forth a bill that sets much looser restrictions on the eligibility of beneficiaries (*Taipei Times* 20 December 2001).

10 Insurance companies were dissatisfied with this decision in that Taiwan has only 2358 companies employing 200 or more employees. Also, they criticized the lack of tax exemption and the government's requirement that any annuities run by private insurance companies guarantee that investment return will equal or exceed that of the average for two-year term deposit rates (*Taiwan Business Topics* 2004).

References

Babb, J. (2002) Politics, business, and the inescapable web of structural corruption in Japan, in E. T. Gomez (ed.), *Political Business in East Asia*, New York: Routledge.

Bureau of Labour Insurance (BLI) (2004) Welfare allowance, at: http://www.bli.gov.tw/en.

Chen, H.H.N. and Chen, H.H. (2003) Universal values vs. political ideology: virtual reform experience of Taiwan's national pension plan, paper presented at the APPLE Workshop, March, University of Birmingham.

Cheng, W.H.P. and Wu, M.J. (1997) The construction of the supplementary pension system in Taiwan, paper presented at the International Conference Toward the 21st Century: State, Family, and Social Welfare, 14–16 March, Academia Sinica, Taiwan.

China Post (2004) Legislature faces debate on pension reform today, 11 June.

Chu, Y.H. (1994) The realignment of business–government relations and regime transition in Taiwan, in A. MacIntyre (ed.), *Business and Government in Industrialising Asia*, Sydney: Allen & Unwin Pty Ltd.

Chung, D.H. (1999) Economic growth and the role of small to medium enterprises in Taiwan, *Korean National Economic Research*, 8(1): 1–21.

Council on Economic and Fiscal Policy (CEFP) (2002) *Koizumi Structural Reform: Accomplishments and Strategic Roadmap*, Tokyo: CEFP.

Cowling, K. and Tomlinson, P.R. (2001) The problem of regional hollowing-out, in *Japan: Lessons for Regional Industrial Policy*, Warwick Economic Research Papers. No. 625, Warwick: University of Warwick.

Evans, P.B. (1995) *Embedded Autonomy: States and Industrial Transformation*. Princeton, NJ: Princeton University Press.

Federation of Economic Organizations (FEO) (1997) *Seeking a Fundamental Reform of the Corporate Pension System*, Tokyo: FEO.

FEO (1998) *Rebuilding the Public Pension System Which Earns the Confidence of the Citizens*, Tokyo: FEO.

FEO (2003) *Outline of Proposal on Pension System Reform for 2004*, Tokyo: FEO.

Federation of Korean Industries (FKI) (2001) *Assessment and Reform Options of the National Pension*, Seoul: Federation of Korean Industries (in Korean).

Feenstra, R.C., Yang, T.H. and Hamilton, G.G. (1999) Business groups and product variety in trade: evidence from South Korea, Taiwan and Japan, *Journal of International Economics*, 48: 71–100.

Fields, K.J. (2002) KMT, Inc.: liberalisation, democratisation, and the future of politics in business, in E. T. Gomez (ed.), *Political Business in East Asia*, New York: Routledge.

Haggard, S. (2000) *The Political Economy of the Asian Financial Crisis*, Washington, DC: Institute for International Economy.

Hill, M. and Hwang, Y.S (2005) Taiwan: what kind of social policy regime?, in A. Walker and C. K. Wong (eds), *East Asian Welfare Regimes in Transition: From Confucianism to Globalisation*, Bristol: Polity Press.

Hiroshi, O. (1991) Intercorporate relations in Japan, in G. Hamilton (ed.), *Business Networks and Economic Development in East and Southeast Asia*, Centre of Asian Studies, University of Hong Kong.

Holliday, I. (2000) Productivist welfare capitalism: social policy in East Asia, *Political Studies*, 48: 706–723.

Hwang, G.J. (2005) The rules of the game: the politics of national pensions in Korea, paper presented at the Second East Asian Social Policy Research Network Conference, 30 May–2 June, University of Kent.

Iwasaki, I. (2002) *Asian Countries and Civil Society*, translated by E. B. Choi, Seoul: Eulyoumoonwhasa (in Korean).

Japan Times, various issues.

Johnson, C. (1987) Political institutions and economic performance: the government–business relationship in Japan, South Korea, and Taiwan, in F. C. Deyo (ed.), *The Political Economy of the New Asian Industrialism*, Ithaca, NY: Cornell University.

Kahal, S.E. (2001) *Business in Asia Pacific: Text and Cases*, New York: Oxford University Press.

Kang, D.C. (2002) Bad loans to good friends: money politics and the developmental state in South Korea, *International Organisation*, 56(1): 177–207.

Khosla, A. (2000) State and economy: some observations and inferences from the Japanese experiences, in K. E. Brodsgaard and S. Young (eds), *State Capacity in East Asia: Japan, Taiwan, China and Vietnam*, Oxford: Oxford University Press.

Kienzle, R. and Shadur, M. (1997) Developments in business networks in East Asia, *Management Decision*, 35(1): 23–32.

Kim, E.M. (1991) The industrial organisation and growth of the Korean Chaebol: integrating development and organisational theories, in G. Hamilton (ed.), *Business Networks and Economic Development in East and Southeast Asia*, Centre of Asian Studies University of Hong Kong.

Kim, Y.M. and Kim, K.S. (2005) Pension reform in Korea: conflict between social solidarity and long-term financial sustainability, in G. Bonoli and T. Shinkawa (eds), *Ageing and Pension Reform Around the World: Evidence from Eleven Countries*, Cheltenham: Edward Elgar.

Kono, M. (2005) The welfare regime in Japan, in A. Walker and C. K. Wong (eds), *East Asian Welfare Regimes in Transition: From Confucianism to Globalization*, Bristol: Polity Press.

Kuwayama, P.H. (2000) Postal banking in the United States and Japan: a comparative analysis, *Monetary and Economic Studies*, May: 73–104.

Kwon, H.J. (1998) The South Korean national pension programme: fulfilling its promise?, in R. Goodman, G. White and H. J. Kwon (eds), *The East Asian Welfare Model: Welfare Orientalism and the State*, New York: Routledge.

Kwon, H.J. (2005) Transforming the developmental welfare state in East Asia, *Development and Change*, 36(4): 477–497.

Lue, J.D. (2004) Can the East Asian capitalism sustain the challenge of globalisation and democratisation? Taiwan's social policy regime in transition, paper presented at the workshop on Comparative Social Policy Reform in East Asia, 31 May, University of Chi-Nan, Taiwan.

Manow, P. (2001) Globalisation, corporate finance, and coordinated capitalism: pension finance in Germany and Japan, in *MPIfG Working paper 01/5*, Cologne: Max Planck Institute for the Study of Societies.

McLellan, S. (2004) Corporate pension reform in Japan: big bang or big bust?, in *Pension Research Council Working Paper 2004–2005*, Philadelphia, PA: Wharton School of the University of Pennsylvania.

Ministry of Health, Labour and Welfare (MHLW) Japan (2004) *Overview of the Corporate Pension*, Seoul: MHLW.

Minns, J. (2001) Of miracles and models: the rise and decline of the developmental state in South Korea, *Third World Quarterly*, 22(6): 1025–1043.

Moon, C.I. (1994) Changing patterns of business–government relations in South Korea, in A. MacIntyre (ed.), *Business and Government in Industrialising Asia*, Sydney: Allen & Unwin Pty Ltd.

Mulgan, A.G. (1999) Electoral pressures for change: the effects of political reform, discussant paper presented to the Beyond Japan Inc.: Transparency and Reform in Japanese Governance International Conference, 20 September, Australian National University.

NLI Research Institute (2003) *Encouraging Informed Debate on the 2004 Pension Reform (A Summary)*, Tokyo: NLI Research Institute Pension Reform Forum.

Noh, K.P. (2005) Hollowing-out of Japanese industry and responses of labour, *Labour Society*, May: 121–131 (in Korean).

Park, G. (2004) The political-economic dimension of pensions: the case of Japan, *Governance*, 17(4): 549–572.

Pempel, T.J. (1999) The developmental regime in a changing world economy, in M. Woo-Cumings (ed.), *The Developmental State*, Ithaca, NY: Cornell University Press.

Pricewaterhousecoopers (2000) *Corporate and Individual Taxes 1999–2000 Worldwide Summaries*, New York: Pricewaterhousecoopers.

Schaede, U. (2004) What happened to the Japanese model?, *Review of International Economics*, 12(2): 277–294.

Seikeiilbo (1996) FKI choose 100 tasks for deregulation, 3 December.

Shin, D.M. (2003) *Social and Economic Policies in Korea: Ideas, Networks and Linkages*, London: Routledge.

Shinkawa, T. (2005) The politics of pension reform in Japan: institutional legacies, credit-claiming and blame avoidance, in G. Bonoli and T. Shinkawa (eds), *Ageing and Pension Reform Around the World: Evidence from Eleven Countries*, Cheltenham: Edward Elgar.

Shizume, M. (2005) Typology of public pension reform and future of 2004 pension reforms in Japan, paper presented at the Second East Asian Social Policy Research Network Conference, 30 May– 2 June, University of Kent.

Taipei Times, various issues.

Taiwan Business Topics (2002) Business and the DPP, 32(7), at: http:// www.amcham.com.tw/publication_topics_view.php?volume=32&vol_num=7& topics_ id=239.

Taiwan Business Topics (2004) Pension law not wholly satisfactory, 34(6), at: http:// www.amcham.com.tw/publication_topics_view.php?volume=34&vol_num= 6&topics_id=489.

Takayama, N. (2004) Changes in the Japanese pension system, Discussion Paper No. 227, Institute of Economic Research Hitotsubashi University.

Takegawa, S. (2005a) Pension reform in 2004: towards a pension, paper presented at Sociology Workshop on the Welfare States in Japan and Korea, 19–20 March, Tokyo (in Korean).

Takegawa, S. (2005b) Pension reform in 2004: birth of welfare politics?, *Social Policy Research*, 14: 193–230.

Tang, K.L (2000) *Social Welfare Development in East Asia*, Houndmill: Palgrave.

Tu, I.C. (1991) Family enterprises in Taiwan, in G. Hamilton (ed.), *Business Networks and Economic Development in East and Southeast Asia*, Centre of Asian Studies University of Hong Kong.

Wad, P. (2002) The political business of development in South Korea, in E. T. Gomez (ed.), *Political Business in East Asia*, London: Routledge.

Whitley, R. (1996) Continuity and change in East Asian capitalism: the limited effects of internationalism and domestic change on the business system of Japan, Korea, and Taiwan, in Working Paper No. 347, Manchester: Manchester Business School.

Woo-Cumings, M. (1999) Introduction: Chalmers Johnson and the politics of nationalism and development, in M. Woo-Cumings (ed.), *The Developmental State*, Ithaca, NY: Cornell University Press.

Yoshimatsu, H. (1997) Business–government relations in Japan: the influence of business on policy-making through two routes, *Asian Perspective*, 21(2): 119–146.

11 Private education policy at a crossroads

Comparing Hong Kong and Singapore

Michael H. Lee

Introduction

Both the Hong Kong and Singapore education systems have been affected by the trend of marketization over the two decades since the 1980s. Major concerns of education reform have been to improve the overall quality of education by allowing more choice for parents and students, granting schools more autonomy, and bringing about a more diversified education system. While the Hong Kong government has introduced and implemented the Direct Subsidy Scheme (DSS) policy with an aim of building up a strong and independent private school system since the early 1990s, the Singapore government has introduced independent and autonomous schools, institutionalized a school ranking system, and conferred quality school awards since the late 1980s and early 1990s.

This chapter reviews major private education policies in Hong Kong and Singapore, and examines and compares the motives of both governments to advocate the growth of private or perhaps more appropriately pseudo-private, education and the changing role performed by the governments in their education policies. The chapter is divided into five sections. The first sheds some light on the concepts and theories of private education with a brief literature review. The second reviews the development of private education in Hong Kong and Singapore after the end of the Second World War. The third examines and compares the ways that both governments have enhanced school autonomy since the late 1980s and offers a comparison between major characteristics of private school education in Hong Kong and Singapore. The fifth analyses the reasons for both governments' proactive role in pushing forward the development of private, or pseudo-private, school and university education, and discusses and compares the impact of such development on the Hong Kong and Singapore education systems in recent years. Finally, the conclusion offers a brief summary of the changing role of the Hong Kong and Singapore governments in relation to their education policies.

Some concepts and theories of private education

Most research on private school education has been undertaken in European and American countries at a time when both public and private elementary and secondary education needs to confront increasing pressures derived from fiscal and regulatory changes. It is rare to have an education system that comprises purely public schools or private schools. A mixed educational system, in which public and private schools coexist, is commonplace to achieve four major objectives: parental choice, pluralism, social unity and educational quality. Firstly, parental choice means the ability of parents to choose the kind of schooling they wish for their children. Pluralism means diversity in schooling and society. Social unity means assuring all citizens share social norms and knowledge and have equal access to educational opportunity. Educational quality means that schools meet minimum standards and exhibit high quality, which includes not only instructional effectiveness but also responsiveness and resource allocation efficiency (Hirschoff 1986: 34–35).

In some developing countries, governments cannot satisfy the needs of education through the public sector because of financial constraints or governance inability. The problem of insufficient supply of educational services by public schools is solved by the emergence and growth of private schools. Performing a supplementary role in the education sector, private schools are always perceived as inferior compared with public schools, in terms of both educational quality and social prestige. In developed countries, however, such as Australia, the UK and the US, the provision of education services is relatively sufficient as a result of the policy of universal or compulsory education. The problem of under-supply of education does not appear in these countries. What attracts parents' attention is whether there are opportunities available for their children to receive quality education. Instead of performing a supplementary role in education, private schools are more welcomed than public schools because they are more eager to enhance the quality of education and thus maintain their social prestige in the educational community and society at large. Therefore, private schools may enjoy a superior status as compared with public schools in those developed countries (Bray 1995: 184).

Other scholars, such as Adnett and Davies (2002) and Chubb and Moe (1990), have indicated that the core function of private schools is to stimulate the running of market principles and mechanisms in order to enable competition between public and private schools. The core aim of market-led competition is to act as a signal for schools to improve their teaching and learning environments and also enhance the quality of education in accordance with the needs and demands of parents, who are simultaneously customers selecting and paying for educational services (Smith and Meier 1995). It is believed that the adoption of a market-oriented approach in the school sector may solve the problem of a lack of innovation among the government-run or public schools, which should be more responsive to social needs, and improve their operational efficiency and effectiveness, and strengthen their account-ability to the general public (Patrinos 2000). The operation of an education market is founded on the basis of the interactions between parents as con-sumers and schools as service providers. While parents have to choose high quality schools for their children, both public and private schools have to strive for their competitiveness in the education market and, more import-antly, their own survival in the sector amidst the growing inter-school com-petition for resources and students (Gewirtz et al. 1995; Pring 1987). There is a widespread belief that education can be run efficiently and effectively within the context of the marketplace, in which the role of the state should be confined to facilitating smooth and effective operation of market mechanisms rather than dominating or monopolizing the provision of education services. In Hong Kong and Singapore, there have been debates about the impact of developing private school and university education. Moving towards a more diversified education system seems to be a common goal for both city-states to justify the development of private education in order to supplement the finance and provision of education that is dominated by the public sector. Meanwhile an increasing number of debates on private education focus on whether such a development would affect negatively the equality of edu-cational opportunities by discriminating against those who cannot afford expensive tuition fees in exchange for better quality of education. While it is still uncertain whether private education would have more positive or negative effects on both education systems, one thing that can be foreseen is that both governments will need to adjust their prominent role in education – either financing or providing education services within the preset regulatory framework – in order to accommodate the revival of private education.

Private education in Hong Kong and Singapore

This section reviews the development of private education in Hong Kong and Singapore in the post-war period from the 1940s onwards, and describes the historical background of private education in both city-states.

Hong Kong

In Hong Kong, private school education has been changed from performing a supplementary role since the inception of compulsory universal education in the late 1970s to providing more alternatives for parents to choose from. The implementation of the DSS policy has been aimed at building up a more diversified education system with the repositioning of the role of private schools in Hong Kong since the early 1990s.

Private school education in Hong Kong has a long history. According to Ng-Lun (1997), the British colonial administration had run western-style schools and provided grants to schools operated by churches since 1860. The foundation of a small-scale modern public school education system was laid down but the government's emphasis was placed on English, not Chinese, education. In the meantime, most private schools were still run by local communities and family tribes in the New Territories, which were leased to Britain for 99 years in 1898.

In the twentieth century, the British colonial government paid much more attention to education policy and development. Not until 1913, however, did the government impose regulations on education, in the form of the Education Ordinance. Apart from empowering the Director of Education to register schools, to remove registered schools or refuse registration, it stipulated that private schools with nine or more students would be required to register and would be subjected to the rules of school management and inspections delegated by the government. Since then, the role of the government in regulating the provision of education had been consolidated (Ng-Lun 1984).

The development of private school education did not reach its climax until the end of the Second World War, in the mid-1940s. The rapid growth of private schools during the post-war period was definitely related to the continuous growth of the population as a consequence of the huge influx of mainland Chinese immigrants by the late 1940s. At that time, about 60–70 per cent of local primary students were studying in private schools, and more than 260,000 students were enrolled in private primary schools by 1964. When the government implemented the policy of six-year free and compulsory primary education in 1971, there were still about a quarter of students studying in private primary schools. Subsequently, the number of private primary schools declined steadily because the government increased the quantity of subsidized schools in place of private ones in order to cater for the growing demands for free primary education (Tam 1999).

According to the official statistics, out of 847 primary schools in 1997, 748 were government and aided schools, 64 private and 35 international. In other words, the proportion of private primary schools was 7.56 per cent by that time. In 2004, the total number of primary schools dropped to 759, in which 653 were government and subvented schools, 59 private and DSS, and 46 international. Similar to the situation in 1997, less than 8 per cent of primary schools were private (Census and Statistical Department 2003: 253; see Table 11.1).

As for the secondary education sector, the two decades of the 1960s and 1970s were a golden time for the development of private secondary schools; they enrolled about three-quarter of local secondary school students. In 1963, there were more than 80,000 students studying in private secondary schools. The policy of six-year free and compulsory primary education in 1971 and, more importantly, the policy of nine-year free and compulsory primary and junior secondary education in 1978, gave rise to a further expansion of the private secondary school sector. At the end of the 1970s, private secondary schools still accommodated about 70 per cent of local students or 280,000 students. At the early stage of compulsory education, the government relied

Table 11.1 Primary schools in Hong Kong, 1992–2004

Year	Government and aided	Private[1]	International[2]	Total
1992	n.a.	n.a.	n.a.	946
1997	748	64	35	847
1998	732	67	33	832
1999	721	63	35	819
2000	719	60	37	816
2001	714	63	38	815
2002	698	60	45	803
2003	678	61	46	785
2004	653	59	47	759

Notes:
1 Figures include Direct Subsidy Scheme (DSS) schools.
2 Figures include schools under the English Schools Foundation and other international schools.

Sources: Census and Statistical Department (2003: 253, 2005: 267–268).

on private secondary schools to supplement the insufficient supply of places provided by government and aided schools. A Bought Place Scheme (BPS) was set up, in which the government bought places from private schools with the use of public money, that is, the students did not pay tuition fees. At that time, BPS schools provided one-third of secondary school places in Hong Kong. In the meantime, following the expansion of primary education since the early 1970s, the government adopted a similar approach to increase the number of subsidized secondary schools to solve the problem of insufficient supply of secondary school places (Cheng 1997; Tam 1999). The number of students educated through BPS reached as high as 150,000 during 1981–82, but dropped drastically to a mere 30,000 by 1993–94 (Bray 1995). In 2004, there were 139 private and DSS secondary schools, together totalling approximately 38,000 students. Although one-fifth of secondary schools were categorized as private, their students shared about 10 per cent of the total secondary student population in Hong Kong (Census and Statistical Department 2005: 267–268, 274; see Table 11.2). The BPS scheme was eventually abolished in 2000 with the institutionalization of DSS – unquestionably a watershed moment in the development of private school education in Hong Kong.

Singapore

Comprising Chinese, Malays, Indians and Eurasians, Singapore was a British colony for more than 140 years, since Stamford Raffles set up a free trading port and settlement for the British East India Company in 1819. The colonial government in Singapore did not support Chinese and Tamil vernacular

Table 11.2 Secondary schools in Hong Kong, 1992–2004

Year	Government and aided	Private[1]	International[2]	Total
1992	n.a.	n.a.	n.a.	485
1997	378	101	24	503
1998	384	100	23	507
1999	394	101	24	519
2000	400	101	24	525
2001	404	110	23	537
2002	405	113	24	542
2003	405	108	24	537
2004	408	139	23	570

Notes:
1 Figures include private evening secondary schools and Direct Subsidy Scheme schools.
2 Figures include schools under the English Schools Foundation and other international schools.

Sources: Census and Statistical Department (2003: 253, 2005: 267–268).

schools, which were privately owned and run, whilst English and Malay schools were run or subsidized by the colonial government. One of the most famous Chinese schools is the Chinese High School, which was opened in 1919 by the Chinese community leader, Tan Kah Kee. A year later, in 1920, the British government passed the Education Ordinance, which required the registration of all schools, teachers and managers. It also granted the government the necessary powers to impose regulations on all schools, including those in the private sector run by the local Chinese community; these, it was believed, were strongly influenced by the political powers in China in the early twentieth century. The political affiliation of those private Chinese schools would become a problem for their survival during the final colonial years from 1946 to 1959, when both Singapore and the Malay Peninsula were under communist threat and believed these schools and their student unions to be closely involved (Turnbull 1989).

In 1959, Singapore achieved self-government under the People's Action Party (PAP), lead by Premier Lee Kuan Yew. Following a two-year merger with Malaysia from 1963, Singapore unexpectedly became an independent nation on 9 August 1965. Over the past four decades, Singapore has experienced rapid and magnificent social and economic development and is now a First World country. For a tiny multi-racial island-state with no natural resources, the importance of education is demonstrated in its function of preserving racial and social harmony and in providing the country with quality human resources to cope with the demands of social and economic developments. In fact, education is always a priority for the Singapore government, as displayed by the fact that more than 20 per cent of total public expenditure has been allocated to the education policy area, second only to national defence throughout the years (Ministry of Finance 2004: 6).

After PAP and Lee Kuan Yew, then Prime Minister and now Minister Mentor, won the first general election in May 1959, the self-government of Singapore emphasized mathematics and science in education policy development. More schools were built in an attempt to ensure equal opportunity to education for all children on the island-state. The policy of free universal primary education was implemented in 1966 with the adoption of a uniform school curriculum. In the meantime, a bilingual medium of instruction policy was enforced in order to enable students to study both the English language and their own mother tongue, including Chinese, Malay and Tamil. Furthermore, another important function of education was to cultivate younger generations with a strong sense of national consciousness. Therefore it was stipulated that all schools should perform the flag-raising ceremony, sing the national anthem and recite the national pledge on a daily basis. Citizenship or civic education has been included in the school curriculum so as to preserve harmony and solidarity in such a multi-racial society. A watershed moment in educational development occurrred in 1979, when a review committee of the Ministry of Education, under the chairmanship of former Deputy Prime Minister Goh Keng Swee, recommended the setting up of a 'New Education System' – a policy of streaming according to students' language and academic abilities. This came into effect and created revolutionary changes in the development of Singapore's education system (Goh 1979; Yip et al. 1997).

The role of the government in education cannot be ignored, particularly in such a state-oriented country as Singapore. The state developed a uniform school curriculum and increased the quantity of school places; government schools still outnumber government-aided and private schools. In terms of regulation, finance and even provision, the Singapore education system, not suprisingly, is dominated by the government (see Tables 11.3 and 11.4).

Tables 11.3 and 11.4 reveal that the number of government primary and

Table 11.3 Primary schools in Singapore, 1960–2005

Year	Government schools	Government-aided schools	Total
1960	166	279	445
1970	198	220	418
1980	199	137	336
1990	157	50	207
2000	155	40	195
2001	151	41	192
2002	137	41	178
2003	132	41	173
2004	131	41	172

Sources: Ministry of Education (2004a: 25, 2005).

Table 11.4 Secondary schools in Singapore, 1960–2004

Year	Government schools	Government-aided schools	Independent schools	Autonomous schools	Total
1960	28	52	0	0	80
1970	68	47	0	0	115
1980	84	46	0	0	130
1990	102	34	6	0	142
1994	103	34	8	6	151
2000	112	24	8	18	163
2001	113	21	8	23	165
2002	114	22	8	22	166
2003	113	21	8	23	165
2004	110	20	9	24	163

Sources: Ministry of Education (2004a: 25, 2004b, 2005).

secondary schools in 1970 and 1980 far exceeded government-aided schools. It is noteworthy that private schools have been excluded from the official statistics. Surprisingly, in such a state-dominated education system, some breakthrough developments did occur in the 1980s and 1990s when the government set up independent and autonomous schools. Those schools demonstrating outstanding academic achievements are basically eligible for conversion and will be granted more autonomy for higher operational efficiency and more responsiveness to students' needs.

From this perspective, the Singapore government adopted a mode of centralized control to regulate the development of education by increasing significantly the quantity of government-run primary and secondary schools. Nevertheless, the government recognized the fact that centralization cannot cope with individual schools' needs and thus negatively affects the efficiency of school management.

Government and school autonomy in Hong Kong and Singapore

After reviewing the background of the private education development in Hong Kong and Singapore, this section aims to provide an account on the ways that both governments attempt to promote school autonomy by encouraging the development of private education.

Hong Kong

As mentioned in the previous section, DSS was the Hong Kong government's most important policy initiative, allowing it to diversify the school education system, which was largely dominated by the public sector. The Education Commission (EC) first introduced DSS in 1988, when *Education Commission*

Report No. 3 was released. The government was strongly recommended to build up a strong and independent private school education system in Hong Kong. In the past, private schools were treated by the government as a buffer to supplement the insufficient supply of school places following the implementation of the universal basic education policy in the late 1970s (EC 1988). It was proposed that DSS schools receive subsidies, which should be equivalent to the annual unit cost of each student studying in government or subsidized schools. For DSS schools, the number of subsidies received is linked to the number of students enrolled. Furthermore, those schools can levy tuition fees within the limits set by the government. However, it was also stipulated that the higher the tuition fees levied, the lower the grants received from government.

The DSS policy was implemented in 1991 and only five pro-China 'left-wing' or patriotic schools and four international schools joined the scheme. In order to receive full government subsidies, DSS schools could set their tuition fees at no more than one-third of the unit cost. Such a strict restriction on charging tuition fees could not attract any aided schools to join the scheme. Since 2001, aiming to attract more subsidized primary and secondary schools to join DSS and encourage the setting up of new DSS schools, the government has increased the maximum limit of tuition fee levied by the DSS schools to up to 2.33 times of the unit cost. In 2001–2002, a DSS primary school could charge as much as $48,000 per student per year, whereas a DSS secondary school could charge as much as $68,000. In the meantime, the government also required those DSS schools charging relatively high tuition fees, exceeding $20,000 per student per year, to set aside a portion of tuition fee income for providing financial assistance or scholarship to students from low-income families (Education Department 1991, 2001; Ip 2003). DSS and other government and aided schools differ not only in the arrangement of charging tuition fees, but also in the mode of school policy-making and management. DSS schools enjoy a higher degree of autonomy in their curriculum designs, student admission, employment and deployment of staff, and the use of financial and human resources (Tam 1999).

Although DSS has been implemented for more than a decade, only recently has the scheme become more popular and attractive among aided schools because of the relaxed limits on the levying of tuition fees. The growing popularity of the scheme in recent years has partially resulted from the conversion of some traditional prestigious grant and aided schools into DSS schools; this is in marked contrast to 1991, when the scheme was launched, when only a minority of schools, including left-wing and international schools and subsequently some BPS schools, applied (Tsang 2002).

The DSS group has expanded tremendously over the past five years, as revealed by the statistical figures for 2003–05. While the number of DSS schools increased to 51 (40 secondary, nine primary, one 'through-train' or primary cum secondary and one international school) in the academic year

2003–04 (Education and Manpower Bureau 2003), that in 2004–05 reached 55 (44 secondary, ten primary and one 'through-train') (Education and Manpower Bureau 2004).

Although the number of DSS schools is much smaller than that of aided and government schools in Hong Kong, an increase in the number of DSS schools over the past few years has actually revealed that more school sponsoring bodies would prefer to have their schools join the DSS rather than become aided schools. By joining the DSS, schools can have more freedom and autonomy in areas like student admission, curriculum, medium of instruction, resource allocation, and staff employment and deployment. The case is similar for a small number of prestigious schools wishing to join the DSS as a means of getting rid of unfavourable policy changes and reforms. The most significant among these changes included the implementation of using the mother tongue (Cantonese) as the medium of instruction in most secondary schools in Hong Kong (Education Department 1997) and the reduction of the number of bands for school place allocation from five to three (EC 2000). While the former policy has been argued to be detrimental for students' English language learning ability and proficiency, the latter policy has been deemed harmful for prestigious schools as they may not be able to get as many top students as in the past because of a sharp increase in the number of 'Band 1' students, who are supposed to be good academic performers. There were also some occasions on which an aided secondary school joined the DSS as a means of maintaining a connection with their feeder primary schools – some of which were originally run as private schools – and thus to form a 'through-train' school offering education services from primary, through secondary to matriculation levels.

At this moment, despite increasing steadily every year, DSS schools are still a minority in the Hong Kong education system. There are several reasons accounting for a much smaller number of DSS schools than other government and aided schools in Hong Kong. One of these reasons concerns geographical differences within the territory. The terms of joining DSS offered by the government are more attractive in a sense that those schools enjoy more freedom and autonomy in daily operation. Nonetheless, the income of DSS schools depends on both government subsidies given according to student enrollments and tuition fees levied from students' parents. Some DSS schools located in high income areas, such as the Mid-level on Hong Kong Island, can charge fees as high as HK$48,000 per annum. It is doubtful whether aided schools located on public housing estates can really join the DSS to enjoy more freedom and autonomy because residents in those estates, most of whom are working class, cannot afford to pay high tuition fees for their children's education. Therefore, geographical disparity really matters for schools when deciding whether joining the DSS is a possible way for them to maintain their quality and competitiveness amidst education reforms.

Another reason accounting for the small number of DSS schools in Hong Kong is related to the beliefs of most religious schools, such as those run by the Catholic Diocese Church and Christian organizations. Although some prestigious Christian schools have joined the DSS, a majority of aided schools run by Catholic, Christian or other religious organizations, such as Buddhist and Taoist associations, still remain in the mainstream school system. These schools avoid the DSS because their religious ethos subscribes provision of educational opportunity to all people regardless of their socio-economic status and economic power.

On the other hand, not a single government school has joined the DSS. The government has failed to persuade teachers, who work as civil servants in government schools and enjoy more generous remuneration, to join the DSS because it is not linked with government remuneration systems. Relatively strong resistance among government schoolteachers and also headteachers or principals to joining the DSS is therefore expected. Although the government tried to persuade some highly performing government schools to join the DSS few years ago, none of them were really interested in the DSS policy.

Singapore

In the 1980s, government officials in charge of education talked about the intention of the government to devolve management power to individual schools. Two advantages of decentralization were identified. On the one hand, it can improve school effectiveness and enable schoolteachers and principals to become more innovative. Students can also benefit from the effective leadership of school principals. On the other hand, individual schools can make decisions and policies according to their own students' needs. It is believed that the bottom-up, school-based mode of making decisions is far more effective than the top-down approach dominated by the government. Although the government tends to shift towards a school-based management policy, schools continue to be held responsible to the Ministry of Education (MOE) and to comply with national education policies.

In 1985, then Deputy Prime Minister Goh Chok Tong, who was Prime Minister between 1990–2004 and is now Senior Minister, announced a policy granting schools more autonomy in such areas as staff appointment and deployment, curriculum design and textbook selection; they still had to comply, however, with the national education policies, including bilingual teaching and public examinations. Lee Kuan Yew admitted that education dominated by government would lead to lack of competition among schools and thus hamper diversification of the education system. Subsequently, in December 1986, the government invited 12 school principals to visit 25 well-established schools in the UK and US with then Minister for Education Tony Tan Keng Yam, who is now Deputy Prime Minister. On their return, the group recommended that the government grant schools more autonomy in order to enable them to make swift responses to students and parents' needs (MOE 1987).

The government subsequently declared the setting up of independent schools, allowing a limited number of prestigious and traditional schools to convert. In 1988, three famous boys' schools, including the Chinese High School (CHS), converted to independent schools. Two famous girls' schools, including Singapore Chinese Girls' School, were converted. Raffles Institution was the first government school to convert, in 1990. Independent schools continue to receive government subsidies, which are calculated according to the average unit cost incurred in government and subsidized schools. The only difference is that those independent schools can set and levy tuition fees. The monthly tuition fees for independent schools range from S$150 to S$200, whereas those for non-independent schools are between S$12 and S$32. Moreover, independent schools are granted relatively more autonomy in the area of student admission.

Referring to Table 11.4, from 1993–2003, there were a total of eight independent schools. Not until 2004 does that number increase, to ten, with the addition of Singapore Sports School (SSS) and Hwa Chong Junior College (HCJC). SSS has operated under the auspices of the Ministry of Community Development, Youth and Sports, which was formerly known as the Ministry of Community Development and Sports, since 2004. There are 141 students, who have to pay S$6,000 annual tuition fees (Singapore Sports School 2004). The school plans to run pre-university programmes from 2005 (Goh 2004). HCJC was granted the right to convert into an independent school in 2004 in order to make a 'through-train' link with CHS to provide a six-year 'integrated programme' at the secondary level (MOE 2002). Its tuition fees would be maintained at S$24 per month (HCJC 2003).

Although the government intended to increase the quantity of independent schools, there were widespread doubts about the negative impact of elitism resulting from the policy at the early stage of the policy implementation in the early 1990s. Moreover, PAP performed unsatisfactorily in the 1991 general election, in which it faced a reduction in its parliamentary seats. This drove newly incumbent Prime Minister Goh Chok Tong to restrict the growth of independent schools in order to placate social controversies over the issue. At a later stage, the government set up autonomous schools to allow 18 non-independent schools with outstanding academic performance to convert between 1994 and 1997. Each autonomous school receives 10 per cent more of the government subsidies than non-independent and non-autonomous schools, but its tuition fees are relatively lower than those of independent schools (Tan 1993, 1996, 1998).

In early 2000, MOE announced that it would allow about one-quarter of secondary schools to convert to autonomous schools. The prerequisites for the conversion are twofold. On one hand, those schools should demonstrate good academic achievement. On the other hand, they should provide well-rounded education in tandem with well-developed community linkage. Those autonomous schools can admit 5 per cent of students with outstanding non-academic performance based on their own discretionary power. In 2004, the number of autonomous schools jumped to 24 and aimed to reach 25 in 2005 (MOE 2003a, 2004b).

The institutionalization of independent and autonomous schools reveals the government's intention to make use of some outstanding and managerially efficient schools as model examples for a majority of government and subsidized schools to follow. More importantly, independent and autonomous schools are expected to stimulate inter-school competition and thus improve the quality of education and the efficiency of school management as viewed by the government. It signifies the ascendancy of the trend of marketization in the Singapore education system. Those independent and autonomous school are naturally labelled as quality schools. With the implementation of a school ranking system in the early 1990s, schools have become more conscious of their own academic and non-academic performance as they become more accountable to the government, parents and society at large.

Independent and autonomous schools symbolize the decentralization of school management power from the government to individual schools. These two types of school still belong to the public sector because they are still subsidized by the government, even though their subsidies are granted in relation to their student enrolments. The development of private school education has lagged far behind that of public school education for a long period of time. There are two private schools providing normal school education, namely San Yu Adventist School and St. Francis Methodist School. These two schools are not related to the government and are completely run by private religious organizations. While the former runs local primary and secondary education, the latter runs local and overseas secondary and pre-university programmes. Their annual tuition fees range from about S$1,700 to S$14,000.

The development of private education has been caught in the spotlight recently; firstly, after Goh Chok Tong expressed in his Teachers' Rally Day speech in 2001 that the government would encourage more private schools to operate on the island-state in the future (Goh 2001; Nirmala 2001), and secondly, after the delivery of Goh's speech, CHS, one of the eight independent schools at that time, announced its intention to convert into a fully private school in exchange for even more autonomy in teaching and curriculum arrangements (Davie 2001).

Not until 2003 did private education make a breakthrough development when Minister for Education Tharman Shanmugaratnam announced the government's decision to accept new applications for setting up private secondary schools and junior colleges. Such brand new private education institutions are totally different from the existing international schools, in the sense that the former have to enrol at least 50 per cent local Singaporeans or permanent residents, while the latter are exclusively for foreigners. In addition, these private schools are bounded by national education policies such as bilingual teaching and learning and national education. Private schools cannot receive government subsidies, but they can enjoy absolute autonomy in curriculum design, school fees and public examination formats (Chong 2003; Lee 2003; Lin 2003; MOE 2003b).

MOE received a total of five proposals for setting up private schools (MOE

2004c). Two of them were made by the governing boards of the CHS and Anglo-Chinese School, where were granted the right to run their own brand-new private schools (MOE 2004d). The two private schools opened in 2005, with the admission of about 200 students at Secondary 1 and 3 in each. Their tuition fees will be set at S$15,000 per annum (Ng 2004a, 2004b). On the other hand, National University of Singapore (NUS) has run a specialized independent school, namely NUS High School for Mathematics and Science, since 2005. The school runs a six-year secondary school curriculum concomitant with the mixture of local A-level and overseas high school examinations. Students will receive diplomas upon their graduation and they can apply for credit exemption when they further their studies in NUS. About 250 students were admitted at the early stage but the number will eventually be increased to 1,250 by 2010 (MOE 2004e; NUS 2004).

Similar to Hong Kong, the number of independent and autonomous schools in Singapore remains a minority compared with a majority of government and government-aided schools. All eight independent schools and one independent junior college are among the top academically performing schools to be handpicked by the government to join the independent school scheme. On the other hand, the 24 autonomous schools are amongst the most popular and well-performing neighbourhood schools in the hinterland or public housing estate districts. In other words, the granting of more autonomy and resources to independent and autonomous schools is closely related to their academic achievements, social prestige and popularity among parents. Both independent and autonomous schools are supposed to serve as model examples for other non-independent and non-autonomous schools to follow to improve the quality of education and school management. Nevertheless, it is rather the case that it is difficult for non-independent and non-autonomous schools to compete with those independent and autonomous schools for attracting the best students. The creation of independent and autonomous schools, which are for elite and talented students, indeed reflects the government's intention to preserve the ideologies of elitism and meritocracy in Singaporean society. Whether the different types of school in the Singapore education system can compete on a fair basis is a critical issue to be carefully examined.

Comparing private school education in Hong Kong and Singapore

This section analyses major characteristics of private school education in both territories, comparing: system, development, government, school and market.

Table 11.5 summarizes and demonstrates some similarities and differences between the development of private school and higher education in Hong Kong and Singapore.

Firstly, at the system level, there are a lot more aided schools than government schools in Hong Kong. This situation reveals that the government

Table 11.5 Private school education in Hong Kong and Singapore

	Hong Kong	*Singapore*
System	• Dominated by aided schools at the primary and secondary levels • Government schools are minority • DSS schools are minority but have been growing much faster in number in recent years	• Dominated by government schools at the primary and secondary levels • Aided schools are minority • Independent and autonomous schools are minority but growing very slowly
Development	• DSS was launched in 1991 and five 'left-wing' or patriotic schools joined • First aided school, St. Paul's Co-educational College, joined the DSS in 2002 • There were 51 and 55 DSS schools in the academic years 2003–04 and 2004–05, respectively	• Independent school was launched in 1988 • Autonomous school was launched in 1994 • There were eight independent secondary schools and one independent junior college in 2004 • There were 24 autonomous schools in 2004
Government	• Diversifying the education system • Encouraging more competition in the schooling system • Allowing more choices for parents and students • Granting DSS schools more freedom and autonomy	• Diversifying the education system • Independent and autonomous schools to set model examples for other schools • Quality of education • More flexibility and autonomy in school management
School	• Some DSS schools charge tuition fees as high as HK$48,000 per annum • DSS schools are not selected by the government • Not all DSS schools are top or elite schools	• Independent schools charge no more than S$200 per month • Independent and autonomous schools are handpicked by the government • All independent and autonomous schools are elite or well-performing schools
Market	• Market competition is not necessarily in favour of all DSS schools • Keen competition between local private, DSS and international schools	• Market competition is always in favour of independent and autonomous schools • Emergence of private schools for both local and international education marketplaces

Sources: Lee and Gopinathan (2005), Mok (2006) and Tan (2005).

refrains from expanding the number of government schools at both primary and secondary levels but keeps providing substantial funding or subsidies to a huge number of aided schools. Aided schools, which are owned by school-sponsoring bodies, are required to comply with the Code of Aids and other regulations as stipulated by the government. The Hong Kong government claims to be the sole financier of basic education but not necessarily the most prominent service provider in the schooling system. In contrast, government schools at both primary and secondary levels dominate the schooling system in Singapore. Aided schools are a minority in the Singapore schooling system. Most aided schools are run by religious organizations, such as the Catholic Diocese Church. While government schools are under the direct control of the Ministry of Education, aided schools also need to comply with the government's education policies. Apart from being the financier of basic education, the government is also the main provider of education services in the schooling system in Singapore. Hong Kong and Singapore are similar in a sense that DSS, independent and autonomous schools are a minority in their schooling systems. Recent years have witnessed a steady growth in the number of DSS schools in Hong Kong, with the conversion of some formerly aided elite schools into DSS schools amidst the process of education reforms. On the other hand, the growth of independent and autonomous schools in Singapore has been placed under strict control of the government in order to avoid arousing public controversy over allegations of favouritism to certain top elite schools at the expense of the principle of equal opportunity of education for all.

Secondly, in terms of development, the DSS in Hong Kong was introduced in 1991 and was not well received: only five left-wing or pro-China patriotic schools joined the scheme. The government's intention of attracting a critical number of aided schools to join the DSS was only realized in 2002 when St. Paul's Co-educational College became the first aided school to convert to a DSS school. The number of DSS schools sharply increased from five in 1991 to 51 in 2003–04 and to 55 in 2004–05. Both primary and secondary schools can join the DSS; international schools cannot. In Singapore, independent and autonomous school policies were introduced in 1988 and 1994, respectively. In 1988, the government handpicked three renowned aided secondary schools, including the Chinese High School and the Anglo-Chinese School, to convert to independent schools. Raffles Institution was the first government school to become an independent school, in 1990. In 1994, the government also identified 15 well-performing neighbourhood schools to be converted into autonomous schools. Not a single primary school in Singapore is independent or autonomous. There were nine independent schools, of which one was a junior college, and 24 autonomous schools in 2004.

Thirdly, at the government-level, DSS in Hong Kong was introduced and promoted with the aim of creating a more diversified education system thus encouraging more competition between different types of school, including government, aided, DSS, private and international schools. Parents, especially those who are willing to pay for better quality of education, have been allowed more alternatives from which to choose. In other words, students from families in higher socio-economic groups may have more options to choose from with the addition of DSS schools, especially those elite schools which are charging high tuition fees. DSS schools are guaranteed greater freedom and autonomy in crucial areas such as curriculum, medium of instruction, student admission, and the use of financial and human resources. Offering such favourable terms and conditions to DSS schools as compared with mainstream government and aided schools, reveals the government's intention to increase the number of DSS schools, which are subsidized by the government according to the number of students enrolled. Similarly, in Singapore, the creation of independent and autonomous schools has served to diversify the schooling system by providing some alternatives to government and aided schools. Furthermore, because independent and autonomous schools are necessarily well-performing schools in terms of academic achievements and school management, both types of school are supposed to set model examples to their counterparts in the school education system to improve the overall quality of education. Nevertheless, there is always a question regarding whether independent and autonomous schools will improve the quality of education system-wide, or will only widen the gap between those independent and autonomous schools and other non-independent and non-autonomous schools in terms of students' academic achievements and the availability of resources.

Fourthly, as seen at the school level, DSS schools in Hong Kong differ from independent and autonomous schools in Singapore. While DSS school tuition fees can be as high as HK$48,000 per annum, independent school tuition fees should be no more than S$2,000 (HK$9,600) per annum. The tuition fees for DSS schools in Hong Kong are much higher than independent schools in Singapore. In Hong Kong, unlike Singapore, the government does not handpick DSS schools. In other words, all aided and private schools can apply to join the DSS; only international schools are excluded. On the contrary, in Singapore, the selection of independent and autonomous schools is under the control of the MOE, which makes decisions according to schools' track records in academic achievement and managerial effectiveness and efficiency. Not all schools are eligible to apply to be independent or autonomous schools. Independent or autonomous schools serve as a benchmark for being recognized as well-performing schools on the island-state; therefore, in Singapore, all independent and autonomous schools are equivalent to top elite schools and well-performing neighbourhood schools, respectively. This is not necessarily the case in Hong Kong, where types of DSS schools vary. While some DSS schools are well-established elite schools with a long history in Hong Kong, some of them are new 'through-train' schools, pro-China patriotic schools, and formerly private BPS schools. In short, the quality of education in the DSS subsystem may vary significantly according to the background of individual DSS schools. This is in absolute contrast to the strict control excercised over the quality of independent and autonomous schools in Singapore.

Finally, from the market point of view, the creation of DSS schools in Hong Kong may have contributed to keener market competition between different types of school in the territory. It is certainly true that a small number of top elite schools have jointed the DSS and an increasing number of new 'through-train' schools have also done so. Because of the decreasing number of school children as a result of the low birth rate in Hong Kong, much keener competition between local mainstream government and aided schools, DSS schools, private schools and international schools for smaller number of students is expected. However, school success in relation to market competition in Hong Kong is not related DSS membership. It is more important for schools to compete successfully by showing their own track record of academic achievement, students' public examination results, and prestige and social standing in the community. The label of DSS does not necessarily guarantee success for a school in Hong Kong. On the contrary, in Singapore, the label of 'independent school' or 'autonomous school' naturally guarantees a school's marketability and competitiveness in the education marketplace. Independent and autonomous schools are not competing on a level playing field with other government and aided schools. Provided with the best students and more flexibility and autonomy in daily operation, both independent and autonomous schools are believed to gain competitive advantages in the market without much difficulty. The social standing of those independent and autonomous schools could be further consolidated without improving the overall quality of education throughout the island-state. Most recently, such independent schools as Hwa Chong Institution (HCI) and Anglo-Chinese School (ACS) have even embarked on setting up private schools to woo full-fee paying international students. In short, 'independent and autonomous school' status does indeed guarantee a better position for schools in competing not only in the local education market but also in the international marketplace, as revealed by the cases of HCI and ACS as mentioned above.

Discussion: changing government's role in education

Over the past two or three decades, private schools have played a supplementary role in addressing the insufficient supply of school places under the policy of free and compulsory education in Hong Kong. That role has been skewed towards the triggering of market competition among schools to improve the quality of education. Private schools are no longer necessarily inferior as compared with other government and aided schools, as seen from the conversion of traditional grant and aided schools into DSS schools over the past few years. DSS enables parents, who are more like consumers, to proceed with more choices in a more diversified education system. The survival of the existing and new DSS schools depends on whether they can appeal to the education market by pursuing a higher quality of education and improving school management (Benveniste et al. 2003).

The rise of private schools implies that the government will not be the only financier for education and more resources from society will be absorbed in the education sector. DSS schools can make use of additional income derived from tuition fees for improving teaching and learning facilities. Performing as a producer of educational services, those schools are more eager to respond to the needs of parents or consumers. It is not surprising that such schools are even more conscious about their own academic achievements and quality of teaching and learning, even though the government has developed a detailed system of quality assurance for the school sector to ensure it is highly responsive to market needs (Ball 1999). Although there is no sign that the government tends to curtail the growth of public expenditure on education with the rise of DSS and private schools, there is a significant message that government and society as a whole need to share the responsibility and cost of education.

Moving towards a diversified education system and offering parents more choice are two major aims of the government in rigorously promoting the DSS policy. Nevertheless, a critical question to be asked is whether all social classes are entitled to enjoy educational equality. Arguably, because some DSS, private and international schools charge much higher tuition fees, more choice is only available for high income or middle class families. Does it mean that the diversified education system is exclusive to higher income or middle class groups, which can choose from a much broader range of educational services within the local school sector or even overseas. The inequality of educational opportunity may inevitably create a certain amount of discontent in society, when the government is accused of providing more subsidies for those who can afford high fees charged by DSS or private schools. From the schools' perspective, new DSS schools are more eager to improve themselves in order to attract parents and students. They are entitled to make use of extra resources to hire native English or native Putonghua teachers to improve the students' language skills, to reduce the number of students per class for better care during the lessons, and also to upgrade the existing computing facilities. Schools and students are not competing on a level playing field; thus the dilemma between choice and equality of education provision has not yet been resolved. The worst result will be a widened gap between social classes in society because education is seen as instrumental in reproducing social classes and reaffirming the superiority of certain privileged social classes and social elites in modern society (Ip 2003).

In Singapore, the development of independent, autonomous and private schools reveals that when the government devolves more management and governance power to educational institutions for improving their effectiveness and quality, it also shifts to a more indirect means of monitoring the running of those institutions. An example can be cited from the implementation of the School Excellence Model (SEM) in 2000. The SEM requires all public primary and secondary schools, and junior colleges, to establish their own self-assessment systems for inter-school comparisons in tandem with the regular supervision by MOE in the areas of teaching effectiveness, school management, and the utilization and distribution of resources in line with the principle of accountability (Ng 2003). SEM is modelled on school-based management, operating in most western countries, which imposes even closer scrutiny of school performance within the policy trend of decentralization.

Apart from this, the government has adopted a school ranking system for assessing and comparing schools' performance. MOE has disclosed the ranks of secondary schools and junior colleges and published them in local newspapers since 1992. The ranking system is conceived as a means to stimulate inter-school competition and to provide parents and students with more detailed information on which to base decisions when choosing schools. The ranks of secondary schools are made in accordance with three major criteria. First, overall academic results in O-level examinations; second, the value-addedness of students' performance in the public examinations compared with their abilities at Secondary 1; and third, the performance of students in the national physical fitness tests and the proportion of overweight students.

Some critics have pointed out that the school ranking system will widen the gap between schools. Best performing students naturally choose highly ranked schools, which are simultaneously independent and autonomous schools that are entitled more resources guaranteed by both government subsidies and school fee incomes. This results in the 'stratification of schools', i.e. schools are competing with each other on an unequal basis as some of them are endowed with better quality students and more resources than others. Therefore, it is questionable whether the overall quality of school education can be improved under the current situation.

More recently, MOE has proposed a reform of the school ranking system, which will divide schools into different banding in place of ranking according to their students' performance in the public examinations. School ranks are determined not only by academic results but also students' characters, physical fitness and academic value-addedness. The reformed school banding system aims to eliminate the negative effects resulting from the existing ranking exercises applied to schools across the board. The new banding system, which has been adopted since September 2004, also aims to accommodate individual schools' self-assessment mechanisms for identifying their own strengths, weaknesses and areas for further improvement (MOE 2004f).

As discussed above, the Singapore government has altered the top-down approach of monitoring the operation of schools and universities to the bottom-up approach of autonomous school-based management in exchange for public and financial accountability (Teo 1999; MOE 2000). Educational institutions are held responsible for their own performance and are subject to market mechanisms for scrutinizing the quality of education. The devolution of managing power means also the decentralization of responsibility. In

Singapore, well-performing schools can be awarded the status of independent or autonomous schools that are entitled to more resources, autonomy and, not surprisingly, the best students. Students and parents normally discriminate against lower-ranked schools. This may give rise to the polarization of school education under the present ranking practice. A more in-depth discussion on the impact of the rise of private education on the education system as a whole and on different stakeholders such as school managers, teachers, students, parents and government is worthwhile.

Conclusion

This chapter has reviewed and compared the development of and major changes within private education policy in Hong Kong and Singapore. In Hong Kong, more autonomy, flexibility and diversity are the selling points upheld by the government to promote DSS and private school and university education. Furthermore, a strong and independent private school sector is widely expected to contribute to a more diverse education system generating more choice for parents. Nevertheless, the issue of the equality of educational opportunity should also be taken into account to evaluate the impact of private school educational development in Hong Kong and elsewhere.

For the state-centred education system of Singapore, the growth of private educational institutions is unquestionably a major development and is worthy of further discussions. Educational development is intimately related to the historical development of Singapore. Since the premiership of Lee Kuan Yew in 1959, the government has steadily strengthened its role in the provision of finance and educational services, resulting in the dominance of government schools over subsidized and private schools. The government's direct interference in both basic and higher education is readily observable, for example in the case of the 'forced' merger in 1980 between the English-medium University of Singapore and the Chinese-medium Nanyang University thus creating the NUS (Gopinathan 1989).

Since the mid-1980s, when the quantitative expansion of education was accomplished, the government has focused on ways of improving the efficiency and effectiveness of school management and the quality of education. Through the institutionalization of independent and autonomous schools, some traditional prestigious schools can reinforce their own social status and outstanding academic and non-academic performance and thus keep their comparative advantage in the local education market. Although such a policy is aimed at creating some model examples for the rest of the schools to follow, thus improving overall educational quality, it is argued that the difference between schools may be worsened because of the widespread prejudice among students and parents against non-independent and non-autonomous schools. Whether market forces are conducive to a higher quality of education is being questioned.

Instead of witnessing a retreat on the part of the government in relation to education, the development of private education means the repositioning of the government to ensure a favourable environment for transforming education as a lucrative export industry for the country's long-term economic development. A proactive role played by the government is justified when it has been working on building up alliances between local and renowned universities over the past few years. Meanwhile, private school education is aiming at serving foreign students coming from other Asian countries. By doing so, Singapore will be developed as a Southeast Asian regional hub of educational services in the foreseeable future. In short, for about 40 years after Singapore's independence, both the government's interference and the ascendancy of market forces have significantly affected the development of education in the city-state. In a nutshell, the role of the government in education can never be neglected.

References

Adnett, N. and Davies, P. (2002) *Markets for Schooling: An Economic Analysis*, London: Routledge.

Ball, S.J. (1999) *Educational Reform and the Struggle for the Soul of the Teacher!*, Hong Kong: Hong Kong Institute of Educational Research, Chinese University of Hong Kong.

Benveniste, L., Carnoy, M. and Rothstein, R. (2003) *All Else Equal: Are Public and Private Schools Different?*, New York: RoutledgeFalmer.

Bray, M. (1995) The quality of education in private schools: historical patterns and the impact of recent policies, in P. Siu and T. Tam (eds), *Quality in Education: Insights from Different Perspectives*, Hong Kong: Hong Kong Educational Research Association.

Census and Statistical Department (2003) *Hong Kong Digest of Statistics: 2003 Edition*, Hong Kong: Government Logistics Services Department.

Census and Statistical Department (2005) *Hong Kong Digest of Statistics: 2005 Edition*, Hong Kong: Government Logistics Services Department.

Cheng, K.M. (1997) Review of education, Part II, in G. Wang (ed.), *New Perspectives in Hong Kong History*, Hong Kong: Joint Publishers (in Chinese).

Chong, V. (2003) MOE unveils private school guidelines, *Business Times*, 14 August.

Chubb, J. and Moe, T. (1990) *Politics, Markets and America's Schools*, Washington, DC: Brookings Institutions.

Davie, S. (2001) The Chinese High wants to go private, *The Straits Times*, 8 December.

Education and Manpower Bureau (2003) List of Direct Subsidy Scheme schools 2003/04, Hong Kong: Education and Manpower Bureau.

Education and Manpower Bureau (2004) List of Direct Subsidy Scheme schools 2004/05, Hong Kong: Education and Manpower Bureau.

Education Commission (EC) (1988) *Education Commission Report No. 3*, Hong Kong: Government Printer.

EC (2000) *Learning for Life, Learning through Life: Reform Proposals for the Education System in Hong Kong*, Hong Kong: Printing Department.

Education Department (1991) General administration circular No. 14/91: the Direct Subsidy Scheme (DSS), Hong Kong: Education Department.

Education Department (1997) *Medium of Instruction Guidance for Secondary Schools*, Hong Kong: Education Department.

Education Department (2001) Circular memorandum No. 210/2001: the Direct Subsidy Scheme (DSS), Hong Kong: Education Department.

Gewirtz, S., Ball, S. and Bowe, R. (1995) *Markets, Choice and Equity in Education*, Buckingham: Open University Press.

Goh, C.T. (2001) Shaping lives, moulding nation, speech by Prime Minister Goh Chok Tong at the Teachers' Day Rally on 31 August, Singapore: Ministry of Information and the Arts.

Goh, C.T. (2004) Speech by Prime Minister Goh Chok Tong at the official opening of the Singapore Sports School on 1 April, Singapore: Ministry of Information, Communications and the Arts.

Goh, K.S. (1979) *Report on the Ministry of Education 1978*, Singapore: Ministry of Education.

Gopinathan, S. (1989) University education in Singapore: the making of a national university, in P. G. Altbach and V. Selvaratnam (eds), *From Dependence to Autonomy: The Development of Asian Universities*, Dordrecht: Kluwer Academic Publishers.

Hirschoff, M.-M.U. (1986) Public policy toward private schools: a focus on parental choice, in D. C. Levy (ed.), *Private Education: Studies in Choice and Public Policy*, New York: Oxford University Press.

Hwa Chong Junior College (HCJC) (2003) *Hwa Chong Junior College goes independent*, Singapore: HCJC.

Ip, K.Y. (2003) Conversion of public schools into Direct Subsidy Scheme schools and the issue of educational equality, *Academic Research* [*Xueshu Yanjiu*], 3: 104–107 (in Chinese).

Lee, J. (2003) Door is open for new private schools, *Straits Times*, 14 August.

Lee, M. and Gopinathan, S. (2005) Convergence or divergences? Comparing education reforms in Hong Kong and Singapore, in J. Zajda (ed.), *International Handbook on Globalization, Education and Policy Research*, Dordrecht: Springer Science.

Lin, P. (2003) There will be private secondary schools and junior colleges in 2005, *Lianhe Zaobao*, 14 August (in Chinese).

Ministry of Education (MOE) (1987) *Towards Excellence in Schools*, Singapore: MOE.

MOE (2000) *Fostering Autonomy and Accountability in Universities: A Review of Public University Governance and Funding in Singapore*, Singapore: MOE.

MOE (2002) *Report of the Junior College/Upper Secondary Education Review*, Singapore: MOE.

MOE (2003a) New autonomous school, press release on 2 August, Singapore: MOE.

MOE (2003b) Privately-funded schools for more choice and greater diversity, press release on 13 August, Singapore: MOE.

MOE (2004a) *Education Statistics Digest 2003*, Singapore: MOE.

MOE (2004b) New autonomous school for 2005, press release on 7 July, Singapore: MOE.

MOE (2004c) Five proposals received for setting up privately-funded schools, press release on 6 January, Singapore: MOE.

MOE (2004d) MOE has approved two proposals for setting up privately-funded schools, press release on 12 April, Singapore: MOE.

MOE (2004e) The education landscape in 2004 and beyond: more choices for students, Singapore: MOE.

MOE (2004f) A more broad-based school ranking system, press release on 17 March, Singapore: MOE.

MOE (2005) *Ministry of Education Factsheet 2005*, Singapore. MOE.

Ministry of Finance (2004) *The Budget for the Financial Year 1 April 2004 to 31 March 2005*, Singapore: Ministry of Finance.

Mok, K.H. (2006) *Education Reform and Education Policy in East Asia*, Oxford and New York: Routledge.

National University of Singapore (NUS) (2004) Revolutionizing secondary school: NUS High School of Mathematics and Science to adopt different pedagogy, *Knowledge Enterprise*, January, p. 3.

Ng, J. (2004a) Private school to let students opt for own final exam, *Straits Times*, 22 March.

Ng, J. (2004b) $15,000-a-year school fees won't faze parents, *Straits Times*, 19 April.

Ng, P.T. (2003) The Singapore school and the School Excellence Model, *Educational Research for Policy and Practice*, 2(1): 27–39.

Ng-Lun, N. (1984) *Interactions of East and West: Development of Public Education in Early Hong Kong*, Hong Kong: Chinese University Press.

Ng-Lun, N. (1997) Review of education, Part I, in G. Wang (ed.), *New Perspectives in Hong Kong History*, Hong Kong: Joint Publishers (in Chinese).

Nirmala, M. (2001) Private schools the answer to better education? *Straits Times Weekly Edition*, 29 September.

Patrinos, H.A. (2000) Market forces in education, *European Journal of Education*, 35(1): 61–80.

Pring, R. (1987) Privatization in education, *Journal of Education Policy*, 2(4): 289–299.

Singapore Sports School (SSS) (2004) About us, Singapore: SSS, at: http://sport-school.edu.sg/legal/sss/aboutUs.htm.

Smith, K.B. and Meier, K.J. (1995) Public choice in education: markets and the demand for quality education, *Political Research Quarterly*, 48(3): 461–478.

Tam, M.K. (1999) Private schools in Hong Kong, in M. Gu and Z. Du (eds), *Hong Kong Education: Past and Present [Xianggang Jiaoyu: Guoqu yu Xianzai]*, Beijing: People's Education Press (in Chinese).

Tan, J. (1993) Independent schools in Singapore: implications for social and educational inequalities, *International Journal of Educational Development*, 13(3): 239–251.

Tan, J. (1996) Independent schools and autonomous schools in Singapore: a study of two school privatization initiatives aimed at promoting school innovation, unpublished PhD dissertation submitted to the Faculty of the Graduate School of the State University of New York at Buffalo.

Tan, J. (1998) The marketization of education in Singapore: policies and implications, *International Review of Education*, 44(1): 47–63.

Tan, J. (2005) The marketization of education in Singapore: what does this mean for Thinking Schools, Learning Nation? in J. Tan and P. T. Ng (eds), *Shaping Singapore's Future: Thinking Schools, Learning Nation*, Singapore: Prentice Hall.

Teo, C.H. (1999) Ministerial Statement by the Minister for Education RADM Teo Chee Hean at the Committee of Supply Debate, FY1999 in Parliament, 17 March, Singapore: MOE.

Tsang, W.K. (2002) *New Elitism and New Direct Subsidy Scheme: Critique on the*

Erosion of Education Capital, Hong Kong: Hong Kong Institute of Education, Chinese University of Hong Kong.

Turnbull, C.M. (1989) *A History of Singapore, 1819–1988*, Oxford: Oxford University Press.

Yip, J., Eng, S.P. and Yap, J. (1997) 25 years of educational reform, in J. Tan, S. Gopinathan and W. K. Ho (eds), *Education in Singapore: A Book of Readings*, Singapore: Prentice Hall.

12 Struggling among economic efficiency, social equality and social stability

Housing monetarization reform in China[1]

Yapeng Zhu

Introduction

In the pre-reform period, China was considered 'a welfare society in a lower income country' (Guan 2000) operating a large social programme in both urban and rural areas. In the urban area, the state provided a wide range of social welfare such as healthcare, pensions and housing, mainly through the work unit system (Gu 2001a, 2001b; Lu and Perry 1997). Ever since the launching of economic reform, the government has striven to build up an economic state during the transitional period (Chen 2003), when economic efficiency is prioritized over social equality.[2] In line with the economic transition, social policy in the country has undergone fundamental changes. The state has made great efforts to 'societalize' the welfare system, seeking to share the responsibility of providing social welfare between central government, local government, work units and individuals (Gu 2001a, 2001b; Guan 2000). The orientation of the reform of social policy in China is following a 'neo-liberal' pattern, aiming to reduce the role of the state in the provision of welfare and to increase individual responsibility for social welfare and wellbeing (Guan 2000).

However, since China's market transition began in the late 1970s, work units, especially the state-owned enterprises (SOEs), have had to bear increasing heavy burdens or 'policy burdens' (Lin et al. 1998) of providing welfare to their employees. They thus became less competitive in comparison to their counterparts in the non-state sector. This was an institutional impediment to the formation of a unified market (including the labour market) and further SOE restructuring reforms. In order to reduce the burdens of the SOEs and to pave the way for further enterprise reforms, the Chinese government launched a new comprehensive welfare reform transforming the Chinese work unit-based mini-welfare state into a system with greater emphasis on welfare pluralism (Gu 2001a, 2001b) in the late 1990s when the reformist Zhu Rongji presided over the government. This chapter examines the implementation and impacts of the reform package with reference to one of the important components – housing monetarization reform. It starts with an overview of housing reform, followed by an exploration of the aims and considerations of the different reform approaches. It then discusses implementation situations and impacts of the housing monetarization reform. It is argued that the adoption of the incremental approach of housing monetarization indicates that more emphases were put on economic efficiency than on social equality, while poor implementation and growing housing inequality put the state under a high risk of social instability. It is concluded that the Chinese government is facing a challenge of balancing economic efficiency, social equality and social stability. If the government is to overcome the challenge, more government capacity and commitment are needed and the social welfare system has to be revamped.

Restructuring the housing system: an overview

Housing reform began with the legacy of socialist institutional arrangements. Since the 1950s, the Chinese government has solely taken the responsibility of housing its urban citizens. Generally, local governments and work units obtained housing investment from the state budget, then built housing and distributed it among employees. Housing was viewed as a right and a kind of welfare for the employees. Urban residents paid a seminal rent, which was far below the maintenance expenditure, needless to say the full cost (Chen 1998). This state housing provision system caused serious problems, such as housing shortage, poor housing quality, insufficient maintenance, and corruption (Shaw 1997; Tong and Hays 1996; Wang and Murie 1999; Zhao and Bourassa 2003). All these problems mainly stemmed from rapid population growth, lack of housing and a chaotic land utilization policy (Chen 1994; Tong and Hays 1996). In response to these problems, the Chinese government tried to restructure the housing system from the end of 1970s onwards. Commercializing and privatizing public housing and gradually building up the real estate market were among the major strategies employed. The ultimate aim is to establish a market-oriented housing system and to shift the housing responsibility from the state to a division between the central government, local government, work units and, most important of all, households and individuals. Despite the general direction of the reform and the adoption of major strategies, slow progress and unstable policies have characterized the process of housing reform (Zhu 2000).

After nearly two decades' efforts, marketization and privatization of housing led to fundamental changes in housing responsibility between central government, local governments, work units and individuals. In spite of the 'incremental approach' of housing reform, fundamental changes had taken place in terms of housing investment, distribution, consumption and management. With the advancement of reform, the central government successfully shifted housing responsibility along the central–local continuum. Local governments had reluctantly taken up more housing responsibility and played a more active role in formulating strategies to meet housing needs.

However, they had their interests and sought to maximize them. It is suggested that local governments now play the role of entrepreneurs in the housing market (Haila 1999). They may try to channel foreign investment into their cities and benefit from leasing urban land to development corporations. The property market is considered a pillar of their economy and land lease and redevelopment are treated as vehicles for economic growth. Land revenue generated from urban redevelopment has become a major source of revenue for local governments. Land-generated income even accounted for 25–30 per cent of local revenue in some coastal cities (Wu 1996). However, local governments tended to be reluctant to implement reform programmes that cost them a loss of revenue. For example, local authorities in many provinces provided very limited affordable housing and social rental housing to low-income households in their jurisdiction.

While the state has changed its role in the housing market from 'provider' to 'enabler' in line with housing privatization and the introduction of the market mechanism (Zhang 2000a), the role of work units in housing distribution is almost intact. Work units used to receive housing investment from the state and provided affordable housing to their employees in accordance with employees' wage levels (Huang 2000). This work unit-based welfare housing distribution system led to distinct housing inequality among and within work units owing to the unbalanced distribution of housing funds among different work units and possible unfairness and corruption in the process of housing distribution within individual work units (Bian et al. 1997; Tong and Hays 1996; Zhu 2000). Along with economic reform, the disparity in housing benefits between work units has been exacerbated by the different economic performance of work units within a mixed economic environment (Zhu 2000). Divorcing housing from work units and shrinking housing inequality among work units has thus become one of the major objectives of the reform as proposed by the World Bank economists in the early 1990s (World Bank 1992). Housing reform in China did move in this direction; nonetheless, the outcome seems rather discouraging. Prior to 1998, work units still played a key role in housing provision: bearing the final burden of rent increases and acting as a major force in public housing production. During the reform period, with the formation of a dual-track housing market – the co-existence of an open market with competitive house prices and an internal public market with discounted house prices – work units even entered the housing market as unavoidable intermediates to bridge poor salaries for ordinary public employees and comparatively high house prices (Bian et al. 1997; Zhang 2000a). Work units had become principal participants in fostering the housing market in the 1990s (Logan et al. 1999) and most commercial housing had been transformed into welfare housing through the intermediate role of work units. Meanwhile, the commercial market had remained a minor channel for urban residents to acquire homes before the launching of housing monetarization reform in 1998. Work units maintained their important role in providing housing as employment benefit to employees, either through housing construction or through acquisition in the market (Fu et al. 2000). The entry of work units as irrational players in the housing market resulted in aggravating housing inequality as well as the creation of a distorted housing market, i.e. soaring house prices and a mismatch between housing production and residents' needs (Zhang 2000b). Generally, housing reform had not weakened the role of work units in housing redistribution as was expected but rather strengthened it (Logan et al. 1999; Zhu 2000). As a consequence, work units, SOEs in particular, had to bear an increasing financial burden resulting from housing provision, which not only made them less competitive compared to their counterparts in the private sector but also impeded further enterprise restructuring reforms.

Housing monetarization reform: a thrust to boost the economy

In the late 1990s, the Chinese government was facing many thorny policy problems. As a result of the Asian financial crisis, China's exports considerably decreased and millions of workers were laid off. In order to offset the impacts of the unfavourable external environment, stimulating domestic demand became an inevitable alternative to maintain rapid economic growth, which was also crucial for the government to ease the unemployment problem and to maintain social stability. Under such circumstances, the housing industry was positioned as 'a new growth point' for the economy. It was hoped that the growth of the real estate sector would help to channel individuals' consumption into property purchase and to stimulate the development of related sectors such as construction materials, home furnishing, electricity supply, and so on. It was against this background that the State Council, which was then presided over by the reformist premier Zhu Rongji, initiated housing monetarization reform in July 1998.

Housing monetarization refers to the provision of direct cash subsidies and allowances to urban residents by the government or work units in the place of in-kind housing distribution. With the cash subsidy or allowance, urban residents are supposed to satisfy their housing needs in the open market, assisted by other financial means such as family savings, housing provident fund (HPF) and bank loans. The policy comprises several aspects. First, the provision of in-kind public rental housing through work units is to be brought to an end. Second, work units are prohibited to build or buy housing for employees. Third, housing funds previously planned to buy or build welfare housing must be transformed into in-cash housing subsidies. Meanwhile, rent reform continues while sales of public flats are given priority. Moreover, households with different income are differentiated in the policy design. A multi-layer housing provision system is to be established, aiming to provide housing to people in accordance with their different economic situations. High salary earners are expected to buy private housing; medium- to low-income households are given chances to buy low-cost housing; low-rent social housing is tailored for the poorest income groups in cities. The whole idea behind the new housing policy is thus reminiscent of a housing ladder, as commonly found in western industrial societies.

The new approach in 1998: objectives and principles

Although housing monetarization as one major goal of housing reform is not a novel approach,[3] its announcement in 1998 was considered a watershed in China's housing reform. The new reform embodies two major goals: to restructure the housing system and to boost the economy. First, it aims to promote housing commercialization and socialization, and to gradually establish a new housing system that conforms to a socialist market economy. Second, it seeks to speed up housing construction and prompt real estate to become 'a new growth point of the economy'. Housing reform is endowed with the strategic goal of stimulating the economy. It is expected that the reform will promote the development of real estate, which is positioned as an engine for economic growth. It is also envisaged that the reform will push individuals to enter the housing market. In this way, vacant flats in the market will be 'digested'. What's more, the reform is also anticipated to cure the problem of unfairness in housing distribution (Xie 1998). To some extent, these objectives are contradictory and offer an open arena for local varieties in implementation.

Several general principles are proposed to guide the reform: (1) allowing local governments to make decisions under the guidance of the unified central policy, suiting the local, particular socio-economic setting as well as their own capabilities; (2) sharing the duty of housing provision appropriately among the state, work units and individuals; and (3) directing the reform by the principle of 'old housing old rule, new housing new system', maintaining policy continuity and assuring a smooth transition. It is clear that the central government envisaged difficulties in executing the reform and allowed for local flexibilities.

The unifying central directive:

- Requires that provinces and cities terminate material housing distribution in the second half of 1998.
- Sets the eligibility criteria for the provision of housing subsidy. Local governments and work units *can* (*keyi*) provide housing subsidies to eligible employees in the public sector when the price of a 60m² Economic and Appropriate Housing flat is more than four times a couple's annual income and when their original funds for housing construction can be transferred for provision of housing subsidy. Housing subsidy will only be provided to employees in the public sector who have not accessed any public dwellings and whose current flats do not reach the housing standard.
- Opens the secondary housing market for exchange of sold public housing (*yi shou gong fang*) and Economic and Appropriate Housing.
- Tightens discipline inspection in the reform process (Xie 1998).

Main strategies of housing monetarization

The tenet of the housing monetarization reform is to change the mode of housing provision from in-kind housing to monetary subsidies. Different strategies can be utilized to 'monetarize' housing provision:

- Wage increases.
- Provision of housing subsidies.
- Sale of public housing at *chengben* (cost) price with full property rights, plus the provision of housing subsidy.
- Raising employers' contributions to the housing provident fund scheme (Chang 1998).

Cash compensation for relocation is also a particular means of monetary distribution (Zhang and Chen 1999). In practice, most cities adopt more than one strategy to restructure the housing system. Housing monetarization reform takes on distinct local characteristics.

Social stability weighing over social equality: the adoption of the incremental approach

Two contending approaches to monetarization reform

Two contending approaches to housing reform were proposed in the 1990s: one by the State Committee of Economic System Reform and the other by the Ministry of Construction (Ji et al. 2001). Both approaches agreed that elderly employees should be subsidized because their low wages did not cover housing expenditure, but differed in their strategies for providing such housing subsidy. Broadly, the former adopted an holistic reform strategy (hereafter, 'the holistic approach'), insisting that the whole housing system be restructured, including all public housing stock, all state-run work units and sectors, as well as all employees in the public sector. The latter suggested an incremental and conservative approach (hereafter, 'the incremental approach'), which was embodied by the guiding principle of 'old housing old rule, new housing new system' and 'old people old way, new people new system', applying different policies to different types of housing and employee.

The holistic approach suggested that both the housing stock and all employees should be covered in the new system. Unlike the incremental strategy of 'new housing new system, old housing old rule', advocates of this approach held that both rent and house price of public flats could be raised to a market level when subsidizing employees who did not earn enough for housing consumption in the (old) wage system. Housing subsidy should be arranged and issued for the whole society within a city according to employees' working age, wage and job rank. That is, the cards of housing benefits need to be reshuffled and housing assets should be redistributed among all public work units and their employees. The provision of housing subsidy aimed to bridge the gap between housing price and employees' poor salaries. In the near future, it could take the form of depositing the subsidy into a special account or issuing coupons. In both situations, the money could only be used for home purchase or rent payment. In response to one of the main worries that the government and work units could not afford the burden of subsidy provision, these proponents contended that the housing stock was an enormous asset which was sufficient for providing housing subsidy and restructuring the housing system.

Proponents of the holistic approach strongly opposed the strategy of 'old housing old rule, new housing new system'. According to the incremental approach, 'old people' were entitled to continue benefiting from the welfare housing system, namely low rents and heavy discounts in house prices; while new people and old employees who had not accessed public flats were forced to purchase or rent in the open market. These measures were considered to both create housing inequality and aggravate it further because they did not deal with existing housing inequality and different social groups had uneven access to housing subsidies. Selling off public dwellings at heavy discounts meant extra income to the buyer but deprivation to those who did not occupy public flats (Cao 1998; Guo 2000a, 2000b). Herein, the amount of housing subsidy was not determined by one's contribution but by the space of the flat purchased or occupied: the bigger the flat, the more subsidies received. This kind of policy would fossilize housing inequality among work units and employees. It was unfair to those who could not get access to public flats before the reform. Obviously, this approach could not cure the problem of unequal housing distribution; rather, it would aggravate housing inequality and even provoke social instability. What's more, since there would always be employees who received no housing or insufficient housing, work units would thus become involved in a new wave of 'competition for housing subsidy'. A new vicious circle might appear and, if so, the reform would achieve no more than a change from distribution of in-kind housing to cash subsidy. The prospects for establishing a new market-oriented housing system looked bleak (Cao 1998).

On the contrary, advocates of the incremental approach pointed out some difficulties in putting the holistic reform proposals into practice (ibid.):

- The money needed for subsidizing employees in government departments and public institutions was much more than the state could provide.
- Most enterprises had difficulty in providing housing subsidies.
- There was no strong legal foundation to deny the ownership of work units over their housing assets.
- Given the fact that about 60 per cent of the saleable public housing had been sold to urban residents, it was difficult to merge the old policies with the proposed one. Attempts to readjust and redistribute these sold public

flats (*yi shou gong fang*) would not only bring about resentment from the homebuyers but also harm the authority of the government.

In order to avoid these obstacles, they put forward a conservative solution: while continuing preferential sales of public housing and not touching the housing benefits of 'old' employees who had bought public flats, the new housing system applied only to 'new' employees. Namely, work units provided housing allowance to young employees and urged them to purchase houses or rent in the market. This approach had advantages. It needed less direct financial support. More importantly, resources for the reform would be easier to mobilize because it covered only young employees and old employees in government departments who had no flats or whose flats had not met space entitlement. Thus, it could stimulate housing demand within a short time. In short, the incremental approach offered the advantages of low cost, minimal social shock and rapid results (see Table 12.1).

In fact, the biggest controversy in the policy discussions concerned whether

Table 12.1 Comparison of two housing reform approaches

	The incremental reform approach	The holistic reform approach
Coverage of housing	New housing new system; old housing old policy	Housing stock and new housing
Coverage of employees	New people and old people without public housing or with less space than entitled	All employees
Coverage of work units	Mainly in government sectors and public institutions funded by the state budget; enterprises are granted autonomy to work out their housing plans	All kinds of work units, including government sectors, public institutions, state-owned enterprises and collective-owned enterprises
Priority	'Looking forward' and giving priority to efficiency	Redistributing housing benefits and taking social justice into account
Potential resistance	Less resistance	More resistance
Resource needed	Needing more funds to provide subsidy	Needing much fewer state subsidy
Property rights structure	Leading to a complicated and ambiguous property rights regime; unfavorable to opening the second-hand housing market	Clear property rights; facilitating the openness of the second-hand housing market
The role of work units in housing provision	Work units more involved in housing provision	Work units less involved in housing provision
Marketization level	Low marketization level	High marketization level

old employees should be subsidized, and how. The fundamental difference between the two approaches was interest distribution (Ji et al. 2001).[4] As the salaries of old employees were inadequate for housing expenditure, they deserved compensation; any other approach would be unfair (Yuan 2001).[5] In addition, since the welfare housing system had led to unequal housing distribution among work units and employees, the incremental reform would only fossilize the previous housing inequality without touching the existing distributive structure of housing benefits. Allowing public flats to be exchanged in the secondhand market might widen the gap between different social groups. In this way, housing inequality between work units and employees would be transformed into income and wealth disparity among households. Hence, explicitly, the holistic reform approach would be better with regard to achieving equal housing distribution.

Semi-official groups supported the suggestions of the holistic reform approach. Reviewing the development of housing reform and analysing its achievements and problems, Zhang and his associates (1998a, 1998b) proposed that the solution to the stagnant situation of slow rent increases and low-price sales in housing reform was to change the in-kind housing distribution system into a cash system under the principle of distribution in terms of labour. They put forward three schemes to create a new housing finance regime, on which a new housing distribution mechanism could be based: (1) a foundation of the assets of the housing stock, (2) a housing provident fund scheme, and (3) housing saving banks. Supported by these financial arrangements, it would be possible to adjust rent and house prices to a market level and to merge public and private housing markets. Employees could thus afford to meet their housing needs through the private housing market. In this way, the target of housing commercialization, socialization and monetarization could be realized and a new market-oriented housing system be established (Zhang 1998b).

In fact, policy-makers did not necessarily oppose the holistic reform approach (Cao 1998; Xie 1998). For example, Xie Jiajin, director of the Bureau of Real Estate of the Ministry of Construction (Xie 1998), thought that in an ideal world, housing reform rent increases should be applied to both the housing stock and newly-built housing. If so, there would be a rational ratio of rent to price and individuals would be motivated to purchase homes. When rent elevation was comprehensively implemented in the society and both rent and housing price came to a reasonable (market) level, the government would provide housing subsidies to all employees to help them rent or purchase flats through the market. This approach would facilitate the establishment of a new housing system. However, Xie pointed out that the current socio-economic situation was not conducive to this kind of reform. The majority of SOEs were in 'difficulty' as structural reform was carried out and millions of workers were laid off. Under such circumstances, the holistic reform strategy could not be widely adopted because most work units could not bear the burden of rapid rent increase.

What's more, steep rent adjustment might also lead to inflation. This might harm social stability.

Controversy raged between these two approaches for three years, from 1995 to 1997 (Ji et al. 2001). In 1988, the discussion ended with the adoption of 'old housing old rule, new housing new system' and 'old people old policy, new people new system' as the guiding policy principles (ibid.). Maintaining social stability and avoiding social shock was deemed more important than concerns about social justice in the policy-making process. The conservative strategy of protecting the interests of beneficiaries was prioritized. Most cities adopted the incremental approach. However, the holistic approach was not totally excluded. It was adopted in Guizhou province and has proved to be quite successful, despite implementation problems encountered in the Guiyang housing reform process, largely due to the political structural factor, which makes it difficult to gain cooperation and coordination from related government departments at various levels (Zhu and Guo 2004; Zhu and Lee 2004).

Poor implementation and the enlarging housing inequality

Poor implementation and major difficulties

On the whole, housing monetarization reform has proceeded very slowly since it was announced in July 1998. The deadline for terminating in-kind housing distribution was postponed several times. Initially it was required that local governments terminate the old system within 1998 (Liu 1998). However, most provinces and cities postponed. For example, Guangzhou was one of the earliest cities to create a monetarization reform plan. However, it extended the deadline of termination of housing distribution until June 2000 so that some 60,000 households could catch 'the last train' (Luo 2000). In April 1999, Yu Zhengsheng, Minister of Construction at that time, demanded that: 'in principle implementation plans for the housing monetarization reform in all cities should be worked out before the end of September' (Xie 1999). However, by April 2000, only 24 of the 35 major cities had worked out implementation plans. In these cities, only ten (Tainjing, Shanghai, Chongqing, Shenyang, Dalian, Qingdao, Jinan, Nanjing, Guangzhou and Guiyang) had really begun to implement the reform (Xie 2000). The other 14 cities just formulated reform plans or began tests or other preparations. The execution of the reform was so slow that the Ministry of Construction had to change the deadline for local governments to publicize their implementation programmes until the end of March 2000 (Sun and Huang 2002). By the end of 2002, all 31 provinces, autonomous regions and municipalities directly managed by central government had created implementation programmes for housing monetarization reform. All 35 major cities, except Urumqi, had worked out specific reform plans. Twenty-nine of them had begun to carry out the reform in their jurisdiction and six (Beijing, Hohhort,

Yingchuan, Xining, Urumqi and Nanchang) had not really carried out the reform yet.

Table 12.2 shows that 219 of the total 269 prefecture-level cities (covering 81 per cent of the total) in China had launched a housing subsidy scheme. That is, in these cities the price of a 60m^2 flat was four times average household annual income. Among these eligible cities, 93 per cent of them (204) made out implementation plans and 155 cities began to carry them out.

As for counties (including county-level cities), more than half (1031) of the total 2053 counties should have carried out a housing subsidy scheme in terms of the central criterion that house price is more than four times household income. However, only 506 counties created implementation plans, accounting for 49 per cent of the eligible cities and 25 per cent of the total number of counties. Only 155 counties had begun to carry out the reform plan.

The reform was unevenly implemented all over the country. The implementation situation was much better in the East than the Middle and the West. For instance, in the East, 97 per cent of eligible prefecture-level cities had worked out implementation plans, compared to 93 per cent in the Middle and 83 per cent in the West. Also, as shown in Table 12.3, 95 per cent of prefecture-level cities in the East had actually begun to implement the reform, compared to 62 per cent in the Middle and 52 per cent in the West.

In terms of the amount of housing subsidy that has been provided, implementation is quite poor. It is estimated that in the 35 major cities about 28.6 billion *yuan* is needed to cash the subsidies, of which 27.4 billion *yuan* is targeted at 'old people'. However, by the end of 2002, only 3.368 billion *yuan* had been cashed, covering only 11.7 per cent of the total amount needed. Old employees received only 3.1 billion *yuan*, which is only slightly more than one-tenth (11.3 per cent) of their entitled subsidies. Interestingly, more housing subsidies have been provided in the East and the West than in the Middle (Table 12.4). To some extent, the reform has not really started in the Middle judging by the small amount of housing subsidy cashed to eligible employees (3 per cent of the total amount needed). At this rate, it will cost 20 to 30 years to finish providing housing subsidy to 'old people', let alone the major target group of the reform, 'new people'. This means that to some extent the reform is merely symbolic. The establishment of a new market-oriented housing system is a long way off.

As most of these housing plans do not necessarily cover enterprise workers, housing monetarization reform in enterprises is even worse. The reform has only been implemented in some major enterprises because funds for providing housing subsidy to workers are provided mainly from revenue of enterprises (under the 'cost' item) and sale of public flats. Table 12.5 and Figures 12.1, 12.2 and 12.3 show that enterprises in the East and West largely depend on their own revenue to launch the reform (respectively accounting for 52 per cent and 73 per cent), while in the Middle, revenue of sale of public flats is the major source of housing subsidy, covering 72 per cent of the total

Table 12.2 Implementation situation in prefecture-level cities

Region	Total No. of cities (A)	No. of cities ought to work out implementation plans (B)	Percentage of (B) out of (A)	No. of cities having worked out implementation plans (C)	Percentage of (C) out of (A)	Percentage of (C) out of (B)	No. of cities carried out implementation plans (D)	Percentage of (D) out of (B)	Percentage of (D) out of (C)
East	110	100	91	97	88	97	92	92	95
Middle	107	84	79	78	73	93	48	57	62
West	52	35	67	29	56	83	15	43	52
Total	269	219	81	204	76	93	155	71	76

Source: Bureau of Real Estate of Ministry of Construction (2003).

Table 12.3 Implementation situations in counties (county-level cities)

Region	Total no. of counties (A)	No. of counties ought to work out implementation plan (B)	Percentage of (B) out of (A)	No. of counties having worked out implementation plans (C)	Percentage of (C) out of (A)	Percentage of (C) out of (B)	No. of counties having carried out the implementation plan (D)	Percentage of (D) out of (B)	Percentage of (D) out of (C)
East	630	390	62	252	40	65	155	40	62
Middle	689	363	53	118	17	33	17	4.7	14
West	734	287	38	136	19	49	40	14	29
Total	2,053	1,031	50	506	25	49	212	10	42

Source: Bureau of Real Estate of Ministry of Construction (2003).

Table 12.4 Situation of provision of housing subsidy in the 35 major cities

Region	Total amount of funds needed (A) (10,000 yuan)	Total amount of housing subsidy issued (B) (10,000 yuan)	Percentage of (B) out of (A)	Amount of funds needed to subsidize 'old people' (C) (10,000 yuan)	Amount of funds issued to 'old people' (D) (10,000 yuan)	Percentage of (D) out of (C)
35 cities	2,868,284	336,800	11.7	2,742,805	309,477	11.3
East	1,271,866	198,794	15.6	1,186,222	183,142	15.4
Middle	899,150	30,923	3	872,141	23,242	2.7
West	697,268	107,084	15.4	684,442	103,093	15.1

Source: Bureau of Real Estate of Ministry of Construction (2003).

Table 12.5 Sources of funds for provision of housing subsidy in SOEs and institutions funded by themselves

	Nation	East	Middle	West
No. of implementation plans made out	24,873	16,578	7527	768
Housing subsidy issued (10,000 *yuan*)	1,173,338	886,819	101,909	184,610
Transferred from original funds for housing construction (10,000 *yuan*)	37,600	23,814	13,786	0
Percentage out of the total funds	3.2	3	14	0
Revenue from sale of public flats (10,000 *yuan*)	517,949	395,993	74,298	47,658
Percentage out of the total funds	44.1	45	73	26
Under the 'cost' item (10,000 *yuan*)	606,191	457,485	13,766	134,940
Percentage out of the total funds	51.7	52	14	73
Other sources (10,000 *yuan*)	11,598	9527	59	2012
Percentage out of the total funds	1	1	0.1	1

Source: Bureau of Real Estate of Ministry of Construction (2003).

funds needed. The reform has been launched mainly in enterprises with good profits or with a large amount of housing stock. Most enterprises cannot arrange for necessary funds. By the end of 2002, only 24,873 enterprises in the whole country had formulated reform plans and 11.733 billion *yuan* had been provided to workers for housing improvement.

It is difficult to abolish a housing system that has been operating for so long. Many impediments are deeply embedded within the implementation process. First, the socio-economic situation is unfavourable for the reform. When most SOEs began to engage in structural reforms, millions of workers were laid off. Second, the biggest bottleneck of the reform is insufficient resources. Whether local governments and work units can mobilize enough

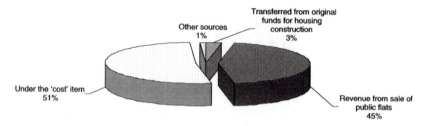

Figure 12.1 Composition of sources for housing subsidy in enterprise in the East.

Source: Bureau of Real Estate of Ministry of Construction (2003).

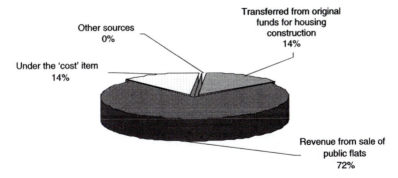

Figure 12.2 Composition of sources for housing subsidy in enterprise in the Middle.

Source: Bureau of Real Estate of Ministry of Construction (2003).

money is a crucial issue. According to the central directive, housing funds come mainly from: (1) the financial budget, (2) funds transferred from the state and work units that were originally planned for building or buying housing, (3) revenue from the sale of public housing, and (4) other sources. The first source is always limited. It changes with the significance of housing in the political agenda and with the financial conditions of local governments. Funds from 2, 3 and 4 are unstable; they will be used up quickly during the reform. That is to say, no stable and regular resource is assigned for implementation of the reform. Table 12.6 reveals resources for implementing the reform in governmental departments. In the 35 major cities, revenue mostly comes from the sale of public dwellings and the government budget, accounting for 43.2 per cent and 40.6 per cent, respectively. The proportion of funds from the government budget is much higher in the East (49 per cent) than in the Middle (37 per cent) and West (23 per cent) (see Table 12.6 and Figure 12.4). The main source for providing housing subsidy in the Middle and West is revenue from the sale of housing stock, covering 56 per cent and 63 per cent, respectively, of total funds (see Figures 12.5 and 12.6). Funds transferred from original sources for housing construction cover only a small

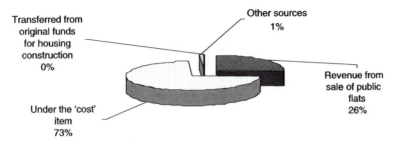

Figure 12.3 Composition of sources for housing subsidy in enterprise in the West.

Source: Bureau of Real Estate of Ministry of Construction (2003).

Table 12.6 Sources of funds for provision of housing subsidy in government departments and institutions in the 35 major cities

Source of funds and their percentage	35 cities	East	Middle	West
Transferred from original funds for housing construction (10,000 *yuan*)	19,420	9800	1620	8000
Percentage of the total funds	7.3	6	6	12
Revenue from sale of public flats (10,000 *yuan*)	115,012	52,544	20,468	42,000
Percentage of the total funds	43.2	32	55	63
Government budget (10,000 *yuan*)	108,121	79,225	13,826	15,070
Percentage of the total funds	40.6	49	37	23
Other resources (10,000 *yuan*)	23,530	20,700	1200	1630
Percentage of the total funds	8.8	13	3	2

Source: Bureau of Real Estate of Ministry of Construction (2003).

proportion (7.3 per cent) in provision of housing subsidy in the 35 major cities. However, funds accumulated from sale of housing stock are running out. As a result, the cashing of housing subsidies will depend on government budgets in the future. Because of common financial constraints faced by local governments in the Middle and the West, the implementation of housing reform will be more difficult.

In fact, even wealthier regions are confronting funding problems in conducting the reform. Take the wealthier Jiangsu province, which had provided 4 billion *yuan* housing subsidy in the five years from 1998–2003, the largest amount in the 31 provinces (Ren and Zhu 2003). This province was also

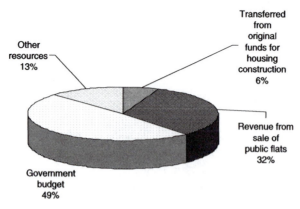

Figure 12.4 Composition of housing funds for housing subsidy in the East.

Source: Bureau of Real Estate of Ministry of Construction (2003).

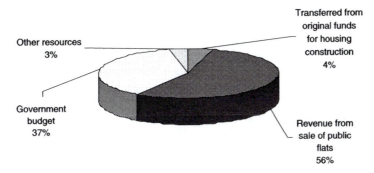

Figure 12.5 Composition of housing funds for housing subsidy in the Middle.

Source: Bureau of Real Estate of Ministry of Construction (2003).

facing funding problems. In March 1999, the Housing Reform Office of Jiangsu Province investigated the implementation situation. It was found that insufficiency of funds was the most serious problem in the implementation process (Huang 1999). Although it was stipulated by the provincial government that funds for housing subsidy mainly came from the government budget and housing funds for housing construction controlled by work units, few cities in the province really transferred the funds that were listed in the budget into resources for cashing housing subsidy. Instead, most funds were invested in housing construction. Some local governments and work units even arranged extra resources to build houses in order to catch the 'last train' (ibid.).

In addition, the revenue from sales of public housing, the major source for provision of housing subsidy, was also shrinking. The total sum of revenue from sales of public dwellings in 1999 was about 7 billion *yuan* in Jiangsu

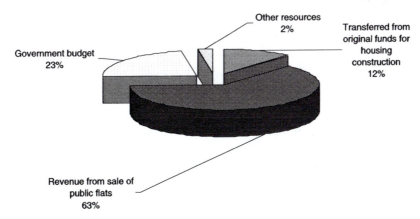

Figure 12.6 Composition of housing funds for housing subsidy in the West.

Source: Bureau of Real Estate of Ministry of Construction (2003).

province. It was far from enough to provide housing subsidy. In fact, new employees could not receive a regular allowance because few government departments and institutions had allowed for this expenditure in their budget.

Things are even worse in enterprises. For example, in Yangzhou city (a prefecture-level city), the majority of SOEs (86.9 per cent of the total) are in deficit or performing poorly. Workers in these enterprises account for 74.2 per cent of the total number of employees. Many of them do not even receive a salary regularly. Housing monetarization reform is almost impossible in these enterprises. As to the small number of well-run enterprises, they are unable to itemize this expenditure under the current accounting system (ibid. 1999). This problem has been solved by a new Ministry of Finance (2000) regulation. Expenditure for provision of housing subsidy can be itemized under 'cost' in the accounting. However, funds from the sale of housing are running out and the revenue needed for implementing the reform has to come from enterprise. This will impose an extra financial burden and harm their competitiveness in the market.

Third, the attitudes and disposition of local governments and work units are an important factor affecting reform implementation. After more than two decades, the duty of housing provision has been shifted from central government to local governments and work units and from the state and work units to the individual. The attempt to build a monetary housing system means further reduction of the responsibility of the state and work units and more involvement of individuals in housing provision. Hence, the success of the reform depends on commitment and cooperation of local government and work units as well as compliance of urban residents.

However, the significance of housing monetarization reform has not been adequately recognized (Yu 2001). Because most local leaders and enterprise managers own good flats, they do not have much motivation to promote the new reform. In fact, they tend to be inactive in mobilizing resources to carry out the reform. To many officials, housing monetarization reform means only contributing to the HPF scheme and providing a small amount of housing allowance. As the central policy stipulates, the provision of housing subsidy is selective, subject to local financial situations. As a result, many of them feel little commitment to the reform and merely passively implement it following the central directive: subsidize the old by using the revenue from the sale of housing and provide housing allowance to the new from the government budget. But, this does not solve housing problems. Instead of being really concerned about alleviating the housing problems of the needy, they are eager to gain from the development of real estate. Heavy levies and fees are imposed on real estate and property exchange, which have become a major source of local revenue. Local officials can use this money to pursue priorities other than ameliorating the residential situation of local citizens. Meanwhile, heavy taxes and levies largely account for high house prices and make private houses less affordable for ordinary people. All these undermine the main objective of housing reform: improving the living conditions of urban citizens.

For instance, in many cities, Economic and Appropriate Housing programmes targeted at providing affordable housing for medium- and low-income households cannot gain preferential treatment in the reduction of taxes and levies to which they are entitled by central policies and regulations (Qin 2002). Rising house prices are a huge impediment to housing monetarization reform, as households find the entitled housing subsidy means nothing in relation to soaring house prices and they tend to expect in-kind housing from their employees. For instance, most residents in Beijing are reluctant to receive housing subsidies and would rather wait for Economic and Appropriate Housing.[6] Consequently housing monetarization reform has not really been implemented in the capital city.

In addition, many local officials and those responsible for implementation have misperceptions about the reform. For instance, some think housing reform is finished since most public flats have been sold to individuals. Some argue that housing monetarization means that the state and work units will no longer bear housing responsibility. These misperceptions and the insufficient significance attached to the new reform account for poor implementation.

Housing monetarization reform and growing housing inequality

Contrary to the expectation of policy-makers, housing monetarization has actually increased housing inequality rather than improved it. Why? First, the stipulation of 'old housing old rule, new housing new system' draws a line between former beneficiaries and the less privileged in terms of housing benefits. Former beneficiaries were, and still to some extent are, entitled to buy public flats at low prices or pay very low rents, whereas those who have not obtained any in-kind housing benefits can only receive small subsidies. As current occupiers of public flats had benefited from free housing before the reform, the policy of preferential sale of public housing provides them with an opportunity of gaining an extra income because the house price is set at an extremely low level, only 10–20 per cent of the market price (Zhang 1998a). According to Ministry of Construction statistics, about 650 million m^2 or 75 per cent of the total saleable public housing stock had been sold to sitting tenants by March 2000 (Xie 2000). The average *chengben* price in major cities was less than 1,000 *yuan* per m^2, far below that of commercial housing (see Table 12.7). Meanwhile, the rent increase is very moderate. By the end of 2000, the average rent in 35 cities was only about 1.5 *yuan* per m^2 per month (see Table 12.8). Generally, the rent has not changed.

As prices of public flats are always arbitrarily set by local governments without taking into account housing quality, land value and differential rents, the policy of selling off public housing stock created new inequalities. According to a survey conducted by the State Statistics Bureau Urban Social and Economic Survey Team (2002), average housing value per household is 109,000 *yuan*. The average worth of private flats is 98,900 *yuan* (139,600 *yuan* per household in big cities; 89,500 *yuan* in middle-size cities and 74,600 *yuan*

Table 12.7 Space of public housing in the 35 major cities sold and *chengben* price in major cities (March 2000)

City	Total area of saleable public housing (million m²)	Public housing sold (million m²)	Proportion of public housing sold out of the total saleable housing (%)	chengben price (yuan/ m²)
Beijing	135	80	60	1485
Tianjing	32	19.2	60	1100
Shanghai	92	47.29	50	1198
Chongqing	36.459	30.99	85	880
Ha'erbin	31.76	27	85	954
Changchun	32	17.5	54	860
Shenyang	40	27.22	68	924
Dalian	21.45	13.84	65	1,320–1,540
Hohhot	9.14	6.95	76	850
Shijiazhuang	23.4	21	89.7	905
Zhengzhou	19.8	14.8	74.7	920
Taiyuan	21	18	85	845
Jinan	16	12.35	78	1138
Qingdao	26.65	20.54	77	1123
Nanjing	29.08	22.39	77	820
Hangzhou	18.655	15.34	82.27	860
Ningbo	11.154	8.762	78	806
Hefei	14	12	85	760
Nanchang	19	10	52.6	680
Fuzhou	14.9	10.43	70	960
Xiamen	6.292	4.7188	75	1208
Guangzhou	36.1	32.675	90	1416
Shenzhen	17.1	10.27	87.80	1700
Nanning	–	–	–	760
Haikou	4.0588	3.8568	95	1177
Changsha	17.1	15.4	90	785–1020
Wuhan	40.55	36.5	90	900
Kunming	19	17	90	759
Guiyang	12	8.5	65	850
Chengdou	25.99	16.38	63	830*
Xi'an	32.38	31.41	96.7	960
Yinchuan	–	–	–	–
Lanzhou	30	20.2	67	960
Xining	10.3887	9.3498	90	840
Ulrumqi	20.605	18.59	90	952
Total	867.2288	650.0274	75	–

Source: Xie (2000).

in small cities), while the average worth of public rental flats is only 7000 *yuan*. On average, urban residents spend 3,500 *yuan* on decorating. Properties (including their interior decoration) account for nearly half of household wealth (47.9 per cent), with slightly different weights in cities of different

Table 12.8 Rent for the public housing sector in provinces and major cities in 2000

Province	Average rent in the province	Major cities	Rent
Beijing	3.05	Beijing	3.05
Tianjing	1.08	Tianjing	1.08
Shanghai	2.3	Shanghai	2.3
Chongqing	1.56	Chongqing	1.56
Heilongjiang	1.3	Ha'erbin	1.44
Jilin	1.2	Changchun	1.65
Liaoning	1.63	Shenyang	2
		Dalian[1]	1.76
Inner Mongolia	2	Hohhot	3.32
Hebei	2	Shijiazhuang	2
Henan	1.42	Zhengzhou	1.45
Shanxi	1.11	Taiyuan	1.4
Shandong	2.55	Jinan	1.75
		Qingdao[1]	2.33
Jiangsu	2	Nanjing	2
Zhejiang	1.85	Hangzhou	1.8
		Ningbo[1]	2.16
Anhui	1.98	Hefei	1.85
Jiangxi	1.05	Nanchang	1.6
Fujian	2.1	Fuzhou	2.79
		Xiamen[1]	3.7
Guangdong	2.47	Guangzhou	3
		Shenzhen[1]	6.6
Guangxi	0.72	Nanning	1.5
Hainan	1.9	Haikou	3.3
Hunan	2.1	Changsha	2.5
Hubei	–	Wuhan	1.42
Yunnan	1.33	Kunming	1.2
Guizhou	3.48	Guying	8
Sichuan	1.65	Chengdou	2
Shannxi	1.17	Xi'an	1.51
Ningxia	0.7	Yinchuan	1
Gansu	1.3	Lanzhou	0.9
Qinghai	–	Xining	1.32
Xinjiang	2.01	Ulrumqi	0.66

Note:
1 Refers to non-capital cities.

Source: Office of State Committee of Planning and Ministry of Construction (2001).

sizes: 49.3, 45.1 and 48.1 per cent, respectively in big, middle-size and small cities. Clearly, residents who are lucky enough to buy public flats get an extra income compared to those in the public rental sector and the private housing sector.

The increase in housing inequality is confirmed by a survey conducted by the China Academy of Social Science in 1999. According to the survey, conducted in 13 cities at different administrative levels, in relation to ownership structure, housing owned by work units and local government accounts for 20 and 12 per cent, respectively, and individuals own 65 per cent. Eighty-five per cent of homeowners bought flats at discounted prices; only 5 per cent purchased homes at market prices. The average imputed rent of owned flats is 5,940 *yuan* per year, with an average imputed rent of 139 *yuan* per m². The average annual hidden housing subsidy for public rental housing (the rental market value minus rent being paid) is 5,873 *yuan* per household. This reveals that housing reform has not changed the welfare nature of the public housing sector; the way that housing welfare is distributed has only hanged from rent subsidy to discounted sale of public housing stock. Considering the big gap between house prices in the public sector and the private sector, housing inequality resulting from housing privatization schemes can be transformed into immense income disparity. At the outset, there were some restrictions on resale of purchased public housing. For example, homeowners were not allowed to sell purchased public flats in the first five years after they bought them. They were required to pay taxes and levies when they sold these flats and, in order to maintain social justice, sellers would have to share the revenue with former owners of the flats. However, these restrictions were soon loosened. Shanghai began experimenting with opening up the secondary housing market for purchased public flats in 1996 (Xie 1998). Learning from the Shanghai experience, the Guangzhou housing authority also allowed privatized public housing to enter the housing market in 1999. In 2003, aiming at boosting real estate and forming a 'ladder' of housing consumption, the central government encouraged urban residents to deal in the secondary housing market. Local governments were required to loosen all kinds of restrictions on exchange of purchased public flats (Zhu 2003). Sellers are now allowed to retain all revenue from the sale after they pay related taxes and only 1 per cent of the original purchase price as *land revenue*. Housing inequality is thus being transformed into income disparity.

The policy implementation process further exacerbates this inequality. First, in most cities many groups cannot get in-kind housing or have not understood and taken advantage of housing benefits to which they are entitled. 'Old people' who have not met their space entitlements and 'new people' are differentiated and covered by different housing subsidy schemes (for instance, in Nangjing, Wuhan and Guangzhou). Old employees are provided with one lump-sum housing subsidy, while young employees are eligible for monthly housing allowances. To many old employees, it seems that things have changed from in-kind housing distribution to cash payment.

Given the fact that old employees generally have more savings, they find it easier to improve their residential situation. As to 'new people', they are generally covered by monthly housing allowance schemes. Housing subsidy will be issued over a long period of time (say, 20–25 years), according to how the allowance is provided. They have to spend a large amount of their salary on accommodation. Considering the rapidly increasing house prices, most of them find it difficult to buy properties on the open market. Without more financial support from the government, work units and banks, the ambitious target of homeownership for most employees in the public sector is a far cry from reality.

Second, the unequal treatment of employees within different work units has been emphasized by institutional arrangements in housing plans. Housing inequality has been institutionalized in some reform plans. For example, civil servants in Shenzhen benefited more from the sale of welfare housing or renting at subsidized prices before 1999. In contrast, enterprise workers had to wait for years to buy more expensive *wei li* (low profit) houses without a definite promise of accessibility (Lau 1997: 16). In Xi'an and Jinan, all employees are eligible for housing subsidy in relation to a certain proportion of their salary, regardless of whether or not they have a dwelling. Although new employees most need assistance for solving housing problems, they benefit less from this policy because of their low wage base; old employees get more, although most of them own flats.

Third, housing inequality is further exacerbated by uneven access to housing subsidies. Work units with more power and housing stock (mainly government departments, financial firms, etc.) have more resources to provide housing subsidies to eligible employees; whereas workers in SOEs and COEs suffer poorer residential situations but have less chance to gain their share of compensation for housing consumption. The continuing operation of the work unit system fossilizes housing inequality between work units and the employees within them. Before the reform, the centralized investment system led to distinct housing inequality between work units. Different types of work unit controlled different resources under the planned economy system. Under rapid housing privatization reform, most saleable housing has been sold to individuals. Because it is explicitly stipulated that work units keep the revenue from the sale of public housing, which comprises a major source of housing subsidy, work units which used to have more housing stock instead now have more housing funds with which to carry out monetarization reform. Work unit ownership of public housing increases housing inequality among work units. Housing inequality between work units and employees is being transformed into income disparity following the loosening of restrictions on resale of privatized housing in the secondary housing market.

Lastly, housing inequality has also been worsened by the affordability problem. In the public rental sector, a large number of renters have difficulty in affording the rising rent. Although in theory the rent will inevitably increase, the impediment remains. Rent elevation will impose an extra burden on employees, who are expecting subsidy from work units to offset it because, otherwise, living conditions will be reduced. As cadres had always occupied better and bigger dwellings, they (always policy-makers) felt reluctant to increase the rent. As a consequence, both work units and those who live in better housing strongly oppose rent increases (Bian et al. 1997). Rent reform has proceeded very slowly since 1988. However, things have changed. With rapid privatization reform in the 1990s, most saleable public housing had been sold at low prices. As most cadres and implementers of housing reform have benefited from the policy of selling off public dwellings, opposition to rent reform has lessened. Now, the public rental sector has been residualized, similar to what happened in the UK. Good flats are sold out. Sitting tenants are generally low-income households, with little ability to afford higher rent. In addition, many employees are obliged to rent private flats (households with 'housing difficulties' in cities and the 'floating population'); they will suffer a great deal from rent rises. According to a survey on the attitude of residents to the news that public housing rent would increase from 1.30 to 3.05 per m² in Beijing, 76.6 per cent of respondents were indifferent because they had bought public housing and 23.4 per cent displayed great concern either because their work units were unable to distribute subsidies or because they had not been able to afford a public flat and had to rent from the private sector. Although the increases would not involve the private sector, rents in the private renting market would be bound to adjust due to interlocking effects. Albeit a small-scale rent adjustment, far from the market rent of 35 *yuan* per m², its influence on the tenants in the private sector would be great (Dong and Wang 2000).

Lack of housing security

Acknowledging the importance of balancing economic efficiency and social equality,[7] the Chinese government does make efforts to assist medium- to low-income households and the urban poor. For the former group, affordable housing schemes have been launched. The Comfortable Housing Project (*anju gong cheng*) was implemented in 1995. It aimed to provide 25 million m² of new affordable housing for medium- and low-income households in cities each year from 1995–2000. However, approximately half of the 232 cities that applied to join the scheme had dropped out by 1999. Although this programme has helped hundreds of thousands of people get decent accommodation, it has also encountered many problems. First, many flats were vacant[8] because: (1) local governments always allocated land in suburban areas with poor transportation and public facilities; (2) many projects were ill-equipped and poorly-designed as developers had scrimped on building costs to increase profit;[9] (3) house prices were still much higher than medium- and low-income households could afford; and (4) there was no means-test for purchases. Many better-off people benefited from this scheme.

Anju project was merged with the Economic and Appropriate Housing (*jing ji shi yong fang*) scheme in 1998. The new programme also targeted medium- to low-income households but the target groups were much larger. As levels of subsidy in most cities' housing plans are calculated based on prices of Economic and Appropriate Housing (*jing ji shi yong fang*), this scheme has become a major means of housing provision. It also plays a critical role in stabilizing house prices in the market and assisting many residents to become homeowners. However, it also encounters similar problems to the *anju* project: Economic and Appropriate Housing projects do not get preferential treatment in relation to land acquisition and tax rebates; provision is limited; house prices are too high for the target group and many better-off people purchase the low-cost houses; many developers abuse the preferential policy, etc. (Cui and Peng 2003). Policy-makers are currently reviewing the rationality and feasibility of the scheme. Central government should set reasonable house prices and implement a strict means-testing mechanism so that the programme meets its goal of providing housing security for medium- and low-income households (Qin 2002).

The *lian zu fang* (social rental housing) scheme is positioned as an important component in the multi-layer housing provision system; it was launched after the 1998 housing monetarization reform and targeted mainly at the urban poor. This scheme was embodied in the State Council's Notice on Further Deepening Urban Housing Reform and Speeding up Housing Construction in Cities and Towns, issued in July 1998 (State Council 1998). It is quite different from the welfare public rental housing that is under reform. *Lian zu fang* is targeted at providing decent dwellings to low-income households in cities who cannot afford to buy either commercial houses at market prices or Economic and Appropriate Housing (*jing ji shi yong fang*) at government-designated prices. Rent for *lian zu fang* is much lower than that for public rental housing. It is a residual system for officially recognized urban poor. *Lian zu fang* includes public dwellings controlled by either local housing bureaus or work units that are vacated or new housing built by local governments. Despite the importance of the scheme in establishing a housing security system for low-income urban residents, it is currently under experimentation. By the end of 2002, half of the 35 major cities had only worked out related regulations and programmes to guide the implementation of the scheme. In most cities social rental housing is provided only to households in 'double difficulties' of both economic difficulty and extremely serious housing shortage, and hence coverage is very limited. Even worse, the scheme suffers from insufficient funding and unstable resources no matter what means are adopted to assist the lowest-income households. It thus far has played a very limited role in solving housing problems of the urban poor. Only a small number of residents have begun to gain benefit from it. For instance, Guangzhou was one of the earliest cities to launch the social rental housing scheme, making implementation plans as early as 1998. However, in the six years from 1998 to 2003, only 1,041 households had solved their housing problem through the scheme, 2,900 households were on the waiting list, and the number of officially recognized lowest-income households increased annually by more than 400–500 households in the city (Zhu and Chen 2005). Even in terms of the eligibility of 'double difficulties', the provision of social rental housing is extremely insufficient. For instance, by 2003 only 632 households had been provided with social rental flats in Chongqing, accounting for less than 3 per cent of the 23,500 eligible households.[10] The slow development of social rental housing hinders the establishment of a multi-layered housing provision system (Office of State Committee of Planning and Ministry of Construction 2001).

As explored, eligible groups targeted by the affordable housing and social rental housing schemes cannot solve their housing problems through the current housing security system due to poor implementation and limited housing provision. There are also a great number of households who belong to the 'sandwich' class. It is estimated that 20 per cent of the urban population needs assistance from the government (Zhu and Chen 2005). In Guangzhou, the registered and officially recognized lowest-income households number 50,000, accounting for 0.03 per cent of the city's population; the 'sandwich class' in Guangzhou is calculated at no less than 20,000 households (ibid.). They are too well off to be eligible for social rental housing but not well off enough to buy an Economic and Appropriate Housing flat.

In addition, housing inequality is made even worse by insufficient institutional arrangements for the urban poor (Lau 1997; Wang 2000). According to the fifth Chinese census, official documents record the existence of a 'floating population' of 121 million, the majority of whom are peasant workers (around 99 million people).[11] Although they have contributed greatly to China's economy, they do not belong to the officially recognized urban poor, who are entitled to some kind of social welfare (Wang 2000) and their accommodation problems are not on the government agenda. Clearly, China might not achieve sustainable development and build up a harmonious society' without tackling this issue. Excluding such a large percentage of the population could constitute a huge political risk.

Concluding remarks

Housing monetarization is a critical step towards a market-oriented housing system. Its initiation shows the resolution of the government to establish a market-based housing system while reducing its responsibility for providing housing welfare. The discussion on the direction housing reform is taking and its adoption in incremental stages indicates that economic efficiency and social stability have been prioritized above social equality during the housing reform decision-making process.

Concessions made for former beneficiaries of the old housing system and previous reforms and poor implementation of the reform across the country have also hugely exacerbated housing inequality among different work units and social groups. The distinctive gap in housing benefits between urban citizens has gradually been transformed into an amazing disparity in household wealth. People who had access to public flats obtained a large amount of extra income while those who had not, mainly workers in SOEs, suffered greatly as a result of the new reform initiatives. To a large extent, both the socialist institutions before the reform and the market mechanism along with housing marketization and privatization doubly deprived workers who had no chance to access public flats. The social welfare to which the socialist regime entitled them has shrunk as a result of the economic reform. Even worse, with the gradual dismantling of the so-called 'mini-welfare state' based on the work unit system, many poor workers are suffering from the transition to a market economy as the social welfare system in line with western market economies is insufficient, if not absent, in China.

A general exploration of the incremental approach throughout the country reveals that housing plans adopting it suffer from limited coverage – meaning exclusion of enterprise workers – and insufficient and unstable resources for implementation. As a result, the reform has not alleviated the problem of housing inequality. In fact, it has created greater housing disparity between different social groups, such as beneficiaries of the former in-kind housing system. Housing inequality has been *fossilized* in a way and further exacerbated as a result of housing monetarization reform and the opening up of a secondary housing market for privatized public flats.

As a result of the difficulties encountered in housing monetarization reform, the policy has had limited success. It has generally undermined ordinary people's dependency on their employers for housing and made them channel their money into buying their own home. Housing monetarization reform is still in its very early stages: only a small amount of housing subsidy (20–30 billion *yuan*) has been provided in recent years, and its implementation has not even started in half of China's cities. It is largely a policy intention or example of government rhetoric rather than a successful outcome in dealing with the housing crisis as declared by the Ministry of Construction.

Wider implications for understanding the development of social policy in transitional China can be inferred from the housing reform practice. Many urban citizens in China, especially those workers who are employed in poorly performing SOEs, are victims of the economic reforms; they are exploited and deprived by both pre-reform institutions and marketization and privatization reforms. Under the rhetoric of the reform, they have discovered that they have quietly lost their social status and social welfare. Excluding a great number of citizens, including the 'floating population', incurs huge risks for social stability and political legitimacy in the long run. The Chinese government is still facing the huge challenge of addressing economic efficiency, social stability and social equality in making and implementing social policy.

Notes

1 This research is supported by the Humanities and Social Science Youth Foundation Project of the Ministry of Education of the People's Republic of China (Project No. 07JC810004) and the Centre for Public Administration and School of Government, Sun Yat-sen University. Their support is most gratefully acknowledged.
2 This is clearly stated in Deng Xiaoping's strategy of economic reform in China: efficiency is prioritized while social justice is also taken into consideration.
3 In fact, housing monetarization reform was firstly put forward in a discussion meeting in 1987, when Yantai and other pilot cities shared their reform experiences.

A consensus was reached in the meeting that the objective of urban housing reform was 'to realize housing commercialization in accordance with the demands of a socialist planned commodity economy, namely, to change the current in-kind housing distribution into monetary distribution through the way that residents purchase or rent housing and make the biggest commodity item – housing – enter the consumption market and realize a healthy circulation of housing funds, so as to to figure out a new way of solving housing problems with Chinese characteristics' (Chen zhen zhu fang zhi du shi dian gong zuo zuo tan hui ji yao [Summary of discussion meeting of experimentation in urban housing reform] 1987). This notion was incorporated in the central reform policy in 1988. The government explicitly stipulated that the objective of housing reform was 'to realize housing commercialization in accordance with the demand of a socialist planned commodity economy. Starting with rent reform, the reform aimed to change the current in-kind housing distribution into monetary distribution (General Office of State Council 1988). The objective of realizing monetary distribution was reiterated in the later reform programmes. It was stressed in the central documents in 1994 that one of the major components of the housing reform was to change the in-kind housing distribution system into a cash distribution mainly based on the principle of distribution according to labour (State Council 1994). Obviously, the transformation from in-kind to monetary distribution has been one of the major objectives of China's housing reform.

4 Professor Wu discussed the hot economic issues of great concern to ordinary people on 9 March 2001. When talking about housing reform, he strongly praised the Guizhou housing model (see Ji et al. 2001).

5 On March 12 2001, Professor Wu, a member of the Standing Committee of the National People's Political Consultative Congress, answered questions about housing reform (see Yuan 2001).

6 According to fieldwork conducted in June 2004.

7 Attention to social welfare can be seen frequently in government documents and officials' speeches, especially the principle guiding China's development and reform proposed by Deng Xiaoping: 'economic efficiency is prioritized while social justice is also taken into consideration'.

8 By the end of 1997, 3.4 million m^2 of *Anju* housing stood vacant (see Rosen and Ross 2000).

9 In fact, the profit that can be made from Economic and Comfortable Housing and Economic and Appropriate Housing is not low. The officials set the rate at no more than 3 per cent. In fact, it ranged from 3–15 per cent, depending on the project, and was always higher than 10 per cent.

10 See www.cin.gov.cn/cxjs/ml/040404.doc.

11 Ibid.

References

Chen zhen zhu fang zhi du shi dian gong zuo zuo tan hui ji yao [Summary of discussion meeting of experimentations of urban housing reform] (1987) in Bureau of Real Estate of Ministry of Construction (ed.), *Selected Documents of State's Policies about Real Estate (1985–1987)*, Beijing: Nengyuan Chubanshe [Energy Press].

Bian, Y., Logan, J.R., Lu, H., Pan, Y. and Guan, Y. (1997) Work units and housing reform in two Chinese cities, in X. Lu and E. J. Perry (eds), *Danwei: The Changing Chinese Workplace in Historical and Comparative Perspective*, Armonk: M. E. Sharpe.

Cao, J. (1998) On monetary distribution of housing, *Housing and Real Estate*, 44(11): 4–9.

Chang, S. (1998) Symposium on monetarization of housing distribution and the second housing market, *Housing and Real Estate*, 36(4): 6–7.

Chen, A. (1998) China's urban housing market development: problems and prospects, *Journal of Contemporary China*, 7(17): 43–60.

Chen, G. (1994) Urban housing problems in China, in C. H. Marc and G. Chen (eds), *China: The Challenge of Urban Housing*, Meridien: Laval, Que.

Chen, S. (2003) The context of social policy reform in China: theoretical, comparative and historical perspective', in C. J. Finer (ed.), *Social Policy Reform in China: Views from Home and Abroad*, Aldershot: Ashgate.

Cui, Y. and Peng, L. (2003) Jing ji shi yong fang shui jing ji? Shui shi yong? [Who benefits from the *jing ji shi yong fang* scheme?], *Jingji Ribao* [*Economic Daily*], 3 April, p. 5.

Dong, M. and Wang, X. (2000) Gongfang zujin jiang dafu tisheng, wei mai gongfang zhe fanying qianglie [Rent in public houses to be raised considerably; those not buying public housing much concerned], *Jingji Cankao Bao*, 29 February, p. 7.

Fu, Y., Tse, D.K. and Zhou, N. (2000) Housing choice behaviour of urban workers in China's transition to a housing market, *Journal of Urban Economics*, 47: 61–87.

General Office of State Council (1988) Guo wu yuan ban gong ting guan yu zhuan fa guo wu yuan zhu fang zhi dou gai ge xiao zu gu li zhi gong gou mai gong you jiu zhu fang yi jian de tong zhi [Notice of State Council on encouraging employees to buy public flats], in Bureau of Real Estate of Ministry of Construction (ed.), *Selective Collection of Documents of State Real Estate Policy (1988–1990)*, Beijing: Tianing she hui ke xue yuan chu ban she [Tianjing Academy of Social Science Press].

Gu, E.X. (2001a) Beyond the property rights approach: welfare policy and the reform of state-owned enterprises in China, *Development and Change*, 32: 129–150.

Gu, E.X. (2001b) Dismantling the Chinese mini-welfare state? Marketization and the politics of institutional transformation, 1979–1999, *Communist and Post-Communist Studies*, 34(1): 91–111.

Guan, X. (2000) China's social policy: reform and development in the context of marketization and globalization, *Social Policy and Administration*, 34(1): 115–130.

Guo, S. (2000a) Guan yu zhu fang zhi du gai ge de jian yi [Suggestions on housing reform], in S. Guo (ed.), *Guizhou Zhu Fang Fen Pei Huo Bi Hua Gai Ge* [*Housing Reform of Monetarisation Distribution in Guizhou*], Beijing: Zhongguo caizheng jingji chubanshe [China Finance and Economy Press].

Guo, S. (ed.) (2000b) *Guizhou Zhu Fang Fen Pei Huo Bi Hua Gai Ge* [*Housing Reform of Monetarisation Distribution in Guizhou*], Beijing: Zhongguo caizheng jingji chubanshe [China Finance and Economy Press].

Haila, A. (1999) Events and debates: why is Shanghai building a giant speculative property bubble?, *International Journal of Urban and Regional Research*, 23(3): 583–588.

Huang, Q. (1999) Jiang su sheng zhu fang fen pei huo bi hua mian lin de zhu yao wen ti he dui ce [Major problems faced in the housing monetarization reform in Jiangsu Province and solutions], *Housing and Real Estate*, 9: 28–29.

Huang, Y. (2000) Housing tenure choice in transitional urban China, paper presented at the Housing Policy and Practice in the Asia Pacific: Convergence and Divergence conference, Center of Urban Planing and Environmental Management, 5 June, University of Hong Kong.

Ji, W., Du, D. and Ru, Q. (2001) Wu jing lian zong lun jing ji re dian [Wu Jinglian talks about hot economic issues], *Zhongguo Jingji Shibao* [*China Economic Times*], 10 March, p.1.

Lau, K.Y. (1997) *Housing Inequality and Segregation: An Exploratory Study on Housing Privatization in Shenzhen City of the People's Republic of China*, working paper, Hong Kong: Department of Public and Social Administration, City University of Hong Kong.

Lin, J.Y., Cai, F. and Li, Z. (1998) Competition, policy burdens, state-owned enterprise reform, *American Economic Review*, 88(2): 420–427.

Liu, Z. (1998) Liu zhifeng fu bu zhang zai bu fen sheng, shi guan che guo wu yuan guan yu ji yi bu shen hua chegn zhen zhu fang zhi dou gai ge, jia kuai zhu fang jian she de tong zhi zuo tan hui shang de jiang hua [Speech on the discussion meeting of provinces and cities about implementation of the State Council's notice to promote housing reform and to speed up housing construction], *China Real Estate*, 12(216): 4–9.

Logan, J.R., Bian, Y. and Bian, F. (1999) Housing inequality in urban China in the 1990s, *International Journal of Urban and Regional Research*, 23(1): 7–25.

Lu, X. and Perry, E.J. (1997) *Danwei: The Changing Chinese Workplace in Historical and Comparative Perspective*, Armonk: M. E. Sharpe.

Luo, J. (2000) Mo ban che bu deng ren, zhi liu ke xu zhua jin [The last train waits for no man and passengers have to hurry up], *Yangcheng Evening News*, 29 February, p. 5.

Office of State Committee of Planning and Ministry of Construction (2001) *Guanyu 2000 nian Quanguo Gongyou Zhufang Zujin Gaige Qingkuai de Tongbao* [*Announcement of national rent reform in the public housing sector in 2000*], at: http://www.cin.gov.cn/fdc/file/2001062601.htm.

Qin, H. (2002) Jia da dui zhong di shu ru jia ting zhu fang bao zhang li du [Increasing the scale of housing secrurity on medium–low income households], *China Real Estate*, 7: 40–43.

Ren, B. and Zhu, X. (2003) Fang gai: Xing bao li zhe ban jiu shi 'zhu fang huo bi hua' [Housing monetarization reform has not been well implemented], *Caijing* [*Business and Finance Review*], 23: 48–54.

Rosen, K. and Ross, M. (2000) Increasing home ownership in urban China: notes on the problem of affordability, *Housing Studies*, 15(1): 77–88.

Shaw, V.N. (1997) Urban housing reform in China, *Habitat International*, 21(2): 199–212.

State Council (1994) Guo wu yuan guan yu shen hua cheng zhen zhu fang zhi du gai ge de tong zhi [Notice of State Council on deepening housing reform in cities and towns], in Office of Leading Group of Housing System Reform of the State Council and Institution of China Housing System Reform (eds), *Zhongguo Zhufang Zhidu Gaige* [*China's Housing System Reform*], Beijing: Gaige Chubanshe [Reform Press].

State Council (1998) Guan yu jin yi bu sheng hua cheng zhen zhu fang zhi du gai ge jia kuai zhu fang jian she de tong zhi [Notice on further deepening urban housing reform and speeding up housing construction], in Editorial Committee (ed.), *Chang Yong Zhufang Zhidu Gaige Falu Fagui* [*Commonly Used Laws and Regulations on Housing System Reform*], Beijing: Renmin Fayuan Chubanshe [People's Court of Justice Press].

State Statistics Bureau Urban Social and Economic Survey Team (2002) Household Wealth Situation, at: http://www.stats.gov.cn/tjfx/ztfx/csjtccdc/t20020927_36428.htm.

Sun, Y. and Huang, T. (2002) Zhu fang fen pei huo bi hua ji hua you wan 3 yue chu tai [Housing monetarization programmes supposed to come out by March], *Shichang Bao [Market News]*, 5 February, p. 1.

Tong, Z.Y. and Hays, R.A. (1996) The transformation of the urban housing system in China, *Urban Affairs Review*, 31(5): 625–658.

Wang, Y. (2000) Housing reform and its impacts on the urban poor in China, *Housing Studies*, 15(6): 845–864.

Wang, Y.P.I. and Murie, A. (1999) *Housing Policy and Practice in China*, New York: Macmillan.

World Bank (1992) *China: Implementation Options for Urban Housing Reform*, Washington, DC: World Bank.

Wu, F. (1996) Changes in the structure of public housing provision in urban China, *Urban Studies*, 33(9): 1601–1627.

Xie, J. (1998) Jin yi bu shen hua cheng zhen zhu fang zhi du gai ge cu jin guo min jing ji de zeng zhang [Further deepening up urban housing reform and promoting national economic growth], *China Real Estate*, 10(214): 8–12, 21.

Xie, R. (1999) *Jia kuai fang gai bu fa* [Speed up the pace of housing reform], *Jing ji ri bao [Economic Daily]*, 12 August, p. 2.

Xie, R. (2000) Zhong guo fang gai ge de ru he [How far has China's housing reform gone?]. *Jing ji ri bao [Economic Daily]*, 22 May, p. 5.

Yu, Z. (2001) Yu jian she bu zhu zhang yu zheng sheng mian dui mian guan zhu xiang fang gai zhi du [Discussing new housing system face to face with the Minister for Construction Yu Zhengsheng], *Dong fang shi kong*, 19 January, CCTV.

Yuan, R. (2001) Fang gai yao li qiu gong ping [Housing reform must seek for justice]. *Zhong guo jian she bao [China Construction News]*, 12 March, p. 1.

Zhang, M. and Chen, Y. (1999) *Ti chang duo yang hua de zhu fang huo bi hua fen pei zheng ce* [Advocating diversified policies of monetary housing distribution], *China Real Estate*, 225(9), 18–20.

Zhang, X.Q. (2000a) Housing reform and the new governance of housing in urban China, *International Journal of Public Sector Management*, 13(6): 519–525.

Zhang, X.Q. (2000b) The restructuring of the housing finance system in urban China, *Cities*, 17(5): 339–348.

Zhang, Z. (1998a) Jia kuai zhu fang huo bi fen pei ji zhi zhuan huan, pei yu zhu fang jian she xin de jing ji zeng zhang dian [Speed up the transformation of the mechanism of monetary distribution and build up a new economic growth pole of housing construction, Part II], *China Real Estate*, 210(6): 4–10.

Zhang, Z. (1998b) Jia kuai zhu fang huo bi fen pei ji zhi zhu huan, pei yu zhu fang jian she xin de jing ji zeng zhang dian [Speed up the transformation of the mechanism of monetary distribution and build up a new economic growth pole of housing construction, Part I], *China Real Estate*, 209(5): 4–10.

Zhao, Y. and Bourassa, S.C. (2003) China's urban housing reform: recent achievements and new inequities, *Housing Studies*, 18(5): 721–744.

Zhu, H. and Chen, M. (2005) Guangzhou lian zu xin zheng: bian 'bu zhuan tou' wei 'bu ren tou [New social rental housing policy in Guangzhou: changing from 'subsidizing bricks' to 'subsidizing target groups'], *Nangfang Zhoumo [Southern Weekend News]*, 28 April.

Zhu, J. (2000) The changing mode of housing provision in transitional China, *Urban Affairs Review*, 35(4): 502–519.

Zhu, J. (2003) Zhu fang xin zheng ce gei lao bai xing dai lai shen me? [What has the new housing policy brought to ordinary people?), *People's Daily*, 15 September.

Zhu, Y. and Guo, W. (2004) Inter-governmental relations and policy implementation: a case study of Guiyang housing monetarization reform, *Hong Kong Journal of Social Sciences*, 28(Autumn/Winter): 35–57.

Zhu, Y. and Lee, J. (2004) Redistributive justice and housing benefits in China: the Guiyang model, *Journal of Societal and Social Policy*, 3: 47–62.

Part IV
The challenge for urban governance

13 Managing the chaotic city–social cohesion

New forms of urban governance and the challenge for East Asia

Ray Forrest

Introduction

Chaos is no more a prominent feature of East Asian urbanization than it is of urban settlements in other parts of the world. Some East Asian cities are, however, growing at an extraordinary rate and some villages have transmogrified into major cities in the space of a decade. The scale and pace of these changes present new challenges for urban management, urban planning and occasional major transformations in social life and the structure of civil society. But, of course, this is only a partial picture of urbanization in the region. There are also the more mature and relatively settled cities such as Singapore and Hong Kong, where notions of disorder and chaos hardly seem apt.

It is important, however, to recognize that a measure of disorder is in the very essence of city life. Indeed, Sennett (1970) persuasively argued that it was, and should be, at the core of the urban experience. Thus, the title of this chapter is not intended to convey a problem that has to be solved. On the contrary, it describes a universal truth – that cities have multiple, overlapping and often double-edged qualities. Cities are exciting and vibrant, threatening and dangerous, ordered and disordered. They are the crucibles of creativity and entrepreneurialism, at the cutting edge of social, economic and cultural change. They are also the epicentres of conflict, friction and social inequality. Great cities tend to be all these things.

We want different things from our cities. We want them to be risky but safe. We want to feel a certain edginess, a roughness rather than a smooth blandness. We do not want anarchy but neither do we want to feel we are sleepwalking through an overplanned superficiality. Moreover, these are more than merely aesthetic or emotional considerations. The ambience of a city, its texture and feel are increasingly important ingredients of its competitiveness – ingredients that contribute to innovation, technological development, its attraction for the 'creative class', for transnational professionals and tourists. Diversity is good for business.

These considerations may seem far removed from some of the fundamental problems of providing decent housing, health, education and the other basic essentials of life, which are the core functions of urban government. But as populations worldwide become increasingly urbanized, as environmental issues come more to the fore and as cities find themselves in a more competitive global environment, the quality of the urban experience has become a more important and contested concept. For East Asia, at the forefront of economic development in the twenty-first century, the challenge is to create cities that are also leading the way in terms of the lived experience of urbanism.

Of course, cities reflect and act upon the cultures in which they sit. And institutional changes, transformations of the built environment, new policies and coalitions of interest derive from and build on a legacy of the past. The prescriptions for how to manage the cities of the twenty-first century may have a pervasive neo-liberal discourse but local outcomes will be path dependent. Where new cities have rapidly emerged on what may have been essentially green field sites, as is the case in many parts of East Asia, the institutional foundations may be sparse and inadequate to the task of managing an expanding metropolis. Equally, however, the opportunities are there to create social and physical infrastructures geared to a new set of needs and demands without the encumbrances of a previous eqoque. One dimension of this relates to the technological hardware of modern cities that is a more disruptive and problematic process in older, historical cities than in newer urban environments. The social software dimensions are more elusive to define and encourage in the new city in which there are not long-established and sedimented routines and practices.

From urban government to urban governance

Underlying what may seem these rather abstract notions is the question of what urban governance is for, and for whom? The idea of 'governance' rather than government has become a rather taken-for-granted positive in the urban as in other spheres. It is imbued with ideas of inclusion, partnership and democratic participation. But it also has strong elements of technocracy, efficiency and market dominance, and suggests a process of sanitization of the 'messy' but valuable qualities of urban life referred to above. It is also, as Maloutas and Malouta (2004) argue, inextricably bound up with the general globalization discourse in which 'solutions' have to be found for previously 'inefficient' welfare systems in the context of a new social and economic order which is 'inevitable'. But one aspect of the solution, closely tied to ideas of social capital, is to mobilize and encourage the informal routines and practices of daily urban life for the greater welfare good. Or to put it another way, in the context of low levels of formal provision, to help people to help themselves and each other rather than be reliant on state welfare. These ideas, of course, seem highly compatible in an East Asian context where more traditional customs and practices appear to be more resilient than in western cultures. The problem, however, is that powerful economic and social forces may be undermining these very qualities that can supposedly substitute for state provision.

In 1970, Ray Pahl, a British sociologist, posed the question: Whose City? At that time the answer was that cities were in the main shaped and controlled by a relatively small group of officials, elected representatives and urban professionals (Pahl 1970). The old model of city government was top down. The key actors were these local government officers, urban professionals and elected representatives. They were the gatekeepers who controlled access to scarce urban resources: housing, education and other key amenities. Cities were environments of constraint rather than choice, in which households negotiated bureaucratic rules and procedures or sought private alternatives in relatively regulated markets. Pahl also recognized that these urban gatekeepers managed but did not create scarcity. This echoed and was partly a response to Marxist critiques of urban policy and urban theory in the 1970s and 1980s, which argued that more fundamental structural solutions were required to combat deep-seated urban inequalities (for example, Pickvance 1976). The root of the problem was argued to be in the nature of cities as capitalist cities. The solution was to seek for a more inclusive, socialist model of the city.

We have come a long way from that theoretical discourse and it would be difficult to find actually existing socialist cities, even in East Asia. References to an 'inclusive city' are now more likely to be embedded in a neo-liberal model. The management of cities revolves around the agenda of partnership, privatization and reregulation. We no longer have urban gatekeepers but stakeholders, which include state, quasi-state and business interests as well as local NGOs, community-based groups and international organizations. The organization and shaping of cities should now, it is argued, be the product of a tripartite partnership between the various organs of the state, private sector and civil society. The Global Development Research Centre (2007) summarizes this approach to cities as follows:

> Good governance assures that political, social and economic priorities are based on broad consensus in society and that the voices of the poorest and the most vulnerable are heard in decision-making over the allocation of development resources.

This is clearly an aspiration rather than necessarily a description of an existing urban order. Moreover, there are ample critiques of the conception of governance in general and urban governance in particular which argue that partnerships are anything but equal. The voices of the poor may be heard but not acknowledged and it is corporate interests that increasingly dominate. Moreover, in the contemporary city the competition for that scarce resource of prime urban space is even more acute evidenced by more intense gentrification of city centres and desirable waterfront locations and the displacement of the urban poor to remoter suburban locations. These processes of revalorization and the reordering of urban space are highly visible in East Asian cities such as Beijing, Seoul and Tokyo (He 2007; Hirayama 2005), often encouraged and facilitated by urban policies.

One of the clearest articulations of the new realities and priorities for urban governance is contained in *Urban Future 21* (Hall and Pfeiffer 2000). This positions sustainable urban development as the core concept of contemporary governance but also emphasizes the centrality of market forces. 'Since the collapse of the communist system at the end of the 1980s, the market economy has literally spanned the globe. It has shown its superiority to any other model for generating capital accumulation and increasing the world's wealth' (p. 166). The report goes on to acknowledge that there are, of course, different kinds of capitalism, and that by implication, cities sit within very different cultures, economies, institutions and policy histories. 'But urban policies do best when they work with market forces, not against them' (op. cit.).

It is worth noting that in these debates about cities and good governance it is not entirely clear in which direction the policy transfer traffic is flowing – from west to east or in the opposite direction. Conceptions of the competitive city of the global age as essentially entrepreneurial would seem closer to the East Asian than the European model. Equally, however, cities such as Tokyo, Singapore and Hong Kong have been shaped by strong states – albeit working with the grain of market forces. The more pertinent point might be in relation to what lessons might be drawn about effective urban governance from East Asia. The contemporary rhetoric of participation, empowerment and inclusion does not resonate obviously with the governance and developmental histories of many cities in the region. If anything, one might conclude that city command economies with strong centralist tendencies had achieved considerable progress in relation to inward investment and rising affluence. And the idea of the entrepreneurial or 'developmental' city fits easily with broader productivist (Holliday 2000) conceptions of East Asian economic and political strategies.

There are numerous critiques of the kinds of visions of future urban governance encapsulated by the Hall and Pfeiffer report. Jessop (2002), for example, whilst acknowledging the strengths of the *Urban Future 21* report in its attention to the different problems and pressures facing different kinds of cities, nevertheless discerns a familiar, underlying neo-liberalism. Welfare states are assumed to be costly and inefficient, cities are essentially engines of economic growth, top-down government is bad and networks and partnerships are good. Jessop observes that throughout the report there is an underlying guiding neo-liberalism which is all the more powerful for its implicit rather than explicit ideological position. He does not suggest that this necessarily reflects a conscious neo-liberal project on the part of the authors: 'More important for my purposes is how this document implicitly endorses neoliberalism in the ways it describes recent economic and political changes, ascribes responsibility for them, and prescribes solutions for the problems they create' (p. 464). Jessop goes on to summarize their prescription for the high-growth East Asian cities: 'a mix of neo-liberalism with public–private partnerships to improve the infrastructure and environment for international as well as local capital. Here the developmental state is allowed to remain pro-active provided it is rescaled and becomes more open to market forces' (p. 467).

The problem of social cohesion

Debates around new models for urban government and governance are inextricably connected to debates about social cohesion. Indeed, Maloutas and Malouta (2004) argue that urban social cohesion has become the new political goal and new governance is the way in which that goal is achieved and implemented. But what constitutes a socially cohesive city? What are the various dimensions of cohesion? Like governance, it is a concept that is easily bandied around as self evidently good but often without a necessary elaboration of what it actually is, and what key areas policy-makers need to address. There is insufficient space in this chapter to explore this in depth (see, for example, Forrest and Kearns 2001) but we can point to the principal dimensions that need to be addressed, particularly in cities that are experiencing rapid expansion and an influx of migrants. The substantial literature on social cohesion emphasizes different aspects that act to bind people together or, alternatively, create barriers and divisions. Of particular relevance in the context of urban governance is the extent to which there is a strong sense of place, social belonging and social identity; whether social networks are weak or strong, introverted or extroverted; and whether social inequalities are widening or narrowing. These dimensions are interlinked and impact more generally on the social order of cities and reflect shifts in wider societal values. But clearly in circumstances when the social and physical fabric of a city is being rapidly transformed amidst far-reaching economic changes, these dimensions are under severe strain. Cities in such situations will have an influx of newcomers, new housing areas, new employment patterns and an almost inevitable weakening of the intermediate institutions that have previously constituted much of the social cement. This may relate to the weakening of traditional family structures, trade unions and other political organizations, religious groups or the erosion of less visible norms and routines which have grown up in more settled times. Moreover, whilst those who govern and shape the city have to contend with the disruptions of rapid change, the influences that act on these dimensions of cohesion operate at different spatial scales (Kearns and Forrest 2000). International, national, regional and local factors all come into play in varying ways over time and space to affect processes of social solidarity, cultural and behavioural norms, trust and participation. It has become conventional wisdom to argue that regions or cities with strong social capital and dynamic social networks are likely to be both economically competitive and socially cohesive. And much of the lexicon of new urban governance – partnerships, stakeholders, participation and inclusion – is associated with building and maintaining social capital to achieve positive social and economic outcomes. However, both the conceptual and empirical foundations of social capital and the practical implications of pursuing policies to achieve it remain highly contested (see, for example, Fine 2001; Maloutas and Malouta 2004). There are also evident conflicts of spatial scale in all this. A strong and cohesive regional identity could conflict with the aim of promoting a strong sense of identity and pride at the city scale. And a city of strong and cohesive neighbourhoods could be riven with turf wars and social conflict.

The challenge, then, is to maintain social harmony in the face of global competitive pressures. But this involves an understanding of what constitutes a competitive and cohesive city as a sustainable proposition. For example, the attraction of domestic and foreign investment is only one dimension, which may have side effects in term of social instability and physical degradation, and which, if pursued too single-mindedly, may damage that competitive edge in the longer term. More importantly, the cohesive city is not one where conflict has been muted and concealed by real or imaginary walls and divisions. And these divisions come in many forms. In contemporary debates we tend to think in stark terms of income differentials, race or ethnicity. But cities, and especially rapidly expanding cities, are by their very nature concentrations of people from different backgrounds and with different expectations and aspirations. That is what gives them their dynamism but which also creates more subtle forms of differentiation related to lifestyle and stage in the life course.

Old problems, new problems, new geographies

The pervasive concern by policy-makers with the problems of social cohesion or social harmony in the contemporary city reflects, perhaps, a feeling that we are at another moment in the history of urbanzsation where there is a loss of control rather than ordered and manageable chaos – negative friction rather than positive juxtoposition. Writing in 1925, Robert Park, one of the first urban sociologists, observed that,

> . . . cities are in unstable equilibrium. The result is that the vast casual and mobile aggregations which constitute our urban populations are in a state of perpetual agitation, swept by every new wind of doctrine, subject to constant alarms and in consequence the community is in a chronic condition of crisis.
>
> (p. 25)

Park was writing mainly with the expanding cities of the United States in mind, particularly his case study city of Chicago. At that time, it was the cities of the US that were growing rapidly through immigration and rural–urban migration and there was widespread concern about social instability. However, Park's observations would not seem too out of place with some contemporary commentaries on urbanization. For example, in 1996, the United Nations Centre for Human Settlements referred to,

> The mass exodus to the cities [which] has already led to sharpened urban poverty, especially among women and dependent children; scarcity of housing and basic services; unemployment and underemployment; ethnic tensions and violence; substance abuse, crime and social disintegration.
>
> (p. v)

Of course, the crucial difference between now and then is that both the geography and scale of urbanization have dramatically shifted. Cities are larger, the majority of people now live in urban environments and the largest cities are now to be found outside the former core capitalist countries of Europe and North America. It is in Asia, Africa and Latin America where we now find the largest and fastest growing urban agglomerations. And it was at the beginning of this century, not the last, when we finally reached the urban age. That process continues to accelerate and is nowhere more apparent than in China, where a vast rural–urban migration is taking place, dwarfing similar developments in earlier periods in Europe and the US. Official estimates suggest that some 18 million people are migrating from rural to urban areas in China every year and this is likely to continue until around 2020 (United Nations 2007). Some 100 Chinese cities now have populations of over one million and cities such as Beihai and Chongqing are among the fastest growing urban agglomerations in the world. The speed and size of this development involves massive infrastructural investment. Chongqing, for example, now encompasses an 'official' population of some 32 million people. Over the last decade, infrastructural projects have included a new international airport, a light transit railway, six motorway links to other cities, eight new bridges across the Yangtse and six tunnels through mountains (Li et al. 2006). This is urbanization on a mammoth scale, involving unprecedented physical and social transformations. And the impacts on social and physical resources are inevitably profound. Longstanding and deep-rooted social networks are disrupted, villages obliterated, rivers dammed and diverted and natural resources strained to the limit.

With this growing affluence many cities in China and other parts of East Asia are experiencing major problems of air pollution and traffic congestion as bikes becomes motorcycles and motorcycles become cars. Beijing, has seen car ownership double in the last five years and a survey carried out by the Chinese Academy of Environmental Planning in 2003 found that more than a quarter of Chinese cities suffered from serious pollution – with air pollution blamed for over 400,000 deaths (Watts 2005). Vietnamese cities are experiencing similar problems as economic development outstrips inadequate or non-existent regulatory and institutional frameworks. For example, river pollution around Hanoi and Ho Chi Minh City is having major consequences for the supply of usable water (Environmental News Network 2007).

Cities in East Asia do not all face similar challenges of rapid growth and extensive redevelopment. But the most common features are population expansion, rising incomes, extensive new development and pressure on basic infrastructural needs. These can be seen as the positive challenges of economic development in contrast to the corrosive effects of deindustrialization and economic decline. But they do bring with them severe environmental and social pressures and the need to reshape existing institutions. With regard to the former, the nature of these problems varies according to local economic circumstances, and the maturity or otherwise of urban systems. Bai and Imura (2000) have, for example, offered a sequential, stage model of environmental problems in which the fast developing Chinese cities most typically suffer from industrial pollution whereas in Japanese cities the problems are more consumption related. Essentially, as societies become more affluent the environmental impact shifts from poverty-related pollution (for example, contaminated water supplies) to affluence-generated pollution (for example, waste disposal, traffic congestion). Thus, fundamental issues of social and economic sustainability are central to all East Asian cities but the nature and dimensions of the challenge will vary from the problems of marginal subsistence to the consequences of the voracious consumption aspirations of an expanding middle class.

So the cities of East Asia face the combined challenges of social and environmental sustainability and are expanding in a profoundly different global context from those of nineteenth-century Europe or the US. Widening social divisions pose a significant threat to social cohesion but both affluent and poor have a shared urban experience of congestion and environmental degradation. But institutional structures are often rooted in a recent past and have not yet adapted to a turbulent and fast changing present. As Rohlen (2002) observes, 'It is no surprise that urbanization creates problems for governance systems created for a largely agricultural world' (p. 25).

Moreover, globalization and more open economies mean that there is less local influence and control over what happens in cities. The major cities themselves are differentially integrated into a global network of capital investment and labour flows, which involve a changed relationship with national governments and the wider economies in which they are situated. Lead cities are likely to be driven and shaped by extranational forces to a much greater extent than their provincial counterparts – and their economic performance may contrast with that of the national economy. This has particular significance in an East Asian context in which cities such as Tokyo, Seoul, Bangkok and the Chinese East Coastal cities exert increasing economic power. In this context, Douglass (2000) refers to the 'extrovert' urbanization associated with the conscious creation of globally significant metropolitan urban regions as the higher-income East Asian countries seek to position themselves as high technology, information-rich centres in the global economy. For Douglass, this strategy involves the intentional planning and creation of dominant urban agglomerations as a key element in the shift from being 'low wage assembly platforms to technologically advanced production and higher order corporate service centres' (p. 2322). However, the increasing dominance of these sprawling, mega city regions is often running ahead of institutional capacity to cope with housing and transport needs, is producing growing contrasts between urban and rural areas and creating stark contrasts between minorities gaining from market-driven urban systems, those struggling to survive and adapt, and the chronic casualties.

These problems are most evident in China, where the shift to market provision, rising income inequalities and often lagging institutional capacities have now driven policy towards giving much greater priority to trying to achieve greater social harmony. However, corruption, waste and inefficiency are still pervasive problems at both national and city levels, with frequent exposure and prosecution of high-level officials. Hutton (2007) refers to endemic corruption, which is 'chronically dysfunctional' and quotes research evidence that estimates that losses due to corruption amounted to almost 15 per cent of GDP between 1999 and 2001 (p. 127). Transparency and accountability, core elements of good urban governance, are still seriously lacking.

Divided and fragmented cities

One of the major urban challenges is that amidst all the rhetoric of good governance, and the stated aspirations for more enlightened and unifying urban policies, the dominant trends appear to be in the opposite direction. East Asian cities, like their western counterparts, are experiencing new forms of social and spatial stratification. The transformations in living standards, employment opportunities and lifestyles brought about by economic progress are driving new wedges between different sections of the population. For example, travelling into Hanoi from the airport in early 2006, it was impossible to avoid noticing an enormous archway in the middle of fast-disappearing rice fields, topped with what appeared to be a chariot with warriors in Greco-Roman style. One might have assumed that this mock Arc de Triomphe was a memorial to the glorious victory of the Vietnamese people over the imperialist French or Americans. It was, however, a memorial to something rather less grand – the imposing entrance to a newly planned up-market gated community for Hanoi's growing middle class. These kinds of development are sprouting everywhere (see, for example, Wu 2005) in East Asia, very visible evidence of the widening gulf between majorities and minorities. Gated communities are, of course, by no means confined to East Asian cities. Millions of US households now live in such developments (Blakely and Snyder 1997). They are a growing part of the social topography of cities worldwide. It is a novel form of segregation in which the rich retreat into protected enclaves behind security guards, CCTV and a variety of high tech devices. It is symptomatic of what Davis (2001) has referred to as the 'fear economy', in which residential owners seek to protect their lifestyles, living standards and property values from what is perceived to be an increasingly hostile world beyond. This residential self-segregation of the rich is part of a more pervasive privatization of urban space in which toll roads, privatized leisure facilities, privileged parking and other facilities enable those with resources to negotiate an urban environment untroubled by those less fortunate (Atkinson and Flint 2004).

From the point of view of urban governance, or indeed, in respect of the notion of shared urban citizenship, the effect (and indeed that is precisely the intention) is to fragment the social contours of cities and to undermine any commonality of interest in the urban fabric. The citizens of Beijing or Hanoi may share a common geographical space but different groups occupy sharply and increasingly differentiated social worlds. The connections between people and places are increasingly diffuse. This is most evident in relation to cities in which transnational migration is prominent or, as in the case of many Chinese cities, where there is a large 'unofficial' population with only limited rights of access to urban resources. Those only tangentially connected to the space in which they work and live will also have a limited sense of loyalty or sense of belonging to that city. They may be in Guangzhou or Manila or Bangkok but they may not feel themselves to be of that place. This has important implications for the degree of participation and collective involvement in urban governance. Moreover, those transient groups are represented by both the urban poor and the urban elite and are likely to be among the most segregated sections of the community. They include the executive transnational elite in their protected communities of up-market housing, often with exclusive leisure and retail facilities, as well as the migrant workers in dormitories or in peripheral or inner city ghettos. Both these groups essentially look to somewhere else for a sense of identity, commitment and in terms of the income they extract from their pragmatic engagement with their current location. Holston and Appadurai (2003) argue that these sites of transnational activity produce a highly differentiated urban citizenship; neither migrant workers nor capital managers feel 'much loyalty to the place in which they are perhaps only temporary transplants. They need state government for their economic activity. But they have reduced moral and personal commitment to it. Instead, they are likely to retain primary loyalty – at least in cultural terms – to diasporic identities' (pp. 303–304).

Cities, of course, have highly diverse characteristics and not all are 'transnational' sites in terms of cultural diversity. They may be highly unequal in terms of incomes and lifestyles but culturally homogeneous. Even the most cosmopolitan of East Asian cities, such as Singapore, Hong Kong or Bangkok, is hardly a cultural melting pot when compared with cities such as New York or London. And Tokyo, usually grouped with the latter two cities as the global power points of the world economy (Sassen 1991), has a very small immigrant population reflecting Japan's historic policies on immigration.

Different cities present, therefore, different challenges for those who formulate and implement governance policies. The mature, cosmopolitan cities may have sharp ethnic divisions but the policy priorities and social tensions will not revolve around the provision of, and access to, basic amenities such as adequate drinking water and shelter, which dominate in the sprawling mega cities. Hall and Pfeiffer (2000) contrast inter alia the very different demographic challenges and potential social conflicts facing mature European cities with, for example, many East Asian cities in which high population growth and low incomes dominate. For Hall and Pfeiffer, the typical, affluent mature city is one in which families are stressed by high participation rates, high housing costs and longer periods in education. In the latter, the family still operates as the primary survival mechanism in the absence of adequate state welfare and household incomes. They go on to suggest that the populations of Asian cities are, however, caught in a different set of circumstances of rising affluence, falling birth rates, ageing populations and undeveloped welfare safety nets in which there continues to be reliance on traditional family structures and roles which are being rapidly eroded.

Social cohesion and governance in the expanding city

For cities to be cohesive, citizens need to have a strong element of trust in officials and in one another. People need to feel safe and secure, and to feel a sense of belonging. Crucially, they need to feel part of the same project, particularly if they are not sharing equally in the gains of a rising economy. As has been suggested, these critical facets of a well-functioning city are inevitably under pressure during periods of rapid social and economic transformation. Populations experience major changes in their living conditions and lifestyles as agricultural employment and rural villages give way to sprawling industrialization. Land prices escalate, housing problems inevitably increase, old neighbourhoods are redeveloped and new residential developments emerge amidst changing social norms and behaviour. Old social and physical boundaries disappear and the new social and physical contours of the city take on an ambiguous and constantly changing shape.

We can explore the extent to which such far-reaching social and spatial transformations do disrupt and erode traditional ties and social practices in slightly more detail with reference to Guangzhou, the city at the epicentre of the Pearl River Delta, one of the most economically dynamic regions in the world. Guangzhou was an important city in world trade in the nineteenth and early twentieth centuries and was one of the first cities re-opened to the wider global economy in 1984; it was also, according to Li and Wang (2003), 'probably the earliest to experience the onslaught of global market forces, largely because of its proximity to Hong Kong' (p. 3).

Describing Guangzhou in the late 1980s, Ikels (1996) described a city in moral chaos in which crime and corruption was rife. According to Ikels, people feared for their safety after dark and shunned public spaces where they might be vulnerable. Old moral codes and conventions were apparently breaking down in the face of rampant marketization and population growth. In a similar vein, Chan (1993) referred to family breakdown and higher residential mobility in Guangzhou threatening 'the kind of social cohesion that encourages the development of strong reciprocal bonds' (p. 215).

Throughout the 1990s, Guangzhou continued to experience both rising per capita incomes and rising inequalities and widening social divisions. Whilst an emergent white collar and entrepreneurial class has become increasingly affluent, the less skilled are in a weak competitive position as rural migrants continue to stream into the city, representing an apparently endless supply of cheap labour. As Nolan (2004) observes, 'Even in the fastest-growing region in China, the Pearl River Delta, there was no increase in the real wages of unskilled labour during the whole of the 1990s' (p. 13).

These images of Guangzhou suggest an urban environment facing major governance problems in the face of a shredded social fabric. However, urban populations and urban social structures may be in a constant state of flux but they also display a remarkable degree of resilience and adaptability. Amidst discontinuities there are also continuities in relation to social networks and social norms, which provide the foundations of social cohesion and a thriving civil society, even in cities in which lifestyles and living standards are being dramatically reshaped. For example, contrary to Ikel's dystopian images of a Guangzhou in the early 1990s in which the social order was apparently disintegrating under the pressures of social and economic change, a more recent study (Forrest and Yip 2007) suggests that levels of trust, sense of community and feelings of belonging in the city are relatively high. Although these feelings of belonging and sense of community were much stronger in the older, less developed areas of the city, even in the newer, commercial estates which increasingly dominate Guangzhou, the majority of residents said that they felt a strong sense of community, a feeling of loyalty towards their neighbours and felt the old values of 'people looking out for one another' were widespread. Perhaps even more strikingly, given external perceptions of the city, the majority of residents felt safe walking alone in their neighbourhood after dark. Levels of trust in one's neighbours, a key ingredient of urban social bonds, were however more varied. In the older areas, almost three-quarters of residents trusted most or many of their neighbours. In the newer estates this fell to around a third. Trust, however, is linked closely to familiarity and these newer estates inevitably contain a high proportion of new arrivals and neighbours who have known each other for a relatively short time. The general impression, however, was of a city where, at the level of the neighbourhood, friendships were maintained and created, people socialized on a regular basis and neighbours were seen as a resource that could be drawn upon in times of need. Of course, one has to avoid presenting too rosy and romanticized a picture of mutuality and informal collective endeavour. But the point is that it is too easy to assume that these practices are becoming a feature of the past and that in China and in other East Asian cities, self-interest and individualism are inevitably beginning to dominate social practices. And it is precisely these qualities of urban life which good govern-ance has to nurture and encourage as the solid foundations of a healthy civil society, without resorting to often lifeless prescriptions for, and measure-ments of, social capital. They are also the qualities that create the 'buzz' of urban life, the civility and respect and a degree of benevolent disorder. Although writing of a different time and a different culture, Jacobs' (1961) descriptions of the hidden subtleties of urban life which make the whole thing work remain as pertinent as ever. She evokes the daily life of mixed use, high density neighbourhoods in which there is a balance achieved between 'people's determination to have essential privacy and their simul-taneous wishes for differing degrees of contact or help from people around. This balance is largely made up of small, sensitively managed details, prac-tised and accepted so casually that they are normally taken for granted' (pp. 77–78).

In cities in China and much of East Asia where there is much more exten-sive new development than in the older, mature cities of Europe or North America, a higher proportion of urban populations are living in unfamiliar surroundings with unfamiliar neighbours. Nonetheless, the evidence from Guangzhou does not indicate that a threatening or unmanageable degree of friction or suspicion is inevitable in such circumstances. And fluidity rather than fixidy in social and spatial structures has its upsides. In new and expand-ing cities, there is an element of 'everyone being in the same boat'. There are fewer barriers to be broken down and less friction between new arrivals and longstanding residents – everyone is new and looking to establish new social networks.

The general point is that the governance of cities is not simply a question of the institutional mix, of the degree to which the business of the city is perceived as a shared project between elected officials, business interests, NGOs, community groups and other elements of civil society. These insti-tutional arrangements sit on a platform of social norms, aspirations and expectations held by the general urban population.

Conclusions: the governance challenge for the changing East Asian city

The dominant policy prescription is to open up cities to market forces. Urban populations worldwide are more exposed to the private market and to greater competition for housing, jobs, education and other resources. At the same time, the previously monopolistic institutions of urban local gov-ernment have generally experienced decentralization and fragmentation. Fordist institutions such as the Hong Kong Housing Authority and the Japanese Government Housing Loan Corporation, which have played a sig-nificant part in the shaping of East Asian cities, have been significantly eroded through processes of privatization and contracting out. And at present it is not clear that extensive decentralization and privatization can necessarily cope with the growing social, economic and environmental pressures of rapid urban expansion.

Cities worldwide face many of the same challenges and it would be wrong to overstate the unique pressures and problems of urban governance in East Asia. There is not a distinctive East Asian urban form or a distinct East Asian urban problematic. Pollution, traffic congestion, social inequalities, spatial divisions, gentrification and ghettoization and all the other features of the urban condition are evident to varying extents in the cities of the region. However, the pace and extent of economic change, and the social transformations associated with it, are certainly more acute in the major metropolitan regions of East and South East Asia than in the more mature cities of Northern Europe. Extensive coastal urbanization in the region could create major environmental problems in the future as sea levels rise. The social fabric of China's cities is undergoing profound transformations as it shifts from one focused around the work-unit system that maintained close links between work and residence. And the upgrading of city centres, commercial development of prime sites and the rising affluence of a new rich are creating acute pressures for poorer households and traditional communities, which are typically displaced to the urban periphery. It is this pervasive and high velocity economic change, combined with often inadequate, outmoded and sometimes corrupt governance structures, which, in some national contexts, will require substantial and far-reaching political and policy responses. Moreover, continuing economic growth has enabled many national and city governments in East Asia to sideline issues of social justice and accountability as urban populations have enjoyed rising, if highly differentiated, gains. The tensions are, however, beginning to grow as gaps widen between rich and poor.

These are cities of oppression as well as opportunity, of defensive and defended communities, of new solidarities as well as alienation. They are also cities seething with the excitement of change and uncertainty. These uncertainties have political, economic and social dimensions in relation to issues of participation, inclusion, democracy and the underlying environmental strains. For East Asia, good urban governance is about the responsible and sensitive management of that positive chaos of economic dynamism. The challenge is to create cities that deliver a high quality of urban life for majorities rather than minorities. But, as has been emphasized at the outset of this chapter, conceptions of success, sustainability and competitiveness in urban governance must also embrace the often subtle richness of the urban experience rather than merely crude measures of development, economic gain and market reform.

References

Atkinson, R. and Flint, J. (2004) Fortress UK? Gated communities and the spatial revolt of the elites and time–space trajectories of gentrification, *Housing Studies*, 19(6): 875–892.

Bai, X. and Imura, H. (2000) A comparative study of urban environment in East Asia: stage model of urban environmental evolution, *International Review for Environmental Strategies*, 1(1): 135–158.

Blakely, E. and Snyder, M. (1997) *Fortress America: Gated Communities in the United States*, Washington, DC: Brookings Institution Press.

Chan, C. (1993) *The Myth of Neighbourhood Mutual Help*, Hong Kong: Hong Kong University Press.

Davis, M. (2001) The flames of New York, *New Left Review*, 12: 34–50.

Douglass, M. (2000) Mega-urban regions and the world city formation: globalisation, the economic crisis and urban policy issues in Pacific Asia, *Urban Studies*, 37(12): 2315–2335.

Environmental News Network (2007) Development waste fouls Vietnam's rivers report says, at: http://www.enn.com/top_stories/article/6369.

Fine, B. (2001) *Social Capital versus Social Theory*, London: Routledge.

Forrest, R. and Kearns, A. (2001) Social capital, social cohesion and the neighbourhood, *Urban Studies*, 38(12): 2125–2143.

Forrest, R. and Yip, N.-M. (2007) Neighbourhood and neighbouring in a Chinese city: aspects of local social relations in contemporary Guangzhou, *Journal of Contemporary China*, 16(50): 47–64.

Global Development Research Centre (2007) Defining urban governance, at: http://www.gdrc.org/u-gov/governance-define.html.

Hall, P. and Pfeiffer, U. (2000) *Urban Future 21: A Global Agenda for 21ˢᵗ Century Cities*, London: E. and F. N. Spon.

He, S. (2007) State-sponsored gentrification under market transition: the case of Shanghai, *Urban Affairs Review*, 43(2): 171–198.

Hirayama, Y. (2005) Running hot and cold in the urban home ownership market: the experience of Japan's major cities, *Journal of Housing and the Built Environment*, 20: 1–20.

Holliday, I. (2000) Productivist welfare capitalism: social policy in East Asia, *Political Studies*, 48(4): 706–723.

Holston, J. and Appadurai, A. (2003) Cities and citizenship, in N. Brenner et al. (eds), *State/Space: A Reader*, Oxford: Blackwell.

Hutton, W. (2007) *The Writing on the Wall: China and the West in the 21ˢᵗ Century*, London: Little, Brown.

Ikels, C. (1996) *The Return of the God of Wealth: The Transition to a Market Economy in Urban China*, Stanford, CT: Stanford University Press.

Jacobs, J. (1961) *The Death and Life of Great American Cities*, New York: Vintage.

Jessop, B. (2002) Liberalism, neoliberalism, and urban governance: a state-theoretical perspective, *Antipode*, 34(3): 452–472.

Kearns, A. and Forrest, R. (2000) Social cohesion and multi-level urban governance, *Urban Studies*, 37(5–6): 995–1017.

Li, S.-M. and Wang, D. (2003) Life course and residential mobility in Guangzhou, Occasional Paper No. 39, Hong Kong: Centre for China Urban and Regional Studies, Hong Kong Baptist University.

Li, S.-M., Leung, Y.-H. and Yi, Z. (2006) Fragmentation or integration? A study of Chongqing, the largest city in China, Occasional Paper No. 72, Hong Kong: Centre for China Urban and Regional Studies, Hong Kong Baptist University.

Maloutas, T. and Malouta, M. (2004) The glass menagerie of urban governance and social cohesion: concepts and stakes/concepts as stakes, *International Journal of Urban and Regional Research*, 28(2): 449–465.

Nolan, P. (2004) *China at the Crossroads*, Cambridge: Polity Press.

Pahl, R. (1970) *Whose City?*, Harmondsworth: Penguin.

Park, R. (1925) The city: suggestions for the investigation of human behavior in the urban environment, in R. Park and E. Burgess (eds), *The City*, Chicago, IL: University of Chicago Press.

Pickvance, C. (1976) *Urban Sociology: Critical Essays*, London: Tavistock.

Rohlen, T. (2002) *Cosmopolitan Cities and Nation States: Open Economies, Urban Dynamics and Government in East Asia*, Stanford, CT: Asia/Pacific Research Center.

Sassen, S. (1991) *The Global City*, Princeton, NJ: Princeton University Press.

Sennett, R. (1970) *The Uses of Disorder*, Harmondsworth: Penguin.

United Nations (2007) *UNFPA State of the World Population 2007*, New York: UNFPA.

United Nations Centre for Human Settlements (UNCHS) (1996) *An Urbanising World: Global Report on Human Settlements*, Oxford: Oxford University Press.

Watts, J. (2005) China, the air pollution capital of the world, *The Lancet*, 366(9499): 1761–1762.

Wu, F. (2005) China's changing urban governance in the transition towards a more market-oriented economy, *Urban Studies*, 39(7): 1071–1093.

Wu, F. (2005) Rediscovering the 'gate' under market transition: from work-unit compounds to commodity housing enclaves, *Housing Studies*, 20(2): 235–254.

14 The governance of urban renaissance in Tokyo

Post-urbanization and enhanced competitiveness

Yosuke Hirayama

Introduction

In Japan, since the mid-1990s, economic globalization has been seen as a more competitive phenomenon. The burst of the so-called 'bubble economy' at the beginning of the 1990s triggered an economic crisis – a long recession, an increase in bad loans, a rising unemployment rate and a chain reaction of enterprise bankruptcies. The prices of land and real estate, which rose tremendously during the bubble period, have been falling since the bubble collapsed. The devaluation of real estate properties reflected and amplified the deterioration in the economy. The 1990s came to be referred to as Japan's 'lost decade', and a growing conviction that Japanese strength in the global economy was waning quickly developed.

In response to the long-standing recession and in the context of an increasingly globalized environment, the government launched 'urban renaissance' as a key policy in the late 1990s, with the aim of re-galvanizing the nation's economic competitiveness. A series of measures, such as the promotion of urban redevelopment and the deregulation of urban planning, has been vigorously put into practice (Igarashi and Ogawa 2003). Of all the big cities, Tokyo has been regarded as being most strongly connected with the global economy, and in addressing international urban competition, the restructuring of Tokyo as a global city has been given top priority. The government has been aiming at restoring the prestige of the Japanese economy within the global economy by using the redevelopment of Tokyo as a catalyst. Skylines and landscapes in the central areas of Tokyo are rapidly changing due to the implementation of the new, aggressive urban policy.

The key principle, which characterizes the basic course of the government in forming urban policy, has shifted from 'development' to 'competition'. The state of Japan, an interventionist state which particularly emphasizes economic development, has continuously pursued economic expansion as a means to legitimize itself and maintain social solidarity (Murakami 1992). During the first half of the post-war period, the combination and interaction of rapid urbanization, industrial development and high-speed economic growth led to a situation where state legitimacy and social cohesiveness were retained relatively successfully. However, in the 1970s, urbanization began to subside and the rate of economic growth declined, and then, together with an increasingly globalized economy, the violent rise and fall of the economic bubble threw Japanese society and economy into confusion. The 1990s, or the 'lost decade', saw the exacerbation of economic conditions and Japan began to drift without clear social direction. It is in this context that the nature of the urban renaissance policy should be understood. The launch of a novel urban policy displaying an aggressive attitude by the government represented the new state strategy to create a new direction for the nation based on the challenge of global economic competition.

This chapter explores the processes and implications of the competition-oriented urban renaissance policy for the restructuring of Tokyo, with particular reference to the strategy of the state in the governance of urban redevelopment. As urbanization pressure has dissipated, the authority for urban planning and policy has been decentralized and the role of partnerships between local governments, the business sector, the non-profit sector and citizen participation has increasingly been emphasized in urban management (Sorensen 2002). It is, however, the face of the interventionist state that has come to the fore as the power driving urban competitiveness in the global arena. This chapter demonstrates that the formation and operation of the urban renaissance policy reflect the desire of the state to re-orientate itself in order to re-establish social solidarity and economic strength.

Crisis and competition

In the latter half of the 'lost decade', the government, in the context of globalizing processes impacting the wider economy, began to put emphasis on regaining the competitiveness of the big cities, especially Tokyo, to address the post-bubble recession. The 1999 report, *Strategy towards the Revitalization of the Japanese Economy*, announced by the Economic Strategy Council (1999) under the Obuchi administration, clearly positioned urban renaissance as a key policy for economic recovery and the amelioration of bad loans. The report regarded 'the revitalization of the big cities to gain global competitiveness' as 'one of the biggest frontiers of the 21st century', claiming that a critical situation was caused by the decline in global competitiveness of Japan's big cities. Following the release of this report, the government began to implement a package of measures to redevelop cities, which included the deregulation of urban planning, the disposal of real estate owned by the former JNR (Japan National Railway) to private developers, the formation of a real estate security investment market and the injection of private funds into the development of public facilities. The Mori administration, which replaced the Obuchi administration in April 2000, continued the policy in order to facilitate urban redevelopment as a pillar of economic recovery measures.

The subsequent administration, led by Junichiro Koizumi, immediately after its establishment in April 2001 started promoting urban renaissance even more vigorously. The prime minister set up the Urban Renaissance Headquarters in the Cabinet with himself as the chief and all the state ministers as members to demonstrate clearly that urban renaissance was a key national policy. The first meeting concluded that a critical issue was the enhancement of the international competitiveness of cities in order to stimulate national growth. Subsequently, the Urban Renaissance Special Measure Law, which is implemented directly by Headquarters, came into force in June 2002 to designate zones that were to be urgently developed, where planning regulation could be radically relaxed and government subsidy could be provided for private developers. Prior governments, before the 1990s, had declared that urban redevelopment, even if it were motivated by profit, was necessary to improve the physical environment of the people. The Koizumi administration, however, stated explicitly that the purpose of promoting urban renaissance was to recover the prestige of the Japanese economy and ensure its survival in conditions of escalating global competition.

The policy for urban renaissance concentrated on the redevelopment of Tokyo in particular rather than all the big cities. The tendency of the government to put more importance on Tokyo has been seen since the 1980s, and has been further strengthened by the Koizumi administration. In a situation where the economic power of all cities was declining, it was assumed that only Tokyo maintained a strong connection with the global economy, and that its regaining competitiveness would lead the whole nation to economic recovery. By December 2005, based on the Urban Renaissance Special Measure Law, 64 districts of approximately 6,567 hectares nationally were designated as priority zones for urgent redevelopment. By region, the area in Tokyo is the biggest, with 2,514 hectares, which is more than double that in Osaka, which is the second largest.

The urban renaissance policy of the Koizumi administration swiftly expanded within a top-down framework. Some commentators looked at Koizumi's strong leadership as deriving from his own personal abilities. His leadership, however, has undoubtedly been built on a new institutional system elaborated by administrative reform. Since the latter half of the 1990s, the structure of government operations has been transformed to reinforce the power of the Cabinet and the prime minister (Noble 2006; Takenaka 2006). Cabinet policies were once formed by time-consuming negotiations with government ministries, political parties and business circles, among others. However, associated with the perceived economic crisis in the 'lost decade', the necessity to build a more efficient, less time-consuming top-down system for decision making was rationalized. Hashimoto assumed the premiership in January 1996, and set up an administrative reform committee in the Cabinet Office in November of the same year, just after his second Cabinet's inauguration. Consequently, the Basic Law on Reforming Government Ministries was established in June 1998, and was put into effect in January

2001. This law effectively restructured the national government to strengthen the power of the prime minister and the Cabinet.

Based on administrative reform, the Council on Economic and Fiscal Policy was formed in the Cabinet Office in order for basic policies to be implemented swiftly under the prime minister's leadership. Koizumi has been fully utilizing the council since immediately after the assumption of his premiership, and has positioned urban renaissance as one of the most important policy issues. The council annually announces basic principles for economic and fiscal policy. As a necessary measure relating to urban renaissance, the 2001 basic principle listed the revitalization of the real estate market and the promotion of urban redevelopment, among other measures. This was followed in 2003 by the assertion of a basic principle stressing the necessity of urban planning deregulation for high-rise housing blocks. Moreover, an advisory body to the prime minister, the Council for Regulatory Reform (from April 2001 to March 2004), and its successor, the Council for the Promotion of Regulatory Reform and Private-Sector Participation (since April 2004), established in the Cabinet Office, aggressively recommended guidelines for wide-ranging reforms concerning urban redevelopment measures.

Business circles increased political pressure on the government to promote urban redevelopment, and in turn, the government formed policies that would increase profits in the construction, real estate and housing industries (Igarashi and Ogawa 2003). The Japan Federation of Economic Organizations (1999), in response to the report by the Economic Strategy Council, expressed its view that the enhancement of a city's attractiveness for business activity was a precondition for the intensification of national competitiveness. The establishment of the Urban Renaissance Headquarters gave rise to an increasing number of proposals from economic circles. The Real Estate Companies Association of Japan (2001) called for the development of urban infrastructure, the reduction of real estate-related taxes and the deregulation of urban planning, while the Japan Federation of Construction Contractors (2001) proposed the formation of an urban renaissance system. The Japan Project Industrial Council (2002) saw urban renaissance as fundamental to economic recovery and, in order to further their interests and influence, reinforced channels with the government.

Along with implementing the urban renaissance policy, the government has formulated a policy discourse to stress the necessity of Tokyo competing with overseas cities, particularly the big cities of East Asia, whose economies have been developing at a striking pace. After the Second World War, Japan began to catch up with the western 'advanced nations' in terms of economic development, and came to assert itself as the sole non-western nation that could be compared economically with western countries. During the peak period of the bubble, it was declared confidently that the Japanese economy had not only caught up with but also was about to overtake the economies of the western 'advanced countries'. The Japanese government determined its success and economic position in relation to economic levels in western nations, and by comparing Tokyo with New York and London. Since the 1990s, however, when the economic crisis deepened, policy-makers have begun to wake up to the stagnant economic condition of Tokyo compared with the growing economies of other big cities in East Asia such as Hong Kong, Singapore, Shanghai, Beijing and Seoul. The government has consequently been asserting that engaging more aggressively in global economic competition is necessary and has developed crisis discourses which emphasize the situation whereby Japan, which used to be trying to catch up with western nations, is now being caught up by East Asian nations.

The TMG (Tokyo Metropolitan Government), led by Shintaro Ishihara who was elected as governor of Tokyo in April 1999, worked out a policy to reorganize Tokyo into a competitive global city in cooperation with the urban renaissance policy of the national government. Governor Ishihara expressed a rhetorical view that the revitalization of Tokyo should be given priority because it would be an opportunity for the nation to be reborn. *The Strategic Plan to Overcome Crisis*, published in November 1999, which outlined the policies of the Ishihara metropolitan government, stated: 'the success or failure in economic activity in Tokyo has a nation-wide impact and determines the rise or fall of Japan in circumstances where competition among individual cities at a global level is growing even more intensified' (TMG 1999: 12). In 2000, this plan was followed by the *Urban White Paper* claiming: 'global urban competition is increasingly intensifying. It is no exaggeration to say that the survival of a city will be determined by whether or not that city is attractive enough to be able to compete with other cities' (TMG 2000a: 5). The *Urban White Paper* also drew attention to the situation whereby Tokyo was being closed in on by cities in East Asia while western metropolises were outdistancing it, showing comparisons between Tokyo and the cities abroad such as New York, London, Hong Kong, Singapore and Seoul. *The Tokyo Plan 2000: Toward a Global City That Attracts a Great Number of Residents and Visitors*, which constitutes a long-term plan of the Ishihara metropolitan government, was issued in December 2000 to envision a future concept of Tokyo as a pre-eminent global city which survives amid intensifying competition between cities and becomes the driving force behind Japan's economy (TMG 2000b). The TMG consequently formulated the *Vision of New Urban Planning in Tokyo* in October 2001, with the goal of 'creating an attractive and exciting Tokyo, a global city to lead the world' (TMG 2001: 9). The policy papers presented in rapid succession by the Ishihara metropolitan administration, in which terms such as 'crisis', 'competition' and 'global city' frequently appeared, have consistently insisted that the recovery of Japan should be lead by an urban renaissance in Tokyo.

Strategic urban redevelopment

In the central areas of Tokyo, urban renaissance policy measures have produced new 'hot spots', where urban redevelopment projects have intensively been implemented and the real estate market has become increasingly active. Many of the mega complexes in the hot spots are comprised of headquarters of transnational corporations, business buildings for finance, information and media companies, luxurious boutiques, restaurants and cafes, tower-type condominiums and amusement facilities, symbolizing that Tokyo has been transformed into a 'global city', a 'post-industrial city' and an 'information city'. Groups of large-scale, high-rise buildings have been re-defining the shape and appearance of Tokyo.

Roppongi Hills, regarded as the flagship of urban renaissance, was completed in 2003 as a result of a redevelopment project operated by the developer, Mori Building Co. Ltd. The 11-hectare development holds offices, housing units, boutiques, hotels and broadcasting facilities. In the 54-story, 238m-high Mori Tower are booming companies from the information and finance sectors, foreign-affiliated companies and cultural facilities. Another redevelopment project in Shiodome Sio-Site, with a vast area of 31 hectares, is also near completion. A forest of super high-rises accommodates offices, hotels, broadcasting facilities, housing units and facilities for consumers. Along with the Shiodome City Centre, a 215m-high commercial complex, a new 210m-high head office building for Dentsu, Inc., the world biggest advertising firm, has already been completed. On the eastern side of Shinagawa station, the 5.3-hectare Shinagawa Grand Commons opened in 2003 with a group of high rise buildings accommodating the head offices of major companies, housing units and commercial facilities, following the 3.5-hectare Shinagawa Intercity. which was completed in 1998. One of the nation's biggest developers, Mitsubishi Estate Co. Ltd., has been a key player in many redevelopment projects in the Marunouchi district in front of Tokyo station. The 37-storey Marunouchi Building, which is one of the results of these projects, opened in 2002 to accommodate offices, boutiques, restaurants and a conference hall. The imperial residence can be looked down upon from the top floors of this building, which has been implicitly considered taboo.

Transformations in the strategies of the government sector in forming and implementing urban redevelopment policy underlie the brand-new and gorgeous landscapes of the city centre. First, both the central government and the TMG formulated the policy to promote the conglomeration of business, commerce and housing in the central areas of Tokyo (Yahagi 2002). In the bubble period the government sector intended to disperse construction works to the periphery of the city because the concentration of building works in the urban centre was considered to inflate land prices and cause overcrowding. In the post-bubble period, however, it is assumed that redevelopment of the city centre should be intensified to make it more competitive in response to the recession. The districts in Tokyo prioritized for redevelopment by the Urban Renaissance Headquarters were all located within the city centre (see Figure 14.1). The TMG was thus able to present the plan as a key policy for redevelopment of the centre core area as an international business centre. As part of the redevelopment of the urban centre, the government

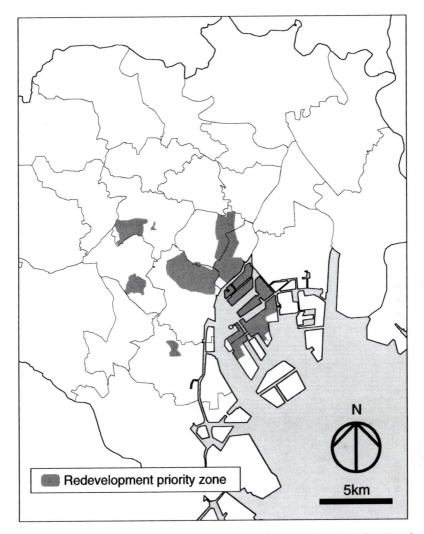

Figure 14.1 Redevelopment priority zones in Tokyo, designated by the Urban Renaissance Special Measure Law.

Source: Tokyo Metropolitan Government.

disposed of a large portion of national land to private developers. Large sites of land owned by the former JNR (Japan National Railway) were utilized for the development of the Shinagawa Intercity, the Shinagawa Grand Commons and the Shiodome Sio-Site. In the Marunouchi district, a group of offices buildings, hotels and facilities for consumers was completed in 2004 on the former site of JNR headquarters. Tokyo Midtown Project, one of the large-scale projects currently in progress, is on a 10-hectare lot where the National Defence Agency used to be located.

Secondly, the government sector adopted a strategy to support specific individual redevelopment projects, putting priority on the creation of hot spots to lead urban reform, rather than setting out a more comprehensive redevelopment of Tokyo as a whole. Many redevelopment projects, which had been planned during the bubble period and which had stagnated due to the post-bubble recession, were revitalized by the kick-start of government intervention. The 1992 revision of the City Planning Law established a system for municipalities to draw up master plans, and the 2000 revision strengthened the institutional position of prefectural master plans. However, the urban renaissance policy of the central government, which is eager to create hot spots, and the local master plans are not actually compatible, although they conform as policy documents (Ishida 2004). The regulations for urban planning and building standards were not simply relaxed, but rather substantially rewritten for some specific target projects. In the case of Roppongi Hills, the average ratio of floor space to land plot size, which had been 327 per cent, was raised to as much as 719 per cent, and from 320 per cent to 670 per cent in the case of Tokyo Midtown Project. With such deregulation of urban planning, the potential building volume for private developers became enormous. These mega complexes within hot spots form complete 'cities within a city', which are cut off from the neighbourhood context. Inside the complex, heavy investment has led to the use of space entirely different to and often disjointed from the surrounding area. Suzuki, an architecture scholar, describes the space tht has emerged from large-scale redevelopments as 'a floating island universe in the chaos of the city' (2003: 162). As a consequence of urban planning regulations associated with measures to promote redevelopment projects, a construction boom of 20 storey-plus condominium towers has been generated, reinforcing the appearance of hot spots in the city centre and the waterfront areas (Hirayama 2005). According to a survey by the Real Estate Economic Institute, in Tokyo, 97 condominium towers or 25,857 units were constructed between 1987 and 2002. Building of high-rise housing is expected to increase. As of January 2003, 228 condominium towers with 78,824 units were planning to be built in Tokyo (see Figure 14.2).

Thirdly, the urban renaissance policy served to accelerate redevelopment. The risk for developers who wish to invest in a redevelopment project increases if too much time is taken to negotiate with the authorities, follow legal procedures, revise construction plans, purchase land and buildings, and negotiate with local people. The government sector, responding to the demand from developers to decrease the investment risk related to time-consuming activities, designed a system to quicken the administrative procedures for redevelopment. Historically only the public sector could initiate urban planning project proposals. The Urban Renaissance Special Measure Law, however, established a system whereby private companies could propose urban planning projects, which must be approved or disapproved by government offices within an exceptionally short time in terms of urban planning

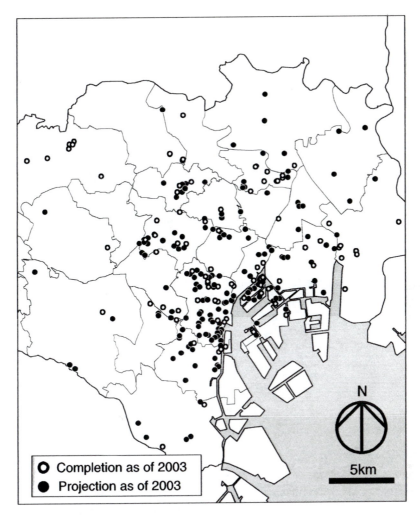

Figure 14.2 Redevelopment priority zones in Tokyo, designated by the Urban Renaissance Special Measure Law completions and projected completions of
tower condominiums, Tokyo.

Source: Real Estate Economic Institute Co. Ltd.

procedure – six months from submission. The TMG has shortened the
procedure further for environmental impact assessments for the construction
of big buildings. In the case of the Tokyo Midtown Project, the procedure for
the environmental assessment, which originally took 24 months to complete,
was shortened to 11 months.

Evidence of the change in Tokyo caused by the urban renaissance policy is
provided in Figures 14.3 and 14.4, which show that the number of super
high-rise buildings, defined by the Japanese Building Code as a building with

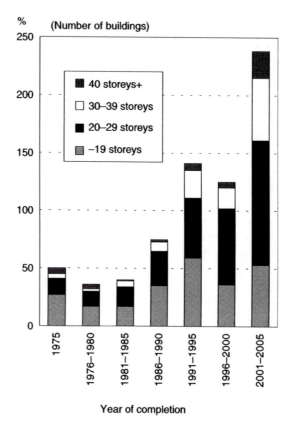

Figure 14.3 Number of high-rise buildings by height.

Source: Tokyo Metropolitan Government.

a height of over 60m, has substantially increased. There are now as many as 705 super high-rises in the Tokyo prefecture. About half of those, 355, are located in three wards (Chiyoda, Chuo and Minato) in the very centre of Tokyo. While 141 were built during the period 1991–1995 and 125 during the period 1996–2000, as many as 238 were built during the period 2001–2005. New super high-rises are even higher and have even more floor space and capacity. A comparison between those built in the period 1996–2000 and those built in the period 2001–2005 shows that the number of buildings with 30 storeys or more has increased from 23 to 77, and the number of those with a ratio of floor capacity to plot size of over 600 per cent, from 30 to 117. As illustrated in Figures 14.5 and 14.6, 146 authorized urban redevelopment projects either have been completed or are currently under way. The number of project permits for redevelopment rapidly increased in the last half of the 1980s, during the height of the bubble period, and has remained high into the 2000s. Super high-rises and high building volumes characterize recent

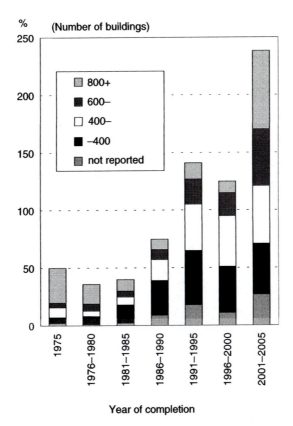

Figure 14.4 Number of high-rise buildings by ratio of floor space to plot size.

Source: Tokyo Metropolitan Government.

redevelopment. Among the 30 cases of projects permitted between 2001 and 2005, 40-storey or higher buildings were built in 11 projects and in 19 cases the ratio of floor capacity to plot size was over 600 per cent.

Competition-oriented urban governance

Japan has often been described as a 'developmental state' (Murakami 1992), which prioritizes economic expansion to maintain its legitimacy and takes a traditional state-guided approach to urban development (Harada 2001; Honma 1996). While Tokyo has been regarded as one of the top three global cities, together with New York and London (Sassen 1991), the political and economic condition of Tokyo is strongly differentiated from those two. In Tokyo the government has been paternalistically protecting major companies and controlling the economic system, rather than treating it as an independent city open to the global economy (Hill and Kim 2000; Saito and Thornley

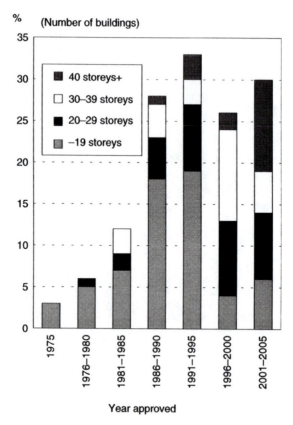

Figure 14.5 Number of urban redevelopment projects by the height of the tallest buildings in the project.

Source: Tokyo Metropolitan Government.

2003; White 1998). Although Tokyo provided other nations with much direct investment during the bubble period, foreign inward investment into Tokyo remained low (Sassen 2001). According to Kamo (2000), while New York voraciously absorbs capital, Tokyo is characterized as a capital supplier. In a global city, there is a tendency for the financial market to be more liberalized and for the financial sector to expand. In Tokyo, however, governmental intervention in the financial market has been strong and the finance industries have grown more slowly compared with New York or London (Kamo 2000). Tokyo was transformed into a global city by the dramatic growth of transnational corporations based in Tokyo. Many of the transnational corporations, however, are Japanese companies. Also, though the number of non-Japanese citizens in Tokyo has been increasing, the labour market in Tokyo is less open and the proportion of foreign citizens is remarkably low compared with New York or London.

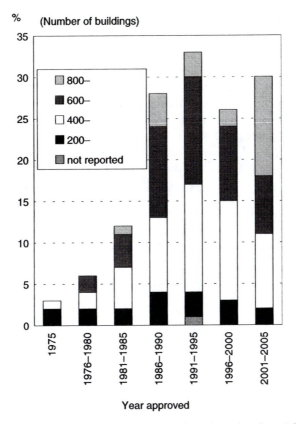

Figure 14.6 Number of urban redevelopment projects by ratio of total floor space to land plot size.

Source: Tokyo Metropolitan Government.

The energy that is restructuring Tokyo into a global city did not originate from free economic activity, but was created by the strategic scheming and policy manipulation of the public sector. As Honma (1996), Machimura (1994), Saito (2003) and Yahagi (2002), among others, argued, redevelopment of Tokyo proceeded within a framework where the state took initiatives and the business sector was protected by the government. Urban policies, since the 1980s, have emphasized partnership and negotiation with local governments, the business sector, citizens' participation and the non-profit sector. Since the forces of urbanization have subsided and related pressure lessened, the management of urban development by a bottom-up approach – with decision making at the local level – rather than a top-down approach has been increasingly regarded as being necessary for the development of good urban environments. At the end of the 1990s, however, the state's initiative to promote large-scale redevelopment projects in Tokyo omitted public consultation processes, which was justified by the perceived economic crisis.

Although the Japanese tradition of state-guided urban development policy is essentially rigid, the structure of urban governance cannot stay stationary in the era of economic globalization. As the key element of the state's agenda has shifted from 'development' to 'competition', the government has begun deploying a policy to enhance the economic openness of the nation and of Tokyo towards the global economy. The Hashimoto government launched the 'Big Bang' policy in November 1996 for the liberalization and globalization of the financial system. When the financial system plunged into crisis in the latter half of the 1990s and major securities firms and banks went bankrupt, the government did not initiate relief measures. This symbolized a significant change in the government's approach, which traditionally had been to protect big business. The 'Big Bang' policy was implemented in phases, promoting financial deregulation (Kuroki and Honda 2003). Japan's inward direct investment being less than outward direct investment was partly caused by the government's refusal to lift controls on inward direct investment for fear of losing control of the Japanese economy to foreign businesses. In the mid-1990s, however, a policy to expand the acceptance of inward direct investment was set up (Suda 2003).

The basic principles announced by the Council on Economic and Fiscal Policy in 2002 and 2005 accentuated the importance of expanding inward direct investment in terms of forming a more competitive economy. Subsequently the council issued the *Global Strategy* report in 2006, which stated that, 'although the trans-border activities of people and enterprises have been expanding, Japan, at present, is not keeping pace with the development of globalization', and demonstrated the necessity of making Japan more open to the world (Council on Economic and Fiscal Policy 2006). In 2004, the council also set up a taskforce to work on Japan's 'Twenty-first Century Vision', which laid out an image for Japan's future as 'an open, cultural, creative country' using phrases such as 'strengthened integration into the global economy', 'an open archipelago' and 'a nation without barriers' (Cabinet Office 2005). In Tokyo, Ishihara metropolitan government policy aimed at the formation of a global city by means of attracting more foreign-affiliated enterprises, more non-Japanese professional workers and more tourists (TMG 2000b).

In Japan, it has been the norm for the government to paternalistically protect the economy of rural areas and smaller cities through the allocation of public works, the redistribution of national taxes and the provision of various subsidies (Honma 1999). In the latter half of the 1990s, however, policies began encouraging provincial communities to be independent and to engage in more economically competitive behaviour. This implies that the government no longer seeks to protect domestic economies equally. While global competitiveness-related issues have been considered more centrally, urban and regional policies have been more decentralized.

The Economic Strategy Council (1999) called for 'the independence of municipalities from the central government' to establish a 'sound, creative, and competitive society'. The Committee on Economic and Fiscal Policy also made the independence of local economies and the promotion of competitiveness a critical part of policy from 2001 onwards. The Urban Renaissance Headquarters launched projects to revitalize cities throughout Japan and started to support the renaissance of provincial cities. It was decided in 2002 to introduce Special Zones for Structural Reform, where various deregulations were implemented. The Headquarters for Regional Revitalization was set up in the Cabinet in 2003, and the Regional Revitalization Law was established in 2005. It was becoming increasingly necessary politically to support provincial economies, which were stagnating due to the prolonged recession. Measures to revitalize provincial areas, however, aimed at encouraging the regions to be independent and competitive, rather than to rely on central government paternalism. The government explained the measures relating to the revitalization of local communities using expressions such as 'spirit of self-help and independence' and 'revitalization by competition using wisdom and means'. In 2004, policies to reduce state assistance and to cut the redistribution of national taxes started to move forward. The government, while it directly intervened in the urban renaissance of Tokyo, regarding it as the centre of Japanese economic competitiveness, has begun to request other areas to be more independent.

The LDP (Liberal Democratic Party), which has been almost continually in office since 1955, had its roots in rural communities, which had led to the tradition of protection of local economies by the national government. The LDP maintained political support through the over-allocation of public works and redistribution of national taxes to local areas. In urbanized Japan, however, it has also become necessary to pander to city dwellers in order to remain in power. People in cities were aggrieved by the fact that resources from the cities were redistributed to rural areas, and regularly chose anti-LDP mayors in the 1970s. In response, during the 1980s the LDP began to court political support from urban citizens. In addition, the government was immersed in the financial crisis of the 1990s, which made allocating public works and redistributing taxes to rural areas unviable. Thus the pattern in which the central LDP government protected local economies began to dissolve.

The urban renaissance policy has followed a traditional Japanese approach whereby the state has taken initiatives in its design and implementation. In this context, Japan could still be described as a 'developmental state'. The government, however, modified the structure of urban governance to challenge global economic competition and stressed the importance of opening up cities to foreign nations, on making local areas independent and also on redeveloping Tokyo as a government initiative. Tokyo is still a closed city compared with New York or London and it is still too early to judge the success of its opening up policy. It is, however, important to consider that the competition-oriented urban renaissance policy reflects a watershed in state urban planning and policy strategies.

A moralistic approach

The government sector, emphasizing the importance of participation in global competition, has been not only promoting strategic urban redevelopment but also attempting to dictate its notion of an ideal Tokyo resident. The state is aiming to achieve social solidarity in the era of globalization by the construction of a narrative projecting a new image for people who live in a globalized city.

Key words such as 'individuals', 'independence' and 'choice' continuously recur in policy documents in an apparent attempt to create an idealized image of the people and values of the future. The implication is that the government is seeking to weaken Japanese traditional values of reciprocity, interdependence and social harmony and instead assert the significance of individuality and individualism. This was plainly indicated in the January 2000 *Japanese Frontier Existing in Japan* report, compiled by the Committee on Japan's Goals in the 21st Century (2000), a private advisory panel to Prime Minister Obuchi. The committee first raised the issue of 'what we should do to utilize individuals' powers and abilities' to deal with globalization, and subsequently considered the creation of a new society involving people changing their way of life as individuals (ibid.: 27). Contextually, the document emphasized a discourse of crisis, and asserted, for example, that 'we share a sense of urgency and apprehension that Japan is going into a decline if nothing is done' (ibid.: 24). The report identified causes for crisis not only in the collapse of the bubble economy and the subsequent recession but also in the erosion of the system of values and moral norms, saying 'our foundation consisting of family ties, the quality of education, especially the attitude to study in elementary and middle schools, and social stability and security, of which we Japanese people have been proud, is now falling apart' (ibid.: 25). This report tried to portray globalization not only from an economic viewpoint but also from a socio-cultural perspective. It specifically described an ideal image of the type of Japanese people necessary for national prosperity in the era of globalization.

Japanese Frontier Existing in Japan (2000) stated, 'we have to change our conventional system and habitual practices, reviewing and reevaluating them from a global point of view and standard', which will bring about an 'era of great competition in systems and international standards'. It then emphasizes that the Japanese traditional way of decision making 'takes too much time to reach a consensus. In the circumstances where rules are not clearly stated and heart-to-heart communication is valued, responsibility is left unclear and individuals' ideas and creativity have not been fully utilized' (pp. 29–30). Then the committee declared, 'while the 20th century was the "century of organizations", the 21st century will be the "century of individuals".' This was followed by a prescriptive description of an 'individual' with illustrative phrases such as 'individuals who act freely with responsibility and self-support', 'the driving force for the 21st century will come from individuals and their pioneering spirits' and 'individuals who make their own independent choices among diverse options to live independently' (pp. 37, 38, 40, 46). The main message of the report was to place top priority on the exploitation of individuals and their potential, which have been buried beneath a tradition that values social harmony.

The committee also mentioned the issue of equality and pointed out that it was necessary to shift the focus of the idea from 'equality of results' to 'equality of chances'. It stated: 'Japanese society tends not to believe in an individual demonstrating a pioneer spirit – we tend to regard "the equality of the result" alone as important and a "tall tree" has been more severely blown about because it has stuck out in a compartmentalized organization with a "going along with the crowd" mentality' (p. 40). There are further assertions that, 'those with a pioneering spirit and creative ideas should be fairly evaluated', 'those who make an effort to demonstrate their pioneering spirit and thereby take a risk should be fully rewarded' and 'the idea of "fair disparity" to evaluate people's achievements and potentialities should be introduced' (p. 41). These discourses demonstrate the construction of an idealization of people as 'individuals', who form a society that accepts 'fair disparities'.

The Council on Economic and Fiscal Policy adopted the 'human resources strategy' in its 2002 basic principle to foster 'world-class, specialized abilities of diverse individuals in the increasingly globalized competitive environment'. The subsequent 2005 basic principle also emphasized the enhancement of human resources as a key policy in terms of overcoming the globalization-related crisis. Furthermore, the Working Group on Competitiveness within the task force on Japan's 21st Century Vision, set up by the council, claimed in 2005 that utilizing varied individuals with various abilities would be one of the fundamental strategies for the formation of a competitive society (Cabinet Office 2005).

Inevitably, a democratic state has to be able to control society and gain its support to maintain its legitimacy. As emphasis on state policy shifts from 'development' to 'competitiveness', it seems that political rhetoric and discourse regarding the importance of 'individuals' is commensurate with the new logic of its strategy. The 'independence of individuals' and social solidarity may appear to contradict each other. The increase of 'free choice' may seem to weaken the cohesiveness of society, especially a society that achieved industrial modernity while asserting principles of harmony and community. The image of 'independent individuals', however, promotes the consolidation of society in a different sense but still one where people share certain norms. The establishments of a consensual strategy to overcome both the economic crisis and the socio-cultural crises by having 'independent individuals' participate in the 'competition' and by requesting people to make a 'free choice'

320   *Yosuke Hirayama*

has been increasingly important. National policy regarding the nature and structure of social unity appears to be shifting substantially.

In Ishihara's TMG urban policy, the approach has become increasingly morally oriented. *The Tokyo Plan 2000* regarded the decline of global competitiveness not merely as an economic crisis but also as a socio-cultural crisis associated with the loss of 'backbone for self-reliance', difficulties in the 'variety of choice based on self-responsibility', the excess of 'equalities of results' along with the impediments to 'equalities of chances' and the dilution of the 'desire to positively contribute to society' (TMG 2000b: 6–7). This argument is similar to that of the Committee on Japan's Goals in the 21st Century.

The Tokyo Plan 2000 proposed an image of the 'new Tokyoite' and emphasized the necessity of nurturing them. A 'new Tokyoite' is 'a person who realizes a life he/she wants to live with a "life vision" as to what kind of life he/she wants to lead and a "career vision" as to what working life he/she wants to have', 'a person who can act with a high sense of mission and contribute to society', 'a person who can act while recognizing an individual's duty and responsibility considering the harmony between public welfare and an individual's benefit', and 'a person who respects the culture and tradition at home and abroad, and who can act with an international perspective and pride and identity as a Japanese' (TMG 2000b: 40). If the standard image of people in social science is applied, the 'new Tokyoite' is a mixture of a liberalist, an individualist, a globalist, a traditionalist and a nationalist (see Machimura 2003). The 'new Tokyoite' is nothing more than an image of 'a great character who leads a positive life, being faithful to authority'. It is, however, necessary to pay attention to the fact that the government sector has begun to introduce many moral elements into the reconstruction of personalities for people living in a global city. New measures that aim to orient, specify and direct the way of life of the people can now be seen. The proposed 'new Tokyoite' of the metropolitan government who manages the global city implies that Tokyo welcomes people of a certain type and doesn't like other types.

In March 2006, the Tokyo Metropolitan Assembly decided to make a bid to host the 2016 Olympics. Preparation works for the Olympic Games are expected to play the role of a new catalyst for the further redevelopment of Tokyo. Moreover, for the Tokyo government, hosting the Olympic Games will offer a means of addressing the socio-cultural crisis evident in Tokyo in particular and Japan in general. The Tokyo 2016 Olympics Advisory Panel (2006) expressed a feeling of nostalgia for the social unity which, according to the panel, occurred during the era of high-speed growth when the 1964 Tokyo Olympic Games were held. The panel stated, 'it was an undeniable fact that most Japanese people shared an overwhelming emotion', then pointed to the current dismal situation, saying, 'unfortunately, after 40 years, not only Tokyo but the whole nation is filled with a feeling of deadlock'. According to the panel, 'the Japanese people, having lost a big goal in common . . . are underestimating their own potential, and shrinking', and 'it is high time that we take a step toward Japan's re-emergence with the Olympic Games as a catapult'.

Governor Ishihara explained the importance of bidding to host the Olympic Games in the regular meeting of the Metropolitan Assembly in February 2006. The governor, who believes 'we are caught in a huge swirl where values are in chaos . . . and we have left our Japanese ambition somewhere behind', claimed 'what we should do now is . . . decide which direction we really should go in as a nation'. He went on to declare, 'the recovery of Tokyo will lead to the recovery of Japan . . . as if the sun rises again', and insisted on the necessity of 'clearly showing Japan's real strength and the presence of a mature city, Tokyo' (cited from TMG official homepage).

Concluding remarks

The Japanese government, at the beginning of the twenty-first century, emphasized the urban renaissance of Tokyo as an important policy. It is considered a mechanism for overcoming the economic crisis and for winning the global metropolitan survival competition. The Japanese economy has eventually begun to recover from the long-standing, deep recession and the disposal of bad debts appears almost complete. The vigorous implementation of the urban renaissance policy has been thought to contribute to the upturn of the economy. On the other hand, however, attention should be paid to the limitations of this competitiveness-oriented, aggressive urban policy.

The facts are that the population is decreasing, society is ageing and fertility is declining. These factors will have the greatest impact on Tokyo in the near future and will cast a cloud over an urban policy eager to reinforce competitiveness. The TMG (2000b) estimated that the population of Tokyo will begin to decrease after reaching its peak around 2010. The accuracy of the estimate of population change is extraordinary compared with the vagueness of the future prospects for Tokyo. The urban renaissance planners have been formulating the hypothesis that it is possible to reinforce Tokyo's economic competitiveness even though the population will decrease. There is no doubt, however, that the impact of the change in the population structure on Tokyo's economy cannot be ignored. According to Matsutani (2004), what impacts economic conditions is actually the speed of population change and not the status of the population. The proportion of baby-boomers, who were born in the latter half of the 1940s in Japan, is noticeably higher in Tokyo than in provincial cities. When these people, who have been contributing to the development of Tokyo, age, the composition of the population and workforce will also rapidly age. Tokyo has been attracting a younger population but, since the absolute number of young people will decrease considerably in Japan, because the fertility rate has been sharply dropping, the inflow of young people into Tokyo will decrease and the speed of ageing will not slow. The population composition of Tokyo has been relatively young compared with that of provincial cities, but the ageing of the population will be especially rapid in Tokyo in the near future. According to Matsutani's analyses, Tokyo will experience an excessively rapid population change and its economy will inevitably decline due to the decrease in the population of those who are of productive age coupled with an ageing workforce.

The government sector promoted redevelopment through the construction of office buildings and housing for urban renaissance. However, the demand for offices and housing cannot be expected to increase when the population is certainly decreasing. Urban renaissance, which is a supply-side measure to spur the economy by the provision of buildings in a blind, rapid way rather than based on a building demand analysis, is likely going to endanger the stability of the real estate market by creating an excess of building stock. In Tokyo, housing construction has been booming in hot spots in the central areas. This, however, has been creating cold spots in the suburbs and the outskirts of the city, where housing prices have been continuously decreasing (Hirayama 2005). There also is a credible prediction that a huge office space surplus will exist in the late 2000s when the baby-boomers are retiring *en masse* (Matsumura 2004; Motani 2004; NLI Research Institute 2002).

The competition-oriented urban renaissance policy has not only facilitated the redevelopment of Tokyo but has also divided Japan into Tokyo and the rest of the country, and produced social, economic and spatial cleavages within Tokyo. The tendency of economic activity to be pulled towards and concentrated in Tokyo has become stronger. The government policy to restructure Tokyo has not been leading to the economic recovery of the whole nation but has been widening the economic gap between Tokyo and other regions. The protection of the economies of provincial, smaller cities by the central government has been progressively diminishing. Within Tokyo, urban space and socio-economic conditions have become increasingly fragmented. The government prioritized the creation of hot spots in the centre of Tokyo and brand new, gorgeous landscapes have appeared. The real estate market in the cold spots, however, has remained stagnant, and problems such as the deterioration in the neighbourhood of low-income dwellers and an increase in the number of homeless people living along rivers or in public parks have not been adequately dealt with.

Finally, the urban renaissance policy has been laying out a new direction for the nation within a narrative based on one key concept, 'competition', which represents the national strategy to reform the sense of unity of society. The fundamental question is whether or not people find the direction attractive and approve of it. During the period of urbanization and high-speed economic growth, the description of the nation focusing on 'development' attracted many people and played a significant role in consolidating and stabilizing society. Compared with this, it is not clear, at least at present, whether the government can form a social consensus at the same time as re-moralizing people, or force people to engage in heightened competition and to tolerate the expanding economic disparities caused by the growing global economy.

References

Cabinet Office (2005) *Nihon 21 Seiki Bijon [Japan's 21st Century Vision]*, Tokyo: Kokuritsu Insatsu Kyoku.

Committee on Japan's Goals in the 21st Century (2000) *Nihon no Furontia ha Nihon no nakani Aru [Japanese Frontier Existing in Japan]*, Tokyo: Committee on Japan's Goals in the 21st Century.

Council on Economic and Fiscal Policy (2006) *Gurobaru Senryaku [Global Strategy]*, Tokyo: Council on Economic and Fiscal Policy.

Economic Strategy Council (1999) *Nihon Keizai Saisei heno Senryaku [Strategy towards the Revitalization of the Japanese Economy]*, Tokyo: Economic Strategy Council.

Harada, S. (ed.) (2001) *Nihon no Toshi Hou [Japanese Urban Laws]*, Tokyo: Tokyo University Press.

Hill, R.C. and Kim, J.W. (2000) Global cities and developmental states: New York, Tokyo and Seoul, *Urban Studies*, 37(12): 2167–2195.

Hirayama, Y. (2005) Running hot and cold in the urban home-ownership market: the experience of Japan's major cities, *Journal of Housing and the Built Environment*, 20(1): 1–20.

Honma, Y. (1996) *Doboku Kokka no Shisou [The Philosophy of the Construction State]*, Tokyo: Nihon Keizai Hyoron Sha.

Honma, Y. (1999) *Kokudo Keikaku wo Kangaeru [Exploring National Land Development]*, Tokyo: Chuo Koron Shinsha.

Igarashi, Y. and Ogawa, A. (2003) *Toshi Saisei wo Tou [Denouncing 'Urban Regeneration']*, Tokyo: Iwanami Shoten.

Ishida, Y. (2004) *Nihon Kingendai Toshikeikaku no Tenkai: 1868–2003 [Evolution of Urban Planning in Modern Japan: 1868–2003]*, Tokyo: Jichitai Kenkyu Sha.

Japan Federation of Construction Contractors (2001) *Toshi Saisei no Arikata ni tsuite [How Urban Renaissance Should Be]*, Tokyo: Japan Federation of Construction Contractors.

Japan Federation of Economic Organizations (1999) *Toshi Saisei heno Teigen [Proposal for Urban Renaissance]*, Tokyo: Japan Federation of Economic Organizations.

Japan Project Industrial Council (2002) *Heisei 14 nen Jigyo Houkokusho [Business Report 2002]*, Tokyo: Japan Project Industrial Council.

Kamo, T. (2000) An aftermath of globalization? East Asian economic turmoil and Japanese cities adrift, *Urban Studies*, 37(12): 2145–2165.

Kuroki, Y. and Honda, Y. (2003) Kinyu: kinyu seido to kinyu seisaku [Finance: financial institution and policy], in T. Tachibanaki (ed.), *Sengo Nihon wo Kenshou Suru [Inspecting Post-war Japan]*, Tokyo, Tokyo University Press.

Machimura, T. (1994) *Sekai Toshi Tokyo no Kouzou Tenkan [Restructuring of Tokyo as a Global City]*, Tokyo: Tokyo University Press.

Machimura, T. (2003) Narrating a 'global city' for 'new Tokyoites': economic crisis and urban 'boosterism' in Tokyo, in H. Dobson and G. D. Hook (eds), *Japan and Britain in the Contemporary World: Responses to Common Issues*, London: RoutledgeCurzon.

Matsumura, T. (2004) Dankai sedai taishoku no fudosan shijo heno eikyo [Effects of baby-boomers' retirement on the real estate market], in M. Higuchi (ed.), *Dankai Sedai no Teinen to Nihon Keizai [Retirement of Baby-boomers and the Japanese Economy]*, Tokyo: Nihon Hyoron Sha.

Matsutani, A. (2004) *Jinkou Genshou no Atarashii Kousiki* [*A New Formula for Population Decrease*], Tokyo: Nihon Keizai Shinbun Sha.

Motani, K. (2004) Dankai sedai no chiriteki henzai to sono koreika ni tomonau eikyo [Geography of baby-boomers' aging], in M. Higuchi, M. (ed.), *Dankai Sedai no Teinen to Nihon Keizai* [*Retirement of Baby-boomers and the Japanese Economy*], Tokyo: Nihon Hyoron Sha.

Murakami, Y. (1992) *Han Koten no Seiji Keizai Gaku* [*Anti-Classical Political Economics*], *Tokyo*: Chuou Koron Sinsha.

NLI Research Institute (2002) *Tokyo Ofisu Shijo no '2010' Mondai* [*The '2010 Problem' of the Tokyo Office Market*], Tokyo: NLI Research Institute.

Noble, G.W. (2006) Seijiteki ridashippu to kouzou kaikaku [Political leadership and structural reform], in Institute of Social Science, University of Tokyo (ed.), *Ushinawareta Junen wo Koete: Koizumi Kiakaku heno Jidai* [*Beyond the Lost Decade: The Era towards the Koizumi Reform*], Tokyo: Tokyo University Press.

Real Estate Companies Association of Japan (2001) *Toshi Saisei ni Kansuru Iken* [*Opinion on Urban Renaissance*], Tokyo: Real Estate Companies Association of Japan.

Saito, A. (2003) Global city formation in a capitalist developmental state: Tokyo and the waterfront sub-centre project, *Urban Studies*, 40(2): 283–308.

Saito, A. and Thornley, A. (2003) Shifts in Tokyo's world city status and the urban planning response, *Urban Studies*, 40(4): 665–685.

Sassen, S. (1991) *The Global City: New York, London, Tokyo*, Princeton, NJ: Princeton University Press.

Sassen, S. (2001) *The Global City: New York, London, Tokyo*, second edition, Princeton, NJ: Princeton University Press.

Sorensen, A. (2002) *The Making of Urban Japan: Cities and Planning from Edo to the Twenty-First Century*, London: Routledge.

Suda, M. (2003) Kokusai boeki [International trade], in T. Tachibanaki (ed), *Sengo Nihon wo Kensho Suru* [*Inspecting Post-war Japan*], Tokyo, Tokyo University Press.

Suzuki, H. (2003) Chou-kousou toiu Shima Uchu [The super high-rise island universe], *Chuou Koron*, (1431): 157–165.

Takenaka, H. (2006) *Shusho Shihai: Nihon Seiji no Henbo* [*Prime Minister Domination: Transformation in the Japanese Political System*], Tokyo: Chuo Koron Shinsha.

Tokyo 2016 Olympics Advisory Panel (2006) *Tokyo Orinpikku no Jitsugen ni Mukete* [*Towards the Realization of the Tokyo 2016 Olympics*], Tokyo: Tokyo 2016 Olympics Advisory Panel.

Tokyo Metropolitan Government (TMG) (1999) *Kiki Toppa Senryaku Plan: 21 Seiki heno Daiichi Steppu* [*Strategic Plan to Overcome the Crisis: The First Step to the 21st Century*], Tokyo: TMG.

TMG (2000a) *Toshi Hakusyo 2000* [*Urban White Paper 2000*], Tokyo: TMG.

TMG (2000b) *Tokyo Kousou 2000: Senkyaku Banrai no Sekai Toshi wo Mezashite* [*The Tokyo Plan 2000: Toward a Global City That Attracts a Great Number of Residents and Visitors*], Tokyo: TMG.

TMG (2001) *Tokyo no Atarashii Toshizukuri Bijon* [*The Vision of New Urban Planning in Tokyo*], Tokyo: TMG.

TMG (2002) *Toshi Hakuhyo 2002* [*Urban White Paper 2002*], Tokyo: TMG.

White, J.W. (1998) Old wine, cracked bottle? Tokyo, Paris, and the global city hypothesis, *Urban Affairs Review*, 33(4): 451–477.

Yahagi, H. (2002) Tokyo no risutorakucharingu to sekai toshi no yume futatabi [Restructuring Tokyo into a global city], in T. Kodama (ed.), *Daitoshiken heno Kousou [Perspectives on the Restructuring of Metropolitan Areas]*, Tokyo: Tokyo University Press.

15 Urbanization, low-income housing and urban governance in South Korea

Seong Kyu Ha

Introduction

Urban governance matters for the low-income group in South Korea (hereafter Korea). The actions of governments, both central and municipal, can make matters worse for the low-income group, through inappropriate and repressive policies and interventions, or they can be supportive by ensuring access to essential infrastructure, particularly shelter.

The economic growth of Korea has often been referred to as an 'economic miracle'. In 1960, annual per capita GNP in Korea was US$69. By 2004, this figure had increased to US$14,162. Despite this economic performance, the Korean housing situation has experienced serious problems. An important phenomenon to emerge has been the increasing polarization between the housing conditions of the better off and those of the worse off.

The Korean government has played a large role in almost all aspects of housing production and consumption. The rationale for government intervention in housing has generated a lengthy debate on the relationship between political structures and the established housing system. The government plays a significant role in determining the distributional aspect of growth prospects in Korea, whether for better or for worse. Democratization and the growth of civil society offer some possibilities for the urban poor to influence what happens.

Since the late 1980s, structural adjustment polices, privatization and deregulation have reduced the scope for government intervention on behalf of the low-income group, or made that intervention more indirect. The interconnections between low-income housing and urban governance are receiving increased attention in Korea. The urban low-income group (or urban poverty) and governance are both issues high on the agenda of Korean governments. Thus it is timely to look at how the governance of the Korean cities affects the prospects and livelihood of the low-income group in those cities.

This chapter focuses on the relationship between issues of urban governance and low-income housing in Korea. The main questions addressed in the chapter are:

1   Do the urban poor benefit from economic growth in general and urban (or housing) regeneration in particular and, if so, how?
2   How can the low-income group bring their influence to bear on the agenda of the various institutions of city governance?

The key message from this chapter is that the wellbeing of the low-income group can be improved by access to economic opportunities, supportive social networks, and greater access to assets (notably housing), and services.

Urbanization, economic growth and low-income housing

Urbanization and economic growth

Korea, as is well known, has limited land and a large population. More than 45 million people live in less than 100,000 km^2. From this position, Korea has experienced a very rapid urbanization process. The first phase of Korean urbanization was characterized by the sudden flow of population into the cities resulting from external factors such as independence (1945), partition and the Korean War (1950–1953). An urban explosion occurred on a massive scale after the Second World War. An unexpectedly large group of returnees and refugees from neighbouring countries settled in urban areas. Some of them simply settled in open spaces, such as military reservation areas, hillside park areas, and public open spaces near railroads. Here, squatters constructed their own houses without the consent of the city government. In addition, mass spontaneous urban squatter settlements began just after the end of the Korean War, in 1953. Over a million persons displaced by war returned to the ruined cities. Finding no suitable housing, they built temporary shacks of wooden boards – so-called *panjajib* and *panjachon*.

The second phase of urbanization occurred during 1960–1990, together with rapid economic growth. During the 1960s, urbanization was the result of the increasing industrial activity in the urban areas and spread of social services. In 1960, urban dwellers comprised only 28.3 per cent of the total population, but this figure rose to about 79 per cent in 1990. The 1960s and early 1970s were characterized by very rapid urbanization; between 1965 and 1970 the urban population increased by about 13 per cent. During 1970–1990, the Seoul Metropolitan Region (SMR) grew much faster than the rest of the country (Table 15.1). Many of the increased city population lived in shantytowns.

The third phase of urbanization was characterized by the slowdown of population growth in urban areas, especially the capital city of Seoul. While the metropolitan area has hardly changed in size, its population has increased threefold over the last 40 years, reaching 21.4 million – more than 46 per cent of the total population as of 2000. The rate of increase recently fell in Seoul but grew in the surrounding region. As shown in Table 15.1, the population of the SMR has been growing faster than the national average. The population

Table 15.1 Population growth in SMR

	1970	1980	1990	2000	Annual growth rate			
					70–80	80–90	90–95	95–00
Nation	31,466	37,436	43,411	46,136	1.74	1.48	0.54	1.12
SMR	8,791	13,298	18,587	21,354	4.14	3.35	1.65	1.12
(A + B + C)	(27.9)	(35.5)	(42.8)	(46.3)				
Seoul (A)	5433	8364	10,613	9895	4.31	2.38	–0.73	–0.67
Incheon (B)	646	1084	1818	2475	5.18	5.17	4.77	1.40
Kyonggi (C)	2712	3850	6156	8984	3.50	4.69	4.35	3.21

Sources: NSO (2003: 45–78) and Ko (2003: 2).

of Seoul begun to decrease from 1992, and Kyonggi province is gaining a momentum of rapid population growth. Despite the fact that the rate of increase has slowed down, the increasing concentration of population and economic activities into the SMR has continued over the years (Table 15.2). Seoul and its environs have created many problems in the course of their fast growth and change. Many claim that the alarmingly high concentration of people, activities, services and resources in the capital region has come to outweigh the merits of agglomeration.

In the pattern of Korea's urbanization, the following points are of major importance: first, the growth rate of larger cities has been higher relative to smaller cities for most periods, and so their share of the total population has been increasing. Second, the most recent census revealed in 2000 the extent of the spillover growth of small cities and counties adjacent to the larger cities. Except those surrounding the largest cities, almost all counties showed a

Table 15.2 Concentration in SMR (2000)

Variables	Nation(A)	SMR(B)	Share (B/A%)
Size (km^2)	99,461	11,705	11.8
Population	46,136	21,354	46.3
Industry			
• No. of workers (thousand)	21,362	9,912	46.4
• Gross regional product (billion won)	465,183	223,081	48.0
Manufacturing			
• No. of establishments (thousand)	98,110	55,874	57.0
• No. of workers (thousand)	2653	1235	46.6
Bank			
• Deposits (billion won)	404,661	275,394	68.1
• Loan (billion won)	310,804	202,797	65.2
No. of universities	162	66	40.7
Public Administration Office	276	234	84.8

Source: NSO (2003).

population decrease in the last census. The rapid increase of population in the fringe areas of Seoul and its satellites has led to a new phenomenon, the metropolitanization of Seoul.

Third, when Korea's export-oriented economic development took a giant step forward during the late 1960s, yet another tremendous population surge from rural to urban areas occurred. As more jobs resulting from this robust economic growth were available in many large cities, many young men and women who were either unemployed or not satisfied with farm-related activities took part in this population shift.

Fourth, in terms of spatial impact, the Korean government has adopted 'growth pole' or 'growth centre' strategies since the 1960s. All these policies were accompanied by rapid economic, spatial and social change. The government's policy for industrialization was centred on cities maximizing their efficiency in existing facilities. Modern industrial and service activities benefited greatly from the economies of agglomeration. This spurred the growth of the industrial economy in the cities. In Korea, since the early 1960s, the government consistently continued the 'growth first' approach. Economic growth was represented by the principle of growth first, redistribution later – the philosophy of national policy. The dominant thinking among the powerful technocrats in the public bureaucracy was that reducing unemployment and forming self-sufficient economic structures could solve national poverty, and that this could be achieved through industrialization rather than rural development. Thus industrialization was first directed to labour-intensive and import-substitution industries based in urban areas.

Industrialization made it necessary for people to move among occupations, industries and areas. Those who could not or did not readjust to the changes were left out of mainstream society. This was often described in terms of informal sectors, dual labour markets, marginal or peripheral jobs or people, under-employment or latent unemployment. Problems of unemployment or under-employment, low income, irregular working, wage discrimination and wage exploitation tended to be concentrated on the poor and on the same families and neighbourhoods. These factors all contributed to the creation of shantytowns in urban Korea.

Low-income housing

Despite many measures to improve housing quality over the past two decades (Table 15.3), the housing conditions of low-income households have not improved as much as expected and the gap in housing conditions between income classes is still large. Analysis of the data of the Population and Housing Census in 2000 shows that about 3.3 million households, 23.1 per cent of the total number of households, are living in very poor dwellings, which do not meet the minimum housing standards.[1] Also, their burden of housing costs has been growing heavier due to a sharp increase in house prices after 2001

Table 15.3 Population, households and housing indicators, 1980–2000

Variable	Whole nation		SMR[4]	
	1980	*2000*	*1980*	*2000*
Housing supply ratio[1]	71	94	60	69
Average size of dwelling (m²)	68.4	83.8	41.0[2]	61.3
Per capita floor area (m²)	10.1	20.1	9.3[3]	19.1
No. of rooms per household	2.12	3.39	2.16	3.37
Hot water (%)	9.0	87.4	22.1	90.8
Flush toilet (%)	18.4	87.0	39.2	92.6
Ratio of apartment to housing stock	7.1	47.7	14.4	37.1

Notes:
1 The ratio of the dwelling to households. According to the government, the ratio of dwelling to
  households in the whole nation, Seoul and SMR in 2004 was 102, 89 and 94%, respectively.
2,3 Indicate urban areas only.
4 The SMR includes the city of Seoul itself, Kyonggi province and Inchon city.

Sources: EPB (1983), KNHC (1981, 1997) and NSO (2003).

and the inequality of housing wealth distribution has become worse than that of income distribution.

The proportion of the population living in slums and squatter settlements varies from city to city,[2] but figures of 20–30 per cent were common during the 1960s and 1970s. Since the early 1980s, particularly in Seoul, substandard housing has decreased due to urban redevelopment projects. In addition, since the early 1980s, poor housing conditions, such as physical deterioration, lack of facilities and security and overcrowding, have been associated with two new kinds of settlement: *Jjogbangs* and vinyl houses.

Jjogbangs[3] have emerged as an important part of the rental sector, the result of housing renewal projects in inner city areas and of the IMF crisis. A number of squatter settlements have been demolished since the early 1980s as part of city beautification or redevelopment projects. Even though the number of squatter settlements has decreased as the result of redevelopment projects, the number of poor tenants has not decreased. Evicted squatters have tended to scatter around the city, but some still remain in inner city areas. For these evicted tenants, *Jjogbangs* have emerged as an alternative form of shelter. Since the IMF crisis, *Jjogbangs* have bridged the gap between the unemployed and the poor's housing needs and the housing supply in Seoul.[4] *Jjogbangs* are based on an illegal lodging or rental system, are available at a relatively low cost and are centrally located. Most *Jjogbangs* suffer from a lack of facilities and poor services. In addition, the tenants of these *Jjogbangs* are mostly poor and homeless people. One of the main characteristics *Jjogbangs* is the daily payment system (Ha 2004a).

Vinyl houses are constructed with thin wood board layers and vinyl covering on the outside. Most vinyl house occupants are poor tenants who have been forcibly evicted from housing renewal areas. Vinyl house squatters simply settle in vacant hillside areas or public open spaces without no land ownership rights or building permits. The majority of residents in squatter settlements (75.7 per cent) had lived there for more than 11 years. Most of the remainder had lived in vinyl houses for between six and ten years and only about 9 per cent of residents had lived for less than five years in this community (KOCER 2002). This relatively low degree of mobility is reflected in the fact that the vast majority of people are working to create a stable community even though they are faced with forced eviction.

Housing is very expensive in Korean cities, especially Seoul. The ratio between the average apartment price and average household income (price–income ratio: PIR) in Seoul was 9.19 at its peak in 1990, declined to 6.25 in 1997, but rose to 8.9 in 2003 (Kim 2004; Kookmin Bank 2003). Also, the urban low-income group's rent-to-income ratio (RIR) is very high, implying that they cannot afford adequate housing without public assistance.

The per capita housing size Gini coefficients decreased between 1993 and 2002, from 0.35 to 0.235, but the housing-related assets Gini coefficients have increased from 0.489 to 0.51. In 2002, the housing-related assets Gini coefficients were greater than the income Gini coefficient, indicating that housing-related asset distribution is worse than income distribution (Chung 2005).

One of the main reasons for the housing poverty problems described above is the inability of institutions and institutional frameworks to develop and manage human settlements. Governments have often helped destroy or stifle the 'social economy' in cities – i.e. the capacity of the inhabitants in each locality to identify and act according to their own priorities. This social economy is central to prosperity and making full use of the potential that cities have to offer requires 'good governance'.

A salient feature of the Korean housing sector is pervasive intervention by government to stabilize housing prices. In relation to low-income housing, direct provisions of public rental housing and housing redevelopment programmes have faced several problems, including inconsistent and unrealistic policy implementations. In Korea, successive governments have been locked into a historical model as monopoly suppliers of basic public services, with decision making concentrated in the hands of a small but often ill-equipped group of officials, and minimal participation by, or accountability to, citizens.

The challenges for urban governance

An understanding of urban governance stems from a definition of governance itself. McCarney et al. (1996) describe governance as 'the relationship between civil society and the state, rulers and the ruled, the government and the governed'. Devas (2004) states that:

> Our analysis of urban governance includes a whole range of actors and institutions, and it is the relationships and interactions between them that

determine what happens within the city. Urban governance also, crucially, involves individual citizens and households, of all income groups, inasmuch as they have any influence over what happens. Within this, city (or municipal) government is but one element, albeit often the largest and most obvious.

(p. 25)

Urban governance allows us to reconsider local government as more than just a technical or administrative arm of central government in Korea. When urban governance is introduced as the relation between actors in civil society engaging with local state structures, new territory is opened up for reviving local government. In this study I use the term 'governance' in a neutral sense to refer to a range of relationships and interactions between the government and civil society. The use of the term governance in Korea is a recognition that this view of government is no longer valid, if it ever was, and that outcomes depend on the interaction between many actors.

The term governance has been widely adopted in the discourse on international developments in recent years, but with varying connotations. It is often associated with normative values, as in the term 'good governance', which features so heavily in the discourse of donor agencies (UNCHS (Habitat) 2001; World Bank 1999). According to the UNCHS (Habitat), the Global Campaign on Good Governance will promote four specific goals for realizing the 'inclusive city': decentralization and local participatory democracy, efficiency, equity and security. The campaign will encourage central and local governments to strive for policy and institutional change to achieve these normative goals (UNCHS (Habitat) 2000: 200–201).

In most countries, the governance of human settlements has become a major issue over the last two decades. The term 'governance', as it refers to the relationship not only between governments and state agencies but also between government and communities and social groups, means more than government or management. The failure of cities to integrate excluded groups into their decision-making process is often also a function of inertia, and bureaucratic and unresponsive forms of government. Exclusion and marginalization create and reinforce housing poverty in urban areas.

With respect to low-income housing, I would like to explore the performance of urban governance in Korea in terms of the five key indicators (or normative goals): participatory democracy, decentralization, efficiency, equity and security.

Participatory democracy

The governance of cities in Korea has been profoundly affected by three separate but related shifts in the discussion of policies for human settlements: (1) democratization, (2) the role of NGOs, and (3) decentralization (Cho 2000; Chung 1999; Ha 2004b).

The military coup d'etat of 16 May 1961 ushered in an era of authoritarianism under the guise of development. Korea was an authoritarian regime for three decades (1961–1992), but anti-dictatorial drives swept the country in the 1970s and 1980s, prompting a transition to democracy, the fruits of which began to be experienced in the mid-1980s. In the late 1980s, the military regime (led by General Chun Doo Hwan) was faced with a serious political crisis as a result of the so-called 'June Uprising' (1987). The June Uprising was a national movement against the military regime that sought to bring about the restoration of democracy in Korea. The Chun regime eventually succumbed to citizens' demands for a constitutional amendment to allow the direct election of the president.

Moreover, the 1980s were, from a historical point of view, a period of important transformation in the pursuit of a democratic political system as well as in social development. In order to create a more democratic rule of law and administrative system, several amendments and radical policy changes were brought about. These kinds of social and political reform policies provided the foundation for the new civic government that took office in 1993. This development marked an important transition stage in Korea's pursuit of democracy, and eventually led to the replacement of the authoritarian military government by a civil government. The political democratization of Korea was brought about as a result of the efforts of a grassroots civil society movement.

NGOs under authoritarianism may be classified broadly into three types: government-patronized organizations, militant resistant social movement organizations, and depoliticized or apolitical organizations. Under an extreme dictatorship, government-patronized and depoliticized NGOs exist as legal entities, but militant resistant organizations can hardly exist as legal entities, and consequently become illegal bodies. 'Life-risking' militant anti-dictatorial democratization campaigns could be only waged in the illegal arena (Cho and Kim 1998).

The June Uprising of 1987 provided a watershed for democracy in Korea. This anti-dictatorial democratization movement grew gradually and continuously under successive military authoritarian regimes, thus paving the way for their retreat and the advancement of democracy in Korea. NGO revitalization signifies the empowerment of civil society, and the June Uprising represented a starting point of such empowerment in the modern history of Korea. This incident provided an important momentum for the 'renaissance' of Korean NGOs.

Toward the end of the 1980s, sweeping changes were made in Korea, and democracy was enhanced as a result. This in turn brought about an explosive growth in non-governmental and non-profit civil movements. The NGOs[5] surveyed totaled 2914 in the *1997 Directory* (3898 if academic societies and overseas organizations are included) and 4023 in the *2000 Directory* (6159 if academic societies and overseas organizations are included). With branches added, the figure stood at over 9400 in the former and some 20,000 in the latter (*Citizen Times* 1999). See Table 15.4.

Table 15.4 NGOs by year of foundation (%)

	%
Pre-1960s	5.7
1960s	7.2
1970s	9.0
1980s	21.0
1990s	56.6

Source: Citizen Times (1999).

Housing movements in Korea can be categorized as either residents' or intellectual movements. Residents' movements have formed almost spontaneously, particularly tenants' groups. Well-known examples of such residents' movements in Seoul are the Sanggedong and Mokdong redevelopment area squatters' associations. The objectives of residents' movements are to assist others in eviction cases and to solve other common problems. Moreover, they actively lobby government in order to force it to promulgate policies that will help to resolve the problems of the urban poor. In the late 1980s, resisting renters from different areas began to demonstrate solidarity. During this period, the main issues raised by renters and CBOs revolved around their right to form their own interest group, and their demand that forced evictions be prohibited.

In contrast to residents' movements, intellectual movements are usually composed of religious organizations and NGOs, with the Citizens' Coalition for Economic Justice (CCEJ) standing out as a prominent example (Cho 2000; Ha 2002).[6] The CCEJ believe that the fruits of economic development should be shared by all common people and not just by a small group of 'haves'. Moreover, the CCEJ has proposed a new methodology of gradual, but thorough, reform of the economic system. On top of this, in recognition of the need for continuous, cooperative efforts by civil society to bring about the reform of urban policies and systems, the CCEJ Urban Reform Centre was established to deal comprehensively with urban problems (Kwon 2003). This urban reform movement strives to transform Korean cities into good healthy places to live, based on sustainable and environmentally-friendly lifestyles.

In addition, a new housing NGO, the Citizens for Decent Housing (CiDeH), was established in 2001. The primary goals of CiDeH are as follows: (1) to work in partnership with all those who have a stake in the process and outcome of housing policy-making; (2) to conduct comprehensive research and formulate effective strategies to enhance housing welfare for people, particularly those in low income brackets; (3) to evaluate and analyse government housing policies and make policy recommendations; and (4) to build consensus and public opinion on housing policy and translate them into workable public policy and effective societal actions. The CiDeH is now deeply involved in evaluating and analysing government housing policies and making recommendations for low-income housing policy.

Decentralization

After liberalization in 1945, the local governments in Korea experienced many complications. For three decades, from 1961 to 1991, Korea had only a central administration handling local affairs without local governments. The local assemblies have been resurrected since 1991 and the chief executives of local governments have been elected directly by the local residents since 1995. However, these could not secure local autonomy due to restrictions and interventions implemented by central government agencies (Chung 1996).

It was not until the 1980s that a wider debate was initiated on the issue of the balance of power and the distribution of functions between the central and local government. Decentralization takes a variety of forms. Assuming that decentralization involves the delegation of autonomy from a higher, or more general, level of the state to a lower, or more specialized, unit (or area), three major variants can be identified: deconcentration, devolution and privatization.

Since decentralization in 1991, locally elected governors and councillors have led local authorities. The election of local governors and councillors representing opposition parties challenged the traditional relationship between the central and local government, that is, the authoritarian and hierarchical pattern. In 1999, the Presidential Commission on Devolution Promotion for Local Authorities was established in order to transfer powers to certain parastatal agencies of the central government. While these parastatal agencies have certain autonomy in day-to-day management, ultimately the government controls them. Devolution, on the other hand, is considered by some to be real decentralization as power and functions are actually transferred to sub-national political entities, and as such these entities are invested with real autonomy in many important respects.

Another body involved with the distribution of functions is the Presidential Commission on Government Innovation, established in 1999, which deals with issues relating to: (1) reducing the workforce and slimming down the central and local government structure, with state-owned enterprises (SOEs) and other quasi-governmental institutions focused on the core competencies of public functions; (2) implementing privatization programmes for SOEs and their subsidiaries, significantly increasing efficiency and performance; and (3) introducing competition and performance oriented compensation in the public sector through programmes such as the Open Career System.

Since the early 1990s, the introduction of local autonomy has certainly played an important role in the democratization and decentralization process in Korea. However, city governments themselves face a number of specific constraints on their ability to respond to the needs of citizens, particularly the housing poverty group. First, in Korea, where different parties may be in power at each level, state government may oppose actions by municipal governments simply on political grounds. Political conflicts between municipal, provincial and central governments can undermine the capacity of municipal governments to respond. Furthermore, in the case of conflicting matters relating to urban planning and management, municipal governments are no longer a mere agency of central government and can make independent decisions. Disputes can now occur between central government and municipal governments: a new situation. The diffusion of power can contribute to the opening and democratizing of local authorities in practice, creating a new arena for policy formation and urban governance.

Second, there are still a number of specific control mechanisms included within the various policies of the planning system by which central government can limit the actions of local governments. For example, local governments' decisions on planning proposals or authorizations are still subject to the Ministry of Construction and Transportation, i.e. the minister still holds numerous reserve powers. But, recently, much of the actual implementation of planning policy for which the central government is responsible tends to be, in fact, delegated to local governments.

Third, lack of financial resources is the most significant factor preventing urban governments from addressing the needs of the poor. In many cases, however, most local governments are only interested in securing the terms of the local budget and have a shortsighted approach to development benefits (Kwon 2003). Extreme regionalism and economic concentration on specific areas are obviously detrimental to long-time governmental efforts to promote equal development.

Efficiency

Cities must be financially sound and cost-effective in their management of revenue sources and expenditures, the administration and delivery of services, and in the enablement, based on comparative advantage, of government, the private sector and communities to contribute formally or informally to the urban economy. According to UNCHS (Habitat), practical means of realizing this efficiency norm include the need for cities to, inter alia:

> . . . encourage delivery and regulation of public services through partnerships with the private and civil society sectors; promote equitable user-pay principal services and infrastructure; encourage municipal departments to find innovative means of delivering public goods and services through management contracts; promote integrated, inter-sectoral planning and management; remove unnecessary barriers to secure tenure and to the supply of finance; adopt clear objectives and targets for the provision of public services, which maximize the contributions all sectors

of society can make to urban economic development; encourage volunteerism.

(2000: 198)

With respect to low-income housing in Korea, the issue of efficiency focuses on two policy areas: (1) the importance of encouraging business development, particularly construction companies, for a city's economic wellbeing and housing production through urban redevelopment; and (2) public housing for sale programmes and filtering strategies.

In urban areas, housing renewal projects, through the demolition of substandard housing, were one of the measures used to achieve mass housing construction and high-density development. The so-called Joint Redevelopment Project (JRP) has been introduced based on a spirit of partnership between homeowners and construction companies. This project, intended to build high-rise flats and share profits, was initiated on the basis of voluntary agreements between homeowners and construction companies selected by representatives of homeowners' associations.

In a JRP, the city government designates an urban redevelopment area and grants approval for all the plans, large construction companies provide financing and carry out the construction, and an association of homeowners takes responsibility for the project. Introduced in 1983, JRPs are now the most typical and prevalent method of improving substandard housing areas. All houses in a projected area are demolished and new high-rise apartment buildings – from 15–25 stories high – are constructed. Apartments are the most common housing type in JRP areas. Most have three rooms and are on average 118m^2 in size. This means that the average floor space per household in redeveloped areas is higher than those in other areas of Seoul.

JRPs are basically profit-oriented and do not take into account the whole urban housing system. Rather, housing is treated as a commodity in the open market. Open market mechanisms, however, are not protected unless social welfare and security are built into the housing equation. Housing renewal projects have changed the spatial patterns of low-income residential areas in Seoul. Since the 1960s, these projects have forced low-income residents out of the inner city toward middle ring areas, and finally to the outskirts of the city. In the 1990s, most of the substandard settlements in the Seoul metropolitan area were located in satellite cities and suburban areas where the housing and land prices were relatively cheap. Urban redevelopment projects have played a decisive role in creating urban sprawl in Seoul.

Korea's basic housing strategy has essentially been based on the filtering concept: expansion of the supply of housing for sale will eventually improve the housing available to lower-income households and reduce the rate of increase in the price of housing services. In Korea, housing policies during the last three decades have not effectively achieved their purposes. While the major objective of Korean housing policy has been to increase homeownership, housing construction policy has focused on middle-income households rather than on the most needy.

The Korea National Housing Corporation (KNHC), which acts as a public housing construction institution supplying housing for low-income groups, is the most important agency of its kind. Since the early 1960s, the KNHC has concentrated on the expansion of state-developed housing for sale rather than on the provision of rental accommodation. Of total housing constructed, 62 per cent is available for sale. Even though the Corporation has also produced rental dwellings, these houses have generally been sold once the five-year period has passed.

Since the early 1980s, housing redevelopment has mainly produced multi-family housing for reasons of efficient land use and to solve the quantitative housing shortage. But multi-family housing provision neglects community development. Urban residential redevelopment planning and housing policy have concentrated on physical improvement and ignored aspects of community tradition and culture. Because housing provision is the central concern, community facility installation and public facility construction are provided only at the minimum level and imsufficient attention is paid to socio-economic considerations.

Equity

In order to tackle the issue of equity in terms of urban governance in the field of low-income housing in Korea, we need to look at the role of the public sector. The Korean government has played a large and increasing role in almost all aspects of housing production and consumption. A social housing programme was launched at the end of the 1980s. These efforts reflect not only the acute housing shortage in urban areas, but also the government's introduction of welfare provision for the low-income group. In the late 1980s, comprehensive housing development planning was instituted to determine the extent to which national resources should be allocated to public housing development for the poor.

In 1993, the new government announced a Five-year New Economy Plan in which, within the context of deregulation, greater emphasis would be placed on the role of the private sector. The social housing system (permanent public rental housing) was abolished in early 1993 and, when compared to the previous five-year housing construction plan (1988–92), financial support for new programmes for the poor continued to decline. Meanwhile, the government implemented a phased lifting of price controls on new housing beginning in 1995 in all regions.

With respect to state-developed housing for sale and five-year rental housing, this system is administratively simple and easily understood by the public. The applicants for state-developed housing for sale are required to deposit a considerable amount of money in the Housing Bank (H&CB). There are no subsidies for the poor who have no ability to pay a deposit in the

H&CB. Only those who have the ability to save can obtain state-developed housing. This prevents low-income people obtaining the bank's loans. Many homeless people and tenants do not deposit their money in the bank because their income is so small. This system has been criticized on the grounds that public housing nominally targeting low-income people have often been allocated to middle-income households.

For Korea, the critical issue in housing policy and urban redevelopment is its reliance on the process of filtering-down as the best means of improving the quality of housing available to those of lower incomes. In fact, it is hard to demonstrate how the profit making mass housing provision in line with the filtering process encourages distributional equity. In addition, classification and identification of target groups is another important distributional equity issue. In relation to the low-income group, serious consideration has not been given to levels of income, how much they can afford, or what programmes are better suited to improving housing welfare and conditions. According to a recent survey on public rental housing, 10–50 per cent of tenants residing in public housing were middle-income households who no longer qualified for public rental housing (Yoon and Kim 1997). This mismatch and equity problem is created by not considering the community housing situation, affordability or market conditions in the region where the public housing is constructed. Therefore, there has been criticism that public housing programs do not improve horizontal and vertical equity.

Security

Security goals are related to issues surrounding eviction in housing renewal projects. Millions of poor people, or squatters, have been evicted over the past two decades in Korea. In Seoul, 720,000 squatters were evicted, often violently, between 1985 and 1988 (Murphy 1990). Most evictions are of renters who refuse to move out of the areas where they live. It has been observed that JRPs typically involve serious human rights violations as poor tenants are forcibly removed from their homes. In many redevelopment project areas, groups of thugs, sometimes right under the eyes of police officials, are brought in to demolish the houses and push people out. Renters – who usually comprise 60 per cent of the population in redevelopment areas – are excluded by law from sharing any benefits accruing from their homes. The economic reason for this unseemly situation, i.e. evictions, is that these projects are intended to make a profit for the developers rather than to improve the quality of life of low-income tenants.

One significant change that occurred during the 1980s and early 1990s was government actions being increasingly influenced by international laws and civil movements concerned with people's rights to housing.[7] Since the early 1990s renters evicted from urban redevelopment areas have been offered two alternatives: receive compensation for moving expenses, usually three months' living expenses; or receive the right to move into government rental housing following construction on the project site. Only renters excluded from compensation (because they have been residents for less than three months) or those demanding on-site temporary housing have undergone forcible eviction. About 10–20 per cent of all renters come to such arrangements. While the first alternative may seem attractive, given the steep rise in rent in the Seoul area, this amount of compensation is insufficient for tenants hoping to relocate near the redevelopment site, and thus most have to move outside of the city. The second alternative allows residence in the same neighbourhood, but there is scant provision for interim housing during the four-year period during which the project is brought to completion. These alternatives have resulted in the destruction of communities.

The 2003 Housing Law details the government's responsibilities regarding housing rights. According to the law, the government should set a minimum housing standard and policy priority should be given to households who live below this standard.

Table 15.5 presents an evaluation of the performance of urban governance goals. The rating uses a very limited scale and so can only present the crudest approximation of the differences between cities in Korea. Despite this caveat, the table does give some indication of relative performance. Good governance is characterized by participatory democracy, decentralization, efficiency, equity and security; and these norms must be interdependent and mutually reinforcing. The most important message from the table is that equity and security goals are the most difficult issues in Korea.

Toward good urban governance

During the 1960s and 1970s, urban governance in terms of low-income housing was characterized by a rather *laissez faire* approach. During the 1990s, however, government policy focused on the role of the private sector within the context of deregulation and privatization. Since the IMF crisis in 1997, market forces have been regarded as of greater importance in the housing sector than the role of the state (or municipal government).

Even though the role of local government is very important in the light of the decentralization of state power and an increasing philosophy of local autonomy, most local governments have not devised housing programmes for low-income residents. Lack of both funds and trained and experienced government officials to implement housing programmes are inherent problems.

Table 15.5 The relative performances of urban governance goals in Korea

	Participatory democracy	Decentralization	Efficiency	Equity	Security
Performance	●	■	■	▼	X

Notes: ● positive, ■ modest, ■ neutral, ▼ poor, X bad.

Despite many measures to improve supply and quality over several decades, housing remains a persistent and divisive social and urban governance issue in Korea. As the inequitable distribution of housing becomes even more prominent as overall prosperity increases, this divisiveness becomes ever greater. After the IMF crisis the poor have suffered more than any other group.

One of main questions addressed in this study was: how can the low-income group bring their influence to bear on the agenda of the various institutions of city governance?

From the above discussion, some key points can be elicited. First, it is important that NGOs and CBOs continue to explore ways of developing a more efficient working process in order to tackle the issues of equity and security and ensure that NGOs can participate in and support the grassroots struggle more actively. Second, the enabling approach has been much more important than other approaches.

Today, a more pluralistic and participatory approach to planning, in which state agencies function more in partnership with NGOs and community organizations, is needed. According to Drucker (1994), nations immersed in the current climate of social transformation need to expand their two-sector notion of society (these two sectors being government and business), to include a third sector. He stresses that this third sector, comprised of NGOs, non-profit and grass roots organizations, and a multitude of volunteers, should assume a significant share of the responsibility for taking on the social challenges facing modern societies.

In Korea, symbolic of the 'NGO renaissance' was the inauguration of the Citizens' Coalition for Economic Justice (CCEJ) in July 1989, which espoused the eradication of real estate speculations and the realization of economic justice, among other issues. Civil movements achieved rapid growth due to the imbalance among the state, the market and civil society that arises under authoritarianism. A need to achieve a rational reform of the state and the market with the aid of the purging power of civil society and NGOs develops. The state was distorted as a military authoritarian regime, and the market as a pariah, a capitalist structure centred on business conglomerates, or *chaebol*. Collusive political and economic relations were naturally formed between the state power elite and *chaebol*. The state and the market suppressed their challengers, accusing them of being communists or communist sympathizers. The civil social movement grew against this backdrop, and its role of forming proper balance among the state, the market and civil society concurred with the demands of the times (Cho 2000).

In urban areas of Korea, a few successful community development programmes were implemented and linked to newer development concepts such as basic needs, primary healthcare, sites and services and slum upgrading. These programmes eventually faded away for a variety of reasons: lack of funding, bureaucratization, political changes and so on. A neighbourhood is a relatively small local community based on relationships among persons who have a sense of living in close proximity. In neighbourhoods face-to-face relationships play a very important role.

Urban housing redevelopment is defined in Korea as the restructuring of the built environment of the local community or communities in a designated urban area. The legal concept of urban redevelopment in Korea would designate a construction district, its land and buildings, and the affected persons, based on ownership criteria. The reason for adding local community to this concept is that local community needs to be positively fostered in urban areas because it is so gravely disrupted by the restructuring of its built environment. For example, just as large construction projects require an environmental impact evaluation before they are carried out, urban redevelopment projects could require an evaluation of the impact on local communities. Under the present urban redevelopment project administration, impact evaluation is only just being initiated through the requirement of some fraction (e.g. two-thirds) of homeowners to agree to the redevelopment (Park 2004).

In the case of urban housing regeneration projects, the mere designation of an area by local government for urban redevelopment should be assumed to instigate neighbourhood phenomena. Distinguishing in this way the concept of neighbourhood from the structured facilities and services of a municipal administration allows one to consider various models of resident participation in urban governance. These could be scientifically developed as means of building local communities in urban settings in Korea.

To make the enabling processes successful and to achieve good urban governance, the following measures need to be implemented. First, the role communities play with regards to planning and management must be increased. In order to increase equity and security, citizens should be given more control over what happens. Second, active participation of NGOs and CBOs at all levels will ensure the legality of tenure, avoid discrimination, and lead to more access to low-income housing for poor residents. Third, there must be a willingness to recognize and learn from past mistakes so that they are not repeated. Poor residents are not looking to place blame on anyone for the conditions they are in, they are only looking to improve them. Fourth, linkages between neighbouring residents must be maximized. The planners, residents and NGOs must work together to promote community empowerment and regeneration. Finally, the experience and knowledge learned during each stage must be passed on to the next through the efforts of staff members and communities.

Conclusions

In answer to the first question posed in the introduction, 'Do the urban poor benefit from economic growth in general and urban (or housing) regeneration in particular and, if so, how?', economic growth does benefit the low-income group in Korea in a variety of ways, but it also tends to amplify inequalities, so that while some may benefit, others – and particularly the housing poverty group – may be disadvantaged. Even though overall housing quality has improved over the last three decades, the housing conditions of low-income families have not improved as much as expected and the gap in housing conditions between income classes is still substantial. Since the IMF crisis in 1997, inequality in housing wealth distribution has become even worse than that of income distribution. Most housing regeneration projects are basically profit-orientated and do not take sufficient account of housing welfare and community situations.

In answer to the second question, 'How can the low-income group bring their influence to bear on the agenda of the various institutions of city governance?', it is clear that the democratization movements in the late 1980s and recent activities of NGOs have offered expanded opportunities. While Korean democracy has trodden a rough road since the 1960s, the NGOs have had an important impact by promoting democracy and have played a valuable role in supporting and articulating the interests of the low-income group. Some examples can be cited of the poor and NGOs bringing pressure to bear on government. Consider the success of the Housing Law (2003) dealing with setting a minimum standard of housing. But community or grassroots organizations are vulnerable to some problems; for example, conflicting interests and unaccountable leadership.

Following a 30-year period of pursuing state development, with an unbalanced emphasis on efficiency, Korea is now entering a period in which issues of equality are being prioritized. Urban governance is inextricably linked to the welfare of the citizenry, in housing as in other areas. Through good urban governance, citizens are provided with a platform that allows them to use their talents to the fullest in order to improve their social and economic conditions. These talents can effectively be applied to the realm of low-income housing. An 'enabling framework' should be strengthened that would draw on the energy and skills of citizens in responding to housing problems and to the failure of conventional approaches. Recent shifts in national governance and the increasingly large role played by civil society, both in decision making and service delivery, have meant that community participation in urban governance is coming to be accepted as the norm in Korean society.

In terms of governing agendas in urban development and regeneration politics in Korea, social reform agenda should be concentrated on community development and centred on perceived issues of social or redistributive justice. Community development strategies target disadvantaged groups and neighbourhoods as the locus of development efforts. The expansion of affordable housing, the support of cooperatives and the improvement of neighbourhoods figure prominently on social reform agendas.

Notes

1 The housing minimum standard set by the Korean government is based on three factors: (1) minimum floor space (adequate space and privacy); for example, the

dwelling floor space area for a household of four persons must exceed 37m². (2) Facilities (provision of basic services): any housing lacking basic services and facilities, such as running water, electricity or a sewer system, is judged to be below standard. (3) Structure and environment: housing with poorly built structures such as tents, communal huts, and barracks using inadequate building materials are also judged to be below standard.

2 The population and housing census taken in 2000 did not include illegal settlements, slums, or squatter settlements such as vinyl houses, tents or barracks. These were not included in the survey because such settlements were not registered in the list of housing stock provided by local housing authorities. Moreover, the census covered legal residential areas only. Therefore, it is hard to figure out what exactly is the real situation with regards to substandard housing.

3 According to the Korean dictionary, the literal meaning of Jjogbang is a divided room or a room where the emphasis is on its smallness. 'Jjog' means a part of a divided thing or a unit to calculate a split article, and 'bang' means a room or sleeping space.

4 Even though Jjogbang is a very popular accommodation for the urban poor, little information is available in terms of conditions and trends. There are no data available on Jjogbang in the census or in any other government statistics. All that is known is that there were approximately 5000 Jjogbang in the areas studied, areas located mainly in the inner city of Seoul (Ha 2004a).

5 NGOs in Korea may be classified into three parts: public interest-orientated organizations, vocational organizations seeking to realize the interests of members of specific bodies, and other organizations concerned with fraternal or social relation pursuits. Under such premises, about 60 per cent of the organizations may be classified into public-interest and vocational organizations. Organizations involved in civil social movements, women, youth, human rights, formers and fishermen, the urban poor, the environment and unification were overwhelmingly public interest-oriented. Vocational orientation was predominant with organizations engaged in business, the press, publications, and health and medical care (*Citizen Times* 1996).

6 The CCEJ is an influential NGO that was founded in 1989. Their slogan, Let's achieve economic justice through citizens' power,' reflects their belief that deep-rooted economic injustices cannot be resolved by the government alone, but ultimately must be addressed through organized citizens' groups.

7 The national constitutions of fifty-three countries have some provision within them for housing rights. Housing rights have long been included within international covenants or conventions, such as the Universal Declaration on Human Rights of 1948 and in the resolution of the UN Commission on Human Rights adopted on 10 March 1993.

References

Cho, H.Y. (2000) Democratic transition and changes in Korean NGOs, *Korea Journal*, 40(2): 45–67.

Cho, H.Y. and Kim, E.M. (1998) State autonomy and its social conditions for economic development in South Korea and Taiwan, in E. M. Kim (ed.), *The Four Asian Tigers: Economic Development and the Global Political Economy*, San Diego: Academic Press.

Chung, C.M. (1999) The new perspective for Korean local government, *Korea Journal*, 39(2): 72–98.

Chung, E.C. (2005) Low-income housing policies in Korea: evaluations and suggestions, paper presented at the Korea Development Institute Conference, 2–3 June, Seoul.

Chung, Y.T. (1996) The intergovernmental relations for sustainable development of Korea, *Korean Journal of Policy Studies*, 11: 13–29.

Citizen Times (1996) [article title], December 16.

Citizen Times (1999) *Directory of Korean NGOs*, Seoul: *Citizen Times*.

Devas, N. (2004) *Urban Governance, Voice and Poverty in the Developing World*, London: Earthscan.

Drucker, P. (1994) The age of social transformation, *Atlantic Monthly*, 274(5): 53–80.

Economic Planning Board (EPB) (1983) *Korea Statistical Yearbook*, Seoul: EPB.

Ha, S.K. (2002) The role of NGOs for low-income groups in Korean society, *Environment and Urbanization*, 14(1): 219–229.

Ha, S.K. (2004a) New shantytowns and the urban marginalized in Seoul Metropolitan Region, *Habitat International*, 28: 123–141.

Ha, S.K. (2004b) Housing poverty and the role of urban governance in Korea, *Environment and Urbanization*, 16(1): 139–154.

Kim, K.H. (2004) Housing and the Korean economy, *Journal of Housing Economics*, 13: 321–341.

Ko, B.H. (2003) The strategy and task for national balance of building the new administrative capital, paper presented at the Forum for Building the New Administrative Capital, Administrative Capital Relocation Team, 20 June, Seoul.

Kookmin Bank (KB) (2003) *Survey of Demand for Housing Loans 2003*, Seoul: Kukmin Bank (in Korean).

Korea Center for City and Environment Research (KOCER) (2002) *The Resting Place of Destitute Families*, Seoul: KOCER.

Korea National Housing Corporation (KNHC) (1981) *Collection of Housing Statistics*, Seoul: KNHC.

KNHC (1997) *Handbook of Housing*, Seoul: KNHC.

Kwon, Y. (2003) Citizens' role in metropolitan governance, in K. B. Lee (ed.), *Global City Region*, Seoul: Korea Research Institute for Human Settlements.

McCarney, P. (ed.) (1996) *Cities and Governance: New Directions in Latin America, Asia and Africa*, Toronto: Centre for Urban Community Studies, University of Toronto.

Murphy, D. (1990) *A Decent Place to Live*, Bangkok: Asian Coalition for Housing Rights.

National Statistical Office (NSO) (2003) *Social Indicators in Korea*, Seoul: National Statistical Office.

Park, M.S. (2004) Nonprofit organizations and housing rights in urban redevelopment in South Korea, in M. Kang (ed.), *Urban Squatter Policies (IV): The cases of Korea and United Kingdom*, Korea Research Institute for Human Settlements, KRIHS Research Report 2004–07, Seoul: KRIHS.

United Nations Centre for Human Settlements (Habitat) (UNCHS (Habitat)) (2000) The global campaign for good urban governance, *Environment and Urbanization*, 12(1): 197–200.

United Nations Centre for Human Settlements (Habitat) (UNCHS (Habitat)) (2001) *Good Urban Governance: A Normative Framework, Summary for the Preparatory Committee for the Special Session of the General Assembly for an*

Overall Review and Appraisal of the Implementation of the Habitat Agenda, Nairobi.

World Bank (1999) *Urban and Local Government Strategy*, Washington, DC: World Bank.

Yoon, J. and Kim, H.S. (1997) *Evaluation and Reform of Housing Welfare Policy*, Seoul: KRIHS.

Index

accountability: China 6, 61, 295;
  democratization 149–50; good
  governance 1, 151; higher education
  127; hospitals 100, 110; urban
  governance 300
accumulation 43, 44
Ackerman, B. 78
administrative licenses 11, 159–82
Administrative Licensing Law 166–8,
  171–3
advisory committees 188
AFC *see* Asian financial crisis
agricultural trade 173
allowance systems 144, 145, 146
Appadurai, A. 296
Argentina 161
'argumentative turn' 67–8, 74
Asia, concept of 89–90
Asian financial crisis (AFC) 1, 26, 142,
  154, 185; China 256; Korea 17, 27,
  213; Taiwan 214; urban governance
  15; welfare states 31–2, 43
assistance systems 144, 145, 146
'authoritarian liberalism' 4, 133
authoritarianism 10, 70, 201, 333,
  341
autonomization: hospitals 8, 100,
  105–6, 109, 111, 112; universities
  126, 127
Axford, B. 142

Bai, X. 294
Bangkok 294, 296
banking 190, 200, 213
Beck, U. 78
Beijing 271, 290, 293, 296, 307
benchmarking 132, 134

bilateral relations 90, 91, 92–3
Blair, T. 152
Bought Place Scheme (BPS) 232,
  236
Brazil 161
Bresser-Pereira, L.C. 149
Bressers, H.T. 142, 147
'bubble economy' 83–4, 303, 306,
  318
bureaucracy 41, 42; China 176, 178n4;
  Hong Kong 186–7
Bush, George W. 85, 86
business interests: China 12, 186,
  194–201, 202–3; developmental
  states 206–8; Hong Kong 12, 186,
  187–93, 202–3; urban
  redevelopment in Japan 306,
  315
business organizations 197–8,
  199

capital 186, 188, 207, 208
capital requirements 161, 162
capitalism 3, 42–3, 44; China 5;
  corporate influences on public
  policy 12; Hong Kong 185; three
  'worlds' of 29; urban governance
  290; welfare development 144
Castells, M. 134
Castles, F.G. 29
CCEJ *see* Citizens' Coalition for
  Economic Justice
centralization: administrative licenses
  168–70, 175; education 235
CEPA *see* Closer Economic
  Partnership Agreement
Cerny, P. 133

chaebol 207, 209, 211–12, 213, 341
Chan, C. 298
change 51–2, 64–5
chaos 15–16, 287, 292, 300
Chen Shui-Bain 84–5
Cheung, Anthony B.L. 3, 4, 25–48,
   188, 192
China: academic collaboration with
   Hong Kong 124; Beijing 271, 290,
   293, 296, 307; business interests 12,
   186, 194–201, 202–3; corruption
   295; development 4–5, 49–66;
   globalization discourse 135;
   Guangzhou 16, 173, 262, 277, 278,
   297–8, 299; healthcare 9; Hong
   Kong 185, 188–90, 191; housing 14,
   253–84; Japan relations with 7, 81,
   83, 84, 89, 90–4; market
   liberalization 10–11; non-state
   sector 195–201; policy paradigms
   5–6; policy studies 6, 68; regional
   order-making 93; regulatory reform
   11, 159–82; rural-urban migration
   293; SARS crisis 59–61, 63; social
   policy 144; social welfare 253,
   278–9; state sector 193–4, 202;
   Taiwan relations with 84–5; urban
   divisions 296, 300
Choi, Young Jun 13, 206–27
Chongqing 277, 293
Chou, Bill 11, 159–82
CiDeH *see* Citizens for Decent
   Housing
cities *see* urban governance
Citizens' Coalition for Economic
   Justice (CCEJ) 334, 341, 344n6
Citizens for Decent Housing (CiDeH)
   334–5
civil society 2, 118; China 62, 64;
   education 119; Korea 333, 341, 343;
   urban governance 299, 332
civil unrest 49, 56, 58–9
Closer Economic Partnership
   Agreement (CEPA) 124
clusters 106, 108, 109, 111, 112
'co-production' 118, 119, 131
Cold War 82, 86, 210
collaboration 123–4
Collingridge, David 69–70
colonial rule: Hong Kong 186–8, 190,
   191, 230–1; Singapore 232–3

commercialization 12, 118, 257, 261,
   280n3
commodification 10, 12, 14
communism 174
Communist Party (China) 85, 193,
   198, 199, 200–1, 202
community development 341–2,
   343
competition 3, 8; education 13, 229,
   245, 247; global 41; higher education
   122; hospitals 99, 110, 111, 112, 113,
   114; Japan 84, 303, 304, 307, 316–17,
   322; Korea 335; pro-competitive
   regulation 130, 133–4, 135
corporate culture 12
corporatism 199
corporatization 12, 118; China 160;
   education 33–4; higher education 9,
   10, 117, 120–30, 134; hospital
   reforms 8, 100, 104, 105, 108, 114;
   see also commercialization;
   marketization; privatization
corruption 6, 57, 58–9, 162, 164, 295,
   297
Cowling, K. 212
crime 297
criticism 73–4
Cultural Revolution 54, 195
Cyberport, Hong Kong 192

Dahl, Robert 74
Davis, M. 295–6
decentralization: China 4, 55, 56,
   162–3, 194; education 119, 134, 238,
   240, 247–8; good governance 1;
   higher education 10, 127, 130, 132;
   Korea 17, 332, 335–6; neo-liberalism
   2; new forms of governance 118;
   Tokyo 304; urban governance
   299–300, 332, 340
deLeon, P. 72
democracy 10, 32, 68; deliberative 67,
   74, 75, 78–9; Korea 17, 333, 343;
   participatory 17, 332–5, 340;
   post-modernism 69; voluntary
   associations 154; welfare
   development 144
Democratic Progressive Party (DPP)
   (Taiwan) 34, 214, 219–20
democratization 39, 140, 206; Hong
   Kong 188–9, 192, 202; Korea 27, 30,

37, 211–12, 326, 332–3, 336, 343;
Taiwan 27, 30, 37, 211; welfare
policy 10, 31, 43, 148–50, 155
demographic changes 27–8; Japan 95,
321–2; pension reforms 222; urban
governance 15
Deng Xiaoping 50, 54, 56, 279n2,
280n7
deregulation 8, 12, 18, 132; China 55,
56, 160; higher education 130; Japan
303, 306, 310; Korea 211, 213, 326,
338; urban governance 15; urban
redevelopment in Tokyo 310;
see also liberalization; privatization
Devas, N. 331–2
developmentalism 3, 25, 26–7, 33,
39–44, 134; China 201–2; Japan 86,
313, 317; legacies of 206–10;
pensions 208–10; productivism 30,
32; transformation to post-
developmentalism 210–12; trust 153,
160
Dickson, B. 198
Direct Subsidy Scheme (DSS) 228,
230, 232, 235–8, 242, 243–6
discourse 75
discrimination 230
Dixon, Norman 70
Douglass, M. 294–5
DPP *see* Democratic Progressive Party
Drucker, P. 341
Dryzek, John 67
DSS *see* Direct Subsidy Scheme

'East Asian economic miracle' thesis
26
economic growth: administrative
licenses 11, 176; China 49, 50, 53–9,
60, 61–3, 64, 91, 164, 201, 256;
developmental state 26; 'East Asian
economic miracle' thesis 26; higher
education reforms 134; Hong Kong
201; housing reform 257; Japan 7,
27, 82, 95, 303–4, 305, 306–7, 321;
Korea 326, 327–9, 342; performance
appraisals 164, 178; sustainability
203; urban governance 15,
300
economic integration 189
economic policy 38–9; China 200, 201;
Japan 83; Korea 209

education 9–10, 33–4; China 56;
developmentalism 33; private 13–14,
228–52; public expenditure 28;
restructuring 118–20; school
ranking system 247–8;
see also higher education
efficiency 254, 332, 335, 336–8, 340,
343
Eliadis, P. 141, 150
'embedded liberalism' 7, 81–2, 94–5
employers' liability systems 144, 145,
146
empowerment 68, 69, 78, 152
energy 82
entrepreneurialism 125, 126, 129, 185,
196
environmental issues: China 57, 62, 63,
64; urban pollution 293–4, 300
equity 332, 338–9, 340, 342, 343;
see also inequalities
Esping-Andersen, G. 29, 30, 143
Evans, P.B. 26–7
evictions 339–40

fairness 18, 152–3
family structures 297
financial sector 206; Hong Kong 190;
Japan 314, 316; Korea 211, 213, 217;
trust 154
fiscal policy 38–9, 210
Fischer, F. 73, 74, 77
Fishkin, S. 78
foreign investment: China 53, 54, 56,
91–2, 93–4, 164, 171, 173; Hong
Kong 186; Japan 95n5, 316; Taiwan
214; Tokyo 314; urban governance
292
Forrest, Ray 1–22, 287–302
Forrester, J. 74
Fraenkel, E. 4, 133
Friedman, Milton 12
Fukuyama, Francis 12, 153
functionalism 42, 43

gated communities 295–6
GDPism 5, 49, 50, 54–5, 56–7, 63, 64
gentrification 289, 300
Giddens, Anthony 151, 152
Giroux, H. 12
Global Development Research Centre
289

globalization 3, 7–8, 39, 134, 140, 206; higher education 121; impact on cities 294; Japan 316, 318; new forms of governance 117, 118; pro-competition tools 135; Singapore 125, 130; welfare states 30–2, 43

Goh Chok Tong 238, 239, 240

Goh Keng Swee 234

good governance 1, 289, 332; social economy 331; trust 151–2; urban governance 15, 299

Goodstadt, L. 187, 190–1

Gopinathan, S. 130

Gough, I. 31, 33, 34, 148

Gray, J. 42

Great Leap Forward 54

'groupthink' 70

'growth first' approach 329

Guangzhou 16, 173, 262, 277, 278, 297–8, 299

Guo, Weiqing 6, 67–80

Ha, Seong Kyu 17, 326–46

Hajer, M.A. 78

Hall, Peter 5, 50–2, 63, 64–5, 290, 297

Hallak, J. 134

Hanoi 294, 295, 296

Harvard Report (1999) 106

healthcare 34–5; China 56; Hong Kong 121; hospital reforms 8–9, 99–116; Japan 85; public expenditure 28; Singapore 135; welfare instruments 146

Heilmann, S. 175

Hewison, K. 31

high-rise buildings 310, 311–13, 314

higher education 9–10, 117–39; Japan 85; reforms 33–4; undergraduate-level exchanges between China and Japan 92

Hirayama, Yosuke 16–17, 303–25

holistic reform approach 258–62

Holliday, I. 25, 30

Holston, J. 296

Hong Kong 185, 201, 290, 296; bureaucracy 41; business interests 12, 186, 187–93, 202–3; civil service 42; colonial rule 186–8, 230–1; economic growth 307; economic

policy 39, 40; health expenditure 101–2, 104, 105, 111–12, 114; healthcare reforms 8, 34, 99, 100–7, 110–12, 113–15; higher education 9, 117, 120–4, 128–30, 132, 134, 135; housing reforms 35; infant mortality 101; life expectancy 101; non-interventionism 26, 42, 187, 191; policy shifts 39; private education 13, 33, 228, 230–2, 235–8, 241–6, 248; privatization 299; public expenditure 28, 36, 40; SARS crisis 60; self-regulation 131–2; social welfare 28, 30, 36–7, 144; welfare instruments 140, 146–8, 155

Hood, Christopher 69–71

hospitals 8–9, 99–116

housing: China 14, 56, 253–84; high-rise housing in Tokyo 310; Hong Kong 121; implementation problems 262–71; incremental vs holistic approach 258–62; Japan 82, 322; Korea 17, 326–46; low-income 17, 35–6, 255, 256, 271, 276–8, 326–7, 329–31, 337–43; reforms 35–6; security 276–8, 339–40

Howell, J. 1

Howlett, M. 143

Hu Jintao 5, 49–50, 60, 63, 64, 201

Hulme, D. 1

Hutton, W. 295

ICA *see* Industry and Commerce Association

ICF *see* Industrial and Commercial Federation

Ikels, C. 297

IMF *see* International Monetary Fund

Immergut, E.M. 150

Imura, H. 294

incentive systems 11, 175, 176, 178

income inequality: China 57–8, 63; housing 273, 274

incremental approach 254, 258–62, 279

India 161

individualism 298, 318–19

Indonesia 43, 161

Industrial and Commercial Federation (ICF) 198, 199

industrial policy 207, 210

industrialization 195, 297, 329

Industry and Commerce Association
(ICA) 197, 198, 199
inequalities: China 5, 6, 49, 57–8, 59,
63, 64; education 246; housing
255–6, 259, 261, 271–6, 278–9, 330,
331, 341, 342–3; Japan 7, 322; urban
15, 16–17, 289, 298, 300, 322;
see also equity
infant mortality 101
information disclosure 109–10,
164–5
information technology (IT) 38, 125,
213–14
informational asymmetry 174
instrument-choice perspective 141–3,
150, 155
intellectual movements 334
interest groups 56, 176–7;
see also business interests
International Monetary Fund (IMF)
1, 2, 118
international political economy
210
international schools 245, 246
Ishihara Shintaro 307, 316, 320,
321
IT *see* information technology
Ito Go 6–7, 81–96

Jacobs, J. 299
Japan 6–7, 81–96; bureaucracy 41;
corporate tax 223n8; developmental
state 26, 160, 313, 317; economic
policy 38, 39; education reforms 33;
factional politics 42; healthcare
reforms 34, 35; housing reforms 36;
pensions 208–9, 210, 215–17, 221–2;
privatization 299; public expenditure
28, 40; social welfare 27, 28, 29–30,
31, 32, 38, 82, 95; state/business
relationship 206–7, 211, 212, 221,
222; Tokyo 16–17, 290, 294, 296,
303–25
Jayasuriya, K. 4, 133
Jessop, B. 290–1
Jiang Zemin 50, 200
Jjogbangs 330, 344n3, 344n4
Johnson, C. 26
Joint Redevelopment Projects (JRPs)
337, 339
joint ventures 211, 214

JRPs *see* Joint Redevelopment Projects

Kamo, T. 314
KDI *see* Korea Development Institute
keiretsu 207, 209, 212
Kienzle, R. 207
Kim Dae Jung 32, 37, 213
Kim Young Sam 212, 213, 223n5
Kissinger, Henry 92
KMT *see* Kuomintang
KNHC *see* Korean National Housing
Corporation
knowledge: 'knowledge-power'
structure 71, 73; local 72
knowledge economy 121, 125
Koizumi Junichiro 6–7, 82, 84, 85–6,
88, 94–5, 304–5, 306
Korea: bureaucracy 41; corporate tax
223n8; democratization 30, 32, 148,
149, 211–12; developmental state
160; economic policy 38, 39;
education reforms 33; factional
politics 42; healthcare reforms 34–5;
housing 17, 36, 326–46; pensions
208, 209, 210, 217–18, 221–2; public
expenditure 28, 40; Seoul 290, 294,
307, 327–9, 331, 334, 337, 340; social
welfare 27, 28, 32, 37, 144; state/
business relationship 207, 211, 213,
221, 222; 'state-led' capitalism 43;
'welfare developmentalism' 25;
welfare instruments 140, 146–8, 155
Korea Development Institute (KDI)
217
Korean National Housing
Corporation (KNHC) 338
Krauss, E. 42
Krugman, P. 185–6
Ku, Yeun Wen 10, 140–58
Kuhn, Thomas 50, 51
Kuomintang (KMT) 28, 85, 208, 209,
211, 212, 214, 219–20, 224n9
Kwon, H.J. 43, 153

labour protection 36–8, 144
Lasswell, Harold 73, 76
LDP *see* Liberal Democrat Party
leadership 141, 305
learning 70, 72, 73–4, 77
Lee Kuan Yew 233, 234, 238, 248
Lee, Michael H. 13–14, 228–52

Lee, M.N.N. 134
legislation: anti-monopoly 39; Chinese
    Administrative Licensing Law
    166–8, 171–3; Chinese Law of
    Legislation 177; Hong Kong Basic
    Law 189; Japanese Basic Law on
    Reforming Government Ministries
    305–6; Japanese pension reform 38,
    216–17; Japanese Revision of Health
    Insurance Law 35; Japanese welfare
    laws 38; Korean Housing Law 340,
    343; Korean pension reform 217,
    218; Taiwanese University Law
    33–4; Taiwanese welfare laws 37–8;
    urban redevelopment in Japan 310,
    317; *see also* regulation
legitimation 43, 44
Levi-Faur, D. 133
Li, S.-M. 297
Li, W. 176
Liberal Democrat Party (LDP) (Japan)
    32, 82, 216, 221, 317; business
    interests 206–7, 209, 211, 212;
    factional politics 42, 84, 86
liberalism: 'authoritarian' 4, 133;
    'embedded' 7, 81–2, 94–5
liberalization: China 10–11, 55, 56,
    160; financial 213, 217; higher
    education 117; Japan 316; Korea
    335; political 201, 202; pro-
    competitive regulation 130, 134;
    trade 210; *see also* deregulation;
    privatization
licensing 11, 159–82
life expectancy 101
Liou, K.T. 57
local government: administrative
    licenses 162–3, 164, 167, 171, 173,
    174–6, 177–8; housing 254–5, 257,
    266–7, 268, 269, 270, 274, 340; Japan
    86; Korea 335–6, 340; rural
    enterprise 196; state-owned
    enterprises 194; urban governance
    332; urban redevelopment in Tokyo
    304, 315
Lü, X.B. 174

Malaysia 134, 135, 161
Malouta, M. 288, 291
Maloutas, T. 288, 291
managerialism 120, 121, 128, 130

Mao Zedong 5, 52, 54, 194, 195
market accelerationist state 4, 133
market access 165, 167, 173
market failure 159–60
market-orientation 55–6, 64; education
    229–30; housing 254, 261, 278; social
    policy 14; urban governance 299
marketization 1, 12, 118; China 5, 55,
    186, 279; education 228, 240;
    healthcare 9, 107, 114, 121; higher
    education 117, 128, 129, 130, 132;
    housing 254, 260, 278; pro-
    competitive regulation 134; social
    policy 14; *see also*
    commercialization; corporatization;
    privatization
Marxism 3, 42, 43, 44, 49, 289
Matsutani, A. 321–2
May, P.J. 72
McCarney, P. 331
medical insurance 34–5, 106, 107, 108,
    146
meritocracy 152–3
middle class 4–5
Midgley, J. 148
migrants 291, 296, 298
Miners, N. 187
Miyamoto, T. 29–30, 31
modernism 71
modernity 29
Mok, Ka Ho 1–22, 117–39
monetarism 119
moral issues 318–21

Nakasone Yasuhiro 83–4
nation-building 53, 134
National University of Singapore
    (NUS) 126, 127, 241, 248
nationalism 91
nationalization 53
neo-liberalism 1, 10, 14, 25, 118, 133;
    China 55–6, 253; critiques of 12;
    education 13; globalization 31;
    higher education 9, 121; Hong Kong
    120, 129; pro-competitive regulation
    130; social policy 4; structural
    adjustment 17; *Urban Future 21
    Report* 290–1; urban governance 15,
    288, 289
neo-traditionalism 174
network society 78

networks: new forms of governance 2, 118; social capital 151; social cohesion 291; urban 298

New Public Management (NPM) 8, 41; competition 99, 114; higher education 129; hospital reforms 100, 104

Ng-Lun, N. 230

Ngo, T.W. 191

Ngok, Kinglun 5–6, 14, 49–66

NGOs *see* non-governmental organizations

Nolan, P. 298

non-governmental organizations (NGOs) 332, 333–4, 341, 342, 343, 344n5

non-interventionism 26, 28, 36–7, 42, 187, 191

Nozick, Robert 12

NPM *see* New Public Management

NUS *see* National University of Singapore

Oi, J. 199

Olympic Games 320–1

O'Toole, L.J. 142, 147, 175

Pahl, Ray 289

Painter, M. 130, 131, 186

paradigm shift 51, 52, 60, 63, 64, 65, 68

Park, Robert 292–3

participation: 'argumentative turn' 68; China 6, 62, 64; deliberative democracy 67, 75, 78–9; good governance 1; policy debate 74, 75–6, 77, 78; social capital 292; trust 154; urban governance 15, 16, 288, 296, 332, 342, 343

participatory democracy 17, 332–5, 340

partnerships: China 62, 64; neo-liberalism 2; new forms of governance 2, 118; social capital 292; Tokyo 304; urban governance 288, 289; *see also* public-private partnerships

party-owned enterprises (POEs) 207, 208, 211, 214

PEA *see* Private Entrepreneurs' Association

peasants 5, 59, 196, 278

Pechtold, Alexander 140

Pekkanen, R. 42

Peng, I. 32, 33

pensions 13, 38, 208–10, 214–22; Japan 85, 208–9, 210, 215–17, 221–2; Korea 208, 209, 210, 217–18, 221–2; Taiwan 208, 209–10, 219–22; trust in provision 154

people-centred paradigm 5, 14, 49–50, 61–3, 64, 65

performance appraisals 11, 163–4, 176, 178

Pfeiffer, U. 297

Philippines 161

POEs *see* party-owned enterprises

Polanyi, K. 42–3

policy evaluation 77

policy failures 69–73

policy instruments 10, 141–8, 150, 155; China 53, 55, 62; new forms of governance 117–18, 120

policy-making style 53, 55, 61, 62

policy paradigms 5, 50–2, 60, 63, 64–5

policy process 6, 74, 75, 76–7, 149; business interests 189, 191, 199, 203; state-owned enterprises 195, 201

policy shifts 39–40

policy studies 50, 67–8, 69, 72, 73–4, 76–7

politics: administrative licenses 11; business interests 185, 187–8, 189, 192–3, 199–200, 202; China 54, 60, 63, 64; factional 42; Japan 82, 85–6, 317; Korea 333, 335–6; liberalization 201, 202; network society 78; pension reforms 222; Taiwan 219–20; welfare provision 10, 28, 32; *see also* democratization; local government; state

pollution 293–4, 300

population changes: Japan 321–2; Korea 327–9; *see also* demographic changes

positivism 67, 69, 74, 75, 76, 77

post-modernism 68–9, 74, 75–6

post-positivism 68, 74

poverty: China 5, 56, 57, 58, 63; exclusion and marginalization 332; Korea 331

principal-agent relationships 174

Private Entrepreneurs' Association (PEA) 198, 199
private sector 11–14; administrative licenses 160, 162; China 159, 195–201; education 13–14, 33, 228–52; healthcare 35, 102, 103, 106, 107, 108–9, 112–13, 114; higher education 122, 123, 132; housing 35, 36, 261, 274, 276, 338, 340; Korean pension reform 218; land development in Tokyo 309; self-regulation 131
privatization 1, 3, 12, 18, 118; China 5, 55, 56, 160, 193, 279; education 13–14, 33–4, 119; higher education 9, 10, 129, 130, 132; hospitals 8, 99, 100, 108; housing 14, 254, 274, 275–6, 278, 326; Japan 83–4, 85; Korea 326, 335; pensions 13; urban governance 15, 289, 299–300; urban space 296; welfare states 32; *see also* corporatization; deregulation; liberalization; marketization
productivism 25, 30, 31, 32–3, 43, 208, 290
property rights 260
protectionism 164, 167, 191–2
provident fund systems: housing 256, 258, 261; welfare policy 140, 144, 145, 146, 147
provincial economies 316–17, 322
public officials: administrative licenses 11, 159, 160, 162, 163–4, 171–3, 174–6, 177–8; housing reforms 270, 271
public-private partnerships 34, 35, 39, 120, 192
public services 12, 192, 336
Putnam, R.D. 151

Qian, Y.Y. 163
Quality Movement 125

RAE *see* Research Assessment Exercise
Rahn, W.M. 151
Ramesh, M. 8, 99–116
real estate market 303, 304, 306, 308, 322
realism 93

redevelopment priority zones 308–9, 311, 322
reflection 73–4
regulation 8, 130–2; financial 38; inter-country comparison 161; neo-liberalism 2; private education 231, 233; pro-competitive 130, 133–4, 135; regulatory reform in China 11, 159–82; reregulation 8, 18, 132–3, 160, 289; urban redevelopment in Tokyo 310; *see also* legislation
regulatory state 3–4, 133
religious schools 237–8, 240, 243
rent-seeking 11, 167–8, 177, 191
rents 261–2, 271, 273, 274, 275–6, 340
reregulation 8, 18, 132–3, 160, 289
Research Assessment Exercise (RAE) 122, 123
residents' movements 334
retirement benefits 209, 210, 220
Ring, P.J. 154
Robison, R. 31, 43
Rohlen, T. 294
Roppongi Hills 308, 310
Ruggie, G. John 81, 85, 94
rural enterprises 195–6, 197, 199

Salamon, L.M. 118, 119–20
SARS crisis 59–61, 63
Sasakawa Peace Foundation 92
School Excellence Model (SEM) 246–7
Scott, James 71–2
Scott Report (1985) 104
Second World War 90, 91
security: housing 276–8, 332, 339–40, 342; Japan 83, 84, 85, 86–90, 94
Self-Employed Labourer Association (SELA) 198, 199
self-regulation 118, 131–2
SEM *see* School Excellence Model
Sennett, R. 287
Seoul 290, 294, 307, 327–9, 331, 334, 337, 340
Seoul Metropolitan Region (SMR) 327–8
Shadur, M. 207
Shanghai 175, 307
Singapore 290, 296; bureaucracy 41; economic growth 307; economic policy 39; health expenditure 101–2, 109, 110, 112, 113, 114; healthcare

reforms 8, 34, 99, 100–3, 107–10,
111, 112–15, 135; higher education
9, 34, 117, 124–30, 132, 134, 135;
housing reforms 35; infant mortality
101; life expectancy 101; private
education 13, 228, 230, 232–5,
238–45, 246–9; public expenditure
28, 40, 233–4; SARS crisis 60;
self-regulation 131–2; social welfare
28, 37, 144; 'state-led' capitalism 43;
welfare instruments 140, 146–8, 155;
World Health Report 100–1
small and medium enterprises (SMEs):
Japan 38; Korea 38, 207, 213;
occupational benefits 210; Taiwan
38–9, 207–8, 209, 211, 212, 213–14,
219
SMR *see* Seoul Metropolitan Region
social capital 151, 153, 154; education
119; urban governance 288, 291–2,
299
social class 244, 246
social cohesion 15, 16, 18, 152, 153,
291–2, 294, 297–9
social housing 277–8, 338–9
social inclusion 15, 152, 288, 292
social insurance 140, 144, 145, 146–7,
208–9
social justice 61, 63, 300; *see also*
equity
social policy 3, 4, 25–48; China 5, 14,
61–2, 63, 253, 279;
developmentalism 153; Japan 82,
86; public expenditure 28;
see also welfare policy
social stratification 295–7
socialism 5, 193, 289
SOEs *see* state-owned enterprises
Solomon, Shane 106
South Korea *see* Korea
sponsorship 198, 200
SPRING Singapore 125
squatter settlements 330–1, 344n2
'stage approach' 76, 77
stakeholders: social capital 292; urban
governance 289
state 3–4, 26–7, 42–3, 44, 206; business
relationship 185, 186–203, 206–8,
211, 212–14, 221–2; China 53, 55,
56; democratization 149;
developmentalism 201–2;

instrument-choice perspective
141–2; Korea 341; *see also* politics
state intervention: China 53;
developmental state 26; healthcare
8–9, 108, 109, 114, 115, 135; higher
education 10, 130–1; Hong Kong
191–2; Korean housing sector 326,
331; urban redevelopment in Tokyo
304, 310, 313, 315–16, 317; welfare
instruments 143–4, 147–8
state-owned enterprises (SOEs) 3, 53,
132; China 162, 173, 193–4, 200–1,
202, 253, 261, 266, 275; Hong Kong
190; Korea 335; Taiwan 207, 208,
211, 214
structural adjustment 17
Stuart, D. 87
sustainable development 290
synarchy 187–9

Taiwan: bureaucracy 41; China
relations with 84–5; corporate tax
223n8; democratization 30, 32, 148,
149, 211, 212; developmental state
160; economic policy 38–9;
education reforms 33–4, 42;
factional politics 42; healthcare
reforms 34; housing reforms 36;
pensions 208, 209–10, 219–22;
public expenditure 28, 40; social
welfare 27–8, 37–8, 144; state/
business relationship 207–8, 211,
213–14, 221, 222; US relations with
83, 84; welfare instruments 140,
146–8, 155
Tanaka Kakuei 82
Tang, J. 191–2
Tang, K.L. 148
tax: China 163; corporate 223n8;
Japan 215, 216; Korea 218, 221;
Taiwan 219
tax for fee reform 59
telecommunications industry 176
terrorism 86, 89
Thailand 43, 135, 161
'third way' 152–3
Tokyo 16–17, 290, 294, 296, 303–25
Tomlinson, P.R. 212
Tow, W. 87
trade 81, 210; China 94, 165;
liberalization 210

transparency: administrative licenses
168; China 6, 61, 164–5, 168, 295;
good governance 1, 151
Transue, J.E. 151
Trow, M. 130
trust 10, 70, 140–1, 150–5, 298
Tu, I.C. 208
tuition fees 236, 237, 239, 240, 244,
246
Tung Chee Hwa 121, 192
Turner, M. 1

UGC *see* University Grant Committee
unemployment benefits 36, 37, 38
United States (US): gated communities
295; global hegemony 94; health
expenditure 101; international
political economy 210; Japan
relations with 81, 82, 84, 85, 86–8,
92–3; Taiwan 83, 84; urbanization
292–3
universalism 25, 30, 32
universities 9–10, 33–4, 134, 249;
Hong Kong 120–4, 128–30;
Singapore 124–30; *see also* higher
education
University Grant Committee (UGC)
121, 122–4
Urban Future 21 Report 290–1
urban governance 15–17, 287–302;
definitions of 331–2; housing
reforms 254; Korea 340–2, 343;
low-income housing 326–7;
social cohesion 291–2, 297–9;
social stratification 295–7;
Tokyo 303–25
urban-rural divide 58, 63
urbanization 287, 292–3, 294, 300;
Japan 303–4, 322; Korea 327–9;
welfare regimes 31

values 318, 321
Vietnam 60, 293–4
vinyl houses 330–1
voluntary associations 154

Wade, R. 26
Wagenaar, H. 78
Walker, A. 10, 144, 148
Wan Jiabo 5
Wang, D. 297
Weil, Robert 5
Weingast, B.R. 163
Weiss, L. 27
welfare-based orientation 5, 14
'welfare developmentalism' 25
welfare policy 140–58; China 253,
278–9; democratization 148–50;
globalization impact on 30–1, 43;
instrument mixes 10, 143–8; Japan
82, 95; labour protection 36–8;
see also social policy
welfare state 3, 25, 26–30, 143–4;
capitalism 43, 44; inclusive 43;
post-crisis transformation 31–2;
social democratic 148; *Urban
Future 21 Report* 290
Wen Jiabao 60, 61, 63, 64
Wildavsky, Aaron 67
Wong, C.K. 10, 144, 148
Wong, J. 149
Wong, P. 188
Wong, S.F. 130, 131
work units: housing reform 255–6, 257,
258–61, 266–7, 269, 270, 274–5;
urban governance 300
World Bank 1, 2, 118
World Health Report (2000) 100–1
World Trade Organization (WTO) 10,
59, 142, 164–5, 166

Xie Jiajin 261

Yep, Ray 12–13, 185–205
Yu Zhengsheng 262

Zeng Qinghong 190
Zhang, Z. 261
Zhao Ziyang 201
Zhu Rongji 253, 256
Zhu, Yapeng 14, 253–84